COGNITIVE APPROACHES TO THE ASSESSMENT OF SEXUAL INTEREST IN SEXUAL OFFENDERS

WILEY SERIES IN
FORENSIC CLINICAL PSYCHOLOGY

Edited by

Clive R. Hollin
Clinical Division of Psychiatry, University of Leicester, UK

and

Mary McMurran
School of Community Health Sciences, Division of Psychiatry,
University of Nottingham, UK

For other titles in this series please visit www.wiley.com/go/fcp

COGNITIVE APPROACHES TO THE ASSESSMENT OF SEXUAL INTEREST IN SEXUAL OFFENDERS

Edited by

David Thornton

and

D. Richard Laws

WILEY-BLACKWELL

A John Wiley & Sons, Ltd, Publication

This edition first published 2009
© 2009 John Wiley & Sons Ltd., except for Chapter 1 (© 2003 Sage Publications, Inc.)

Wiley-Blackwell is an imprint of John Wiley & Sons, formed by the merger of Wiley's global
Scientific, Technical, and Medical business with Blackwell Publishing.

Registered Office
John Wiley & Sons Ltd, The Atrium, Southern Gate, Chichester, West Sussex, PO19 8SQ, UK

Editorial Offices
The Atrium, Southern Gate, Chichester, West Sussex, PO19 8SQ, UK
9600 Garsington Road, Oxford, OX4 2DQ, UK
350 Main Street, Malden, MA 02148-5020, USA

For details of our global editorial offices, for customer services, and for information about how to
apply for permission to reuse the copyright material in this book please see our website at
www.wiley.com/wiley-blackwell.

The right of the editor to be identified as the author of this work has been asserted in accordance with
the Copyright, Designs and Patents Act 1988.

Library of Congress Cataloging-in-Publication Data

Cognitive approaches to the assessment of sexual interest in sexual offenders / edited by D. Thornton
and D. R. Laws.
       p. cm.
    Includes index.
    ISBN 978-0-470-05781-0 (cloth) – ISBN 978-0-470-05784-1 (pbk.)   1. Sex offenders–Research.
2. Child molesters–Research.   I. Thornton, D. (David)   II. Laws, D. Richard.
    RC560.S47C64 2009
    616.85′830072–dc22   2009013394

A catalogue record for this book is available from the British Library.

Typeset in 10/12pt Palatino by Aptara Inc., New Delhi, India.
Printed in Singapore by Markono Print Media Pte Ltd

1 2009

CONTENTS

ABOUT THE EDITORS

David Thornton, Ph.D., is currently treatment director for Wisconsin's program for Sexually Violent Persons at Sand Ridge Secure Treatment Center. He is an adjunct professor in the Clinical Psychology department of the University of Bergen in Norway and holds honorary appointments at the University of Wisconsin and the University of Birmingham. He received his Ph.D. in psychology from the University of Exeter in England. He is a member of the British Psychological Society and a Chartered Forensic Psychologist. He currently serves on the editorial board of *Sexual Abuse: A Journal of Research and Treatment*. He is also a member of the Executive Board of the Association for the Treatment of Sexual Abusers and received that organization's Significant Achievement Award in 2005. Between 1990 and 2001, he headed the multidisciplinary team within Her Majesty's Prison Service's headquarters that was responsible for the development of programs designed to reduce the rate of re-offending by discharged prisoners. He specializes in the development of assessment and treatment programs for sexual and violent offenders. His published research has primarily focused on program evaluation, therapist style, actuarial risk assessment and psychological risk factors. He is co-author of STATIC-99, the most widely used risk assessment instrument for sexual offenders in the world, and of Risk Matrix 2000, the most commonly used risk assessment instrument in the United Kingdom.

D. Richard Laws, Ph.D., is currently Co-Director of the Pacific Psychological Assessment Corp. (PPAC), which markets visual stimuli for assessment and training manuals for use in forensic psychology. He is additionally the Director of Pacific Design Research, which serves as a development arm of PPAC. Dr Laws holds adjunct faculty appointments at Simon Fraser University and the University of Birmingham (UK). He received his Ph.D. in educational psychology in 1969 from Southern Illinois University, Carbondale. He currently serves on the editorial boards of *Sexual Abuse: A Journal of Research and Treatment*, *Journal of Sexual Aggression*, *Journal of Interpersonal Violence* and *Legal and Criminological Psychology*. He is the author of numerous journal articles, book chapters and scholarly essays, and co-editor/co-author of a number of books and manuals. Dr Laws is the recipient of the Significant Achievement Award (1989) and Service Award (1998) of the Association for the Treatment of Sexual Abusers (ATSA) and has served as President of that organization (1992–93).

Editor's note: Co-editor D.R. Laws and contributors C.L.Z. Gress and D. Glasgow have a financial interest in some of the procedures described in this book.

LIST OF CONTRIBUTORS

Anthony R. Beech

Professor, Centre for Forensic and Criminological Psychology, School of Psychology, University of Birmingham, Birmingham, UK.

Caoilte Ó Ciardha

School of Psychology, University of Dublin, Trinity College, Dublin, Ireland.

Vanja E. Flak

Centre for Forensic and Criminological Psychology, School of Psychology, University of Birmingham, Birmingham, UK.

David V. Glasgow

Head, Product Development, Pacific Psychological Assessment Corp., Victoria, British Columbia, Canada, and Carlton Glasgow Partnership, Colne, Lancashire, UK.

Michael Gormley

School of Psychology, University of Dublin, Trinity College, Dublin, Ireland.

Nicola S. Gray

Professor, Cardiff University, Cardiff, and Caswell Clinic, Bro-Morgannwg NHS Trust, Bridgend, UK.

Carmen L.Z. Gress

Faculty of Education, Simon Fraser University and the University of Victoria, British Columbia, Canada, and Co-Director, Pacific Psychological Assessment Corp., Victoria, British Columbia, Canada.

Jeffrey E. Hecker

Professor, Department of Psychology, University of Maine, Orono, Maine, USA.

Glyn W. Humphreys

Professor, Behavioural Brain Sciences Centre, School of Psychology, University of Birmingham, Birmingham, UK.

Matthew W. King

Department of Psychology, University of Maine, Orono, Maine, USA.

D. Richard Laws

Co-Director, Pacific Psychological Assessment Corp., Victoria, British Columbia, Canada.

Kevin L. Nunes

Assistant Professor, Department of Psychology & Institute of Criminology and Criminal Justice, Carleton University, Ottawa, Ontario, Canada.

Susan Sachsenmaier

Sand Ridge Secure Treatment Center, Evaluation Unit, Madison, Wisconsin, USA.

R. Jamie Scoular

Highlands Behavioral Health Systems, Denver, Colorado, USA.

Paul Smith

Associate Principal Lecturer in Forensic Psychology, Department of Psychology, Leeds Trinity and All Saints, Leeds, UK.

Robert Snowden

Professor, Cardiff University, Cardiff, UK.

David Thornton

Sand Ridge Secure Treatment Center, Mauston, Wisconsin, USA

SERIES EDITORS' PREFACE

ABOUT THE SERIES

At the time of writing, it is clear that we live in a time, certainly in the United Kingdom and other parts of Europe, if perhaps less so in other areas of the world, when there is renewed enthusiasm for constructive approaches to working with offenders to prevent crime. What do we mean by this statement and what basis do we have for making it?

First, by 'constructive approaches to working with offenders', we mean bringing the use of effective methods and techniques of behaviour change into work with offenders. Indeed, this view might pass as a definition of forensic clinical psychology. Thus, our focus in this series is the application of theory and research to develop practice aimed at bringing about a change in the offender's functioning in order to reduce re-offending. The word *constructive* is important as it allows a clinical approach to be set against approaches to behaviour change that seek to operate by destructive means. Such destructive approaches are typically based on the principles of deterrence and punishment, seeking to suppress the offender's actions through fear and intimidation. A constructive approach, on the other hand, seeks to bring about changes in an offender's functioning that will produce, say, enhanced possibilities of employment, greater levels of self-control, better family functioning or increased awareness of the pain of victims, with the net result of reduced numbers of victims.

A constructive approach faces the criticism of being a 'soft' response to the damage caused by offenders, neither inflicting pain and punishment nor delivering retribution. This point raises a serious question for those involved in working with offenders. Should advocates of constructive approaches oppose retribution as a goal of the criminal justice system as a process that is incompatible with treatment and rehabilitation? Alternatively, should constructive work with offenders take place within a system given to retribution? We believe that this issue merits serious debate.

However, to return to our starting point, history shows that criminal justice systems are littered with many attempts at constructive work with offenders, not all of which have been successful. In raising the spectre of success, the second part of our opening sentence now merits attention, that is, 'constructive approaches to working with offenders *to prevent crime*'. In order to achieve the goal of preventing crime, interventions must focus on the right targets for behaviour change. In addressing this crucial point, Andrews and Bonta (1994) have formulated the *need principle*:

Many offenders, especially high-risk offenders, have a variety of needs. They need places to live and work and/or they need to stop taking drugs. Some have poor self-esteem, chronic headaches or cavities in their teeth. These are all 'needs'. The need principle draws our attention to the distinction between *criminogenic* and *non-criminogenic* needs. Criminogenic needs are a subset of an offender's risk level. They are dynamic attributes of an offender that, when changed, are associated with changes in the probability of recidivism. Non-criminogenic needs are also dynamic and changeable, but these changes are not necessarily associated with the probability of recidivism (p. 176).

Thus, successful work with offenders can be judged in terms of bringing about change in non-criminogenic need *or* in terms of bringing about change in criminogenic need. While the former is important and, indeed, may be a necessary precursor to offence-focused work, it is changing criminogenic need that, we argue, should be the touchstone in working with offenders.

While, as noted above, the history of work with offenders is not replete with success, the research base developed since the early 1990s, particularly the meta-analyses (e.g. Lösel, 1995), now strongly supports the position that effective work with offenders to prevent further offending is possible. The parameters of such evidence-based practice have become well established and widely disseminated under the banner of 'What Works' (McGuire, 1995, 2002).

It is important to state that we are not advocating that there is only one approach to preventing crime. Clearly there are many approaches, with different theoretical underpinnings, that can be applied to the task of reducing offending. Nonetheless, a tangible momentum has grown in the wake of the 'What Works' movement as academics, practitioners and policy makers seek to capitalize on the possibilities that this research raises for preventing crime. The task for many service agencies lies in translating the research into effective practice.

Our aim in developing this series in Forensic Clinical Psychology is to produce texts that review research and draw on clinical expertise to advance effective work with offenders. We are both committed to the ideal of evidence-based practice and we will encourage contributors to the series to follow this approach. Thus, the books published in the series will not be practice manuals or 'cook books': they will offer readers authoritative and critical information through which forensic clinical practice can develop. We are both enthusiastic about the contribution to effective practice that this series can make and look forward to continuing to develop it even further in the coming years.

ABOUT THIS BOOK

The official crime statistics suggest that compared to some other types of crime, such as burglary and assault, sex offences are relatively low volume. In this light, it may be thought that sex offenders attract a disproportionately large amount of attention. There are journals given to the topic of sex offending, regular international conferences and any number of books – indeed, this is the fifth title in this series solely concerned with sex offenders. However, it is also known that sex offences are massively under-reported and the official figures are but the tip of a very substantial iceberg. Further, the harm and distress caused by sex offences in their many forms and guises, affecting both adults and children, perhaps marks them out as a particularly heinous form of criminal activity.

Of course the study of sex offenders is not new and there is a large research base to draw on. However, it is noticeable that as offender-focused research matures, researchers are addressing increasingly fine-grained issues. An example of this shift to detailed examination of specific aspects of offenders' functioning is seen in the previous book in the series, edited by Theresa Gannon, Tony Ward, Anthony Beech and Dawn Fisher (2007), which focussed on cognitive functioning in aggressive offenders. In this book, David Thornton and Richard Laws examine the precise issue of cognitive approaches to the assessment of sexual interest in sex offenders. This is a topic that covers a large amount of ground: the book's contents range from widely used means of assessment, such as questionnaires, to methods designed specifically for sexual assessment, such as penile plethysmography and encompassing innovative approaches such as the Stroop test and the implicit association test.

The editors of this collection are both acknowledged experts in the field of sex offending, with a weight of experience behind them as practitioners, service managers and researchers. They have drawn together an outstanding collection of chapters written by authorities in the field which, we believe, will make a significant contribution to the work of those engaged in practice and research aimed at preventing sex offending.

Clive Hollin
Mary McMurran

REFERENCES

Andrews, D.A. and Bonta, J. (1994) *The Psychology of Criminal Conduct*, Anderson, Cincinnati, OH.

Gannon, T.A., Ward, T., Beech, A.R. and Fisher, D. (2007) *Aggressive Offenders' Cognition: Theory, Research and Practice*, John Wiley & Sons, Ltd., Chichester.

Lösel, F. (1995) Increasing consensus in the evaluation of offender rehabilitation? *Psychology, Crime, and Law*, **2**, 19–39.

McGuire, J. (ed.) (1995) *What Works: Reducing Reoffending*, John Wiley & Sons, Ltd., Chichester.

McGuire, J. (ed.) (2002) *Offender Rehabilitation and Treatment: Effective Programmes and Policies to Reduce Reoffending*, John Wiley & Sons, Ltd., Chichester.

INTRODUCTION

DAVID THORNTON

Sand Ridge Secure Treatment Center, Mauston, WI, USA

D. RICHARD LAWS

Pacific Psychological Assessment Corporation, Victoria, BC, Canada

WHY MEASURE SEXUAL INTEREST?

More than any other psychological characteristic, the nature of their sexual interests is what distinguishes repetitive sexual offenders from both non-offenders and lower risk offenders. Valid and efficient technologies for assessing the sexual interests of sexual offenders are of critical value in the identification of treatment needs and the assessment of risk. For treatment professionals, they also have the additional value that sharing the results of these assessments with offenders can be used to motivate them to accept that they have a problem that they need to work on. The main purpose of this book is to bring together critical reviews of the more established technologies for assessing sexual interest together with explanations of newly developing technologies by the primary researchers involved in their development.

THE PENILE PLETHYSMOGRAPH

Since about 1975, a psychophysiological method called penile plethysmography (PPG) – direct measurement of circumferential or volumetric changes in the male genital – has been used to assess sexual interest, primarily in sexual deviants. The procedure has, for the most part, proven to be an excellent technology for assessing sexual interest. However, it is expensive, invasive, labour intensive, limited to males and ideally requires a motivated and responsive subject. These problems do not render the procedure useless but they limit its utility and in some circumstances

Cognitive Approaches to the Assessment of Sexual Interest in Sexual Offenders   Edited by D. Thornton and D. R. Laws
© 2009 John Wiley & Sons, Ltd

challenge the validity of results obtained with the method. In spite of these problems, a considerable literature has built up over the past three decades that more or less supports the use of PPG. In Chapter 1, Laws critically examines this literature and identifies developments in this older technology that seek to overcome some of its limitations.

Limitations of the PPG as an assessment technology have led to a search for a viable alternative. Subsequent chapters explore different alternatives.

The best established of these alternatives – the amount of time that a subject views a possibly erotic stimulus – has been tested in various formats since 1942. This technique has been refined within the past 10 years and there are now two commercially available viewing time procedures. The *Abel Assessment for sexual interest (AASI)* was developed and it marketed by Abel Screening Inc. of Atlanta. This is a simple viewing time procedure which measures how long a subject looks at a stimulus. It is a commercial product exclusively marketed by Abel Screening who also controls administration procedures, scoring and data interpretation. The scoring algorithm is proprietary and has not been made available for independent empirical evaluation. This lack of peer review has raised concerns about the validity of the test. In Chapter 2, Sachsenmaier and Gress review the evidence-supporting use of this method, identify its limitations and propose circumstances when the method is appropriate for use and circumstances when it should not be employed.

The second procedure, *Affinity 2.1*, was developed for the assessment of paedophilic interest in persons with learning disabilities. The computer-based procedure uses convergent measures – the ranking, then rating of non-pornographic images while viewing time is measured. A pilot investigation in 2003 was successful in assessing sexual interest in the learning disabled as well as normal subjects. In Chapter 3, David Glasgow, the primary developer of this procedure, describes the way it was developed to enhance its user-friendliness both for the person being assessed and for the clinician interpreting the results. In contrast to the AASI, Affinity is probably best understood as a structured, user-friendly way of eliciting self-reports of sexual attraction. It incorporates measures of the time spent viewing images as a validity check on self-report rather than as primary measure of sexual interest in its own right.

In Chapter 4, Gress and Laws go on to explore the use of *Choice Reaction Time (CRT)* tasks in assessing sexual interest. A particular value of this chapter is its clear introduction to an information-processing model of sexual content-induced delay (SCID). The central notion here is that a salient sexual stimulus will trigger attentional processes that reduce the attentional resources available for other tasks. A common paradigm is to instruct the person being assessed to press a response key indicating the location on a screen of a briefly appearing dot. Neutral or sexual images of different kinds are present during this task and the degree to which they induce errors or slowing in the CRT recorded. To date, research indicates that the methodology can assess gender preference, but it has not yet been developed in a way that allows sexual preference for children to be assessed.

Like the CRT method, a number of other approaches to assessing sexual interest have tried to adapt well-established paradigms from experimental social and cognitive psychology. This has the advantage of being soundly based in academic psychology but has only recently been applied to the assessment of sexual offenders.

In Chapter 5 Gray and Snowden describe their pioneering application of the implicit association test (IAT) in assessing the sexual interests of child molesters. The IAT involves asking the participant to classify stimuli, for example, as *pleasant* or *unpleasant*, or as *insects* or *flowers*. The classification can be made more complex by asking people to classify stimuli by whether they are *pleasant* or *flowers* versus *unpleasant* or *insects*. When category labels are combined like this, it has been found that combinations that involve cognitively compatible categories (e.g. *flower* and *pleasant*) allow faster categorization than combinations that involve cognitively incompatible categories (e.g. *insect* and *pleasant*). By comparing the speed with which categorization judgments are made for different combinations of categories, it is possible to determine the way the categories are implicitly associated within the person's cognitive system. The IAT has been widely used in social psychological research to measure attitudes and affective responses. It has the particular advantage that it does not depend on truthful or insightful self-report as it measures the cognitive side effects of attitudes directly. The challenge in applying this to measuring child molesters' interests is how you develop stimuli that are amenable to the IAT paradigm to represent the contrast *adult* versus *child* and the contrast *sexual* versus *non-sexual*. Gray and Snowden's research represents a brilliant solution to this problem combining verbal and visual stimuli. Findings reported by this research group include that their versions of the IAT can distinguish men who have committed sexual offences against children from other kinds of offender, can distinguish paedophiles from hebephiles and that offenders who are in complete denial of their sexual offences produce responses on the IAT that are just as deviant as those of men who admit their offences.

In Chapter 6, Nunes reports an independent attempt to adapt the IAT to assess child molesters' implicit attitudes to themselves and to children. Like Gray and Snowden, Nunes finds that child molesters can be distinguished from non-sexual offenders by their showing an unusual association between the concept of sex and the concept of children. Nunes adds the additional finding that this association is stronger for those who, according to standard actuarial instruments, present a greater risk of committing further sexual offences.

Cumulatively, the research described in these two chapters makes the IAT the best established of the measures of sexual interest that are based on adapting well-established paradigms from social and cognitive psychology.

In Chapter 7, Flak, Beech and Humphreys draw on the effect of salient stimuli on attentional resources in a way that is different from its use in the CRT. They start from the concept of the attentional blink. This is the well-established phenomenon whereby allocation of attentional resources to a particularly emotionally salient stimulus means that these resources are not available for processing a stimulus that is presented shortly afterwards. Flak *et al.* review the more general literature on the rapid serial visual presentation (RSVP), and identify a more credible process model with associated brain mechanisms. They then go on to describe how this has been adapted to the measurement of sexual interest. Results supporting the paradigm's ability to distinguish gender preference are reported, though the effect seems to depend on the use of unclothed stimuli. And preliminary results are reported finding that clothed images of children produce a greater attentional blink in child molesters than in non-offenders.

In Chapter 8, Smith reviews research by himself and Waterman, and by others, suggesting that the strength of the sexual schema of sexual offenders could be assessed using a version of the Stroop colour-naming task. The general finding shown for a variety of groups is that taking longer to name the colour of words reflects the emotional significance of the words for the individual. Repeated studies have shown aggressive individuals showing slowed colour naming with aggressively themed words and preliminary results indicate that sex offenders may take longer to name the colour of sex-related words. This would seem to imply that sexual words and the associated ideas possess greater emotional significance for them. So far the methods seems to be a potential measure of sexual preoccupation rather than of a particular sexual interest, though it is clear that the method could be adapted to assess specific sexual interests if stimuli were more specific to those interests. A particular strength of this chapter is the detailed guidance on how to set up effective Stroop tasks for identifying individual differences.

In Chapter 9, Ò Ciardha and Gormley demonstrate how the modified Stroop task can be used to assess the direction of sexual interests. They use images instead words so that the task becomes to name the colour of an image rather than of a word. Images can then be used to depict either male adults, female adults, male children or female children. They demonstrate that responses to images of adults in this modified Stroop task could be used to identify adult males' gender preference. This chapter is also of interest because it reports research suggesting that combining IAT and Stroop methods can give more powerful identification of sexual interests.

Finally, in Chapter 10, Hecker, King and Scoular report a series of studies exploring the use of the startle probe reflex to assess male sexual interest. They show that the strength of a man's eyeblink reflex in response to a startling stimulus is lessened when they are viewing a sexual image that they find appealing. This eyeblink response measure of sexual interest is shown to correlate appropriately with both self-report and PPG measures of sexual interest. Additionally, they found that their adult male participants could not exercise voluntary control over the effect of sexual stimuli on their eyeblink startle response. The method has yet to be tried with sexual offenders, but these results suggest that it has considerable potential.

THE WAY AHEAD

Do the methods described in this book represent the new frontier in sexual interest assessment? We believe that they do, although major refinement and establishment of reliability and validity remain the important tasks for the future. The major features that we find attractive about these approaches are that they are:

- Entirely portable and useable in any setting,
- Relatively inexpensive,
- Easy to implement,
- Not labour-intensive,
- Easy to score and interpret,

- Not physically intrusive,
- Relatively hard to fake,
- Potentially useable with males and females of any age, and importantly,
- Completely open to psychometric evaluation.

For decades, the cognitive psychology literature has been testing these and other procedures that meet the above criteria.

WHO WILL FIND THIS BOOK USEFUL?

Researchers may find it a useful resource as it brings together in one place, material that they will otherwise have to search diverse journals for. Additionally, contributors have been careful to highlight limitations of methods and gaps in knowledge. These provide the foundations for further research and development projects, especially for those concerned with better grounding applied psychological practice in academic knowledge. University teachers concerned with training forensic psychologists and clinical psychologists with a forensic specialization may find this book a useful resource in relation to the assessment of sexual offenders. Professionals from a variety of disciplines (e.g. psychologists, psychiatrists, clinical social workers) who are concerned with evaluating sexual offenders either for the courts, as part of offender management or as part of treatment, may find it of value to study the assessment methodologies described in this book, either so they can take make better use of these methods themselves, or so they can understand and critically appreciate evaluations done by others.

Chapter 1

PENILE PLETHYSMOGRAPHY: STRENGTHS, LIMITATIONS, INNOVATIONS[1]

D. RICHARD LAWS

Pacific Psychological Assessment Corporation, Victoria, BC, Canada

STRENGTHS

Penile Plethysmography as Technology

Dorland's Illustrated Medical Dictionary (1994) defines *plethysmography* as 'the recording of the changes in the size of a [body] part as modified by the circulation of the blood in it' (p. 1306). This is done by measuring electrical *impedance*, 'a technique for detecting blood volume changes in a part by measuring changes in electrical resistance'. Impedance changes are detected by a *strain gauge*, 'a technique for detecting blood volume changes in ... circumference employing a rubber tube filled with a conductive liquid; as the tube expands and contracts, the resistance in the fluid changes in proportion to the circumference'. A *plethysmograph* is 'an instrument for determining and registering variations in the volume of an organ' (Dorland's Illustrated Medical Dictionary, 1994, p. 1306, passim).

In medicine, plethysmography is primarily used for 'measuring changes in body volume, used especially in measuring pulmonary ventilation' as well as for 'measuring blood volume taking place in a single finger' (Dorland's Illustrated Medical Dictionary, 1994, p. 1306). This description shows that it is a small step from measuring blood volume in a single finger to measuring circumferential change in a penis. This impressive definition lends an aura of scientific respectability to penile plethysmography.

There are two general methods for measuring changes in penis size. The first, called the *volumetric method*, was developed by Freund in the former

---

[1] This chapter is an adapted version of Laws, D.R., Penile Plethysmography: Will we ever get it right? In T. Ward, D.R. Laws and S.M. Hudson (Eds) *Sexual deviance: Issues and controversies*, 82–102. Copyright © 2003 Sage Publications, Inc.

Cognitive Approaches to the Assessment of Sexual Interest in Sexual Offenders   Edited by D. Thornton and D. R. Laws
© 2003 Sage Publications, Inc.

Czechoslovakia. This method encloses the penis in a glass tube and measures changes in air volume in the tube as the penis expands and contracts (Freund, Sedlacek and Knob, 1965). Although this approach is highly sensitive and favoured by a small coterie of researchers, it has never seen wide use due to its expense and cumbersome nature.

The second approach, called the *circumferential method*, is virtually identical to the medical definition given above. A loop of silicone rubber tubing is filled with mercury or indium–gallium and plugged with electrodes attached to electronic circuitry that passes a weak current through the mercury (Bancroft, Jones and Pullan, 1966). This is called the *mercury gauge*. The transducer loop is fitted over the shaft of the penis. In a state of flaccidity, the resistance in the circuit is zeroed. Following this, any expansion of the penis will thin out the column of mercury and increase electrical resistance. These resistance changes are typically read out as a real-time tracing of the response. An alternative device (the *Barlow gauge*) was developed by Barlow, Becker, Leitenberg and Agras (1970). This method employs a mechanical strain gauge attached to the flat top of a thin band of surgical steel which is shaped like a ring and open on the lower side. It is placed on the penile shaft in the same way as the mercury transducer. When the penis expands, the strain gauge is slightly bent, which increases the resistance and permits the same kind of reading as the mercury gauge. The function of the two gauges is quite similar (Laws, 1977).

These are respectable scientific methods. If used properly, they should produce reliable and valid data. The manufacturers of penile plethysmographs provide extensive instructions for the use of their equipment. Some treatment centres such as Sand Ridge Secure Treatment Center in Wisconsin and HM Prison Service in the United Kingdom have developed highly detailed protocols for implementation and scoring of the procedure, but this is not typical. It is well recognized by researchers in the field that PGG equipment and procedures are often used in highly idiosyncratic ways, likely without continuous reference to user manuals. Despite these shortcomings, there resides a considerable confidence in this technology. 'Machines don't lie', one of the author's assistants once said. Since we know that penile plethysmography (PPG) evaluations can differ wildly from site to site, it matters little whether machines lie or not.

PPG as Procedure

Although PPG has the potential to be creatively used in a variety of ways, there are two typical procedures that have developed over the years.

Age and gender assessment

In this procedure, still images of males and females of various ages are presented to the client. There are typically five or six age categories with two to four exemplars per category. The images are presented for a predetermined period of time, usually 2 minutes. The client is instructed to allow himself to become sexually aroused if he finds the image sexually attractive. The resulting erection response values are scored as millimetres off baseline, percentage of full erection, some kind of deviance index or transformed to ipsative z-scores. Means are computed for each category and the resulting scores per category are used to determine sexual interest by age and gender. This procedure has proven most useful with extrafamilial child molesters.

Sexual activity assessment

In this procedure, scenarios are constructed that describe various forms of consenting and non-consenting sexual activities and recorded on tape or CD. These can be constructed by the client but most often are prepared in a standard set by the researcher/clinician. The scenarios are usually 2–3 minutes in length. As with the age/gender assessment, the client is instructed to allow himself to become sexually aroused if he finds the script to be sexually attractive. This procedure is most often used with child molesters and rapists. The scripts contain different content to reflect the supposed sexual interest of these two groups.

The two procedures are directed primarily at child molesters and rapists because they make up the majority of clients assessed. Incest offenders are frequently exposed to the age/gender assessments but tend to respond like non-offenders. Specially prepared assessments using recorded scripts are sometimes prepared to evaluate clients such as exhibitionists, voyeurs or frotteurs.

PPG as Art

PPG is, in a sense, an art because there are essentially no universally agreed-upon standards for performing the procedure. For example, Howes (1995) conducted a survey of 48 plethysmographic assessment centres in 25 US states and 6 Canadian provinces. He was concerned that

> although the technical adequacy of plethysmographic assessment is the subject of some disagreement, and validity studies are not entirely convincing, plethysmography had nonetheless been accepted as both a reasonably precise quantification of sexual arousal ... and a diagnostic instrument about which there is every reason to be optimistic. ... Perhaps the most substantial criticism of this procedure ... is its apparent lack of standardization. (p. 14)

The agencies responding to Howes's questionnaire reported being in the plethysmographic testing business for an average of 5.5 years ($R = 6$ mo $-$ 25 yr). Technicians performing the assessments reported an average of 3.4 years of experience ($R = 6$ mo $-$ 25 yr). Forty-two per cent of the technicians had been doing the assessments for 2 years or less. Formal training in the procedure was 1 week or less for 76% of the technicians, and 18% had received no training at all. Admittedly, the extent to which Howes's sample of 48 is representative of North American practice is unknown. The data he reported are appalling. The author's several decades of experience with the procedure and with a variety of assessment centres suggest to me that he is right.

O'Donohue and Letourneau (1992) also noted that 'there does not appear to be a standardized penile tumescence assessment, but rather there is a family of procedures which share some common aims and features' (p. 126). They listed the following potential sources of procedural variation. These referred to the assessment of child molesters but would apply equally well to other offender groups:

1. Type of strain gauge used (mechanical, mercury) and transducer placement.
2. Type of stimuli used (audio recordings, slides, videotapes).
3. Content of stimuli used (differences in models).
4. Duration of stimulus presentation (2 s to >4 min).
5. Length of interstimulus (detumescence) interval (fixed time vs. return to baseline).
6. Nature of stimulus categories sampled (Tanner criteria vs. age scales).
7. Number of categories and of stimuli used for each category.
8. Instructions to subjects (imagine sexual behaviour with target vs. no instructions).
9. Whether a warm-up was used and number of assessment sessions.
10. Type of recording instrumentation used (computer-generated graphs vs. strip chart recorder).
11. Whether strain gauge calibration was used to correct for any non-linear characteristics of recording.
12. Data sampling rate (every 5 s vs. every 1 min).
13. Whether methods were used to assess for faking.
14. Gender and other characteristics of the evaluator.
15. Type of data transformation (z-score vs. deviance index).
16. Characteristics of the laboratory (degree of privacy).
17. Type of sample and setting (outpatient, prison).

These appear to be a formidable set of requirements but actually they are not. They are exactly the problems that one encounters every day in performing these assessments. Over the years, the author has visited many assessment centres and spoken to the persons in charge. He has stressed the absolute necessity of standardization to them. He has routinely received responses such as, 'We've always done it this way', or 'We do what works for us', or 'We've tested hundreds of people using this method. Why should we change?' For 8 years, first as president and then as a member of the Executive Board of the Association for the Treatment of Sexual Abusers (ATSA), the largest umbrella organization in the world for workers in this field, the author repeatedly stressed the need for proper training in psychophysiological assessment.

However, ATSA made an effort. In their *Practice Standards and Guidelines for Members of the Association for the Treatment of Sexual Abusers* (ATSA, 1997), they included an appendix (pp. 40–43) dealing with the plethysmographic examination. It should be emphasized that this appendix is *not* intended as a training manual. It is simply a set of recommendations and guidelines. It includes, in part, (a) requirements for training, (b) appropriate client groups, (c) screening of clients, (d) informed consent, (e) appropriate stimulus sets, (f) legislation regarding use of erotic stimuli, (g) stimulus material, visual and audio, (h) documentation of assessment data and

(i) data scoring and interpretation. This set of very general guidelines meets some but not all of the issues raised by O'Donohue and Letourneau (1992). The extent to which practitioners followed the recommendations is unknown. The latest revision of this manual is equally non-specific (ATSA, 2001).

In recent years two highly detailed procedure manuals have been prepared, one by the Sand Ridge Secure Treatment Center in Wisconsin (D.M. Thornton, personal communication, 5 April 2007) and the other by HM Prison Service in the United Kingdom (HM Prison Service, 2005). The author was asked to peer review the latter manual. It describes, in considerable detail, the exact elements of the assessment procedure as well as the clinical protocol that must accompany it. It is a hard read but everything is there. It embodies precisely what many researchers have been recommending for 20 years.

There is also a national effort underway in the United Kingdom. D. Perkins (personal communication, 11 April 2007) has described this process:

> There is now a national PPG forum in the UK, bringing together practitioners from prisons and forensic mental health services. The group has been asked by the BPS [British Psychological Society] to update the current BPS PPG guide-lines, which we are currently doing. Different sites are using slightly different procedures, stimulus sets etc., but the group is helping establish some common practices. It is also a useful forum for considering complex or controversial PPG referrals/results, and this is proving valuable as a peer reference group. We are trying to set up some comparison of visual and auditory stimuli along with other variables. We have a project ongoing on the use of film material in ways that are ethical and legal (including [sic] copywrite), and a couple of us are looking at visual scan technology linked to PPGs.

To date, there has been one major attempt in North America to standardize the age and gender assessment for child molesters. In 1987, a group of senior researchers in penile plethysmography met at the National Institute of Mental Health in Rockville, Maryland. The purpose of the meeting was to define a stan-dard protocol for stimulus type and procedure in that assessment (Abel, Becker, Card, Cunningham-Rathner, Farrall, Jensen, Laws, Murphy, Osborn, Quinsey and Wormith, 1989). This was to be called the Multisite Assessment Study and was to be carried out at five sites in the United States and three in Canada. Only one Canadian site (Laws, Gulayets and Frenzel, 1995) completed the study. The pro-tocol (see Laws et al., 1995, pp. 48–52) specified (a) characteristics of the research participant, (b) characteristics of the individual stimulus slides, (c) characteristics of the slide set, (d) calibration of equipment, (e) details of the assessment proce-dure, (f) informed consent, (g) data reduction and (h) statistical analysis of data. This protocol attempted to address most of the concerns raised by O'Donohue and Letourneau (1992). The study by Laws et al. (1995) reported on only 30 participants. Had the other sites reported that many subjects, we would have had the beginnings of an international database. No further attempt has been made to complete this project.

Murphy and Barbaree (1994) observed that most of the published studies in the literature have originated in the laboratories of a small number of senior in-vestigators. Students and colleagues of these researchers continue to publish their findings. At least for this small coterie of investigators one may reasonably surmise that there is a rough consistency in their procedures and manner of reporting data. But what of the vast majority of clinicians/researchers who were not part of this more experienced group, who learned to do PPG by listening to conference presentations or reading the publications of this group? Therein lies the major continuing problem in standardization.

In the past few years, there have been discouraging as well as encouraging developments. In 2005, a meeting on standardization was held at the annual ATSA conference. About 50 people attended a meeting. The author had reviewed the HM Prison Service procedure manual and protocol a few months earlier and presented the basic idea of a potential nationwide protocol. The organizer of the meeting had set up a web site (phallometrics.com) and people were encouraged to blog on this site. There seemed to be some general interest and then the questions started: 'Why should I devote precious time to this procedure when the one I have works perfectly well?' And that was the end of it. Hardly anyone contributed to the web site and it is now defunct. On the other hand, the remarks by Perkins cited above are encouraging. The United Kingdom is a small country, the persons doing this work are all known to one another, and the likelihood that a reasonably coordinated system will develop is high.

Related to these issues is a multisite study proposed by Marshall, Fernandez, Marshall and Mann (2001). An investigation was proposed that would continue over a 2-year period at multiple sites in Canada and the United Kingdom. The study would compare responses of extrafamilial child molesters, incest offenders, rapists and normals. These authors estimated that the final data set would exceed 1000 participants. The stimulus sets used would be recorded descriptions of sexual activity between adult males and children and of sexual violence against adult women. The sets would be updated versions of stimuli previously tested and reported by Quinsey and his colleagues (Quinsey and Chaplin, 1988; Quinsey, Chaplin and Varney, 1981). The project was proposed to proceed in four phases: standardization, data collection, psychometric analyses and establishment of normative data. All sites would use the same assessment protocol, the same PPG equipment, the same stimulus sets and the same data-reporting format. Three studies were proposed. The first would focus upon internal consistency, the second on test–retest reliability and the third on criterion validity, examining differences between the four groups. The distribution of scores for the normal groups would be determined. Percentile scores for those distributions would be established in order to compare the offenders' responses to them.

The main deficiency in the proposal is the absence of an age/gender assessment. The age/gender assessment using visual stimuli has been the classical plethysmographic procedure with child molesters for decades. Its absence here is regrettable.

Dean (C. Dean, personal communication, 12 April 2007) has provided an update on this research programme. On the noted date, 7 sites were using the standardized PPG protocol. Three sites have been using them for over 2 years. By the end of 2007, it is expected that all 10 sites proposed will be fully equipped and running. Across the sites currently operating, over 100 PPGs have been completed, the majority being pre- and post-intervention. The main addition to the procedure has been the development of an *Interpretation Manual*. Dean stated that this manual 'clearly documents procedures for interpreting and reporting data, including our decision-making criteria regarding when responses should be considered interpretable and indicative of offence-related sexual arousal'.

In the author's judgment, the proposal of Marshall *et al.* (2001) represents a breakthrough study that has been too long in arriving. It will undoubtedly solve many of the problems that have plagued PPG over the years. However, we may reasonably ask: Will this information be accepted beyond the proposed study sites? If it is simply reported in the psychological literature, the answer is probably 'no'. On the other hand, if the researchers package the protocols, the stimulus sets and the normative data, sell them or even give them away, there is an excellent chance that this model could be adopted. We must hope for that result.

Summary on Strengths

The preceding section has included some harsh comments about PPG. Although the method is intrusive, invasive of privacy and very time consuming, it works well if implemented in a relatively consistent fashion. Therein are the problems which compromise what otherwise should be viewed as a scientifically respectable psychophysiological assessment procedure. PPG has been used to evaluate sex offenders since the mid-1960s (Bancroft *et al.*, 1966). It has only been very recently, 40 years later, that we are seeing the emergence of standardized procedures and explicit protocols for the procedure. This should never have happened. The many problems have been detailed for years. It is time to fix them.

Does PPG have strengths in clinical and research use? It most certainly does. However, those strengths reside where they have always resided, in the age/gender and sexual activity assessments. Despite dramatic improvements in equipment, stimulus presentation and scoring of data, these procedures continue to be implemented in the same manner as 30 years ago. The introduction of highly specific procedure manuals is a very welcome addition.

LIMITATIONS

What about Construct Validity?

Vogt (1993) defined a 'construct' as 'something that exists theoretically but is not directly observable. . . . A theoretical (not operational) definition in which concepts are defined in terms of other concepts' (p. 44). 'Deviant sexual arousal' is such a construct. Construct validity, said Vogt, refers to 'The extent to which variables accurately measure the constructs of interest. . . . Do the operations really get at the things you are trying to measure?' (p. 44). In terms of our present concern, is the phenomenon that PPG measures – penile erection – a valid measure of deviant sexual arousal (i.e. deviant sexual interest and preference)? Opinion has been divided on this issue for decades. Many clinicians and researchers believe that PPG is, in fact, a valid measure of deviant sexual interest.

This point of view has not gone unchallenged. For example, O'Donohue and Letourneau (1992) noted that

> [p]enile measurement is often used to gather information so that inferences can be made concerning naturalistic behavior (e.g., Does this individual prefer children over adults as sexual partners?). However, this type of measurement as currently practiced uses neither naturalistic stimuli nor naturalistic responses. ... Penile tumescence measurement is more directly an assessment of penile response to erotica than a measure of actual sexual behavior in naturalistic situations.

> As with any analogue assessment, the nature of this methodology may miss many critical elements that are relevant to sexual behavior and sexual offending (e.g., affection, fear, tactile and olfactory clues [sic]). Moreover, the only sexual behavior measured is penile responding, and other relevant behavior such as verbalizations, approach behavior, touching, cognitions, etc. are usually ignored. ... Thus, penile measurement techniques do not involve a direct sampling of the domain of interest, but, rather, involve an indirect, analogue approach. More bluntly, pen deflection is not directly [sic] sexual preference and viewing a slide is not a naturalistic potential sexual interaction. (pp. 162–163)

An opposing position was advanced by Barlow in 1977:

> The function of behavioral assessment in an ideal world would be the direct and continuous measurement of the ... behavioral problem in the setting where the behavior presents a problem. ... In some cases the behavior cannot be conveniently produced even in contrived situations. When this happens, as in the case of sexual behavior, clinicians move back down the behavioral chain and measure sexual arousal, presumably an earlier component in the chain of sexual behavior. (Cited in Laws and Osborn, 1983, p. 294)

Laws and Osborn (1983, p. 295) acknowledge that the problem of ecological validity is an important one but agree with Barlow that the erection response is measured because it is the one behaviour in the chain that *can* be (more or less) objectively measured.

Murphy and Barbaree (1994) reported that early research in construct validity centred on comparing subjects' reports of their level of sexual arousal with the measured values. Some researchers (e.g. Abel, Blanchard, Murphy, Becker and Djenderedjian, 1981; Wincze, Wenditti, Barlow and Mavissakalian, 1980) found high correlations among these variables. Murphy and Barbaree (1994) also noted that competing stimuli and demand characteristics of the situation could affect self-report of arousal. When some of these competing variables were taken into account, correlations between measured arousal and self-report were quite low (e.g. Farkas, Sine and Evans, 1979).

There has been a movement towards investigating construct validity in terms of convergent validity. This more straightforward approach compares PPG measures with other indicators of deviant and non-deviant sexual interest. For example, Day, Miner, Sturgeon and Murphy (1989) reported a classification study in which they compared PPG responses to slides, audiotapes and videotapes with a self-report measure that was constructed from the item pool of the Multiphasic Sex Inventory (MSI; Nichols and Molinder, 1984). The PPG measures correctly classified 82% of the offenders by sex of victim and 74% by both victim gender and use of force. The MSI measures, on the other hand, correctly classified 86% by sex of victim and 85% by use of violence. The combination of PPG and self-report was not tested.

Laws, Hanson, Osborn and Greenbaum (2000) reported a similar study. Child molesters completed a self-report card-sort measure of sexual interest and PPG responses were obtained from slides and audiotapes. All three measures of pae-dophilic interest significantly differentiated boy-object child molesters from girl-object offenders. The card sort measure showed the greatest classification accuracy and was the only measure to improve accuracy, once the other two modalities were considered. Taken together, all three modalities provided classification accuracy of 91.7%, greater than any single measure.

The investigations of Day *et al.* (1989) and Laws *et al.* (2000) appear to provide evidence for construct validity, that is, there is such a state as 'deviant sexual arousal'. We must ask, however, whether penile responses to a putatively erotic stimulus, a slide or a recorded description of sexual behaviour and endorsement of inventory items that purport to be descriptions of deviant behaviour are in fact measures of sexual interest, not to say preference. Some would say that they are not. It could be argued that acceptance of these data as measures of interest and pref-erence are more an act of faith than an empirical demonstration of fact. To be sure, the data supporting construct validity are encouraging but they are not definitive.

Is PPG a Genuine Test?

O'Donohue and Letourneau (1992) have noted that the PPG procedure is not equiv-alent to typical standardized psychological tests such as the WAIS-R, which uses an invariant administration protocol. They ask whether PPG is a *norm-referenced* test, where a client's scores can be compared to established norms to determine if his score is 'deviant', or whether it is a *criterion-referenced* test, where the purpose is to indicate whether the subject responds to some established treatment criterion such as a 'normal' as opposed to a 'deviant' sexual response. As indicated previ-ously, most PPG practice is so cluttered with procedural inconsistencies and the failure to establish a standard protocol that it could not, in its present state, come close to being termed a norm-referenced test. The cited proposal of Marshall *et al.* (2001) is a move towards resolving some of these issues. At present, the author is aware of only one attempt to produce normative PPG data. Howes (2001) col-lected data on 724 subjects from nine sites. He was able to establish norms for the interpretation of low arousal scores in cases where full erection could not be ob-tained. In treatment, but probably only in behaviour therapy, does PPG approach being a criterion-referenced test. In this application, the aim of the treatment is to decrease deviant arousal and increase non-deviant arousal. These changes are easily observable in behaviour therapy data. In other situations, the magnitude of the response becomes the criterion. If a penile response to a supposed deviant stimulus is greater than a response to a non-deviant stimulus, that is considered a criterion response.

Another possibility, said O'Donohue and Letourneau (1992), is that PPG is not really a test in the typical meaning of that term but is rather a *direct observation* of behaviour. This is a staunchly behaviourist point of view that would argue that sexual response is a phenomenon worth studying in its own right. Examples of this approach can be seen in the work of Abel (1979), Abel, Blanchard, Barlow and Mavissakalian (1975) and Laws (1984). In these investigations, differing levels of ongoing erection responding were compared to the content of concurrently presented audiotaped scripts.

Can PPG Scores Predict Reoffence?

Opinion and empirical research are divided on this question. There have been reports over the past decades that suggest that PPG scores are (usually weakly) related to sexual recidivism (e.g. Barbaree and Marshall, 1988; Quinsey, Chaplin and Carrigan, 1980; Rice, Quinsey and Harris, 1991). In the early 1990s, PPG use lay somewhat dormant due to concerns about the use of stimuli depicting nude children or violent and degrading acts. In 1998, Hanson and Bussière published a large meta-analysis that demonstrated that a 'paedophile index' (deviant responses divided by non-deviant responses) was a robust predictor of recidivism. Historically, this was important. The publication coincided with a continuing intense interest in meta-analysis and a surge of confidence regarding the use of actuarial assessment to predict sexual recidivism. In short, it made PPG respectable again.

The only example of this use of PPG in actuarial assessment may be seen in the *Sex Offender Risk Appraisal Guide* (SORAG) (Quinsey, Harris, Rice and Cormier, 1998, pp. 241–243). The SORAG is a 14-item algorithm based solely upon static risk factors. Item 13 is *Phallometric test results*. There are only two choices for this item:

All indicate non-deviant sexual preferences $= -1$
Any test indicates deviant sexual preferences $= +1$

Note the words *any test*. Does this refer to a single stimulus or a group of stimuli? It seems to say that *any* erection response to a deviant stimulus considered 'significant' by the evaluator adds one point to the total score. Because we do not know what a clinically significant response is, confidence in this item is diminished. Because PPG is not widely used in the typical outpatient forensic evaluation, it seems unlikely that it will be incorporated in future actuarial instruments.

There is a larger problem here. In the United States, some 'sexually violent predator' (SVP) programmes use PPG. When administrators of these programmes are asked why they are using such an assessment procedure on people who have been determined to be so dangerous that they might have to be permanently incarcerated, they are likely to reply that it is to determine 'treatment needs'. The result of this practice could be that, if deviant arousal does not decrease as a result of that treatment, it is a small step to cite Hanson and Bussière (1998) or, more recently, Hanson and Morton-Bourgon (2004) to assert that this is evidence that the person is still too dangerous to release. This is a highly inappropriate use of PPG data (see below).

Does PPG predict reoffence? Researchers citing earlier work by Quinsey *et al.* (1980) and, more recently, Hanson and Bussière (1998) or Hanson and Morton-Bourgon (2004) might argue that it does. Others will argue that simply because deviant sexual arousal has been observed in some recidivists hardly makes it a predictor. How those data are used requires rather careful consideration of many other variables operating in the individual's life which may serve as protective factors to decrease danger.

Legal Challenges to PPG

Lawyers for the defence often argue that their clients are being abused by legal, psychiatric or psychological procedures when PPG testing is ordered. They may argue that the procedure is humiliating to their client, that he is being forced to participate in what is clearly a degradation ritual. It is true that the procedure is highly invasive of personal privacy. It is equally true that the majority of technicians go to considerable lengths to ensure the comfort and well-being of their testees. But sex offenders are not attractive plaintiffs, and this argument may be given little weight.

There are growing legal challenges to PPG based on civil law. Consider the following hypothetical case (adapted from Rulo, 1999, p. 1):

> John Smith is a defendant who has just pleaded guilty to several counts of child molestation. John is awaiting his sentencing hearing when he is told that the court has ordered him to take a test. John is told that in the administration of this test a device will be attached ... to his penis, to monitor its response to various graphic images to which he will be exposed. The results of this test, John is told, will be used as evidence in his sentencing hearing to establish his current status as a sexual deviant and later as a condition of his release, to make predictions about his future as a sexual deviant and to monitor his rehabilitative progress.

> The prosecution will argue that PPG is a well-established procedure for evaluating sexual deviants that has been in constant use for over 30 years and is supported by hundreds of publications in the professional literature. John's lawyer may counter-argue that existing precedents in civil law have determined that PPG is an unreliable and invalid procedure, totally lacking in standardization both for administration and interpretation and therefore is inadmissible as evidence in court. ... John's lawyer is highly likely to win this point.

From 1923 to 1993, the standard for admissibility of scientific evidence in court was the Frye test. The Frye standard is that a scientific finding or practice be generally accepted in the scientific community from which it comes. Frye states:

> Just when a scientific principle or discovery crosses the line between the experimental and demonstrable stages is difficult to define. Somewhere in this twilight zone the evidential force of the principle must be recognized, and while courts will go a long way in admitting expert testimony deduced from a well-recognized scientific principle or discovery, the thing from which the

decision is made *must be sufficiently established to have gained general acceptance in the field in which it belongs* [emphasis added]. (*Frye* v. *US*, 293 F. 1013 [D.C. Cir. 1923])

It is obvious that plethysmographic evaluation of sex offenders is a very small portion of behavioural science inquiry. Even within that narrow band of interest, PPG has never been fully accepted. Some of the reasons for this have been noted above. PPG has never met the stipulation of the Frye test.

A new, more comprehensive standard of admissibility was set in 1993 (*Daubert* v. *Merrell Dow Pharmaceuticals*, 509 U.S. 579, 113 S. Ct. 2786, 1125 L.Ed.2d 469 [1993). Smith (1998) noted that

> *Frye* mandated that scientific evidence was admissible only if 'generally ac-cepted' by the scientific community. ... In 1993 the United States Supreme Court adopted a somewhat more flexible, factor-based approach to the admis-sion of scientific evidence in *Daubert v. Merrell Dow Pharmaceuticals*. ... Where the *Frye* test rigidly adhered to a rule requiring 'general acceptance' ... the *Daubert* standard focuses on the 'reliability' and 'fit' (relevance) of the evidence. (pp. 2–3)

Smith (1998) reviewed much of the legal literature surrounding the admissibility of PPG evidence in court, an account too lengthy to summarize here. The main factors that emerged from *Daubert* are the following:

1. Has the technique been tested?
2. Has the technique been subject to peer review and publication?
3. What is known of the potential rate of error?
4. Do standards exist for the control of the technique's operation?
5. Has the technique been generally accepted within the relevant scientific community?

PPG meets the standard for points 1 and 2, although the results are fraught with inconsistency. The technique has been tested thousands of times but with highly variable results depending upon what 'rules' the examiner is following. It has been peer reviewed and published hundreds of times. Opinions of reviewers vary widely and are rarely unanimous. It is with the remaining points that PPG encounters the most difficulty.

The absolute rate of error is unknown (point 3). The potential for error is large. Smith (1998) stated, 'Penile plethysmography cannot meet Daubert's standard of validity or relevance tests because the test results are not generally accepted, are not sufficiently accurate, the test is subject to faking and voluntary control by test subjects' (pp. 5–6).

To obtain a flavour of the error rate in the procedure, one need only consult primarily favourable reviews by Murphy and Barbaree (1994) and O'Donohue and Letourneau (1992) and the more negative ones by Marshall and Fernandez (2000, 2001, 2003). Taken as a whole, it would appear that the error rate is substantial.

The final point in *Daubert* is a reiteration of *Frye*: Is PPG generally accepted in the relevant scientific community? PPG does not meet this standard for the following reasons:

1. Adequate standards for the administration of the procedure do not exist (Barker and Howell, 1992; Howes, 1995; Simon and Shouten, 1991). There are no centres where technicians can be trained. The first formal attempt at standardization, the Multisite Assessment Study (Abel *et al.*, 1989; Laws *et al.*, 1995), was never completed. As noted above that several attempts at standardization are currently being undertaken.
2. O'Donohue and Letourneau (1992, p. 126) listed 17 potential sources of variation in the procedure. Some of these are present in all testing centres.
3. Marshall and Fernandez (2000, p. 813) stated that the PPG procedure appeared to show reasonable but not impressive internal consistency. Test–retest reliability has not been established.
4. Marshall and Fernandez (2003) stated that there is no strong evidence for the criterion validity of the PPG test. This refers to the ability of the test to differentiate sex offenders from one another as well as from non-offenders. They found that the agreement across studies was much greater for child molesters than for rapists. Further, they stated that the test appears to have limited value if rapists and exhibitionists appear normal at assessment and only those extrafamilial child molesters who admit to being deviant show deviant arousal.
5. Laws and Rubin (1969) demonstrated that it was quite easy for males to suppress their erection responses. Laws and Holmen (1978) later demonstrated that, depending upon the type of instructions provided to a single client, he could produce a credible response or suppress the response at will, even while speaking a fantasy unrelated to the stimulus displayed. Although it may be difficult for some to produce a response in the presence of a non-preferred stimulus, a profile of no responding is uninterpretable.

Within the 'relevant scientific community' that routinely uses PPG, none of the preceding will have any impact. PPG will live on, bolstered by the findings of Hanson and Bussière (1998) and Hanson and Morton-Bourgon (2004) and the perceived absolute need to assess and predict risk.

Inappropriate Uses of PPG

In the conclusion of their monograph, Murphy and Barbaree (1994, pp. 84–85) consider the appropriate and inappropriate uses of PPG. Apart from the numerous classification studies seen in the literature, the most appropriate *clinical* application of the technique is the use of erection responses to indicate the need to target deviant sexual arousal for treatment and to monitor the effectiveness of that treatment. In the punitive contemporary social climate, that is a very small part of the bigger picture.

There are three major inappropriate applications of the procedure:

1. Use of erection responses to determine or make statements about whether some-one has committed a specific sexual offence or whether someone 'fits the profile' of a sex offender.
2. Use of erection responses as a sole criterion to decide someone's release from custody or from a treatment programme.
3. Use of erection responses to screen general populations in search of potential sex offenders.

First, there is no such thing as a 'profile' of any variety of sex offender. The second point is the most egregious use of the technique. Mentioned above is the persisting problem that the meta-analyses of Hanson and Bussière (1998) and Hanson and Morton-Bourgon (2004) have introduced, linking deviant sexual arousal to recidi-vism. This presents a temptation in both custodial and community programmes to use sexual arousal as a key decision-making issue. At the moment, the third point may seem far-fetched. However, for example, given the concern over clerical abuse of children, it is not inconceivable that PPG could one day be introduced in seminaries where these individuals train, or made a prerequisite for employment to work with children, or made a prerequisite to obtain certain types of security clearance. There are many possibilities for improper use and all of them are grim.

Murphy and Barbaree (1994, p. 85) make two additional points that are worth mentioning:

1. Erection measures should always be used with other data. These include psycho-metric evaluations as well as clinical interview data, police reports and victim statements. They should never stand as a single mode of assessment.
2. Offenders are frequently accused of faking when they fail to respond in a PPG assessment. It should be remembered that failure to respond may occur for a variety of reasons, only one of which is faking. Data that show lack of re-sponse or very low responding should be reported as exactly that and viewed as uninterpretable.

Conclusions on Limitations

PPG was introduced as a clinical tool with sex offenders in the mid-1960s. It has actually changed very little since then. From the 1960s to the 1980s most laboratories used very large equipment. In those days, the author's laboratory used a 6-channel Beckman Dynograph which could record other events as well as arousal, with all electronic controls situated in a large power rack. It looked impressive but the functions were quite simple. The only thing that is different today is that we have much smaller and much superior electronics, stimulus presentation and data management by computer. These are artefacts of technological change, nothing more. The basic procedure is what it has always been and is still subject to all the same shortcomings. It is a ponderous procedure that eats up valuable clinical time. And, in the end, the actual yield of new information in the data is typically quite small. PPG often tells us what we already know.

Of one thing we can be certain. Whether empirical evidence supports its continued use or not, whether its procedural faults are remedied or not, PPG will survive. We have wasted a great deal of time on a procedure that has given us too little in return. Things could always have been different. The effort to make them different would require a degree of procedural cooperation among clinicians and researchers that has never been a trademark of this field.

INNOVATIONS

In the 42 years that PPG has been used to evaluate sex offenders (1965–2007) there have been very few innovations reported. As mentioned previously, there have been significant technological improvements in the procedures, but there has been little creative use of PPG in research or clinical applications. Importantly, when innovations have appeared, they have rarely been followed up. This section reports some of them.

PPG + Polygraphy

Considering the interest in polygraphy that has developed over the past decades, this seems a natural extension of the use of PPG. Thornton (D.M. Thornton, personal communication, 5 April 2007) has described the integration of the two procedures. The PPG portion is presented in two parts. The first, called the 'non-suppression PPG', is the standard procedure in which the client is instructed to attend to the stimulus and allow himself to become sexually aroused with no attempt to control the response. The second, called the 'enhanced non-suppression PPG', is the same except that the client is asked a series of questions about the stimulus 30 seconds after it has terminated. The purpose, says Thornton, 'is to encourage him to process it more deeply'. Then, in the following days, the client undergoes a polygraph examination which focuses upon compliance with 'a detailed list of dos and don'ts, and asking more generally whether he has deliberately tried to distort the results'.

Thornton states that, in addition to examining penile changes, clinicians also look at respiration and skin conductance changes. These are compared with the results of the polygraph examination. Then, all of this is put into the context of the client's known history and what he has been saying in group meetings about his sexual interests.

The procedure of Thornton et al. goes well beyond what we have recognized over the years as the standard PPG assessment.

Evaluating Stimulus Content

One of the criticisms justifiably levelled at PPG is that one is never certain about what aspect of the stimulus, visual or auditory, the individual is responding. If the stimulus is judged to be deviant in nature and the individual responds at some criterion level, that response is labelled sexually deviant. One can, of course, ask the subject: 'Why did you respond to that? What did you find attractive about it?' He may provide a straightforward and credible answer and he may not. In an effort to circumvent this problem, attempts have been made to match response patterns to stimulus content.

With regard to audio stimuli, Laws (1984, p. 132) observed:

> Unlike visual stimuli, audiotaped descriptions control the erection response rather precisely. Subjects are instructed to attend to the spoken text and not to try to anticipate the described action or relate it to their own experience. 'If you feel yourself becoming sexually aroused', they are told, 'let that happen'. The result, generally speaking, is a highly variable response record, accelerating to subjectively erotic portions, decelerating to nonerotic portions. And so we find ... the subjective erotic value of a wide variety of sexual activities in a particular individual.

Abel *et al.* (1975) were the first to examine how audiotaped segments could control the erection response. Using a fantasy produced by a proclaimed shoe fetishist they were able to show that segments describing a woman's foot produced substantially greater arousal than segments describing only shoes.

Abel (1979) matched the text of a 120-second audiotape of a frottage offence against a PPG tracing of response to the tape. Broken into 6-second blocks it was possible to see exactly which portions of the text produced the greatest arousal. The subject was incrementally aroused by the whole episode. The greatest uptick in arousal was evident in the final 12 seconds where the text described the *sine qua non* of frottage – a victim trapped in the midst of uncaring, unobserving people while the frotteur calmly performed his offence. The offender even obliged by ejaculating at the finale, confirming the diagnosis. This admittedly is a dramatic example but shows the potential power of the procedure.

Laws (1984) replicated Abel's findings with a rapist, two bisexual paedophiles, two exhibitionists and a sexual sadist. The purpose of Laws' research was to demonstrate that offenders then believed to be not particularly dangerous (paedophiles, exhibitionists) were highly sexually aroused to explicit descriptions of sexual violence.

The Kurt Freund Phallometric Laboratory

This description is included here because the Kurt Freund unit is one of a kind. Wilson (R.J. Wilson, personal communication, March 2007) described the early set-up of the laboratory. There were two unique features at that time.

The first feature was the exclusive use of the volumetric plethysmograph (Freund *et al.*, 1965) described above. This is the only institutional laboratory using this device and thousands of clients have been tested with it. The author is aware of only two other private practitioners who use it.

The second feature was the use of a standardized set of 16-mm films as stimuli for assessment. These were initially developed by Freund in Czechoslovakia and abandoned when he resettled in Canada in 1969 at the Clarke Institute of Psychiatry

in Toronto. The set was reproduced in 1970–1972. In each brief stimulus presentation, the subject is nude, standing in front of a theatre curtain. He or she slowly
approaches the camera. The only thing that changes is the model. The background
and motion are identical and there is no extraneous influence due to context or
activity. This set was revolutionary for its time as most other laboratories were
using slide stimuli. This procedure was in place for decades.

For the past decade, the procedures at the Kurt Freund Laboratory have changed
somewhat in that the motion picture films are no longer used (M. Kuban, personal
communication, 9 May 2007). Kuban described the current procedures:

> In the current testing for gender and age preference, audio-taped narratives are
> presented through headphones and accompanied by slides. Three projectors
> display the images simultaneously on three adjacent slide screens approxi-
> mately two to three metres in front of the patient. In each display is an image
> of a nude model from each of three angles: full frontal view, full back view
> and close-up genital view. In the audio, there are seven categories of narratives,
> which describe mild sexual interactions with prepubescent girls, pubescent
> girls, adult women, prepubescent boys, pubescent boys, adult men, and also
> non-sexual neutral stimuli. The accompanying slides show nude models cor-
> responding in age and sex to the topic of the narratives, and landscape slides
> accompany the neutral stories. The test stimuli are presented in discrete trials,
> each 54 seconds in duration, with between trial intervals for as long as required
> for penile volume to return to baseline. The full test consists of four blocks of
> seven trials, with each block including one trial of each type in a fixed pseudo-
> random order. The full duration of this test is about an hour. There are, however,
> other audio-only tests for sexual coercion, masochistic interests, or cross-gender
> (autogynephilia), which have been employed in slightly differing formats than
> the gender/age test.

The procedure described by Kuban is unique for PPG assessment in the use
of three screens to present visual stimuli accompanied by audio narratives appropriate to the visual material shown. Some investigators would argue that this
represents confounding of stimuli. However, Kuban reported that 'less than 5% of
our tests produce responses below those required for a valid test'.

Fading

In the 1970s, the use of stimulus fading was an attempt to alter sexual preference
by positive rather than aversive conditioning. The following examples illustrate
two of the methods. Only portions of the procedures are described.

Barlow and Agras (1973) attempted to treat three male homosexuals. Using adult
male and female slide stimuli, they positioned two slide projectors so that the images overlapped on the screen. Using a variable voltage transformer they were
able to manually dim or brighten each image. There was a series of 16 equal steps
from 0% illumination to 100%. Subjects wore the Barlow strain gauge (Barlow
et al., 1970) to assess penile circumference. Subjects experienced a 2-min presentation with a male image brightened to 100% and the female image to 0%. If the

subject produced an erectile response equal to 75% of his maximum, he advanced to the next step (6% female, 94% male). This stepping process continued as long as his response remained above criterion. If he failed to meet the criterion, the image was displayed in repeated trials until he did. There were six trials per session. Generalization was evaluated in separate sessions which measured response to single-slide presentations. Although homosexual arousal remained high across sessions, Barlow and Agras reported about a 25–30% increase in heterosexual arousal in the post-fading generalization sessions.

Laws and Pawlowski (1974) presented an automated version of the fading procedure to two paedophiles. Their approach resembled that of Barlow and Agras with these exceptions: (1) they attempted to alter sexual interest *within* a sexual orientation, (2) a continuous session rather than a discrete trial procedure was used and (3) fading was controlled by changes in the subjects' sexual response. Two slide projectors were positioned so that the images overlapped. An electronic sensor detected when the criterion response (70%) was reached. This started a stepping motor which controlled lamp illumination, dimming one lamp and brightening the other. If the erectile response remained above criterion, the stepper continued to operate, bringing the image to full illumination. If it fell below criterion, the fading reversed.

Subjects were asked to pick a child slide that they found highly arousing and an adult slide that they did not find unattractive. The 30-minute session began with a child slide fully illuminated and the adult completely faded out. The sensor was set to detect a 70% erection. Subjects were instructed to fantasize to the slide of the child to produce erection. When fading began and the sexual characteristics of the adult became visible, they were to switch the fantasy to adults, admittedly a difficult requirement. If the subject began to lose his erection and fell below criterion, the adult image faded back to that of the child which would allow him to recapture his erection and fade back to the adult image. A second series of child to adult fading was conducted with different slides. These were randomly selected so that which child would be paired with which adult could not be predicted. Generalization tests were conducted using slides from the fading procedure.

This procedure 'failed to demonstrate the effectiveness of an automated stimulus fading technique. . . . Following child to adult fading, we were unable to show an independent response to adults. After two series of child to adult fading, response to adults presented alone was either lower or insubstantially higher than that shown in the baseline condition' (Laws and Pawlowski, 1974, p. 139).

Automatic Morphing

In recent years, the construction and use of virtual stimuli has appeared. Renaud, Proulx, Rouleau, Bouchard, Bradford, Federoff and Bonin (2006) have demonstrated a procedure where a total change from one stimulus to another can be accomplished through changes in a penile transducer or a vaginal blood flow monitor. Like the fading procedures described previously, the subject first sees an image of an attractive child. In the example presented, when changes occur in the mercury transducer (Bancroft *et al.*, 1966), the attractive image morphs to an image of an ugly old woman. This is a promising development in that it requires much smaller instrumentation than the procedures reported previously. However, it is also subject to the same problems that befell Laws and Pawlowski (1974). To the author's knowledge, this procedure has not yet been tested clinically.

Virtual Reality and Attention Control Technologies

Renaud (2005) has also reported on a variety of procedures developed in cyberpsychology. He proposes 'a new method for assessing and treating sexual deviance based on the combined use of VR [virtual reality], eye-tracking systems (ETS) and PPG' (Renaud, 2005, p. 1). Renaud argues that the immersive potential of virtual reality significantly increases the external or ecological validity of assessment measures. By 'immersive', he means a 'feeling of presence' (p. 3). This 'feeling of presence refers to the illusion of being in a real situation of a sexual or potentially sexual nature. . . . The feeling of sexual presence generated by VR can thus increase the validity of sexual interest and preference measures by making the sensorimotor experience in VR more like that outside VR, that is, in the real world' (p. 3). Renaud's subjects enter a virtual environment (VE), a three-sided enclosure in which three projectors back-project still and moving imagery upon the walls. 'The virtual stimuli that we use to elicit sexual attraction and arousal and fully synthetic animated avatars generated with commercial 3D software. These avatars have been designed, developed and validated in order to ensure that they are perceived to represent the required age and sexual properties' (p. 5). The subject is seated inside the VE, wearing a head-mounted display (HMD) which is able to track eye movements. The gaze and dwell time of the eye movements is recorded, providing 'the subjective perspective of the subject being evaluated in virtual immersion' (p. 9). Concurrent PPG measures are also recorded to compare erectile response to the eye-tracking measures.

Conclusions on Innovations

One cannot help but ask why PPG has remained such a stale technology for all these years when potential innovations were obvious but never exploited. The analysis of stimulus content and use of fading procedures never went anywhere. This is unfortunate because they offer a unique approach. The stimulus morphing procedure is similar to the automatic fading procedure but its utility remains to be demonstrated. The use of motion pictures as erotic stimuli has never been repeated. Pornographic videotapes were used for a time in the 1970s but abandoned because it was impossible to know what the subject was responding to. Thus the Freund stimuli remain unique in that the issues of activity and context are controlled. Some innovations are evolutionary such as the pairing of PPG and polygraphy and the multiscreen presentation of visual stimuli along with matching audio scripts. In the author's judgment, virtual reality is going to change everything. The described combination of eye tracking and PPG and the use of virtual avatars in a virtual environment represent the new frontier in sexual interest assessment.

COGNITION AND PPG

What is the role of cognition in penile plethysmography? In the author's view, cognition is the motor that drives sexual arousal. It is often said that sexual arousal is a mental, not a physiological, event. From this point of view, penile erection is merely an epiphenomenon. We measure penile erection because we can, because it is an approximation of what we are seeking. We are unable to measure mental events directly, although the fMRI procedure is bringing us closer to that.

There are other perspectives on cognition and sexual arousal. For example, Gress (C.L.Z. Gress, personal communication, 29 May 2007) stated:

> I think cognition plays a role, but individual differences occur. A person cannot become aroused until they first become aware of and appraise the object of potential interest. Once aware of something, cognition kicks in. I think there are a number of conscious and unconscious . . . regulatory systems that process information and feed that information into a few different feedback loops. The literature suggests one of the loops goes straight to genital arousal, while others cycle through memories and understandings of the current context, which can also feed into genital arousal.

To be sure, cognition has a role in sexual arousal. However, exactly what that role is and exactly how it functions remains to be determined.

SUMMARY ON PPG: A PERSONAL VIEW

In 2003, I published an earlier version of this chapter. It was very negative in tone. I was one of the pioneers in promoting PPG technology in the United States in the 1970s and 1980s. By the turn of the century, I had become quite disillusioned with it, primarily because of its failure to mature and the continuing lack of standardization. I described myself as a former true believer who had become an apostate.

Having written this new version of the material, I am willing to retract some of that negativism. I do not know how it happened but there is finally some movement in this portion of the assessment field. I am especially encouraged by the implementation of the multisite study in the United Kingdom and the detailed procedure manuals that have been developed. This should at least partially solve many of the problems that have been hanging around for decades. I am also encouraged by some of the innovative procedures that have been too long in arriving.

I believe, however, that the future belongs to virtual reality. This is a giant step forward in that it permits us to tailor entire stimulus environments to a particular individual and promises technological evaluation of a host of behaviours, internal as well as external. For many years, these have been the stuff of dreams. Now, at last, they are at hand.

REFERENCES

Abel, G.G. (1979) Assessment and treatment of child molesters. Grant proposal submitted to the National Institute of Mental Health, No. MH33678-01, Rockville, MD.

Abel, G.G., Becker, J.V., Card, R.D., Cunningham-Rathner, J., Farrall, W.R., Jensen, S.H., Laws, D.R., Murphy, W.D., Osborn, C.A., Quinsey, V.L. and Wormith, J.S. (1989) *The Stimulus Standardization Study of the Multisite Assessment Group. Paper presented at the First International Conference on the Treatment of Sex Offenders, May 1989, University of Minnesota, Minneapolis, MN.*

Abel, G.G., Blanchard, E.B., Murphy, W.D., Becker, J.V. and Djenderedjian, A. (1981) Two methods of measuring penile response. *Behavior Therapy*, **12**, 320–28.

Abel, G.G., Blanchard, E.G., Barlow, D.H. and Mavissakalian, M. (1975) Identifying specific erotic cues in sexual deviation by audiotaped descriptions. *Journal of Applied Behavior Analysis*, **8**, 247–60.

Association for the Treatment of Sexual Abusers (ATSA) (1997) *Ethical Standards and Principles for the Management of Sexual Abusers. Appendix B: Plethysmograph Examination*, ATSA, Beaverton, OR, pp. 44–51.

Association for the Treatment of Sexual Abusers (ATSA) (2001) *Practice Standards and Guidelines for Members of the Association for the Treatment of Sexual Abusers. Appendix A: Phallometry*, ATSA, Beaverton, OR, pp. 40–43.

Bancroft, J.H.J., Jones, H.C. and Pullan, B.P. (1966) A simple transducers for measuring penile erections with comments on its use in the treatment of sexual disorders. *Behaviour Research and Therapy*, **4**, 239–41.

Barbaree, H.E. and Marshall, W.L. (1988) Deviant sexual arousal, demographic and offense history variables as predictors of reoffense among child molesters and incest offenders. *Behavioral Sciences and the Law*, **6**, 267–80.

Barker, J.G. and Howell, R.J. (1992) The plethysmograph: a review of the literature. *Bulletin of the American Academy of Psychiatry and Law*, **20**, 13–25.

Barlow, D.H. (1977) Assessment of sexual behavior, in *Handbook of Behavioral Assessment* (eds A.R. Ciminero, K.S. Calhoun and H.E. Adams), John Wiley & Sons, Ltd, New York, pp. 461–508.

Barlow, D.H. and Agras, W.S. (1973) Fading in increase heterosexual responsiveness in homosexuals. *Journal of Applied Behavior Analysis*, **6**, 355–66.

Barlow, D.H., Becker, R., Leitenberg, H. and Agras, W.S. (1970) A mechanical strain gauge for recording penile circumference change. *Journal of Applied Behavior Analysis*, **3**, 72.

Daubert v. Merrell Dow Pharmaceuticals, 509 U.S. 579, 113 S. Ct. 2786, 125 L.Ed.2d 469 (1993).

Day, D.M., Miner, M.H., Sturgeon, V.H. and Murphy, J. (1989) Assessment of sexual arousal by means of physiological and self-report measures, in *Relapse Prevention with Sex Offenders* (eds D.R. Laws), Guilford, New York, pp. 115–23.

Dorland's Illustrated Medical Dictionary (1994) 28th edn, W.B. Saunders, Philadelphia, PA.

Farkas, G.M., Since, L.F. and Evans, I.M. (1979) The effects of distraction, performance demand, stimulus explicitness, and personality on objective and subjective measures of male sexual arousal. *Behaviour Research and Therapy*, **17**, 26–32.

Freund, K., Sedlacek, F. and Knob, K. (1965) A simple transducer for mechanical plethysmography of the male genital. *Journal of the Experimental Analysis of Behavior*, **8**, 169–70.

Frye v. US, 293 F. 1013 (D.C. Cir. 1923).

Hanson, R.K. and Bussière, M.T. (1998) Predicting relapse: a meta-analysis of sexual offender recidivism studies. *Journal of Consulting and Clinical Psychology*, **66**, 348–62.

Hanson, R.K. and Morton-Bourgon, K. (2004) Predictors of sexual recidivism: an updated meta-analysis. User Report No. 2004-02. Public Safety and Emergency Preparedness Canada, Ottawa, Ontario.

HM Prison Service, Offending Behaviour Programmes Unit (2005) *Penile Plethysmograph Procedure (PPG) Documentation*, Home Office, London.

Howes, R.J. (1995) A survey of plethysmographic assessment in North America. *Sexual Abuse: A Journal of Research and Treatment*, **7**, 9–24.

Howes, R.J. (2001) Interpretation of low arousal in plethysmographic assessment: an empirical basis. Unpublished manuscript, Stony Mountain Institution, Winnipeg, Manitoba, Canada

Laws, D.R. (1977) A comparison of the measurement characteristics of two circumferential penile transducers. *Archives of Sexual Behavior*, **6**, 45–51.

Laws, D.R. (1984) The assessment of dangerous sexual behavior in males. *Medicine and Law*, **3**, 127–40.

Laws, D.R. (2003) Penile plethysmography: will we ever get it right? in *Sexual Deviance: Issues and Controversies* (eds T. Ward, D.R. Laws and S.M. Hudson), Sage, Thousand Oaks, CA, pp. 82–102.

Laws, D.R., Gulayets, M.J. and Frenzel, R.R. (1995) Assessment of sex offenders using standardized slide stimuli and procedures: a multisite study. *Sexual Abuse: A Journal of Research and Treatment*, **7**, 155–66.

Laws, D.R., Hanson, R.K., Osborn, C.A. and Greenbaum, P.E. (2000) Classification of child molesters by plethysmographic assessment of sexual arousal and a self-report measure of sexual preference. *Journal of Interpersonal Violence*, **15**, 1297–312.

Laws, D.R. and Holmen, M.L. (1978) Sexual response faking by pedophiles. *Criminal Justice and Behavior*, **5**, 343–56.

Laws, D.R. and Osborn, C.A. (1983) How to build and operate a behavioral laboratory to evaluate and treat sexual deviance, in *The Sexual Aggressor* (eds J.D. Greer and I. Stuart), Van Nostrand Reinhold, New York, pp. 293–335.

Laws, D.R. and Pawlowski, A.V. (1974) An automated fading procedure to alter sexual responsiveness in pedophiles. *Journal of Homosexuality*, **1**, 149–63.

Laws, D.R. and Rubin, H.B. (1969) Instructional control of an autonomic sexual response. *Journal of Applied Behavior Analysis*, **12**, 93–99.

Marshall, W.L. and Fernandez, Y.M. (2000) Phallometric testing with sexual offenders: limits to its value. *Clinical Psychology Review*, **20**, 807–22.

Marshall, W.L. and Fernandez, Y.M. (2001) Phallometry in forensic practice. *Journal of Forensic Psychology Practice*, **1**, 77–87.

Marshall, W.L. and Fernandez, Y.M. (2003) Sexual preferences: are they useful in the assessment and treatment of sexual offenders? *Aggression and Violent Behavior*, **8**, 131–43.

Marshall, W.L., Fernandez, Y.M., Marshall, L.E. and Mann, R.E. (2001) *A proposal to conduct a multi-site standardization study of phallometric assessments*. Unpublished document, Rockwood Psychological Services, Kingston, Ontario, Canada.

Murphy, W.D. and Barbaree, H.E. (1994) *Assessment of Sex Offenders by Measures of Erectile Response: Psychometric Properties and Decision Making*, Safer Society Press, Brandon, VT.

Nichols, H.R. and Molinder, L. (1984) *The Multiphasic Sex Inventory Manual*. Available from Nichols and Molinder, 437 Bowes Drive, Tacoma, WA 98466.

O'Donohue, W. and Letourneau, E. (1992) The psychometric properties of the penile tumescence assessment of child molesters. *Journal of Psychopathology and Behavioral Assessment*, **14**, 123–74.

Quinsey, V.L. and Chaplin, T.C. (1988) Penile responses of child molesters and normals in descriptions of encounters with children involving sex and violence. *Journal of Interpersonal Violence*, **3**, 259–74.

Quinsey, V.L., Chaplin, T.C. and Carrigan, W.F. (1980) Biofeedback and signaled punishment in the modification of inappropriate age preferences. *Behavior Therapy*, **11**, 567–76.

Quinsey, V.L., Chaplin, T.C. and Varney, G. (1981) A comparison of rapists' and non-sex offenders' sexual preferences for mutually consenting sex, rape, and physical abuse of women. *Behavioral Assessment*, **3**, 127–35.

Quinsey, V.L., Harris, G.T., Rice, M.E. and Cormier, C.A. (1998) *Violent Offenders: Appraising and Managing Risk*. American Psychological Association, Washington, DC.

Renaud, P. (2005) The use of virtual reality and attention control technologies in the assessment of deviant sexual preferences. Unpublished manuscript, Université du Québec en Outaouais, Gatineau, Québec, Canada.

Renaud, P., Proulx, J., Rouleau, J.-L., Bouchard, S., Bradford, J., Federoff, P. and Bonin, M.-P. (2006) *Sexual and Oculomotor Biofeedback Mediated by Sexual Stimuli Presented in Virtual*

Reality. Paper presented at the annual meeting of the Society for the Scientific Study of Sexuality, November 2006, Las Vegas, NV.

Rice, M.E., Quinsey, V.L. and Harris, G.T. (1991) Predicting sexual recidivism among treated and untreated child molesters released from a maximum security institution. *Journal of Consulting and Clinical Psychology*, **59**, 381–6.

Rulo, D.G. (1999) *Can We Identify the Sexual Predator by Use of Penile Plethysmography?* www.forensic-evidence.com/site/Behv_Evid/BeE00005_2.html (accessed 16 June 2001).

Simon, W.T. and Shouten, P.G.W. (1991) Plethysmography in the assessment and treatment of sexual deviance: an overview. *Archives of Sexual Behavior*, **20** 75–91.

Smith, S.K. (1998) Evidence of penile plethysmography, psychological profiles, inventories and other 'Not a Pedophile' character and opinion evidence offered on behalf of a defendant in a child sexual abuse case is inadmissible under *Daubert vs. Merrell Dow Pharmaceutical*, http://www.smith-lawfirm.com/Scientific_Evidence_Brief.html (accessed 14 June 2001).

Vogt, W.P. (1993) *Dictionary of Statistics and Methodology: A Nontechnical Guide for the Social Sciences*. Sage, Newbury Park, CA.

Wincze, J.P., Wenditti, E., Barlow, D. and Mavissakalian, M. (1980) The effects of a subjective monitoring task in the physiological measure of genital response to erotic stimulation. *Archives of Sexual Behavior*, **9**, 533–45.

Chapter 2

THE ABEL ASSESSMENT FOR SEXUAL INTERESTS – 2: A CRITICAL REVIEW[1]

SUSAN J. SACHSENMAIER

Sand Ridge Secure Treatment Center, Evaluation Unit, Madison, WI, USA

CARMEN L.Z. GRESS

Faculty of Education, Simon Fraser University and the University of Victoria, BC, Canada

INTRODUCTION

Singer (1984) suggests that men show three stages of sexual attraction and arousal: (a) increased visual attention to the target of interest, (b) movement towards the target and (c) penile engorgement. Consistent with this hypothesis, the Abel Assessment for Sexual Interest (AASI, versions 1 and 2) was developed with the hope that it could measure the first stage, sexual attraction, with the same degree of accuracy as penile tumescence measures the final stage, arousal, but via a far less invasive procedure. The core component of the AASI is a measure of viewing time (VT), determined by the amount of time slides are retained on a computer screen by the subject being tested. In addition to the VT measure, the AASI includes a measure of self-reported sexual attraction to the VT stimuli, a self-report questionnaire and a client data form filled out by the therapist.

The AASI has gone through several iterations. The forerunner was the Abel Screen (Abel, Lawry, Karlstrom, Osborn and Gillespie, 1994), designed to screen males with no known history of sexual offences for paedophilic interests. The first version of the AASI included a summary report with a risk prediction score (*Abel Screening News*, 1997), developed to emulate the measured recidivism risk factors found by Hanson and Bussiére (1998). The AASI authors eventually dropped this statistic and replaced it with the probability value, the probability that an alleged

---

[1] All opinions expressed in the chapter are of the authors and do not necessarily represent the opinions of the State of Wisconsin Department of Health Services.

---

offender is a child molester. Recently introduced is the AASI-2, which includes questionnaire items on Internet porn use and experience of sexual trauma. This chapter reviews the foundation upon which the core component of the AASI, VT, was developed, including methodology, statistical adequacy, cross-validation and replication, detection of dissimulation and use with adolescents and other special populations. In addition, we include a brief review of significant recent advances in the field of VT research, a discussion of implications for future research, cautionary notes and a summary that includes a recommendation for how the AASI can best be utilized on the basis of existing published research.

DEVELOPMENT OF VT AS A MEASUREMENT OF SEXUAL INTEREST

People have long been interested in determining a person's sexual thoughts and desires. Scientific inquiry eventually asked whether the amount of time a person attends to, or views, presented sexual stimuli indicates sexual interest in that particular stimulus or category of stimuli. As indicated above, VT methods do not measure sexual arousal, as they do not measure a physiological increase in penile tumescence. Instead, researchers and theorists suggest that it may measure sexual interest or attraction, essentially an inference of a cognitive state. If sexual interest is strongly positively correlated with sexual arousal, then measures of sexual interest to certain stimuli might be interpreted as showing the likelihood of sexual arousal to similar stimuli.

Empirical research on VT dates back to 1942, when psychiatric hospital staff members noted that the length of time male patients looked at sexual stimuli presented via a photoscope correlated with staff members' ratings of patients' sexual behaviour (Rosenzweig, 1942). A subsequent study showed that homosexual males looked longer at male nudes than female nudes, while heterosexual males looked longer at female nudes than male nudes (Zamansky, 1956). This research on sexual interest was occurring at about the same time that penile plethysmography (PPG), a way of measuring sexual arousal, was being developed by Freund in Czechoslovakia to help determine which military draftees might be homosexual (Freund, 1957). It is likely, therefore, that research evaluating VT as a measure of sexual interest has been influenced by the parallel objectives of PPG as a measure of sexual arousal.

Subsequent VT studies noted a number of interesting yet commonsense findings. For example, male college students looked longer at pornographic slides than non-pornographic slides (Ware, Brown, Amoroso, Pilkey and Pruesse, 1972; Brown, Amoroso, Ware, Pruesse and Pilkey, 1973; Love, Sloan and Schmidt, 1976) and college students' VT of specific sexual stimuli increased along with their ratings of sexual arousal, sexual stimulation and sexual attractiveness (Lang, Searles, Lauerman and Adesso, 1980; Quinsey, Rice, Harris and Reid, 1993). Factors that influenced interest in and reaction to sexual stimuli included expectancy, alcohol and degree of sexual guilt (Lang et al., 1980).

Interest then turned to investigating VT's ability to measure deviant sexual interest in sex-offending males. The first such study compared normal men with

Table 2.1 Classification accuracy of 1994 version of Abel Screen

Victim category	Per cent identified by VT
Male children	76% TP + 24% FN (paedophiles)
(n = 25)	98% TN + 2% FP (normals)
Female Children	91% TP + 9% FN (paedophiles)
(n = 73)	77% TN + 23% FP (normals)
Male teens	90% TP + 10% (paedophiles)
(n = 30)	98% TN + 2% FP (normals)
Female teens	86% TP + 14% FN (paedophiles)
(n = 57)	77% TN + 23% FP (normals)

admitted child molesters (Abel *et al.*, 1994). The Abel Screen was developed to detect adult males' sexual interest in children using a VT procedure (mislabelled as visual reaction time; Maletzky, 2003) that was less intrusive and less time consuming than PPG. Participants consisted of two groups: men who were referred for AASI testing and who admitted to sexually molesting a child ($n = 185$, grouped by target victim category), and male community volunteers paid for their participation as a comparison group ($n = 101$). The Abel Screen consisted of slides depicting partially clothed and nude people of various ages and both genders. Results were presented in terms of true positives (TP) and true negatives (TN) determined by comparing their longest VT averages in preset categories (male child, female child, male teen, female teen) to their admitted behaviours (see Table 2.1). Neither the raw scores nor the cut-off values were reported. Results are presented in Table 2.1.

As seen in Table 2.1, almost one-quarter of admitted paedophiles with male victims were inaccurately classified as non-paedophilic men, while the comparison sample of men were almost all accurately classified. In the male teens category, only one-tenth of admitted paedophiles were inaccurately classified as normal men; most of the normal men were accurately classified as such. In the female children category, most admitted paedophiles were accurately classified. Interestingly, however, almost one-quarter of the comparison sample of men were more likely to be inaccurately classified as having paedophilic interests when responding to slides of female children. In the female teens category, almost one-quarter of the normal men were inaccurately classified as paedophiles, whereas about five-sixths of admitted paedophiles were accurately classified as such, and the remaining one-sixth were inaccurately classified as normal men. It should be noted that sexual interest in adolescents is not considered to be paedophilic, as paedophilia, by definition, refers to sexual urges, fantasies or behaviour concerning children aged 13 years or younger, typically prepubescent.

After completing a 'cross-validation' using the same set of data, with statistics computed separately for 'partially clothed' and 'nude' slides, and child and teenage categories combined, Abel *et al.* recommended that the test be used in organizations where screening for paedophiles is a concern. Unfortunately, only partial results of this cross-validation were provided, making any direct comparison and an assessment of the possible generalizability of the results difficult, thereby negating the purpose of a cross-validation. The Abel Screen did not undergo further development and is not marketed (Abel, 2000).

Harris, Rice, Quinsey and Chaplin (1996) compared viewing time (VT) with plethysmographic arousal (PPG) in child molesters and a comparison sample of non-offending males. Participants resided in the community or came from minimum-security correctional or psychiatric settings (26 child molestation sexual offenders, 25 community volunteers). Three measures were taken: VT, self-reported attractiveness and PPG. Stimulus categories included adult female and male, pubescent female and male, child female and male, and neutral (landscapes). Non-neutral slides showed one nude person with the genital area visible. The researchers reported that VT discriminated between the non-offenders, who had significantly longer VTs, and child molesters, although PPG was more effective at this discrimination. The non-offending males showed a close correspondence between their VT, self-report of the model's attractiveness and PPG scores. Child molesters' self-reports of the models' attractiveness, however, were inconsistent with their PPG and VT, and their PPG and VT were inconsistent with each other. The authors concluded that the child molesters' VT responses were too inconsistent to use in a classification or prediction scheme specific to sexual offenders against children, but that VT overall appeared promising as an epidemiological screening tool for sexual preference. This is based on the congruence of non-child molesters' VT, PPG and self-report, and the finding that there is a large between-group difference: child molesters as a group could be distinguished from community-based non-offending males. The incongruence of child molesters' VT, PPG and self-report contraindicated use of VT with clinical populations.

Quinsey, Ketsetzis, Earls and Karamanoukian (1996) conducted two studies utilizing VT as a measure of sexual interest in two samples of non-offending heterosexual college students, males ($n = 58$) and females ($n = 24$). They investigated VT from an evolutionary theory of mate preference perspective and found supportive results (see article for further information). Of particular interest to this chapter is the fact that adults viewed their preferred sexual interest categories for significantly longer than all other categories, which included male and female images in three age ranges: child, pubescent and adult. Models were frontal nudes, but otherwise non-provocative. In one of the studies, half of the participants' VTs correlated positively with PPG. In three-fourths of these participants, VT correlated positively with self-reports of the model's sexual attractiveness. These studies provide some evidence of construct and concurrent validity of VT as a measure of sexual interest, but leave room for development.

Abel, Huffman, Warberg and Holland (1998) investigated VT in admitted child molesters ($n = 157$) by comparing participants' VT with self-reported sexual interest, and in about one-third of the participants, with sexual arousal measured by PPG. The PPG included four slides in each of eleven categories, including nude Caucasian males and females of ages 4, 8, 12, 16 and 22 years. No slide depicted coercive, forcible, sadistic or aggressive themes. The VT included seven slides in each of six categories, including clothed males and females at ages 8–10, 14–17 and 22 and older. This subset of 42 slides was embedded in the full set of VT slides, which additionally included a set of slides depicting either (1) exhibitionism, voyeurism, frottage, a suffering male, a suffering female, two males hugging, two females hugging, a male and a female hugging and neutral landscapes, or (2) half Caucasian and half African-American models, with landscapes removed and depictions of

2–4-year-old boys and girls added. While these additional slides were not used in the analysis, they may have affected how participants responded to the set of 42 embedded slides. Participants were divided into five groups: those who admitted to abusing male children ages 13 and under, female children ages 13 and under, male adolescents 14–17 years of age, female adolescents 14–17 years of age and those whose offenses included rape of an adult or a paraphilia other than child molestation. ('Child molestation' in this study included offences against children and adolescents through age 17 years.) The authors report that non-child molesters were then excluded (to maximize the likelihood of finding clearer sexual interest in one of the four groups of child molesters) and used as a control group. Exactly how many were excluded and from which parts of the analysis is not clearly reported. The calculation of internal reliability for VT slides used a sample of 95, while the VT discriminant analysis used a sample size from 148 to 154, depending on the target victim category, while the full sample size was reported as 157.

Participants who were determined to have shown their highest interest (VT) or arousal (PPG) to one slide stimulus depicting a certain sexual target victim category also showed higher interest (on VT) or arousal (on PPG) to other slides depicting the same sexual category. Abel et al. conclude that this offers evidence of internal reliability for each procedure, with VT being somewhat higher. It is important to note that PPG categories had four slides each and VT categories had seven slides each, with an unknown number of VT 'disparate responses' removed prior to analysis; what this means and how it was done is not described. Fischer and Smith (1999) point out that the AASI method of removing outliers may have artificially inflated the internal reliability coefficients. Given the incongruous manner in which internal reliability was calculated in this study, the current authors question the credibility of Abel et al.'s conclusion.

Abel et al. (1998) report that child molesters who reported child female, child male and adolescent male victim targets had 'significant correlations' between VTs and slides depicting those categories, while offenders who targeted adolescent females did not. Unfortunately, the actual correlations were not reported, so the strength of the significance is not ascertainable. These results are contradictory to those reported by Harris et al. (1996), where child molesters' VTs were inconsistent with self-rated attractiveness of the models.

Interestingly, PPG did not significantly correlate with any sexual interest category when 30%, 20% or 10% of full erection was used as the criterion; only 30 of the 56 participants reached the 10% criterion. Researchers then removed any per cent-full-erection criterion and combined results from all PPG participants, including the 26 'flatliners'. When these data were used, PPG significantly correlated with child male and adolescent female categories, but again no actual numbers were published. Surprisingly, from our point of view, Abel et al. state: 'Thus, according to this set of statistical tests, visual reaction time is consistent with clinical impressions in more categories of sexual interest (p. 90)'. This is actually not the case, however, as only admitting participants were included in the study: 'If the therapist believed that sufficient evidence existed to classify a participant as having an interest in children, but the participant denied ... [he was] omitted from the analysis (p. 90)'. It is not clear to us how including non-clinically significant flatline PPG data pushed the correlation between PPG arousal and sexual interest category to a statistically significant level; again, the incongruous manner in which the analysis was performed and the lack of clear description in the published work call the conclusion into question.

In addition to the above, this study (Abel *et al.*, 1998) investigated the ability of PPG and VT to classify child molesters according to their sexual interest category. Methodology is described as 'the discriminant analysis used all of the stimulus categories as independent variables and treated stimulus-specific interest categories as the dependent variable (p. 90)'. Thus, it appears that all PPG indices (with no criterion cut point) were used to predict VT interest category and all VT indices were used to predict the highest VT interest category. This differs from a traditional discriminant analysis in that typically the independent and dependent variables are not correlated as they are here: If we are interpreting the authors' methodological description accurately, it appears that the independent variable, 'all stimulus categories', includes the dependent variable, 'stimulus-specific category'. If self-reported sexual target victim category was used, it is not reported as such. Results provided for true and false positives, true and false negatives, and per cent correctly classified are given in Table 2.2 (Table 3 in Abel *et al.*, p. 91); again, cut-off scores are not provided.

The authors conclude: 'In sum, visual reaction time and plethysmography were similar in their ability to predict categorizations. . . . The findings of this study lend strength to the validity of both measures (p. 92, 93)'. Upon review, however, we find this study to be statistically weak and to offer little clinically relevant information. Only participants who claimed to have molested children in specific age and gender categories were included. Abel *et al.*'s method of VT had over

Table 2.2   Classification accuracy of 1998 version of Abel Assessment and penile plethysmography

Victim category (no. of cases/no. with interest)	Per cent identified by VT	Per cent correctly classified by VT[a]	Per cent identified by PPG	Per cent correctly classified by PPG[a]
Male children ($n = 150/13$ for VT) ($n = 53/8$ for PPG)	38.5% TP + 61.5% FN 95.6% TN + 04.4% FP	90.7%	62.5% TP + 37.5% FN 91.1% TN + 08.9% FP	86.8%
Female children ($n = 154/46$ for VT) ($n = 55/17$ for PPG)	67.4% TP + 32.6% FN 64.8% TN + 35.2% FP	65.6%	No variables entered stepwise analysis	0%
Male teens ($n = 148/10$ for VT) ($n = 52/6$ for PPG)	60.0% TP + 40.0% FN 93.5% TN + 06.5% FP	91.2%	50.0% TP + 50.0% FN 93.5% TN + 06.5% FP	88.5%
Female teens ($n = 150/20$ for VT) ($n = 52/8$ for PPG)	60.0% TP + 40.0% FN 79.2% TN + 20.8% FP	76.7%	37.5% TP + 62.5% FN 77.3% TN + 22.7% FP	71.2%

[a] Per cent correctly classified refers to the per cent of total cases which were correctly predicted to be in the category 'has interest' or 'does not have interest'.

one-third false positives for female children and did not significantly correlate with female adolescents. Offenders who said they had sexually molested boys were likely to be classified as having done so, but not with the same degree of accuracy as their self-report. The PPG method, when using a minimum of 10% of estimated full erection criterion, did not significantly correlate with any of the four sexual interest categories, while the VT method correlated with three of the four categories. When PPG flatliner data were included, PPG correlated with two of the four categories, with only one of those categories overlapping with the three categories that VT correlated with, child male. Self-reported attraction significantly correlated with only one of the four categories, child male, and 'partial significant correlation' is reported for adolescent male. The lack of a comparison group of non-offending males, the exclusion of alleged but denying offenders and including adolescent victims in the definition of 'child molesters' further limits conclusions that can be drawn about the ability of either PPG or VT to classify 'child molesters'. A further anomaly that restricts generalization of this study is the way VT was measured. Abel *et al.* report (p. 87) that VT was recorded while participants rated their sexual attraction to each slide, meaning each slide was viewed only once to accomplish both measures, VT and self-reported attraction. The standard AASI procedure, however, is for the test participant to view the slides twice, once to report degree of self-attraction to the slide models and once to measure VT. All that can be concluded from this study is that both PPG and VT may be more likely to identify admitted sexual offenders whose self-reported victims are male and who deny having committed other kinds of sexual offences. This does not tell us much. In a clinical situation, when an offender's self-report is more accurate than the test, there is little reason to use the test.

METHODOLOGY OF THE AASI

The AASI includes measurement of VT, self-report rating of sexual attraction to the models, a multiple-page self-report questionnaire and a questionnaire that the therapist fills in with information about the test participant. Raw data are transmitted via electronic modem to Abel Screen Inc. and an interpretive report is generated and returned to the health professional (however, the raw data are retained by Abel Screen Inc.). The report includes a VT bar chart and summary of the offender's self-report questionnaire data, as well as the calculation of a probability score, which has changed in form from an earlier risk prediction score (*Abel Screening News*, 1997; for further discussion, see Fischer, 2000), representing the probability of committing sexual abuse in the future, to the current probability value, representing the probability of having sexually abused a child in the past. These two probability scores are entirely unrelated.

Stimuli include 160 slides of clothed Caucasian and African-American children and adults, representing 22 sexual categories, including boys and girls aged 2–4, 8–10 and 14–17 years, women and men older than 22 years, sadism against men, sadism against women, exhibitionism against women, voyeurism against women, frottage against women and fetishism (panties and bras). No slide depicts overt sexual activity, but the slides are designed to be provocative to men with sexual interest in the targeted categories. The client sits in front of a computer on which the slides are presented. He is told that he must keep his non-dominant hand (usually the left hand) on an obviously outdated and non-functional cordless computer mouse that sits to the left of the computer keyboard, and to use his dominant hand (usually the right hand) to advance slides by hitting the Enter key. He views the slide set twice, first to familiarize himself with the photographs (during which time VT is unobtrusively recorded) and then to rate the degree of sexual attraction (or disgust) elicited by the model. Participants indicate their ratings of the model's sexual attractiveness using the number keys 1–7 on the keyboard as a Likert scale, where one end indicates strong sexual disgust with the depicted model and the other end indicates strong sexual attraction. As stated above, VT (aka Abel's VRT) is the amount of time each slide is retained on the computer screen during the first viewing (ratings are made during the second viewing). 'Disparate' VT times are deleted by the scoring programme but 'disparate responses' are not defined in published information or the report. Average VT for each stimulus category is indicated on a bar chart. Scoring is ipsative only, meaning a client's average VT in each category is compared only to his own relative VT in other categories and not to any normative database, nor are actual VT measurements provided. The client's self-report to slide categories are compared with his VT for those slide categories and discrepancies interpreted.

To score the VT measure, the 'rule-of-thirds' method is used to determine which VT categories are considered significantly elevated: 'Clinicians are to isolate the space between the lowest score and highest adolescent or adult score. They are then to divide that space into thirds and consider any child category score VT that crosses the first third as a category that represents probably deviant sexual interest' (Fischer and Smith, 1999, p. 199). In addition to VT, a lengthy questionnaire asks the client to report about his own behaviours, including criminal and sexual history, treatment experience and attitudes about sexual behaviour. Items are designed to identify cognitive distortions, social desirability and the probability of denial, in addition to gathering self-report information.

The risk prediction score emerged as a component of the AASI following the Hanson and Bussiére (1996, 1998) meta-analysis of factors that correlate with sexual recidivism, which included PPG. A newsletter published by Abel Screening Inc. (*Abel Screening News*, 1997) explained that two VT measures were equated with PPG deviant arousal to children (we assume these two VT measures are child males and child females). The article does not list an author and does not explain on what basis VT scores can be equated with a correlation derived from a meta-analysis. Eighteen other risk factors reported by Hanson and Bussiére were likewise matched to questionnaire items and then the items were weighted by the correlation noted in the meta-analysis: 'We then multiplied this standardized variable of sexual interest in children by the Hanson and Bussiére weight of .32; multiplied a standardized variable of deviant sexual preference by their weight of .22; prior sex offense by .19; and so on'. The results of these 20 values were summed and the sum standardized using AASI data from 1454 participants. The higher the z-score, the higher the chance of relapse: 'The average is 0. A client with a +1.1 standard score is at 90%; a client at 1.8 is at 95%. A client who scores 95% is in the top 5% of clients likely to relapse'. Actuarial or other supporting data were not provided. Additional information was distributed in product information pamphlets. Fortunately, due to the speculative nature of the scale, the risk prediction score is no longer reported. Unfortunately, it was replaced by a probability value as of 1 January 2001 (flier distributed in November 2006).

The probability value is based on research reported by Abel, Jordan, Hand, Holland and Phipps (2001). Participants included 747 men who underwent AASI assessment; half were used to develop a prediction model (logistic regression equation) and the other half to cross-validate it. The authors note that incest offenders were systematically excluded because they often offend for reasons other than sexual interest, such as family dynamics and opportunity. Others were excluded if they had income that exceeded US$60,000 the preceding year or had no income. Inability to read the questionnaire without assistance also resulted in exclusion. Three-quarters of the participants were Caucasian. Groups included admitting child molesters, admitting non-child molesters (e.g. rapists), and 'liar-denier' alleged offenders. 'Liar-deniers' were labelled such if the offender's therapist suspected that the sexual molestation allegations were true. VT measures, self-reported attraction, and questionnaire responses were used as potential predictor variables. VT and cognitive distortion variables were forced into the equation for the models for offenders against boys and girls, but not for the liar-denier model, and other variables were statistically selected.

The predictive model for offenders against girls aged 13 years and younger included six variables: longer VT to 8–10-year-old females (determined by a sample regression coefficient of 0.29, not the clinical rule-of-thirds), higher cognitive distortion score (coefficient 1.34), negative response to the question 'I feel I am someone children can look up to' (coefficient −0.68), self-reported attraction to 8–10-year-old females (coefficient 0.31), self-reported disgust to adult males (coefficient −0.20) and number of times married (coefficient 0.39). Although the ROC (receiver operator characteristic) is not reported for overall classification accuracy, the authors report sensitivity and specificity indices at two coefficient cut points: at a cut point of 0.48, this equation correctly identified 74% of true positives and 73% of true negatives, leaving 26% false positives and 27% false negatives. At a cut point of 0.88, 25% of child molesters of girls were identified and 99% of non-child molesters of girls were identified, leaving only 1% false positives, but 75% false negatives.

The predictive model for offenders against boys aged 13 years and younger included four variables: longer VT to 8–10-year-old males (coefficient 0.53), higher cognitive distortion score (coefficient 1.30), being a victim of child abuse more than once (coefficient 2.43) and a higher score on the hobbies and interests scale 1 (coefficient 0.31, which includes these items: visiting the zoo, going to movies or plays, playing team sports, visiting amusement and theme parks, playing video games, science hobbies like astronomy and nature study, collecting things like comic books and arcade games, etc.). At a cut point of 0.21, this equation correctly identified 86% of true positives and 86% of true negatives, leaving 14% false negatives and 14% false positives. At a cut point of 0.83, 28% of true positives were identified and 99% of true negatives were identified, leaving 72% false negatives and 1% false positives.

The liar-denier model was developed using offenders who denied sexually molesting a boy or girl younger than 14 years, but were believed to have done so by a therapist, and non-child sexual offenders. All variables competed for inclusion in this model; a combination of four was found to be predictive. These four included hobbies and interests scale 2 (coefficient 0.27, which includes these items: growing houseplants, building models, watching children's team sports (baseball, football, basketball), going to movies or plays and photography), the higher of the predicted values from the first two models (coefficient 3.97), the behaviour denier scale (coefficient −0.14, which includes these items: exhibitionism, public masturbation, fetishism, frottage, voyeurism, bestiality, obscene phone calls and letters, masochism, rape, sadism, transvestism, affairs and affairs with strangers), and an interaction between the behaviour denier scale and the higher of the predicted values from the two previously described models (coefficient −1.22). Using a cut point of 0.32, 75% of those determined to be liar-deniers were identified (true positives, leaving 24% false negatives) and 76% of those determined to be non-child sexual offenders were identified (true negatives, leaving 25% false positives). A cut point of 0.73 raised the true negative rate to 96%, but resulted in only 33% true positives. As with most sensitivity and specificity indices, as sensitivity goes up, specificity goes down.

It is important to note that none of the participants in this study could be verified as true negatives, as all had been determined to be sexually deviant in some manner. Non-child offenders included persons with paraphilias such as bestiality, rape, exhibitionism or excessive use of pornography. Additionally, some offenders were known to have offended against both boys and girls younger than 14 years and fit into both groups. The number of non-contact offenders in the non-child molester category is unknown.

Information distributed by Abel Screen Inc. in November 2000 stated that the probability value represents 'the extent of the probability that your client matches a set of characteristics of child molesters in that category'. The flier goes on to note: 'The Liar-Denier category is only applicable to individuals accused of child molestation but who deny the offence(s). The probability value for the Liar-Denier category represents the extent of the probability that your client matches a set of characteristics of child molesters attempting to conceal having molested a child. Probability values will be given as percentages, for example, there is a 75% probability that your client matches the characteristics of a Liar-Denier'. Current information (www.abelscreen.com) states: 'Approximately 80% of child sexual abusers attempting to conceal are detected using the Probability of *PAST* CSA Behaviour (emphasis in original)'. When this figure, 80%, is compared with Abel *et al.*'s (2001) published research of a 75% true positive rate for the liar-denier probability value, we do not understand how this has been raised to 80%, and we further question the presentation of a true positive value without corresponding sensitivity and specificity indices across a range of cut points.

Abel *et al.* (2001) emphasize the need for caution when interpreting probability scores, specifically the fact that they do not represent certainty about whether someone has committed a specific act of sexual abuse and therefore *should not be used in legal contexts* (emphasis added), where they may be prone to misuse. Yet the authors tend to overstate the purpose of the probability values themselves; for example, they state, 'Probability estimations have distinct advantages for the evaluator, since they provide an actual probability value that the evaluee has molested girls under 14 outside the home, boys under 14 outside the home, or fits a liar-denier category' (p. 715). In addition to Abel *et al.*'s cautionary note, we would add that the development sample may not match the client in question.

Upon reviewing this study, we have many questions that were not adequately addressed. For example, it would be useful to see the percentage of true and false positives and negatives for cut points between those reported. Second, would it have been necessary to force VT and cognitive distortion scores into the regression equation, or would they have been insignificant predictors if they had to compete with other variables in the regression analysis. Finally, the use of a participant's hobbies and interests to predict sexual offending against a male child, or to predict the probability that the offender is denying a committed sexual crime, when those items appear to be devoid of any rational or empirical association with sexual offending, may be theoretically intriguing but should be further examined before clinical application (Mills, Kroner and Hemmati, 2007).

CROSS-VALIDATION AND REPLICATION ATTEMPTS OF THE AASI VT MEASURE

Due to increasing interest and use of this tool, independent researchers became interested in cross-validating the VT portion of AASI. There could be no truly independent research, as all raw data are owned and controlled by Abel Screen Inc. Notably, all known published or presented research using the AASI stimuli look only at the 16 stimulus categories that depict different ages, gender and race (Caucasian and African-American) and do not look at the remaining six categories, representing exhibitionism, voyeurism, fetishism (bras and panties), sadism against females, sadism against males and frottage. These special categories are scored by Abel Screen Inc. and interpreted by the clinician, however, using either the rule-of-thirds or a variation thereof. Seghorn and Weigel (1999) presented an unpublished study using 39 participants for VT (AASI VRT scored reports) assessment and 11 for PPG. They concluded, 'Even though singly, neither VRT or PPG does a great job of classifying paedophiles, together they are much better'. Seghorn considered the study limited by the small number of participants and it did not receive peer review.

Johnson and Listiak (1999) compared PPG with AASI VT scored data. PPG stimuli used in this study pose a dilemma when considering outcome and generalization of results. The authors report that there were no appropriate (non-pornographic) stimuli available in slide format, so they used two different sets of commercially produced videotape stimuli (by Northwest Media, NWM; and Behavioural Technology Inc., BTI) for PPG assessment. One set included non-nude models in visual vignettes and the other set (also non-nude) included both visual and audio components. A further complication arose when the researchers found that when administering the full set of PPG stimuli, many offenders took too long, from a practical standpoint, so researchers selected stimuli that matched each participant's victim profile and deleted stimuli that were unlikely to elicit arousal, based on the participant's target victim profile. Data from 48 incarcerated sex offenders suggested that PPG (using either method) and VT were about equally effective at measuring sexually deviant arousal or interest in eight categories, including F/2–4 (females aged 2–4 years), F/8–10, F/14–17, F/adult, M/2–4, M/8–10, M/14–17 and M/adult. 'Clinically significant' on VT was defined as any VT that was at least 33% of the maximum z-score achieved in the appropriate racial category; the degree of 'per cent full erection' used to determine 'clinical significance' on PPG was not stated.

When VT is compared with NWM PPG stimuli, the frequency of significant responses on both procedures ranged from 1 to 36 (of 49) and the frequency of 'no response on both procedures' ranged from 5 to 35 (of 49), yielding measurement agreement (defined as both PPG and VT showing the same outcome, either 'significant response' or 'no response') ranging from 63 to 85%. The highest proportion of significant responses on both procedures occurred to F/14–17 (36/85%) and F/adult (32/77%) target victim categories. Interestingly, the lowest number of significant responses on both procedures was with male victim categories, with only 1 for M/2–4 and 3 for M/8–10. Respectively, there were 34 and 31 who responded to neither procedure for these categories. This is in contrast to findings in previous studies (Abel *et al.*, 1994, 1998), where the ability of VT to classify child molesters was greater with male victim categories than with female. In this study, measurement agreement was not a supportive statement for AASI VT. There were a substantial number of subjects who produced 'no response on both procedures'. When no response was shown on both procedures for the same participant, it was counted as a case of measurement agreement. For example, for F/2–4, there was 'measurement agreement' for 30 of 48 participants (63%); but only 4 participants showed a significant response on both procedures, while 26 participants showed no response on either procedure.

Gray (2000) compared PPG and AASI VT scored data in a sample of sex offenders in an outpatient treatment programme. The initial sample pool was 63 participants who had undergone both procedures. Seventeen were excluded for being non-responsive to PPG (less than 10% estimated full erection), another seven were excluded for being non-paedophile sexual offenders, which left 39 paedophiles who had repeatedly assaulted a male or female victim aged 10 years or younger. The AASI correctly identified 31 (79%).

In addition to the above comparison, Gray (2000) reviewed about 200 AASI charts on confirmed paedophiles and noted that many had produced 'normal' VT profiles; in other words, the clients did not demonstrate sexual interest to children. The author discovered a 'pattern of deception' perhaps due to 'reflexive responding'. Reflexive responders, those who responded reflexively rather than following instructions, showed little variation in VT and self-reported attractiveness across stimulus categories. When Gray applied this pattern to his study and identified and removed 11 research participants, the AASI accurately identified 27 (96%) of the remaining 28. Interestingly, the AASI accurately identified 5 (36%) of 11 reflexive responders. PPG accurately identified 25 (64%) of the full sample (reflexive responders included), 19 (68%) of the sample of 28 (reflexive responders removed) and 6 (55%) of 11 reflexive responders. Gray concluded that both AASI and PPG 'were able to identify confirmed paedophiles to a high degree' (p. 12), and reported 100% agreement of the AASI with PPG using non-reflexive responders and 0%

using reflexive responders, with 76% overall agreement for a total of 25 participants. Examination of the data reveals that these 25 participants are those identified
by PPG as paedophiles. In summary, after removing PPG non-responders from the
original sample, then removing those who showed non-paedophilic sexual interest, then removing those that PPG did not identify as paedophiles, AASI agreed
with PPG on 19 of the remaining 25; after removing 6 more identified as reflexive responders, not surprisingly the AASI agreed with PPG 100% of the time on
the remaining sample of 19 of the original sample of 63. Note that these data do
not merit the statement that PPG and AASI showed 100% agreement in the full
study.

Letourneau (1999) reported the preliminary conclusion that using a sample of
57 volunteer offenders incarcerated in a military prison for sexual offences, Abel
et al. (1998) had been 'largely replicated'. Letourneau (2002) later provided more
detail and final conclusions indicating that although the study was replicated, the
results were not. Participants completed self-report measures of sexual interest and
also underwent VT (AASI slides) and PPG with audiotapes. PPG audiotapes were
reported to have adequate internal consistency. VT slides had adequate internal
consistency in all categories except for male children aged 2–4 years. Coefficient
alpha (internal consistency) varied considerably depending on whether trimmed
or untrimmed scores were used. Stronger measures of reliability, such as parallel
forms and test–retest, were not performed. Although Letourneau developed a way
to trim outliers, it did not replicate the way used by Abel Screen Inc., which uses a
confidential, proprietary formula (Fischer and Smith, 1999).

Letourneau (2002) calculated convergent validity in two ways, by comparing
VT with PPG and by comparing VT with index offence target victim categories.
Using trimmed scores stated to be similar to Abel's deletion of disparate responses,
VT and PPG were significantly correlated for child males and child females, but
not for adolescent females or female adult rape categories. Curiously, PPG had a
negative correlation with child females, making the apparent convergent validity
in this category less useful. VT and index offence target victim were significantly
correlated for child males and adolescent females, but not for child females or
female adult rape. Both measures did well identifying molesters of young boys, but
neither was able to identify molesters of young girls. VT did not identify rapists,
resulting in high false negatives for that category, and all but one participant
showed significant VT to adolescent females, resulting in high false positives for
that category.

Letourneau (2002) additionally looked at the accuracy of the rule-of-thirds used
by clinicians when interpreting AASI bar graphs. Data showed accurate identification only with male child target victims. The AASI did not accurately identify
participants with the female child, female adolescent or female adult rape categories. Therefore, neither the statistical validity nor the clinical utility of the AASI
rule-of-thirds was upheld. PPG fared little better; using 10% estimated full erection as the criterion, it accurately identified male child, showed significance with
female child but in the opposite direction expected, and approached significance
for female adult rape. In her conclusion, Letourneau (2002) did *not* consider this
study to be a replication of Abel *et al.* (1998) because of numerous differences in
the stimuli used (correcting her 1999 statement that it had been a replication).

There has been no independent replication or cross-validation of the AASI probability values (Abel *et al.*, 2001) in the last 6 years since the publication of development study. The authors acknowledge the necessity of such research: '*If* these data withstand the rigors of independent review, it strongly indicates that this methodology can be relatively easily applied in answering three important questions for evaluators for those accused of child molestation...' (p. 716, emphasis added). This, therefore, is a fertile area for further research.

STATISTICAL ADEQUACY OF THE AASI

A detailed review of the statistical properties of the AASI procedure is reported by Fischer and Smith (1999), who point out problems with the 'Abel Assessment for Interest in Paraphilias'. According to Fischer and Smith, the form of scoring used by Abel, without the benefit of a normative population and the ability to compare scores across offenders, is being misused, gives misleading results and is an inaccurate indication of specificity that is not justified given the nature of the data and the way it is scored. Fischer and Smith write:

> A single ipsative elevation may appear to be significantly deviant from the mean but in reality may be minuscule. Likewise, differences between categories may appear to be large but actually be quite small. . . . This type of presentation provides an illusion of normative reference which is inadvertently misleading. . . . In the absence of a norm-referenced interval by which to judge category elevations, an arbitrary rule of thirds is imposed as a guide to interpretation (pp. 197, 199).

Abel (2000) refuted these findings, arguing that Fisher and Smith confused the Abel Screen, the Abel Assessment for Interest in Paraphilias and the AASI, each of which is an entirely different method. According to Abel (2000), the Abel Screen existed from its introduction in February 1995 until May 1996, when it was renamed the AASI. Abel states, 'In their statistical analysis of the Abel Assessment *for sexual interest*[(TM)], they have mistakenly included citations and references (Abel *et al.*, 1994) to research surrounding an entirely different test: The Abel Screen (Abel, 2000, p. 159)'.

Abel himself compounds this confusion, however, by equating different forms of the method, as follows: 'These validity results [Abel Assessment] cannot be used to calculate the sensitivity and specificity of the two methodologies [VRT and PPG] since normals were not compared with participants for child molesters. Results reported previously, however have demonstrated a high sensitivity and specificity of visual reaction time when comparing these two groups (Abel *et al.*, 1998, p. 94)'. The implication seems to be that Abel *et al.*'s 1994 data on the sensitivity and specificity of the Abel Screen can be used to assume that the Abel Assessment has similar sensitivity and specificity indices. The reader, like the authors, may be perplexed by Abel's use of specificity and sensitivity data on one instrument to support an instrument he now states is entirely different. Beyond the discussion of the differences among the three Abel methods, Fisher and Smith's criticism of Abel's methodology was largely unanswered.

Fischer and Smith's (1999) point about ipsative scoring can be illustrated as follows. Before scoring, Client A has a mean VT of 0.4 seconds for female child slides and 0.2 seconds for female adult slides; Client B has a mean VT of 20 seconds for female child slides and 10 seconds for female adult slides. Scoring includes applying a z-score formula to individual (rather than group, which is the norm) data. After scoring, both Client A and Client B show twice as much elevation on the female child scale as on the female adult scale, making Client A and Client B look identical on female child VT, when there is an actual difference of 19.6 seconds. Fischer (2000) points out that all previous research on VT measures and sexual interest have analyzed between-group differences, for example, high and low sexual interest, normal and pathological, or heterosexual and homosexual; however, the Abel method does not rely on between-group differences, but on intra-individual differences. Further, Fischer notes, that Abel *et al.* create a method of scoring and interpreting intra-individual differences that makes it appear as though an individual's data is compared to group normative data, when it is not.

The interpretation of scores is always of concern and each scoring method, whether normative or ipsative, has a unique set of cautions due to the significant impact psychosexual assessment results may have on an increasing number of persons' lives. Therefore the quality of the test, the validity of interpretation and the context in which the interpretation is used (e.g. treatment or risk assessment) is a primary concern. Karpatschof and Elkjær (2000) provide an informative view on the caution required to interpret ipsative scores. Ipsative scoring compares a person only to himself on dimensions within himself and interpersonal comparisons are meaningless. This may work well for treatment purposes as each assessment is individualized. Yet inevitably, especially when presented in a manner typically reserved for group comparison such as z-scores, clinicians and non-mental health professional such as probation officers, lawyers and judges make interpersonal comparisons. Unfortunately, this type of scoring and reporting method leads clinicians to compare and decide that one person shows more deviance than another based on the results of AASI VT chart. When comparing individuals, it is appropriate to use only normative data, which has not yet been provided by Abel *et al.* or any other researcher investigating VT. When scoring and interpreting the AASI, it is important to note that like many measures of sexual interest, preference or orientation, the number and type of dimensions are predefined, limited and unidimensional. A person's primary sexual interest may not be represented by any of the slides in the test set.

DETECTION OF DISSIMULATION

When developing the Abel Screen, Abel *et al.* (1994) noted the desirability of research wherein known paedophiles would be asked to try to respond to a VT measure in a way that would make their sexual interests appear normal, and these data compared to VT data from normal subjects. Abel (www.abelscreen.com, accessed 7 September 2000) reported the results of a study to learn whether sex offenders can conceal their sexual interest patterns on the AASI. Research participants comprised two groups, paedophiles who admitted their behaviour and those determined to be paedophiles who denied their behaviour. When sexual offenders were told to alter their visual reaction times and self-report of sexual interest, a change was produced in their raw score, but the rank order of target victim categories was unchanged. Unfortunately, this study does not appear to be on the web site currently and it does not appear to be published. If these results are submitted to and stand up to peer review, this could be an important and useful finding. Publication of the methodology would enable the reader to decide.

Gray and Plaud (2005) published an online report of Gray's (2000) presentation but it did not include any new data. The authors did, however, provide a numerical formula for sorting the supposed dissimulators – those who responded reflexively rather than follow instructions, from the non-reflexive responders, and those who produce a profile consistent with their known sexual offence history. Unfortunately, the numerical formula does not appear meaningful in a clinical application, as to label the process essentially involves knowing the participants are repeat child molesters, deciding that the offence history represents sexual preference and sexual interest, removing data from participants whose VT charts do not agree with this assumption and classifying those as dissimulators, and then classifying the remaining participants as child molesters, a rather circular process. Recall that Gray (2000) initially accomplished much the same thing by simply looking at the AASI VT bar charts.

The process of sample selection in this study (Gray, 2000; Gray and Plaud, 2005) is meaningful to our discussion of dissimulation. The initial sample consisted of 63 participants who underwent both PPG and AASI. Seven non-paedophile sexual offenders were removed, leaving 56 repeat child molesters. Seventeen of these 56 did not show significant arousal on PPG and were removed, leaving 39. Eleven of these 39 did not show significant sexual interest on AASI VT, leaving 28. Hence, fully one-half of the original sample of 56 repeat child molesters did not show significant deviance on either PPG or AASI. This reflects on the lack of ability of both laboratory procedures to 'catch' real-world behaviour. It questions the authors' untenable statement that 'The data clearly show that both the *Abel Assessment for Sexual Interests* and the penile plethysmograph were able to identify diagnosed paedophiles to a high degree' (p. 7).

Further, although Gray and Plaud (2005) conclude that AASI was better at classifying paedophiles than PPG, this conclusion is undermined by the fact that of the sample of 56 paedophiles, PPG correctly classified 11 that AASI did not, until those profiles had been identified as having not been correctly classified by the usual procedure. It must be noted that there is no data reported to support the assumption that the reflexive responders were actually dissimulating; it could be that they were simply not interested in the stimuli. It is known that a substantial proportion of sexual offenders do not show significant arousal to PPG (46% in Abel *et al.*, 1998); it may be that a proportion of sexual offenders will not show significant interest in AASI stimuli. In fact, in an unpublished study, Abel (2004; www.abelscreen.com) reports that reflexive responders are less likely to be child sexual abusers than are non-reflexive responders. This may be an important finding and hopefully will be published. At this time, it remains proprietary and unavailable for peer review; accordingly, details will not be provided.

USE OF THE AASI WITH ADOLESCENTS

Smith and Fischer (1999) examined the psychometric properties of the AASI with 81 adolescent males in treatment for sexually offending against children ($n = 41$) or for non-sexual behaviours ($n = 40$). Standard AASI slides were used and like most studies on the AASI, the authors evaluated the scores produced by the Abel scoring programme (i.e. not the raw scores in seconds). Participants were tested twice for a measure of temporal stability (test–retest reliability), using an average interval of about 2 weeks. Three correlation coefficients were calculated, a test–retest reliability coefficient based on each participants' 22 z-scores (ipsative scores underwent substantial data transformation to be amenable to this analysis), a correlation between the highest z-score at test and retest, and a correlation between the rule-of-thirds method at test and retest. Coefficients were 0.63, 0.58 and 0.48, respectively, none rising to acceptable limits (Crocker and Algina, 1986).

In this study, the authors used two AASI procedures for identifying known offenders, the highest ipsative z-score and the rule-of-thirds (Smith and Fischer, 1999). Results are presented in Table 2.3.

Adolescent offenders' target victim categories were defined as females from birth to 6 years, females aged 7–12 years, males from birth to 6 years and males aged 7–12 years; authors note that there was substantial overlap in those who had multiple victims. The authors determined that classification accuracy was no better than chance using either clinical screening method; however, identifying known sexual offenders was better accomplished using the rule-of-thirds; while identifying known non-offenders was better accomplished using the highest z-score. Only one offender's highest ipsative z-score matched the age and gender of his known victims. Rule-of-thirds designations were correlated with corresponding categories of known victims, yielding eight coefficients, none of which were significant, indicating that diagnostic validity was poor. Screening validity, the ability to distinguish offenders from non-offenders, was also poor, as the AASI was not able to distinguish accurately between adolescent child molesters and non-molesters. The authors (Fischer and Smith, 1999; Smith and Fischer, 1999) offer recommendations

Table 2.3 Classification accuracy of Abel Assessment rule-of-thirds and ipsative z-score

$n = 41$ TPs	Highest z-score		Rule-of-thirds	
$n = 40$ TNs	Test	Retest	Test	Retest
True positives (sensitivity)	10%	15%	61%	56%
False positives	5%	2%	48%	40%
True negatives (specificity)	95%	98%	58%	60%
False negatives	90%	85%	39%	44%
Classification accuracy	52%	56%	59%	58%

for improvement of technical adequacy, including the development of truly norm-referenced scores.

Barboza-Whitehead (2001) used data from 336 male Caucasian juvenile sexual offenders (aged 9–19 years) to examine the ability of a particular section of the AASI (see below) to distinguish between those who admitted sexual offending against children, those who were accused of doing so and denied it and those who admitted to both child molestation and peer/adult sexual assault. Slides depicted males and females in four age categories: 2–4 years, 8–10 years, 14–17 years and 22 years or older. Slides depicting African-Americans, exhibitionism, voyeurism, sadism and fetishism were not analyzed. Barboza-Whitehead (2001) hypothesized that deniers would have longer VTs relative to their self-reported attraction to the same stimuli, while admitters would show a greater concordance. However, for all eight categories (four age groups for each gender), differences between deniers and admitters were insignificant. In fact, for the variable that came closest to significance ($p = 0.072$), males 2–4 years old, deniers were more likely to have shorter VT relative to their self-reported sexual interest than were admitters. It was predicted that admitters would not show a difference between VT and self-reported attraction to stimuli, but this was not supported. In other words, the self-report information on sexual interest of admitters did not correlate significantly with their VT.

Abel, Jordan, Rouleau, Emerick, Barboza-Whitehead and Osborn (2004) assessed the validity of the AASI with 1704 male adolescents (aged 11–17 years). Groups included 1170 adolescent offenders who admitted molesting a child at least 5 years younger and 534 adolescent offenders who were involved in other problematic sexual behaviours (non-molesters). Data were the 'natural logs in seconds' (i.e. the raw data), rather than the standardized values provided in AASI reports, as a way to increase the reliability and predictive power of VT scores (Abel et al., 2004). It was predicted that (a) adolescents whose VT to slides of children were longer were more likely to be the group of admitted child molesters (in comparison to the non-molesting offenders) and (b) those with longer VT to children would have more child victims and more acts of child molestation. The mean VT to slides of children for molesters differed significantly from that of non-molesters, but it is unknown whether that significance was meaningful, as unfortunately the effect size was not presented (nor the standard deviations so a reader could compute the effect size). A logistic regression analysis to address the second hypothesis was also significant, indicating that adolescents who looked longer at slides of children were more likely to be child molesters. Although the area under the curve (AUC) result of 0.64 was significant, it is a clinically poor level.[2] Three different types of correlational analyses (Pearson, Spearman and Kendalls tau-b) were run for admitted child molesters and number of victims and number of acts of molestation, all of which were significant at the 0.001 level and ranged from 0.18 to 0.30, suggesting again a statistically significant yet clinically poor finding.

---

[2]An AUC of 1 represents a perfect predictive ability and 0.5 represents zero predictive ability. Tape (1999) suggests the following rough guide for classifying the accuracy: an AUC of 0.90–1 is excellent, 0.80–0.90 is good, 0.70–0.80 is fair, 0.60–0.70 is poor and 0.50–0.60 is a fail.

Abel *et al.* (2004) point out differences between this study and Smith and Fischer (1999) that Abel suggests may account for Smith and Fischer's lack of support for the AASI with adolescents. According to Abel *et al.*, Smith and Fischer committed a critical error by not attempting to ensure that their control group of non-child-molesting adolescents had indeed never molested a child, as many who have never been accused of doing so actually have done so. In the current study, Abel *et al.* (2004) used a control group who had never been blamed, charged or arrested for molesting a child. This may not be the critical factor that distinguishes Abel *et al.*'s findings from Smith and Fischer's finding; however, as Zolondek, Abel, Northey and Jordan (2001) gathered information from 485 adolescent males who were being evaluated as possible sexual offenders and found that of the boys who reported never being accused of child molestation, 41.5% reported they had, in fact, sexually molested a child.

Abel *et al.* cautioned that the AASI should not be used to identify adolescent males who are accused of child molestation but are denying it, and VT alone should not be used as a classification tool. Abel *et al.* suggested that the AASI might best be used to identify higher risk offenders among known adolescent child molesters to help decide who cannot be safely treated in the community. Although this appears to be a reasonable conclusion, recall that ipsative scores such as those used by the AASI do not allow for inter-individual comparisons. Additionally, while a method with a receiver operator characteristic of 0.64 does offer predictive accuracy above that of chance, it is clinically a poor result and therefore not an appropriate foundation upon which to base decisions regarding a person's confinement. A risk assessment should be based on a larger body of test and other data and use methods designed specifically for risk assessment.

USE OF THE AASI WITH SPECIAL POPULATIONS OR IN SPECIAL CONTEXTS

A common question related to many psychological assessment tools is whether the measures can be used on special or non-typical (for that tool) populations, such as the intellectually disabled, or in non-therapeutic contexts, such as child custody cases or pre-trial judicial proceedings. The AAIS, like all psychological measures, should be used with caution when administered to populations or in contexts not evaluated in research studies, and if used, the resulting report should clearly indicate the scientific basis for their inclusion and limitations of the results. In addition, clinicians should always adhere to the ethical guidelines provided by their associative bodies. The following is a brief summary on the use of the AASI with special populations or in special contexts.

Child Custody

The summary reports issued by Abel Screen Inc. indicate that the AASI probability values should not be used in disputed child custody cases. The warning states: 'You should be aware that child custody dispute cases violate some of the assumptions on which the Denier-Dissimulator probability model is based, and therefore, it should not be used in these situations' (see the *Abel Administrator* manual).

Intellectually Disabled

Research has used participants who were able to read the AASI questionnaire without assistance. Those whose intellectual disability prevents them from doing so should not be tested with the AASI. Abel Screening Inc. offers for sale the Abel–Blasingame Assessment System for individuals with intellectual disabilities. It appears that the main differences are simplified instructions and a simplified questionnaire that is read to the client. Product information does not mention differences among slide sets. We can find no published research using the Abel–Blasingame Assessment System. Blasingame reported that he is gathering data (personal communication, 9 September 2007), but has not yet received permission from Abel Screening Inc. to share preliminary results, as data are owned by Abel Screening Inc. Publication of this research could be an important advance in the field.

Females

Abel Screen Inc. has a questionnaire for female children and female adults (Abel *et al.*, 2004); however, no research has been reported using female participants with the AASI.

Minority Races

The AASI includes African-American slide stimuli that are to be used with that population. The vast majority of the participants in the research have been Caucasian. The AASI questionnaire is offered in Spanish and French, in addition to English (Abel *et al.*, 2004). There is no published research using substantial numbers of participants from these minorities.

Sadism/Masochism

The AASI includes stimuli designed to identify sexual interest in sadism against females and sadism against males. The ipsative scores reflected by the AASI bar chart are scored differently from the age and gender categories, in that the sadism against females score must exceed the adult female score by a full standard deviation and likewise for males, in order for further inquiry to be made of the participant. There is no reported research to support the use of these scores. Abel Screen Inc. currently advises AASI-2 users not to report the sadism scores. Additionally, Letourneau (2002) did not support the use of the AASI with rapists.

Incest Offenders

It is commonly accepted that incest offenders are less likely to show sexual interest in children (Abel *et al.*, 2001) than are other child sexual offenders. Abel *et al.* (2001) excluded incest offenders from the two groups of admitting sex offenders used to construct the probability models for child molesters. Letourneau (2002) speculated that the non-significant findings for sexual interest in female children may have occurred because many of the child molesters were incest offenders. Abel Screen Inc. reports that the probability value for denier-dissimulator (formerly liar-denier) may be applied to alleged incest offenders. Abel *et al.* (2001) do not report how many incest offenders were used in the denier group to construct the model, making investigation of this claim difficult. AASI's use in child custody battles where incest is alleged has recently been forbidden by Abel Screening Inc.; this is stated on the web site and on AASI summary reports.

RECENT ADVANCES IN VT RESEARCH WITH NON-AASI METHODS

Glasgow, Osborne and Croxen (2003) developed the Affinity VT procedure to be used with developmentally delayed males. Participants first rank and then rate their degree of sexual attraction to each of 56 slides; ratings are recorded as a numerical value of 0–18. VT is unobtrusively recorded during the ratings. Software allows the test administrator to view and interpret the results without sending the data in to be scored. Affinity provides raw scores and ipsative scores. Research has been done with adolescents (Worling, 2006) showing that Affinity VT could distinguish adolescents who assaulted male children from other groups, but could not distinguish those who assaulted female children. One of the more significant advances with the Affinity is that normative data are being collected (Fischer and Morgan, 2006) on non-offending male adults. A separate chapter in this book provides detailed information. The Affinity procedure is commercially available.

Laws and Gress (2004) became interested in using computer-modified imagery as VT stimuli in lieu of photographs of real people. The authors took a collection of nude slide stimuli from multiple sites across Canada and used software to morph them into real-looking persons who did not resemble any real person. Interrater reliability for sorting the slides into images that represented different levels of sexual development ranged from 0.39 to 0.89 with an overall kappa coefficient of 0.62 (good reliability) when 'a stringent method was applied to compare the proportion of classification agreement against proportion of classification agreement that could be expected by chance' (p. 189). The authors propose that more accurate assessment of sexual interests and sexual arousal will eventually be facilitated by use of virtual reality, where the participant will interact with the stimuli, and by use of virtual environment, where stimuli will be presented in ways similar to sophisticated video games where the participant not only interacts with the stimuli, but is presented with options and choices along the way. This would hopefully make VT much more effective at discerning sexual interest than it has shown to be to date.

Gress (2005) presents initial research with the computer-generated slide stimuli viewed by 26 sexual offenders in outpatient treatment, 19 of whom had child victims and 7 of whom had adult victims. Slides represented males and females at the ages of 5, 9 and 13 years and adult, both clothed and nude. Sixty-four slides in 16 categories were presented 10 times each. VT was recorded as participants answered questions about the image. Each category's mean score was compared to the overall mean of all 16 categories. For ages 5 and 9 years and adult, a category mean one or more standard deviations above the overall mean was considered significant. The author found that this scoring method was not optimal for the category representing 13-year-olds, which had more statistical variation; for this category, a cut-off of 1.2 standard deviations above the mean was used. Classification accuracy of the slide stimuli was compared to that of the Sexual Deviance Card Sort, which has been found comparable to PPG with known child molesters (Laws, Hanson, Osborn and Greenbaum, 2000). For classification of child molesters ($n = 19$), sensitivity was greater with VT (84.20% vs. 15.79%) and specificity was greater with the card sort (100% vs. 57.10%). There were 42.90% false positives and 15.8% false negatives for offenders with adult victims. Gress (2005) concluded that the findings from this study further support the concept that 'VT classification of sexual interest has the potential to be comparable to results produced by PPG' (p. 124). Further research into scoring procedures and whether nude imagery is necessary is recommended, using larger samples.

Gress (2007) continued work in this area by testing three male samples ($n = 44$ non-sexual offending incarcerated youth, $n = 22$ outpatient sexual offending adults, $n = 60$ university students) with a VT method, a choice reaction time method, and four questionnaires. Slide stimuli were developed by Laws and Gress (2004) and the method for measuring VT was developed by Gress and Limestone Technologies (www.limestonetech.com). All research data and protocols are openly available (Gress, 2007) and the software is obtainable, with hope to eventually (with further research) market the procedure (C. Gress, personal communication, 6 August 2007). The adolescents and offenders viewed all clothed imagery, while the university students viewed half-clothed and half-nude imagery. VT was unobtrusively measured while the participant answered a question about each slide. Internal consistency was good. Only the VTs to clothed imagery (as these were the common slides across all samples) were statistically evaluated.

All participants viewed female subtest stimuli longer than male and neutral subtest stimuli, and adult sexual offenders had significantly higher average VT overall compared to youth offenders and university students. There was no significant difference between youth offenders and university students. Using sexual offenders as the true positive group and university students as true negatives, the AUC was 0.82 (good) for average VT to female images and 0.85 for male images. Using the mean VT to *male child images only* and a decision cut point of 4.23 seconds, the true positive rate (sensitivity) was 64% and the true negative rate (specificity) was 83%. Gress (2007) concluded that overall the method of VT used in this study showed good ability to distinguish between adult sexual offenders and the two groups of non-sexual offenders, upholding the 60/90 benchmark (Lalumière, Quinsey,

Harris, Rice and Trautrimas, 2003) used by phallometric laboratories to identify rapists; that is, 'about 60% of rapists show rape indices that are larger than the rape indices of about 90% of non-rapists' (p. 220). The same benchmark can be applied to identifying paedophilic preference. In the study of Gress (2007), the VT measure for the female mature and male child VT scores demonstrated a 60% sensitivity level when specificity was held above 90%.

DIRECTIONS FOR FUTURE RESEARCH

VT methods of measuring sexual interest have held promise for more than half a century, yet the achievement of good, stable psychometric qualities remains elusive. This is partially due to the lack of published psychometric information and the confidential and proprietary nature of the AASI. Fortunately, the introduction of the AASI initiated additional studies utilizing other VT methods, slowly illuminating applicable theories and appropriate research methods. There is a substantial amount of research still required, however, especially on the AASI, to substantiate its use. First, researchers and clinicians require peer reviewed published information on the AASI psychometric properties. This permits proper evaluation of the AASI and comparison between AASI studies and studies utilizing other VT methods. Second, there has been little to no informative research evaluating the AASI on populations exhibiting exhibitionism, frottage, voyeurism, sadism against males and females and rapists. There are scales in the AASI that assess these areas but unfortunately, there does not appear to be an evaluation of the full AASI (all self-report scales plus all VT scales using the full set of stimulus materials) published in peer review journals.

Third, an area that requires immediate attention is the reliability and predictive ability of this measure's scoring procedures. For example, Abel *et al.* (2004) used raw scores (seconds) to 'increase reliability and predictive ability' that suggests that the raw score means may be more reliable and predictive than the z-score transformation (p. 269). Unfortunately, the latter is what Abel Screen Inc. provides clinicians to use in practice. Although the results of the analysis utilizing raw scores were significant, they were mediocre in strength (AUC of 0.64 when compared to an AUC of 0.82 and 0.85 by Gress, 2007), indicating that a discussion of the AASI's (and VT in general) clinical significance versus statistical significance is warranted. Finally, research is required to determine the effect, if any, of a client's knowledge on the purpose and method of the AASI. This is important for all psychometric measures utilized in forensic settings, as the consequences for alleged and known sexual offenders in civil and criminal contexts can be substantial. Due to this increased personal risk for the client, if he or she knows that they may undergo the AASI assessment (or other psychological measures) they may attempt to learn about the test by searching online.

A search for 'abel assessment' via a popular search engine (e.g. Google) provides a variety of informative web sites including a link to *Innocent Dads*, which provides a detailed description of how the Abel Assessment measures VT. The more persistent web searcher will also find a *New York Times* article (Bergner, 2005) explaining that the AASI measures erotic preference by the amount of time a person looks at the different slides, not the self-report ratings of sexual attraction. This situation is not the fault of Abel Screen Inc., but it is a reality they must live and deal with.

If the accuracy of a test depends upon people's naiveté, and at this time VT measures appear to do just that, authors of these tools are ethically obliged to provide clinicians information on the effect of non-naïve clients. Abel Screening Inc. has begun this process by including instructions that alert clinicians to the fact that VT may not accurately reflect a person's sexual interest pattern: 'The integrity of the AASI-2 is dependent on the client's ability to follow instructions, have reasonable acuity to see the images and not be influenced by auditory or visual hallucinations or brain damage' (http://abelscreen.com/products, retrieved 12 June 2007).

CAUTIONS WHEN USING THE AASI

Much of the integral psychometric information necessary for proper evaluation and interpretation of any psychological instrument is lacking in many of the published studies on the AASI. This includes descriptive numbers (instead of verbal descriptions alone) such as means, standard deviations, correlations and significance levels. The presentation of effect sizes would also greatly improve a reader's ability to evaluate the significance of research on the AASI. Therefore, until the authors complete the task of publishing this information so it is accessible to all clinicians, not just those who bought the measure, we suggest clinicians to be cautious when using and interpreting all components of the AASI. In addition, when administering this tool to special populations or in specific contexts that have not received a thorough psychometric evaluation, such as those described above, the clinician should do so with extreme caution and state the circumstances in any report of the measure's results.

Another area of concern is the clinical application of the AASI probability values (Abel *et al.*, 2001). Importantly, the probability values should not be used due to the substantial number of false positives and false negatives, lack of cross-validation, and other research weaknesses. In addition, there is the inherent potential for committing the error of reversing conditional probabilities. For example, a group of known sexual offenders can be studied and a list made of their most common characteristics, but to take this list of common characteristics and apply it to a non-offending male and use the degree to which that person has these characteristics as a probability that he is a sexual offender demonstrates flawed reasoning. To say, 'If you are a known sexual offender of boy children, we can look at you and see characteristics a, b, and c' is not the same as saying, 'If you have characteristics a, b, and c, you are probably a sex offender of boys'. (See Poole and Lamb, 1998, for a discussion of this phenomenon in child sexual abuse literature.)

Although Abel *et al.* (2001) cautioned against using either AASI VT or probability values in litigious contexts, this has not been heeded (see, e.g. *United States* v. *White Horse*, 2003; *Ready* v. *Commonwealth of Massachusetts*, 2002); consequently, we recommend that use in litigious contexts should be clearly forbidden by the test manufacturer and so stated on reports. Similarly, AASI users should be aware that the lack of published research, lack of independent cross-validation and replication studies and lack of adequate statistical reliability and validity data make the AASI vulnerable to attack under judicial standards for admissibility of expert witness evidence. The first author of this article is currently preparing a review of legal decisions involving the AASI for *Behavioural Sciences and the Law*.

SUMMARY

When compared to PPG, VT is obviously appealing in that it is a kinder, gentler method. Studies have yet to determine, however, whether the measure is at least as accurate as or perhaps more so than PPG. At this time, VT appears to be prone to error, potentially more so than PPG because of the multiple layers of inference required for VT interpretation, and its use with adolescents has not met a high enough psychometric standard to be ethically appropriate. The scoring method in AASI VT, ipsative z-scores presented as if comparable across individuals, is limited in utility and as discussed above, can lead to misinterpretation. Unfortunately, clinical interpretation using the rule-of-thirds does not appear to be statistically supported, reliability is low (when using ipsative z-scores, better but not good when using raw data in seconds) and validity is not strong, with different studies showing variable results across categories of victim targets. In addition, there is little to no research reported for the paraphilic categories of exhibitionism, frottage, voyeurism and sadism. Continued research meeting the standards reported above would address many, if not most, of these issues, and we feel that this research would provide significant benefit to applied settings as VT detection of sexual interest in male children appears promising. We suggest that the AASI (and other VT tools) are best used as clinical interview aids and treatment tools (rather than risk assessment and diagnostic tools) and as a way to gather and organize large amounts of self-report questionnaire data.

REFERENCES

Abel, G. (2000) The importance of meeting research standards: a reply to Fischer and Smith's articles on the Abel assessment for sexual interest. *Sexual Abuse: A Journal of Research and Treatment*, **12**, 149–61.

Abel, G.G., Huffman, J., Warberg, B.W. and Holland, C.L. (1998) Visual reaction time and plethysmography as measures of sexual interest in child molesters. *Sexual Abuse: A Journal of Research and Treatment*, **10**, 81–95.

Abel, G.G., Jordan, A., Hand, C., Holland, L. and Phipps, A. (2001) Classification models of child molesters utilizing the Abel Assessment for sexual interest. *Child Abuse and Neglect*, **25**, 703–18.

Abel, G.G., Jordan, A., Rouleau, J.L., Emerick, R., Barboza-Whitehead, S. and Osborn, C. (2004) Use of visual reaction time to assess male adolescents who molest children. *Sexual Abuse: A Journal of Research and Treatment*, **16**, 255–65.

Abel, G.G., Lawry, S.S., Karlstrom, E.M., Osborn, C.A. and Gillespie, C.F. (1994) Screening tests for pedophilia. *Criminal Justice and Behavior*, **21**, 115–31.

Abel Screening News (1997, September/October) p. 1, Abel Screening Inc., Suite T-30, West Wing, 3280 Howell Mill Road, N.W., Atlanta, GA 30327.

Barboza-Whitehead, S.E. (2001) Discriminant validity of the Abel assessment for sexual interest with juveniles who admit versus deny their sexual offenses. *Dissertation Abstracts International: Section B: The Sciences and Engineering* **61** (12B), 6697.

Bergner, D. (2005) The making of a molester. *The New York Times*, http://www.nytimes.com/2005/01/23/magazine/23PEDO.html?ex=1186977600&en=66c14313bf735778&ei=5070 (retrieved 23 January 2005 and 11 August 2007).

Brown, M., Amoroso, D.M., Ware, E.E., Pruesse, M. and Pilkey, D.W. (1973) Factors affecting viewing time of pornography. *Journal of Social Psychology*, **90**, 125–35.

Crocker, L. and Algina, J. (1986) *Introduction to Classical & Modern Test Theory*. Holt, Reinhart and Winston, Inc., Orlando, FL.

Fischer, L. (2000) The Abel Screen: A non-intrusive alternative? in *Remaking Relapse Prevention with Sex Offenders: A Sourcebook* (eds D.R. Laws, S.M. Hudson and T. Ward), Sage Publications, Thousand Oaks, CA, pp. 303–18.

Fischer, L. and Morgan, D. (2006) Norm Referenced Clinical Decision-Making with Affinity Viewing-Time. *Annual meeting of the Association for the Treatment of Sexual Abusers*, Chicago, IL.

Fischer, L. and Smith, G. (1999) Statistical adequacy of the Abel assessment for interest in Paraphilias. *Sexual Abuse: A Journal of Research and Treatment*, **11**, 195–205.

Freund, K. (1957) Diagnostika homosexuality yu muzu [Diagnosing homosexuality in men]. *Czechoslovakian Psychiatry*, **53**, 382–94.

Glasgow, D.V., Osborne, A. and Croxen, J. (2003) An assessment tool for investigating paedophile sexual interest using viewing time: an application of single case methodology. *British Journal of Learning Disabilities*, **31**, 96–102.

Gray, S. (2000) *Outcome of the Abel Assessment with Penile Plethysmograph in a Sample of Sex Offenders in Outpatient Treatment*. Annual meeting of the Association for the Treatment of Sexual Abusers, Orlando, FL.

Gray, S. and Plaud, J. (2005) A comparison of the Abel Assessment for sexual interest and penile plethysmography in an outpatient sample of sexual offenders. *Journal of Sexual Offender Civil Commitment: Science and the Law*, **1**, 1–10, http://www.soccjournal.org/index.cfm?page=http%3A//www.soccjournal.org/jsocc_home.cfm (accessed on 7 July 2008).

Gress, C.L.Z. (2005) Viewing time measures and sexual interest: another piece of the puzzle. *Journal of Sexual Aggression*, **11**, 117–25.

Gress, C.L.Z. (2007) Delays in attentional processing when viewing sexual imagery: the development and comparison of two measures. Unpublished doctoral dissertation. University of Victoria, British Columbia, Canada.

Hanson, R.K. and Bussiére, M.T. (1996) Predictors of Sexual Offender Recidivism: Meta-Analysis, User Report 96-04, Department of the Solicitor General of Canada, http://www.sgc.gc.ca (accessed on 7 July 2008).

Hanson, R.K. and Bussiére, M.T. (1998) Predicting relapse, a meta-analysis of sexual offender recidivism studies. *Journal of Consulting and Clinical Psychology*, **66**, 348–62.

Harris, G.T., Rice, M.E., Quinsey, V.L. and Chaplin, T.C. (1996) Viewing time as a measure of sexual interest among child molesters and normal heterosexual men. *Behaviour Research and Therapy*, **34**, 389–94.

Johnson, S. and Listiak, A. (1999) The measurement of sexual preference – a preliminary comparison of phallometry and the Abel assessment, in *The Sex Offender: Theoretical Advances, Treating Special Populations and Legal Developments* (ed. B. Schwartz), Civic Research Institute, Kingston, NJ.

Karpatschof, B. and Elkjær, H.K. (2000) *Yet the Bumblebee Flies: The Reliability of Ipsative Scores – Examined by Empirical Data and a Simulation Study*. Research Report no. 1. University of Copenhagen, Copenhagen, Denmark.

Lalumiére, M.L., Quinsey, V.L., Harris, G., Rice, M. and Trautrimas, C. (2003) Are rapists differentially aroused by coercive sex in phallometric assessments? *Annals of the New York Academy of Sciences*, **989**, 211–24.

Lang, A.R., Searles, J., Lauerman, R. and Adesso, V. (1980) Expectancy, alcohol, and sex guilt as determinants of interest in and reaction to sexual stimuli. *Journal of Abnormal Psychology*, **89**, 644–53.

Laws, D.R. and Gress, C.L.Z. (2004) Seeing things differently: the viewing time alternative to penile plethysmography. *Legal and Criminological Psychology*, **9**, 183–96.

Laws, D.R., Hanson, R.K., Osborn, C.A. and Greenbaum, P.E. (2000) Classification of child molesters by plethysmographic assessment of sexual arousal and a self-report measure of sexual preference. *Journal of Interpersonal Violence*, **15**, 1297–1312.

Letourneau, E. (1999) *A Comparison of the Penile Plethysmograph and the Abel Assessment for Sexual Interest on Incarcerated Military Sex Offenders*. Annual meeting of the Association for the Treatment of Sexual Abusers, Orlando, FL.

Letourneau, E. (2002) A comparison of objective measures of sexual arousal and interest: visual reaction time and penile plethysmography. *Sexual Abuse: A Journal of Research and Treatment*, **14**, 207–23.

Love, R.E., Sloan, L.R. and Schmidt, M.J. (1976) Viewing pornography and sex guilt: the priggish, the prudent, and the profligate. *Journal of Consulting and Clinical Psychology*, **76**, 624–9.

Maletzky, B.M. (2003) Letter to the editor. *Sexual Abuse: Journal of Research and Treatment*, **15**, 393.

Mills, J.F., Kroner, D.G. and Hemmati, T. (2007) The validity of risk estimates: an issue of item performance. *Psychological Services*, **4**, 1–12.

Poole, D.A. and Lamb, M.E. (1998) *Investigative Interviews of Children: A Guide for Helping Professionals*, American Psychological Association, Washington DC.

Quinsey, V.L., Ketsetzis, M., Earls, C. and Karamanoukian, A. (1996) Viewing time as a measure of sexual interest. *Ethology and Sociobiology*, **17**, 341–54.

Quinsey, V.L., Rice, M.E., Harris, G.T. and Reid, K.S. (1993) The phylogenetic and ontogenetic development of sexual age preference in males: conceptual and measurement issues, in *The Juvenile Sex Offender* (eds H. Barbaree, W.L. Marshall and S.M. Hudson), Guilford Press, New York, pp. 143–63.

Ready v. Commonwealth of Massachusetts (2002) WL 1255800 (Mass. Super. 2002).

Rosenzweig, S. (1942) The photoscope as an objective device for evaluating sexual interest. *Psychosomatic Medicine*, **4**, 150–58.

Seghorn, T. and Weigel, M. (1999). *Comparative Use of the Abel Assessments and Penile Plethysmograph Laboratory Assessments in an Outpatient Forensic Practice*. Annual meeting of the Association for the Treatment of Sexual Abusers, Orlando, FL.

Singer, B. (1984) Conceptualizing sexual arousal and attraction. *The Journal of Sex Research*, **20**, 230–40.

Smith, G. and Fischer, L. (1999) Assessment of juvenile sexual offenders: reliability and validity of the Abel assessment for interest in Paraphilias. *Sexual Abuse: A Journal of Research and Treatment*, **11**, 207–16.

United States v. White Horse, 316 F.3d 769 (8th Cir.) cert. denied 124 S.Ct. 116 (2003).

Ware, E.E., Brown, M., Amoroso, D.M., Pilkey, D.W. and Pruesse, M. (1972) The semantic meaning of pornography stimuli for college males. *Canadian Journal of Behavioral Science*, **4**, 204–9.

Worling, J.R. (2006) Assessing sexual arousal with adolescent males who have offended sexually: self-report and unobtrusively measured viewing time. *Sex Abuse*, **8**, 383–400

Zamansky, H.S. (1956) A technique for measuring homosexual tendencies. *Journal of Personality*, **24**, 436–48.

Zolondek, S.C., Abel, G.G., Northey, W.F. Jr and Jordan, A.D. (2001) The self-reported behaviors of juvenile sexual offenders. *Journal of Interpersonal Violence*, **16**, 73–85.

Chapter 3

AFFINITY: THE DEVELOPMENT OF A SELF-REPORT ASSESSMENT OF PAEDOPHILE SEXUAL INTEREST INCORPORATING A VIEWING TIME VALIDITY MEASURE[1]

DAVID V. GLASGOW[2]

Pacific Psychological Assessment Corp., Victoria, BC, Canada, and Carlton Glasgow Partnership, Colne, Lancashire, UK

Affinity is a computer-based assessment of sexual interest. It combines self-report measures with an unobtrusive viewing time (VT) validity scale. The primary purpose of this combination is to enable a person being assessed to easily and absolutely unambiguously specify relative sexual interest in male and female individuals of different ages, and for the authenticity of the preference profile thus generated to be corroborated (or otherwise) by an unobtrusive measure. Although it is now used with a wider range of individuals, with varying utility (Worling, 2006), it was originally developed to assist the assessment and management of sexual offenders with significant intellectual disabilities (Glasgow, Osborne and Croxen, 2003).

The first section of this chapter deals with the history and development of Affinity, and describes some of the challenges relating to assessment of sexual interest in sex offenders with significant intellectual impairment.

No attempt will be made to describe all the features of Affinity; attention being focused on those aspects of development and features which convey something significant either about the assessment or the use which can be made of it. The second section addresses some of the issues surrounding normative versus ipsative measurement. In particular, it describes the rationale underlying the very

---

[1]All human images appearing in this chapter are commercially available stock photography licensed to the author for the purposes of software development and publication in print.

[2]The author of this chapter is the developer of the Affinity assessment procedure, which is distributed by Pacific Psychological Assessment Corporation (PPAC). He has received royalties on software sales from PPAC and also subsidized travel to the United States.

Cognitive Approaches to the Assessment of Sexual Interest in Sexual Offenders   Edited by D. Thornton and D. R. Laws
© 2009 John Wiley & Sons, Ltd

deliberate use of ipsatization made within Affinity, and the risks and advantages this confers. The final section describes some of the data emerging from the use of Affinity, some of which are somewhat unexpected and may shed some light on the psychological processes underlying VT measures. Some tentative suggestions are made regarding the possible nature of such processes, and advantages this may confer on assessment and treatment.

THE DEVELOPMENT OF AFFINITY

Any professional who is experienced in interviewing sex offenders regarding their possibly deviant sexual interests will affirm that it involves judicious and often subtle use of both motivational techniques and interrogative pressure. When the person being interviewed has significant intellectual limitations, this process carries with it considerable risks. For example, and most obviously, the interviewee may simply not understand the questions, a fact he may also be very reluctant to acknowledge or disclose. Alternatively, he may or may not understand the questions put, but be sufficiently suggestible and compliant to attempt to give a response perceived to be what is wanted by the interviewer, rather than a reflection of reality. In addition, the interviewee may be unable to either perceive or perhaps articulate anything more than gross determinants of sexual interest. Finally, it is also possible that the question is fully understood but the response given is not honest; the intention is to minimize both personal responsibility and social deprecation.

Where the interviewee has normal or better intellectual functioning, the presumption is that a failure on the part of the interviewee to respond adequately or coherently to an attempt to explore sexual interest necessarily reflects dissimulation. However, when the interviewee has intellectual impairments, it is likely to be impossible to eliminate the potential confounds between incapacity and dissimulation. It simply cannot be assumed that verbal responses, or indeed the absence of a response, reflects an informed answer to any question put. These problems are certainly not the only ones associated with this group (Tudway and Darmoody, 2005), but they are the most salient when attempting to evaluate the possible presence of deviant sexual interest.

Deviant sexual interest is of significance in all sex offender populations, because it has repeatedly been found to be one of the strongest predictors of re-offence (Hanson and Harris (2000); Barbaree and Marshall (1988)). However, it is a particularly important assessment to make in the learning disabled population because of the high prevalence of significant intellectual, emotional and behavioural dysfunction which might suggest that in some cases factors other than sexual deviance lead to sexual behaviour being exhibited towards a child. In other words, the absence of sexual deviance would enable risk mitigation to focus on other pertinent deficits.

It was precisely the problems relating to assessment of sexual interest in the learning disabled population that the earliest components of Affinity were intended to address. The intention was to evolve computer-based procedures which would enable men with intellectual limitations to communicate their relative sexual interest in males and females of different ages. It was thus quite a prosaic goal of minimizing task demands associated with self-reporting sexual interest to the

point where coherent and meaningful self-disclosure was optimized. It was anticipated that in such circumstances, the relative contributions between incapacity,
honesty and dissimulation might be easier to make. There was initially no intention
of incorporating any unobtrusive measures such as VT, although its potential as
a measure had already long been recognized (Rosensweig, 1942; Zamansky, 1956;
Brown, Amaroso, Ware, Pruesse and Pilkey, 1973; Lang, Searles, Lauerman and
Adesso, 1980).

The process of developing Affinity was quite different to that typically employed
in most psychological assessment procedures. Its present form was determined by
an iterative, evolutionary approach, which was made possible by the availability
of what is referred to as Rapid Application Development (RAD) software.[3] As the
name suggests, these powerful tools allow software developers to quickly prototype a procedure, test its utility and then refine it to better achieve any desired goals.
Typically, this involves enhancing the human–computer interface, improving com-
prehensibility, ease of use or reducing errors. From a psychometric perspective, the
intention is to incrementally reduce the contribution of general error to assessment
scores. The process involved is much more akin to undertaking repeated with
small N design generalizability studies (Cronbach, 1990, p. 195) than traditional
test development, standardization and validity studies.

The development process involved repeated prototyping of facets of proposed
assessment tools, with incremental changes being systematically introduced and
evaluated. Typically, the criterion for success or failure of an evolutionary adaptation is quite harsh. The desired advantage must be operationally defined, and if it
is not then demonstrated in five consecutive assessments; the adaptation is either
revised or rejected. The intention is not to achieve a statistically detectable difference between adaptations, rather to make an improvement significant enough
to be self-evident. The ultimate proof of utility is enabling someone who could
not previously engage with or use the assessment to do so. Occasionally, an ABA
form of single case methodology would be necessary to ensure that the apparent
improvement in the assessment was not in fact a practice effect or other artefact.

For example, during development it was noted that a number of men with
relatively poor motor skills tended to miss on-screen 'buttons' on which they had
attempted to click to indicate sexual preference. Sometimes they clicked outside the
on-screen button border, and sometimes they clicked within the on-screen button,
but in so doing moved the pointer outside the button before releasing the mouse
button. It is often not appreciated by users that in the latter circumstances, the
universal convention in software development is that this will *not* register as a
click on the target, which requires (in the jargon) both 'mouse down' and 'mouse
up' events within the target on-screen object. In other words, it is the pressing and
release of the mouse button while the pointer remains over an on-screen button
which causes a 'click' to be registered.

---

[3] Affinity was initially developed using Hypercard (© Apple Computer), http://en. wikipedia.org/
wiki/HyperCard, then rewritten in Visual Basic (© Microsoft corporation), http://en.wikipedia.org/
wiki/Visual_Basic. Shortly thereafter development was switched to Revolution (© Runtime Revolution), which is a remarkably powerful RAD environment for Mac, Windows and Unix, http://
en.wikipedia.org/wiki/Runtime_Revolution.

This might appear to be a trivial problem, and in the vast majority of instances occurring daily all over the world, users simply click again, taking more care than before. However, where an assessment involves timing reactions, any such difficulty introduces significant measurement error. In addition, clicking again will be much more difficult in the presence of motor skill deficits much more prevalent in the learning disabled population. Further, such respondents often display concurrent emotional and behavioural problems. Since they are being assessed regarding a very sensitive matter, it is obviously very undesirable for anything to arise which might cause frustration or other negative emotions. It does not require many minor 'failures' for users to begin to display and express frustration with the procedure. This is likely to reduce cooperation and engagement, and may further impair performance by generating above-optimal emotional arousal and increasing distractibility.

In an effort to reduce this source of error, three adaptations were tested. The first was simply making the buttons larger. The second was placing an invisible 'skirt' around buttons which registered 'near misses' and automatically passed them as a click on the button. The third was constraining the pointer within the area of the buttons until a click was registered.

Somewhat surprisingly, enlarging the buttons only resulted in a modest reduction in missed clicks. This may have been because the buttons were already designed to be fairly large, and further increase in size beyond a certain point delivered diminishing advantage. The 'skirt' appeared to be somewhat better, but using the stringent five cases test did not eliminate the error. However, constraining the mouse pointer virtually eliminated 'missed click' errors. It also became apparent during the evaluation of this adaptation that the most common problem had been respondents moving the pointer to left or right with the intention of registering a click on either extreme left or right buttons, and simply overshooting the target. It was somewhat surprising to discover that the fact that the pointer was constrained within an area and that such overshoots were being artificially prevented appeared to be unnoticed by users.

The above example of iterative development is drawn from a later stage in assessment development. The earliest stages in development involved making 'mock-ups' of the proposed computer-based task, using a white board, paper, card, and sometimes other materials. Various proposed on-screen displays of images, text and buttons can be arranged and rearranged. In conjunction with this, a manual analogue of the proposed procedure can be tested on respondents and progressively refined.

ARCHETYPE RANKING

With respect to Affinity, two distinct paradigms were developed concurrently. The first came to be known as *archetype ranking*. The aim of this procedure was to elicit a rank order of relative sexual preference, but without actually exposing learning disabled respondents to the considerable task demands of rank ordering items.

A range of approaches were manually prototyped and piloted, but the most successful (in terms of ease of use) involved a procedure whereby simple line

Figure 3.1   Archetype ranking figures. (a) Original versions and (b) prototype revision.

drawings of human figure 'archetypes' were printed on cards and laid in front of the respondent. The figures were adapted from those used in another multimedia assessment project under development at the same time (Calam, Cox, Glasgow, Jimmieson and Groth Larsen, 2000), and were chosen because they represented males and females of a range of ages. The archetypes themselves have evolved over time, although figures very close to the originals remain the default set. The original archetypes, along with a recent prototype revision, appear in Figure 3.1. The archetypes correspond (from left to right) to the following categories and codes: small child male (SCM), small child female (SCF), pre-juvenile male (PJM), pre-juvenile female (PJM), juvenile male (JUM), juvenile female (JUF), adult male (ADM) and adult female (ADF).

It was found that asking respondents to rank order images was too difficult a task for a significant minority. A card sort style procedure worked somewhat better, but the procedure most readily understood was to simply ask the respondent to point to the card showing the sort of person they perceived as possessing 'the most' of any attribute. If this card was then removed, the process could be repeated in order to generate a rank order, but ranking was never formally presented as a required task.

This procedure worked well for simple attributes, but not with sexual interest. The problem appeared to be that archetypes were associated with either a degree of potential attractiveness or unattractiveness. Respondents were able to indicate the sort of person they would most like to have sex with, until the remaining archetypes were perceived as all representing unattractive options. At this point, the procedure would either grind to a halt or the respondent protested about the question put. The solution was to ensure that respondents could either choose a figure representing the most sexually attractive category or declare that none was attractive. Once the latter has occurred, the task then switches to selecting the archetype which represented the category of person with whom sexual contact would be most unattractive or aversive.

Computerizing this paradigm proved remarkably easy. The archetype figures all appear on screen, and any one can be selected by clicking on them using a mouse pointer system. Selection is indicated by a highlighted line surrounding the figure, and automatically deselects any previous selection. A button appears under the selected image labelled and coloured differently according to whether the current task is identifying the archetype representing the most attractive or the most unattractive category. Clicking this button confirms the selection made and causes the selected archetype to disappear, and the procedure can be repeated. Before the button is clicked, the respondent can freely change the selection made.

Thus, just as in the paper pilot, the computerized version minimizes the task demands of what is actually, for the intended population, a fairly complex procedure. Expressed relative sexual preference can thus be elicited without the distractions and complexities of real images of people, with minimal reliance on verbal ability, by adopting a relatively simple 'point-and-click' procedure.

Although somewhat unwieldy when described linguistically, computerization renders the *archetype ranking* task very simple to complete. Although it is important not to lead respondents, guidance can be requested or offered at any stage. During the assessment, discussion can take place about the representations available or selected. The procedure rarely takes longer than 5 or 10 minutes, even when it involves a good deal of discussion between the test administrator and the respondent.

The procedure automatically generates a very simple ranked order representation of the archetype images from most to least attractive which is concatenated with a second series representing those from least unattractive to most unattractive. This representation of relative sexual preference itself often facilitated very informative discussions with learning disabled sex offenders. Common themes tended to include the basis of sexual preferences and also discussions about the process of discriminating sexual maturity, particularly where this task can be challenging, either by virtue of disability or in relation to figures whose sexual maturity might be ambiguous, that is, adolescents.

The *archetype ranking* task was typically very well accepted by men in the IQ range of 60–75. Apparent or claimed non-comprehension of the task was quite rare, at around 2% of an inpatient learning disabled forensic population. Initial testing with learning disabled offenders (and non-offenders) suggested that the most common problems which threatened validity were unfamiliarity with mouse pointer system or poor psychomotor skills (Glasgow *et al.*, 2003).

IMAGE-RATING TASK

The second procedure, developed concurrently with the first, was a simple image-rating task. The paper pilot of this procedure consisted of approximately 200 pictures of males and females of different ages (taken from clothing catalogues). Again,

Figure 3.2   Affinity rating scale and sample image.

various procedures were investigated as possible means of eliciting a rating of attractiveness or unattractiveness. It was somewhat surprising to discover that the
idea of a rating scale representing both ranges (with a neutral point in between)
was quite well accepted. The piloting evolved towards a procedure in which the as-
sessor manipulated the cards and registered scores, whereas the respondent either
pointed to or placed a pointer on the rating scale.

Variants of such a scale were evaluated, with little evidence either supporting
or against any particular form. Discriminating the ranges by colour seemed to be
helpful, as was representing 'points' on the scale as boxes rather than check marks
on an analogue continuum.

The scale eventually adopted had a 'neutral box' between the two ranges, and
extended seven 'boxes' in either direction. The final paper form was implemented
almost unchanged into the software (see Figure 3.2).

The computerized rating task prototype involved approximately 150 non-
pornographic images being sequentially displayed on a computer screen. Copyright issues meant that images used in the paper prototype could not be used in
the computerized system, and a research license was obtained for a large number
of commercially available images.[4] These were manipulated using Photoshop to
remove extraneous people and objects, which might distract from or otherwise
complicate the assessment and interpretation process.

The respondent was required to click on an 'on-screen' rating scale displayed
immediately below the image, thus indicating degree of perceived sexual attractiveness or sexual unattractiveness. Once a rating was made, a button appeared
which enabled the respondent to move on to the next image.

---

[4]The source of images was Photodisc Ltd, now part of Getty Images, www.gettyimages.com.

Once the assessment was completed, ratings could then be aggregated in a fairly *ad hoc* and exploratory fashion in order to explore the reported value of almost any salient feature. The simplest means of achieving this was to rank order the images according to rating, and scan the highest and lowest scored image contents for common and apparently salient characteristics. As with the manual version, this then formed the basis for a debriefing interview with the respondent, which often proved enlightening.

The most common considerations in this regard tend to relate to age and gender, but it was discovered that quite often discrepancies in ratings between superficially similar images would reveal idiosyncratic facets of the respondent's sexual interest. This was often most apparent if the salient feature was shared by a subset of images. However, careful debriefing could then elicit important information arising from discrepancies between pairs of ostensibly similar images.

For example, one respondent, who had a history of offending against boys around the age of 8 years scored one such image very high (+7) and another relatively low (−4). During the assessment debriefing session, the images were presented to the respondent, who was asked to explain the difference between his ratings. He indicated that one was blond, clean 'and looks like a choir boy', whereas the other was described as 'a scruffy little tyke'. It emerged that he had a particular attraction to the latter which may well have evolved as a result of his practice of targeting neglected and poorly supervised boys in public places. Whether or not this relative preference actually evolved from his well-established predatory behaviour, it certainly reflected it, and this insight could be incorporated in risk mitigation and management interventions.

The *archetype ranking* and *image-rating* procedures typically generated data that were both consistent and coherent. Further, even when men had significant intellectual impairments, the tasks generated information that facilitated further assessment by interview. These original procedures were systematic and idiographic, with no expectation that normative comparisons would be appropriate or even desirable. However, extensive testing revealed that it was often helpful to directly compare data generated by the ranking with that from the rating procedures in order to look for consistencies and inconsistencies.

Generally speaking, there was a high concordance between the highest ranked archetype and the age and gender of those images which rated most attractive. Following assessment, the most highly rated images could (on an *ad hoc* basis) be matched with an archetype most closely matching them in age and gender. It was very evident that ranked archetypes generally predicted image ratings and vice versa.

When there was a discrepancy between the ranking and rating measures, again, debriefing interviews referring to both archetype and images data were often very informative. It became clear that in order to facilitate this process, it was desirable that images presented in the rating task were much more explicitly related to the archetypes of the ranking task. At around the same time this became apparent, the decision was taken to convert the software from HyperCard (which ran exclusively on the Macintosh operating system) to Visual Basic, which would make the assessment available on the then newly arrived Windows 95 operating system.

The process of rewriting the software from scratch enabled a number of improvements to be introduced, including the closer correspondence between images rated and archetypes. This was intended to increase the predictive power of the ranking procedure in relation to rating scores. Thus, instead of images being associated with an archetype category on an *ad hoc* (and potentially inconsistent) basis, images would be associated a priori and permanently with a category archetype.

This was achieved by requiring five judges (all mental health professionals) to independently allocate all images to one of the eight archetype categories. Only those images upon which all five judges agreed were incorporated into the new software. Perhaps unsurprisingly, the 'juvenile' categories presented the most inter-rater disagreement with respect to category membership. In fact, of over 20 images previously assumed to represent adolescent males, only 7 of these images were agreed by all five judges.

Since the proposal was that each category would contain the same number of images, the level of disagreement with respect to juvenile males limited the overall number of images in all categories to seven. This constituted a substantial reduction from the original prototype assessment which incorporated over 190 images to just 56. Previously, the images had no systematic naming convention, but were now accorded the acronym of the corresponding archetype, suffixed with a number 01–07. This made it much easier to identify concordance and discrepancy between the results of ranking and rating tasks. The 7 images (PJF01 to PJF07) associated with the pre-juvenile female (PJF) archetype can be seen in Figure 3.3.

This development was, however, not without its costs. It had the effect of severely limiting the potential to undertake *ad hoc* exploration of idiosyncratic preferences (as in the case of the choir boy vs. 'tyke' example described above). Notwithstanding this constriction in utility, it was decided to proceed with improved integration

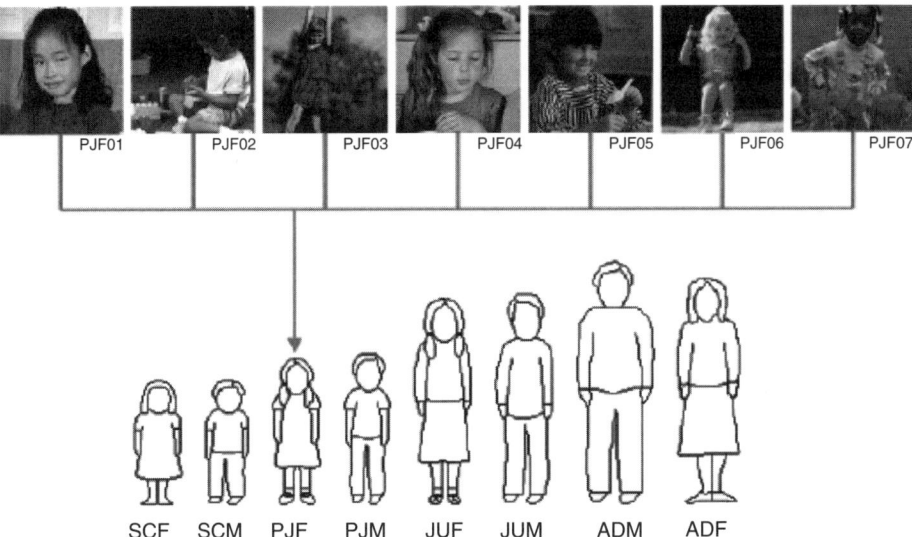

Figure 3.3   The seven exemplar images corresponding to the pre-juvenile female archetype.

of the measures with a view to increasing the number and diversity of images at a later date.[5]

Having reduced the number of images, it also proved necessary to reduce image quality and size. This was in order to make the assessment compatible with the limited capabilities of Windows 3.1 systems, which at that time remained very widely in use. This step was taken reluctantly but with hindsight may have made a significant contribution to beginning to understand some aspects of the VT phenomenon. It became increasingly difficult to reconcile an assessment which worked using fully clothed images, which were small and relatively of poor quality, with the idea that VT necessarily involves sexual arousal.

The rewriting of the Affinity software also offered an opportunity to incorporate a VT measure into the assessment. The potential for this to be of value had been apparent in the research literature for some time. However, early work conducted in 1980 at (the now closed) Moss Side High Security Hospital near Liverpool, England, revealed just how challenging it would be to begin realizing this potential.

A series of assessments were undertaken in the hospital PPG suite on sex offenders who were undergoing routine physiological assessment of sexual interests. Sexually explicit photographic images, similar to those used in PPG assessments, were presented using a slide projector. The respondent was free to view each image for as long as he wished, and was required to indicate how sexually arousing he found each, using a mechanical slide taped to the arm of his chair. A computer system recorded the rating and VT for each slide.

Unfortunately, the system proved to be cumbersome and unreliable. Some of the problems were technical. For example, sometimes the computer or slide projector failed to advance the slide in response to the respondent pressing the button. In response, he would jab repeatedly at the advance button, causing several slides to flash by. Other problems were a more complex interaction of human and technical limitations. For example, it was not unusual for respondents to completely forget to move the rating slider before advancing to the next slide, or to make the rating, but forget to press the slide advance button. Attempts were made to use a stopwatch to time and adjust for these errors, but these were very imprecise and required two people to continuously monitor the equipment and respondent, one of whom communicated with him and the other used the stopwatch.

The difficulties were numerous and effectively insurmountable, resulting in a high rate of aborted assessments. However, in those cases when the procedure worked, consistent with the scientific literature, modest to high positive correlation between VT and rated interested was repeatedly demonstrated. In some cases, VT was strongly consistent with offence history, although in many others it was not. Notwithstanding this, although the data showed promise, it was difficult to see how a VT assessment procedure using the available technology could supplement the data already obtained from PPG.

Fifteen years later, the technological obstacles to combining rating and VT had all but disappeared. The need to connect mechanical devices in order to serve different functions had gone. A computer could be used to present colour images on screen, time such presentations with precision and even present a virtual equivalent

---

[5]The most recent version of Affinity uses 80 images.

of the mechanical slider to register ratings. Perhaps even more important, the human–computer interface could be designed to eliminate the problem of the forgotten rating or multiple button presses. These mechanical components could be replaced with on-screen tools which appear when needed and disappear when not. This not only eliminates significant sources of error, the change in the on-screen layout signals to the respondent a change in the assessment and quickly comes to act as a cue to do what is required at the time.

The relative ease with which a reliable rating and timing system could be implemented into Affinity was also quite astonishing. By 1996, it was possible to time on-screen responses with an accuracy of approximately 1/60th to 1/100th of a second (the latest version of Affinity records milliseconds, with accuracy close to ±3 milliseconds). Not only was it possible to time the duration the respondent took to make a rating, it was also possible to time how long the respondent left the image on the screen after having made a rating but before clicking the virtual on-screen button to advance to the next image. This raised the prospect of measuring different 'fractions' of the VT response. It was hypothesized that the time spent making a rating or on task latency (OTL) might represent different and perhaps more active psychological components to the period after a rating was made, the post-task latency (PTL). If this proved to be the case, it was hoped that having decided an image was sexually attractive, there might follow a period of 'appetitive gazing', and that this might be more highly correlated with actual sexual interest than the time taken to actually make a rating.

Data arising from early prototyping strongly supported the case that the system was an acceptable and effective way of enhancing the self-report regarding sexuality of men with learning disabilities. Data from non-learning disabled non-offenders, both male and female, also indicated a modest to high correlation between self-report and the VT measures particularly the OTL VT component, that is, measurement of the time taken to complete the rating. In some individual cases the PTL VT correlated well with other measures, but generally speaking did not, showing great variance within and between image categories and individuals.

Initially, this was a considerable disappointment, but the fact that a significant source of unwanted variance (i.e. PTL) could be isolated from the overall VT was some consolation. It also offered the first hint that although VT might involve some element of passive, 'appetitive gazing', a substantial and perhaps more predictive element might be active, adaptive psychological processing which would normally take place as an antecedent to courtship.

At this stage, although the VT data could be described as showing considerable potential as a direct measure of interest, rather more conservative use of it as a validity scale in relation to the Affinity self-report scales appeared very effective indeed. In spite of this, it became apparent that both the VT and self-report data presented very significant challenges with respect to statistical analysis. The distribution of scores from most individuals was highly skewed. Further, as with data drawn from any single case methodology, it should not be presumed that observations are sufficiently independent to justify simply transforming the data and then using parametric techniques. On the other hand, some researchers argue that this is in fact justified (Banse, 2006).

Studying the data revealed that there is also very substantial between individual variance in VT range. Some moved through the items relatively quickly, whereas others paused for several seconds apparently reflecting carefully before making a rating. Although examining raw and mean score data strongly suggested the self-report and VT validity scales tended to converge when honest self-report was taking place, how this might best be objectively tested was far from evident.

The Kruskal Wallis is a non-parametric test which does not assume that data are normally distributed (Zimmerman, 1995; Odiase and Ogbonmwan, 2005), or that samples have similar standard deviations. It can be a very powerful technique and has also been recommended for use in single case methodologies (Edgington, 1992). Applying this technique to Affinity data from 20 non-offender assessments indicated significant differences between category responses in all cases, with an adult category higher than any other in all cases (a finding subsequently confirmed by Fischer, 2006). However, the Kruskal Wallis test has limited value because with eight categories it is difficult to clarify where the significant differences lie. Further, whilst significant differences are encouraging, it is impossible to say whether statistically significant differences reflect differences likely to have a real-world significance with respect to expressed behaviour.

IPSATIZED SCORES IN AFFINITY

It has already been indicated that the VT and rating data generated by Affinity are highly skewed. Such data are often viewed with suspicion because extreme scores are likely have an inordinate effect on the mean, particularly with smaller data sets. However, skewed and outlier prone distributions can be highly meaningful and valid, representing the reality of the systems generating the data. For example, measures of rainfall generate highly skewed distributions of scores. The idea of excluding or transforming outlying raw data in this case is patently absurd and misleading.

With respect to data from Affinity, there are no a priori reasons for assuming that extreme rating or VT scores are not similarly valid and meaningful. Although of course a VT *might* be conflated by distraction or inattention, images attended to for the longest time might also turn out to be the most 'diagnostic' of sexual interest. There is also some anecdotal evidence of this arising from the Affinity debriefings described above. In almost all cases, respondents were able to meaningfully contrast an image that had given rise to an extreme VT from one which had not, despite the fact that they were not aware that the discrepancy existed or indeed that VT had been measured. Most graphically, one respondent referred to an image he had examined for several times longer than any other image by simply saying, 'He reminds me of one of my victims'.

Nevertheless, it is certainly true that Affinity data are not readily amenable to parametric analysis, and any attempt to develop norms faces very considerable technical obstacles (Fischer, 2004). Further, although the data from Affinity 1.0 appeared to be highly meaningful in individual cases and with relatively small samples, it is very difficult to obtain a clear impression of the relationship between ratings and VT data, an issue for descriptive as much as differential statistics.

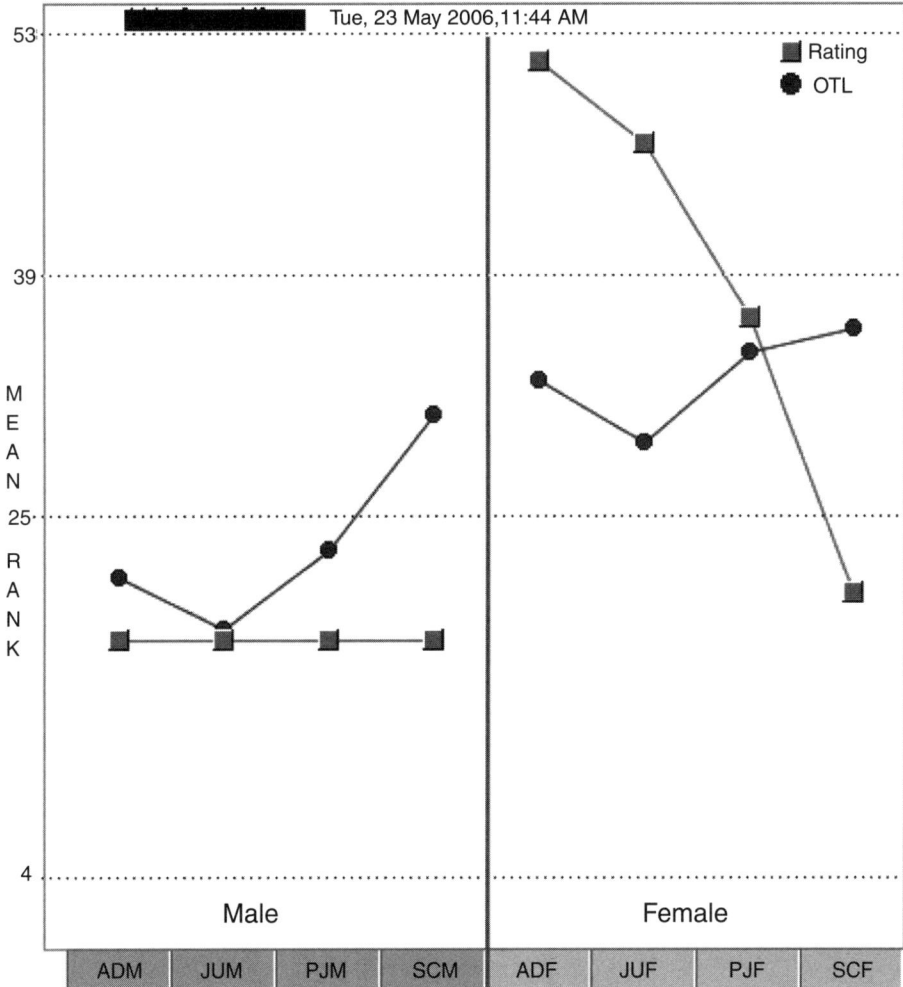

Figure 3.4 Ipsatized viewing time (OTL) and image-rating scores.

In relation to descriptive statistics, a number of significant revisions were undertaken up to Affinity 2.5, one of the most important developments was that in addition to offering raw data and a category means bar chart, the rating and VT scores were ipsatized. This enables VT and rating data to be displayed on the same chart as can be seen in Figure 3.4.

The procedure adopted to ipsatize the scores is conversion to mean ranks, which is in fact an intermediate step in the process of conducting the Kruskal Wallis test referred to above. Although other ipsatization procedures exist, mean ranks are very simple to calculate, are conservative and are very easy to relate back to raw data. It can be seen that the ipsatized data chart gives a very clear visual display of the correspondence between self-report and VT data. Discrepancies between the two measures become quite clear. In the example in Figure 3.4, there are significant discrepancies between self-report in the form of rating and the VT data. Claimed interest in adult females (ADF) and juvenile females (JUF) is much greater than would be suggested by VT, and claimed interest in small female children is much lower than would be suggested by VT.

With a minor modification, it is possible to add even more information to the display and also make discrepancies between self-report and VT even more apparent. The categories along the baseline of the chart can be sorted left to right according to the ranked order derived from the archetype ranking module, with the discontinuity between attractive and unattractive archetypes represented by a vertical line. Thus, categories to the left of the line represent attractiveness increasing to the left, and those categories to the right progressively unattractive categories to the right (see Figure 3.5).

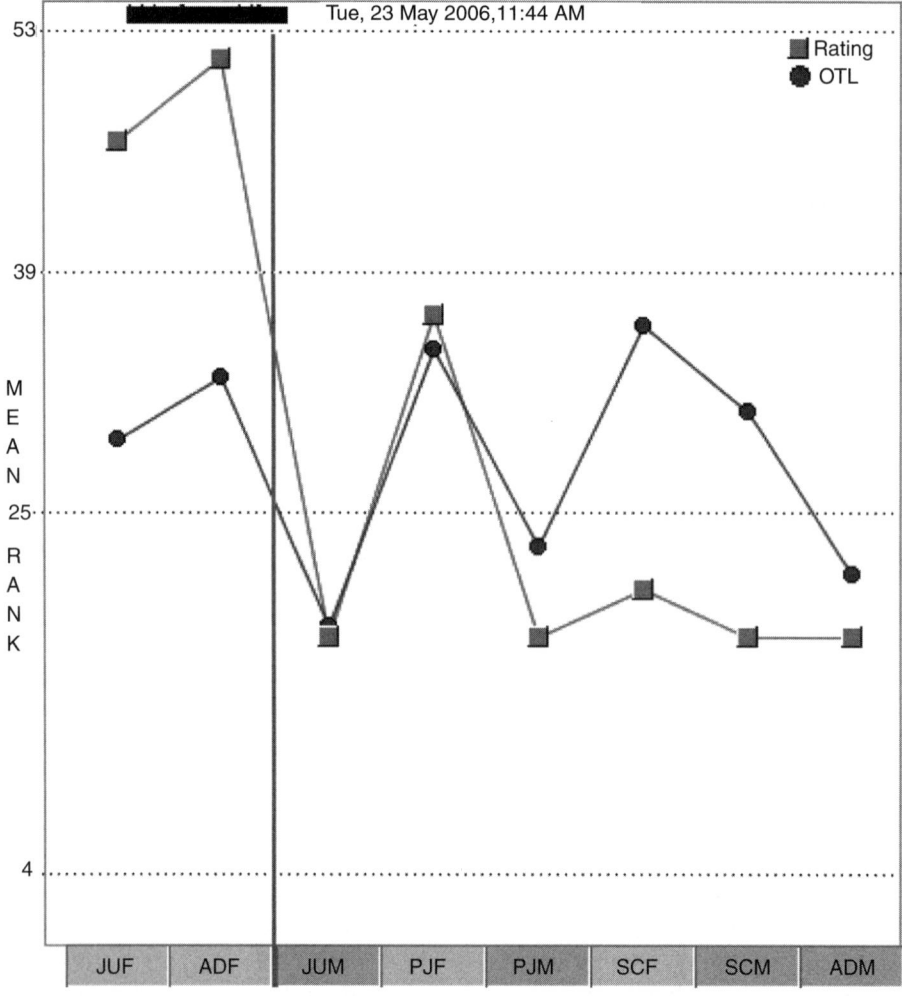

Figure 3.5   Ipsatized viewing time (OTL) and image-rating scores with the horizontal axis sorted according to the order of categories in the archetype-ranking module.

It will be recalled that the highest ranked archetypes typically predict the age and gender of highest rated images, with a modest to high correlation. As a result, the more dishonest a respondent is (i.e. representing a more attractive category as more unattractive), the more readily apparent the discontiguity between ranking and VT (OTL) becomes. Accordingly, in this case, the SCF (small child female) scores stand out as particular cause for concern.[6] Also of interest is the fact that although sexual interest in PJF (pre-juvenile females) was denied in the ranking procedure, it was acknowledged to some degree in the rating procedure. This is indicated by the correspondence between the mean ranks of OTL and rating in this category. This hints at what might be some degree of honesty within an overall dishonest pattern. Focusing on rating responses to PJF images in a debriefing interview might well be an appropriate way forward with this man.

Notwithstanding the above claims for and example of benefits to data interpretation arising from ipsatization, this remains the subject of some debate and even controversy. Although ipsative methodologies have their adherents, it is true to say that many would argue that they are simply an inferior approach to assessment and should be replaced by normative assessments.

The misuse and misinterpretation of ipsative data have quite properly vexed many psychometricians and psychologists alike. Fischer and Smith (1999) detail the dangers of this in connection with VT data interpreted in relation to sex offenders. Some would go so far as to say that the generation of ipsative data should be avoided at all costs, certainly within the domain of personality assessment (Johnson, Wood and Blinkhorn, 1988). The consensus view is very much in favour of normative assessments, probably driven by continuing inappropriate use of ipsative data as if they can legitimately be used to make normative comparisons. This error is quite rightly regarded as an egregious one, but its prevalence and consequent deprecation by others has arguably had the effect of eclipsing any more sophisticated debate about the nature and strengths of ipsative assessments. Further, there is a case to be made that regarding ipsative assessments as inevitably inferior to normative assessments risks disposing of a baby with the bath water (Baron, 1996).

Many assessments generating ipsative data are what might be described as *intrinsically ipsative*, that is to say, because of the way forced choice questions are presented to respondents, only ipsative data can arise. This is important because when intrinsically ipsative assessments measure relatively few traits or dimensions, the fact that at item level, respondents can only endorse one option generates spurious negative correlations between the traits or preferences. This is obviously undesirable and potentially significantly misleading both immediately and also if multivariate analysis of these data is subsequently attempted. It is important to note that Affinity is not intrinsically ipsative in this sense. There are no forced choices between the images in the rating task, and there is absolutely no restriction on the duration with which any item can be viewed. In consequence, raw data arising from the rating module do not have the undesirable correlation of properties seen in many, if not most ipsative assessments. Nevertheless, the process

---

[6]The individual being assessed in this example had offended against girls of ages between 5 and 9 years.

of ipsatization does exaggerate negative correlations between variables, although this effect reduces as the number of variables increases.

Although the mean rank conversion enables direct visual comparison between the three key measures in Affinity, it is entirely open to a user to ignore ipsatized scores and undertake any analyses or comparisons on the basis of the raw data. As has been indicated above, this presents considerable psychometric challenges, but there is no reason to suppose that these are necessarily insurmountable. It is also important to note that whereas any display of ipsatized data can exaggerate discrepancies between raw scores, Affinity offers the facility to switch between raw and ipsatized displays enabling problematic profiles to be scrutinized more closely.

For example, Fischer (2004) reported the case of a woman who completed an Affinity assessment by very rapidly clicking a rating with little evidence whether she was paying attention to the stimuli or the process of rating. This was apparent during the assessment, and also from the raw data which indicated that she had completed the assessment much faster than would be expected. However, if these indications of a problem were overlooked, the ipsatized chart suggested deviant sexual interest. It is therefore very clear that as an idiographic tool ipsative displays can be very informative; they must be interpreted only by those who are conversant with potential pitfalls. Further, the serious human costs of misinterpretation of data pertaining to possible sexual deviance are very high and should be borne in mind at all times.

So far, the origins and strengths of Affinity as an idiographic, single case methodology have been described, and some defence of the inclusion of ipsatized scores has been made. However, it is possible to go further and make the case that when the goal of assessment is to investigate an individual's relative preferences, ipsatized data have unique strengths.

An illustrative example may help explore some of the issues relating to ipsative scores generally and also their legitimate role in the interpretation of data arising from Affinity. It has already been stated that ipsative data reflect relative strengths of traits or preferences within an individual. This might be helpful if one wishes to explore an individual's relative preferences for varieties of a particular product, for example ice cream. That ice cream consumption reflects an appetitive behaviour makes it a somewhat useful analogue for assessment of sexual preference, which can also be regarded as an appetitive behaviour. Table 3.1 shows the data from a hypothetical ice cream preference assessment administered to six individuals.

The fact that the within individual scores all sum to a constant integer (20) is a strong clue that the data are derived from an intrinsically ipsative assessment and therefore there can be no assumptions made regarding the absolute levels of preference, only individuals' preferences, given the available choices.

The issue of available choices is important because the extent to which the choices included in the assessment reflect the universe of actual behavioural choices facing the individuals being assessed reduces measurement error. As it happens, the most popular flavour in the United Kingdom is vanilla, and the omission of this from the assessment might well mean that some of the individuals assessed will be

Table 3.1 Data from a hypothetical ice cream preference assessment

Flavour	Individuals					
	A	B	C	E	E	F
Strawberry	7	4	1	7	0	1
Mint choc chip	2	3	0	2	2	3
Chocolate	1	3	0	3	4	4
Cookie dough	5	3	3	5	0	3
Baileys	0	4	12	0	10	5
Honeycomb	5	3	4	3	4	4

somewhat unenthusiastic about many of the choices; a fact which is completely obscured by the ipsative data.

One can also envisage hypothetical characteristics of individuals which would completely change the interpretation of the data. These can expose a sometimes very strong temptation to aggregate data across columns to attempt to draw general conclusions about the flavours rather than the individuals, despite the absence of an explicit normative reference. A thought experiment such as imagining that you are an ice cream retailer scanning the table regarding changes to a product range can give an insight as to just how insidious this temptation is.

Other thought experiments can make the potential pitfalls even clearer. For example, what is the first impression of person C's feelings towards Baileys flavour ice cream? What if we subsequently discover that person C has temperature-sensitive teeth and also hates ice cream? Further, we then discover that person B is an ice cream aficionado and loves many flavours, eating some at least twice a day. These scenarios together make it clear that person C's 'Baileys flavour' score of 12 may well in fact reflect much less 'ice cream appetite' in absolute terms than person B's 'Baileys flavour' score of 4. These critical differences are obscured by the forced choice nature of an intrinsically ipsative assessment.

The issue of whether the categories regarding which data are gathered represent the universe of behavioural options has already been raised. In contrast to the ice cream flavours example, the categories in Affinity encompass a great deal of the universe of preferred ages, and dominant sexual preferences for the majority of male and female adults are represented in four of the categories (adult + adolescent × male and female). To all intents and purposes, because human beings display very marked sexual bimorphism, the available stimulus options regarding gender effectively encompass primary gender-related sexual orientations, that is, heterosexuality, homosexuality (and bisexuality).

There is an additional point to be made relating to the relationship between age categories. In Affinity, the person being assessed is free to report interest in either males or females in four age categories which are effectively developmentally *consecutive*. Accordingly, there is a special relationship between the categories in Affinity which is qualitatively different to those in the ice cream example above, in which there is no prima facie continuum on which the flavours can logically be placed in any specific order. The age-related continuum of categories might benefit from being extended at either end, but the idea of a respondent wishing to express sexual interest in a category inserted between existing categories makes no sense.[7]

Further, contrary to the passionate arguments of children, the consumption of ice cream is not a biological imperative. The formation of sexual relationships certainly is, at least for the vast majority of human beings. The Affinity procedure is therefore not predicated on the relatively weak expectation of ice cream consumption, but the much stronger and probable expectation of courtship,[8] sexual activity and perhaps attachment (Fisher, Aron, Mashek, Li and Brown, 2002).

Of course, individuals will engage in courtship with different frequencies, levels of motivation and varieties of prospective sexual partners. Nevertheless, adopting Bayesian language, the prior probability of sexual behaviour is high. Consequently, both the VT and self-report components of Affinity generate data in relation to the question, 'When this individual engages in sexual activity, what would be his (or her) relative preferences regarding gender and age of sexual partner?' Once again, the issue is not one of absolute appetite, but relative preference.

The VT data, even when these are relatively moderately correlated with actual sexual interest, ought (with an honest response style) to be manifestly consistent with data generated by known antecedent sexual behaviour, expressed preferences and data from the Affinity rating and ranking modules. If paedophilia is denied by general self-report and archetype ranking, it is a matter of some concern if the ipsatized 'ranking by rating' of prepubertal images contradicts this.

Obviously, there is an important issue relating to how to measure 'contradiction', and what might be an appropriate threshold for reaching either a strong diagnostic conclusion, for example 'denied paedophile sexual interest is present', or a weaker (but nonetheless important) conclusion about the psychometric process and self-report, for example '[t]his person reported exclusive sexual interest in adult males, but a validity scale (VT) did not confirm that this was honest self-report'. Of course, this is not only a statistical issue. The positive and negative utilities of different conclusions in any given circumstances must play a part.

The convergent nature of the three measures of sexual interest in Affinity also means that careful scrutiny of the ipsative and raw data sets *together* can alert a professional to factors which might, in some circumstances, cause false conclusions to be drawn from just the ipsatized data alone. This does not mean that normative references can be drawn; merely the ipsative profile of sexual interest relative preferences may be placed in a more coherent idiographic context.

For example, in one particular assessment, the adult female was evidently (according to ipsatized VT) most preferred by a considerable margin. However, examining the raw and mean ratings chart relating to specific images revealed that on the −7 to +7 rating scale, the highest raw score regarding *any* adult image was +2. This was somewhat surprising because in an earlier interview he had claimed to be strongly and exclusively heterosexual, and very averse to the idea of sex with

---

[7]This is not to suggest that sexual interest might not be significantly determined by facets other than age and gender, like the example of the fat fetishist individual described below.

[8]For the purposes of this chapter, the term 'courtship' is used to include what is generally referred to as 'grooming'; behaviour regarded as a travesty of courtship because the target of the behaviour is a potential victim.

anyone other than an adult. Using the printed debrief facility built into Affinity, a clarificatory interview was conducted. The respondent explained that the images were 'nice enough, but not my type'. With minimal prompting, he explained that he had a long-standing and intense sexual interest in women weighing more than 20 stone (280 pounds or 127 kg). This was confirmed by reference to previous partners and pornographic magazine use.

The essential point is that when considering relative sexual preferences of an individual, ipsatized scores have a unique contribution to make. Indeed, it is difficult to imagine any process of standardization which would not obscure at least some potentially significant differences between individual profiles and relative preferences.

DATA ARISING FROM AFFINITY

Having made a case for careful interpretation of ipsative data, it is important to emphasize that it does not mean to imply that the issue of validity – whether scales measure what they purport to measure – is insignificant; not only is ipsatization an issue here. Roid and Johnson (1998) undertook a detailed review of trends in computer-assisted psychological assessment. In an attempt to explicate advantages, disadvantages and risks of such assessments, they offered a typology. This accommodated the fact that early examples of assessment computerization tended to be little more than digitized versions of a paper and pencil test. The key benefits of this approach were ease of administration and data storage. Validity could be established by simply comparing results from the computerized and paper version. The latter was often assumed to be the 'gold standard', although of course discrepancies between paper and digital versions might conceivably arise from lower validity or reliability of the former. More recent computerized assessments have increasingly adopted novel procedures and scoring systems.

Within Roid and Johnson's framework, Affinity would be described as 'multi-media or specialized test administration'. Assessment procedures falling into this category are, almost by definition, the most difficult to describe and specify, and also present the greatest challenges to those wishing to ensure that they constitute valid procedures. Further, the evolutionary and iterative approach to assessment development, described above in positive terms, presents serious challenges to establishing validity and ensuring that it is not adversely affected by what might appear to be minor changes.

An early study using Affinity 1.0 (Croxen, 2003) involved the assessment of 31 men who had been convicted of committing at least one sexual offence against a child ('paedophile group'). All were detained in a high security psychiatric facility. These data were compared with those of 31 non-offending adult male volunteers ('comparison group'). Cronbach alphas for each of the categories can be found in Table 3.2 below. They range from 0.76 to 0.93. This suggests that those who scored relatively highly on one item in a category were likely also to score highly on other items within the same category.

An obvious measure of the relationship between VT and self-report is to calculate correlation coefficients for each individual's rated sexual interest and VT on all

Table 3.2 Cronbach alphas for Affinity categories using viewing time in paedophile ($n = 31$) and comparison ($n = 31$) groups

	Cronbach alphas	
	Paedophile	Comparison
Child female	0.92	0.89
Child male	0.93	0.93
Preadolescent female	0.87	0.89
Preadolescent male	0.8	0.9
Adolescent female	0.89	0.79
Adolescent male	0.9	0.76
Adult female	0.93	0.88
Adult male	0.89	0.93

images. Spearman's rhos for non-offenders ranged from 0.05 to 0.68. The median correlation was 0.57. Of the 31 correlations, 29 were statistically significant, one at the $p < 0.5$ level and the remainder at $p < 0.01$. Perhaps unsurprisingly, given the likely presence of denied paedophile interest in the offender sample, far fewer (23 of 31) of the correlations in the paedophile group were statistically significant (16 at $p < 0.01$ and 7 at $p < 0.05$). The range in the paedophile group was between 0.02 and 0.70 and the median correlation was 0.35).

Close inspection of the Croxen study data revealed something of a surprise with respect to the VT data of the non-offending comparison group. This sample all claimed to be exclusively heterosexual. The transformed mean VTs showed a very marked pattern by which the men displayed a significant 'gender effect' with female images being attended to longer than male images of the corresponding age category. Although this effect diminished with younger age groups, it remained evident (Figure 3.6). Unfortunately, this was not anticipated, and did not form part of the statistical analysis. However, the pattern was replicated in Fischer's (2004) study of non-offending males ($n = 61$), and a reciprocal pattern found in the profiles of non-offending females ($n = 141$).

One somewhat disturbing conclusion that might be drawn from this is that non-offending heterosexual males exhibit some kind of incipient 'sexual' response to females of all ages, which results in longer VTs. This possibility is a controversial and sensitive issue, because it effectively implies that many if not all males, regardless of what they claim, have some degree of sexual attraction to young female children.

Although VT is a validity measure within *Affinity*, and intended to be an adjunct to systematic self-report, it is appropriate to investigate the extent to which VT alone can discriminate between paedophile and non-offending samples. This is difficult (perhaps impossible) to investigate taking into account the entire profile, because paedophiles have very variable responses to different child image categories. Some express interest in, and have offended against, only one prepubertal category. Others have relative elevations in more than one within-gender category and yet others across both male and female categories. Aggregating these highly heterogeneous data across individuals inevitably obscures individual and between-group differences in the overall variance.

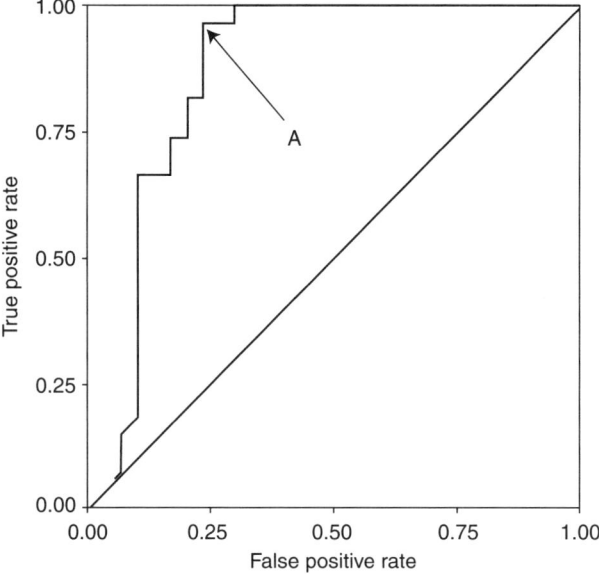

Figure 3.6   Receiver operating characteristic (ROC) curve discriminating sexual offenders against children from non-offending males using a VT-derived *deviance index*. The candidate cut point marked (A) is referred to in the text.

This very problem was faced many years ago by those using PPG to assess sex offenders. In an attempt to simplify and operationalize at least part of the interpretation of phallometric data, the *deviance index* was developed by Harris, Rice, Quinsey and Chaplin (1992). In order to explore the discriminant validity of Affinity VT component, a 'VT variant' of the deviance index was calculated. For each participant, the highest mean VT for a child category (excluding adolescents) was subtracted from whichever of the mean VT of the adult categories was the higher. Obviously, where the child related VT is greater, the deviance index will be negative and where it is the lesser, it will be positive. A receiver operating characteristics (ROC) analysis was used to investigate the effectiveness of this continuous measure to categorize participants into paedophile and non-paedophile groups (see Figure 3.6). Two of the great strengths of ROC analysis are that the procedure is relatively unaffected by either skewed data, or the relative base rates of the categories being distinguished.

The area under the curve (AUC) was a respectable 0.87, suggesting that VT alone is likely to possess discriminant validity sufficiently high to be of practical use (Henley and McNeil, 1982). An obvious candidate cut-off point (marked as 'A' in Figure 3.6) was one at which 96% of paedophiles were correctly categorized at a cost of approximately 23% false positives. Of course, the cut-off point might be shifted to reflect the relative costs of false positives versus false negatives. However, notwithstanding the fact that an AUC of 0.87 would be regarded as very desirable in relation to risk assessment tools, the percentage of false positives at 'A' is a valuable reminder of the potential human costs of miscategorization.

Two concerns which have been expressed regarding the Affinity system related to the possibility that factors other than sexual interest might conflate VT. In particular, it was suggested that same sex images might be viewed for longer because the respondent was evaluating potential sexual competition. This was repeatedly suggested by women anecdotally reporting their own behaviour upon entering a social situation in which courtship was a possibility. The second concern was that filial affection might increase VT. In other words, being the devoted parent of, say, a 6-year-old child might cause longer VTs in relation to images corresponding to that category.

A small-scale study ($N = 25$) investigated both concerns using Affinity 2.2 with adult women who were parents of one prepubertal child. This would allow the specific impact of parenthood to be related to a single category. The study did not focus on the 'raw' categories, but compared mean ranks of categories which were functionally equivalent between subjects. These were preferred adult, non-preferred adult, highest child, own child and opposite sex child.

How the child-related categories were defined require some explanation. The category 'own child' consisted of the images corresponding to the archetype which best represented the age and development of a given participants own child. The 'opposite sex child' category was formed from the images corresponding to the archetype which matched the participants' child by age, but not by gender. Thus, for example, if a woman had an 8-year-old daughter, the 'own child' category would consist of data from (pre-juvenile female) images PJF01 to PJF07. The 'opposite sex child' category would consist of data from (pre-juvenile male) images PJM01 to PJF07. The 'highest child' category was determined *post hoc*, and simply consisted of the data from the child category which generated the highest mean rank scores. This was effectively a 'worst-case scenario' condition, intended to investigate the extent of any overlap between preferred adult score distributions, and the child-related data distribution most likely to threaten a 'false positive' result for deviant interest.

The overall correlations between self-report and VT were higher than in the Croxen study, ranging from 0.57 to 0.74. Further, there was absolutely no evidence that either filial affection or sexual competition confounded VT or self-report measurement of sexual interest. In no case was the mean rank for preferred adult category lower than the mean rank for any other category (Figure 3.7), which obviates the need for discriminative statistics.

Contrary to the filial affection hypothesis, the mean rank VTs for the category corresponding by age and gender to that of the each participants' child tended to be *lower* than all other categories, including that of the same age but opposite sex child. The sample is too small to conduct *post hoc* analysis of such a counterintuitive finding, but it does raise the intriguing possibility that whatever the psychological processes which underlie VT as a measurement of sexual interest, parenthood imposes a cognitive proscription which truncates the process which would otherwise occur, even in response to young children of the 'preferred' gender.

Finally, perhaps the most surprising finding in relation to Affinity is that relatively few, small, low-quality, non-pornographic images can constitute stimuli which generate significant and meaningful VT data relating to sexual interest. Whilst it is just possible that some highly deviant and sexually reactive individuals

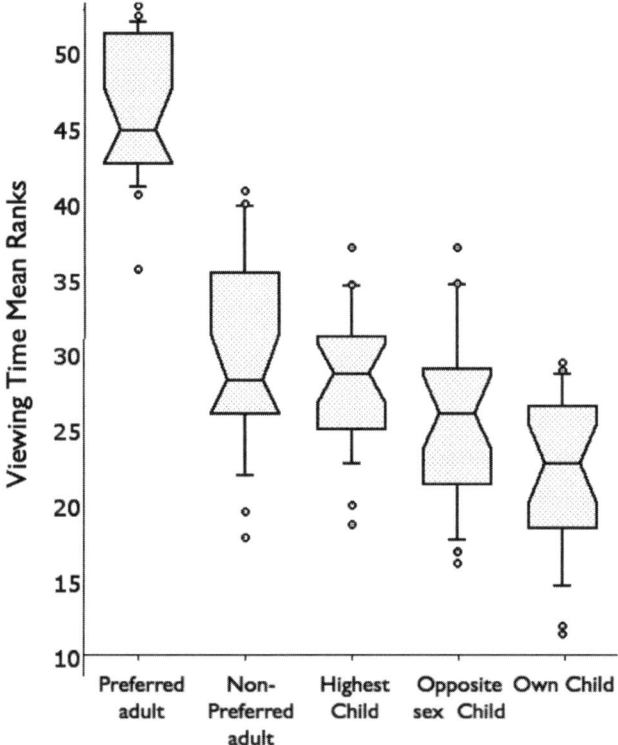

Figure 3.7   Mean rank viewing times of mothers undertaking the Affinity rating task.

might regard the images as sexually salient, this seems highly unlikely in the general population. Taken together with the above findings, this suggests that VT does not necessarily relate to sexual arousal *per se*, but might reflect a more cognitive process, arising from the systematic appraisal of human beings as potential targets for courtship.

CONCLUSIONS AND SOME SPECULATION

On the cognitive VT model suggested above, when people encounter others (and images of others), these are analyzed for the extent to which criteria relating to sexual attractiveness are met. If this is to be an efficient process, highly salient features such as gender and age are likely to be analyzed first and if these criteria are met, then more time might be invested in further processing, perhaps in a cascading 'gated' process unless or until a proscriptive cognition is encountered.

The data relating to differential VTs between gender categories in relation to even very young children suggest that some of this attraction-specific processing takes place before conscious awareness. Thus, in normal heterosexual men, processing of female children proceeds measurably beyond that for children of the non-preferred

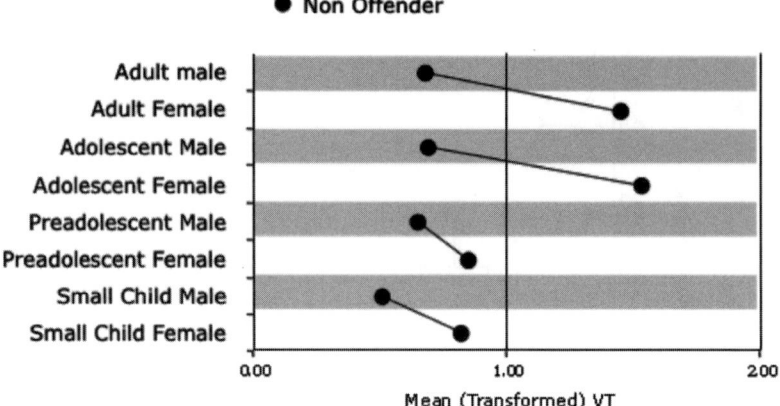

Figure 3.8   Mean VT for heterosexual non-offender males, showing longer viewing times for females across all age categories.

gender, but this is not a conscious process, or one which reflects or presages deviant arousal.

On the other hand, for mothers at least, there is some evidence of a pre-emptive proscription, which prevents even the earliest processing taking place for children of similar appearance to their own children. This suggests that the VT measure in Affinity is not likely to be readily confounded by non-sexual affection in females. It would be very interesting to see if this effect could be replicated with respect to fathers, particularly heterosexual men with prepubertal daughters.

At the 'other end' of the VT continuum, the self-report in relation to long VT images suggests that processing continues into awareness, and sometimes over several seconds, particularly for highly salient images approximating personal sexual preferences. How much of this is appetitive gazing, and how much a more active psychological process linking perception, memory, wishing and willing, is unclear at present, although the activation of courtship schemata would be consistent with cognitive models of human action.

The above is necessarily very speculative at present, but a dynamic cognitive model of VT would certainly fit in with the empirical evidence from Affinity, and also with more general models of sexual relationship and behaviour. Typically, something akin to cognitive or 'romantic' attraction is discriminated from but related to physiological arousal (Palace, 1995), and both are in turn related to attachment (Janssen, Everaerd, Spiering and Janssen, 2000; Fisher *et al.*, 2002).

If subsequent data from Affinity and other VT paradigms prove to be consistent with the cognitive VT hypothesis, some very exciting possibilities in relation to assessment and even treatment arise. For example, Laws, Hanson, Osborn and Greenbaum (2000) made a compelling case for the potential for multiple measures of deviant interest to be combined to improve overall classificatory accuracy. This would only be of benefit if the measures combined accessed different facets of sexual interest. If this is the case, then it in turn raises the possibility that facets combined for classificatory purposes might be discriminated for the purposes of treatment. Whilst it is very likely that there are significant interactions between cognitive and physiological arousal systems relating to sexual attraction, it is possible to speculate about and even envisage quite distinct interventions for cognitive components of attraction, which might potentiate or at least complement other relapse prevention interventions.

Despite the early research in VT having been undertaken many decades ago, development of VT-based assessment and treatment procedures are without doubt in their infancy, and the true nature of VT is only just beginning to be systematically explored (Gress, 2005). Whether a defensible, norm-referenced VT procedure or whether effective VT-based cognitive interventions will ever emerge are empirical questions which may take years to answer. Nonetheless, although many questions remain unanswered, it is certainly a fascinating time to be working in the field of the assessment of deviant sexual interest.

REFERENCES

Banse, R. (2006) *Indirect Assessment of Sexual Preference in Paedophile Sexual Offenders.* Paper presented at the 16th Conference of the European Association of Psychology and Law (www.i-psy.com/eapl).

Barbaree, H. and Marshall, W. (1988) Deviant sexual arousal, offense history and demographic variables as predictors of reoffending among child molesters. *Behavioural Science and the Law*, **6**, 267–80.

Baron, H. (1996) Strengths and limitations of ipsative measurement. *Journal of Occupational and Organizational Psychology*, **69**, 49–56.

Brown, M., Amaroso, D., Ware, E., Pruesse, M. and Pilkey, D. (1973) Factors affecting viewing time of pornography. *Journal of Social Psychology*, **90**, 125–35.

Calam, R.M., Cox, A.D., Glasgow, D.V., Jimmieson, P. and Groth Larsen, S. (2000) Assessment and therapy with children: can computers help? *Child Clinical Psychology and Psychiatry*, **5** (3) 329–43.

Cronbach, L. (1990) *Essentials of Psychological Testing*, 5th edn. Harper Collins.

Croxen, J. (2003) Assessment of paedophlile sexual interest using Affinity 1.0. Unpublished Doctoral Thesis, University of Manchester, England.

Edgington, E.S. (1992) Nonparametric tests for single case experiments, in *Single Case Research Design and Analysis: New Directions for Psychology and Education* (eds T.R. Kratchow-ill and J.R. Levin), Erlbaum, Hillsdale, pp. 133–57.

Fischer L. (2004, October) Psychometric issues in viewing-time research, clinical, and forensic applications, in *Accessible, Standardized, Viewing-Time Measurement* (ed. L. Fischer (Chair)). Symposium conducted at the 23rd Annual Research and Treatment Conference of the Association for the Treatment of Sexual Abusers, Albuquerque, New Maxico.

Fischer L. (2006) *Psychometric Issues in Viewing-Time Research, Clinical and Forensic Applications.* Paper presented at Association for the Treatment of Sexual Abusers 25th Annual Conference.

Fischer, L. and Smith, G. (1999) Statistical adequacy of the Abel Assessment for interest in paraphilias. *Sexual Abuse: A Journal of Research and Treatment*, **11** (3), 195–205.

Fisher, H., Aron, A., Mashek, D., Li, H. and Brown, L. (2002) Defining the brain systems of lust, romantic attraction, and attachment. *Archives of Sexual Behavior*, **31** (5), 413–9.

Glasgow, D., Osborne, A. and Croxen, J. (2003) An assessment tool for investigating paedophile sexual interest using viewing time: an application of single case methodology. *British Journal of Learning Disability*, **31**, 96–102.

Gress, C.L.Z. (2005) Viewing time and sexual interest: another piece of the puzzle. *Journal of Sexual Aggression*, **11**, 117–25.

Hanson, R.K., and Harris, A.J.R. (2000) Where should we intervene? Dynamic predictors of sex offense recidivism. *Criminal Justice and Behavior*, **27**, 6–35.

Harris, G., Rice, M., Quinsey, V. and Chaplin, T. (1992) Maximizing the discriminant validity of phallometric assessment data. *Psychological Assessment*, **4** (4), 502–11.

Henley, J. and McNeil, B. (1982) The meaning and use of the area under a receiver operating characteristic (ROC) curve. *Radiology*, **143**, 29–36.

Janssen, E., Everaerd, W., Spiering, M. and Janssen, J. (2000) Automatic processes and the appraisal of sexual stimuli: toward an information processing model of sexual arousal. *Journal of Sex Research*.

Johnson, C.E., Wood, R. and Blinkhorn, S.F. (1988) Sp{rouser and spuriouser: the use of ipsative personality tests. *Journal of Occupational Psychology*, **61**, 153–62.

Lang, A., Searles, J., Lauerman, R. and Adesso, V. (1980) Expectancy, alcohol and sex guilt as determinants of interest in sexual stimuli. *Journal of Abnormal Psychology*, **89**, 644–53.

Laws, D.R., Hanson, R.K., Osborn, C.A. and Greenbaum, P.E. (2000) Classification of child molesters by plethysmographic assessment of sexual arousal and a self-report measure of sexual preference. *Journal of Interpersonal Violence*, **15** (12), 1297–312.

Odiase, J. and Ogbonmwan, S. (2005) Exact permutation critical values for the Kruskal–Wallis one-way ANOVA. *Journal of Modern Applied Statistical Methods*, **4** (2), 609–20.

Palace, E.M. (1995) A cognitive–physiological process model of sexual arousal and response. *Clinical Psychology: Science and Practice*, **2** (4), 370–84.

Roid, G. and Johnson, W.B. (1998) Computer assisted psychological assessment, in *Comprehensive Clinical Psychology* (eds A.S. Bellack and M. Hersen), Pergamon, New York, pp. 501–23.

Rosensweig, S. (1942) The photoscope as an objective device for evaluating sexual interest. *Psychosomatic Medicine*, **4**, 150–58.

Tudway, J. and Darmoody, M. (2005) Clinical assessment of adult sex offenders with learning disabilities. *Journal of Sexual Aggression*, **11** (3), 277–88.

Worling, J. (2006) Assessing sexual arousal with adolescent males who have offended sexually: self-report and unobtrusively measured viewing time. *Sex Abuse*, **18**, 383–400.

Zamansky, H. (1956) A technique for measuring homosexual tendencies. *Journal of Personality*, **24**, 436–48.

Zimmerman, D. (1995) Increasing the power of the ANOVA F test for outlier-prone distributions by modified ranking methods. *Journal of General Psychology*, **122**, 83.

Chapter 4

COGNITIVE MODELLING OF SEXUAL AROUSAL AND INTEREST: CHOICE REACTION TIME MEASURES

Carmen L.Z. Gress

Pacific Psychological Assessment Corporation, Victoria, BC, Canada

D. Richard Laws

Pacific Psychological Assessment Corporation, Victoria, BC, Canada

INTRODUCTION

Identifying or substantiating a sexual offender's sexual interest leads to enhanced court decisions regarding risk assessment, sentencing, civil commitment decisions and dangerous offender designations, as certain sexual interests are associated with a higher recidivism risk. For example, Hanson and Bussière (1998) state that 'the risk for sexual offence recidivism was increased for those who had . . . selected male victims' (p. 351). More often than not, a mental health professional can determine a client's sexual interest via the offender's self-report information and/or sexual history. On occasion, however, a documented history does not exist, information is not forthcoming, an offender denies his sexual offence history and/or index offence, or he claims his interests have changed. A reliable, objective and standardized sexual preference instrument would, therefore, augment legal and treatment assessment. To meet this need, there is a rise in research on the cognitive models of sexual interest using attention-based measures.

COGNITIVE MODELLING OF SEXUAL INTEREST: A BACKGROUND

Researchers model and measure attention, specifically the performance associated with different aspects or attention processes such as attention span, interference,

---

selective attention or attentional bias, to investigate complex cognitive and behavioural patterns ranging from memory and emotion to the recent examinations of sexual arousal and interest (Geer, Estupinan and Manguno-Mire, 2000). The impetus for cognitive attention-based models of sexual arousal and interest arose from studies investigating the effect of distraction on male sexual arousal (Barlow, 1986). For example, Laws and Rubin (1969) as well as Henson and Rubin (1971) demonstrated that prompting a person to distract themselves with non-sexual thoughts during a physiological assessment of sexual arousal can lead to decreases in penile circumference or blood flow. A study by Rook and Hannen (1977) demonstrated that those participants who identified non-sexual physiological arousal (for example, blood flow in the genital region can increase during fearful events) as sexual arousal consistently interpreted non-sexual situations as sexual if genital sensations occurred simultaneously.

Barlow (1986), informed by his and colleague's work on sexual dysfunction, proposed a cognitive–affective model of sexual arousal focusing on the perception of physiological arousal and the cognitive processing of erotic cues. In his 1986 article, Barlow noted that sexually dysfunctional men (specifically, erectile dysfunction) reacted negatively to sexual situations, suggesting that their sexual experiences begin with awareness and identification of sexual cues and move to negative perceptions and emotions. Geer and Janssen (2000) proposed that after appraisal and recognition, emotional saliency dictates the degree to which regulatory processes focus additional attention on sexual behaviours or sensations and whether that attention focuses on positive or negative aspects. Additional attention to sexual information is evidenced by studies demonstrating that anxiety and/or sexual distractors can increase sexual arousal in sexually functional men (due to additional attention to positive sexual aspects) but hampers it in sexually dysfunctional men due to additional attention to negative sexual aspects (Barlow, 1986). For example, Barlow, Sakheim and Beck (1983) examined the effects of performance anxiety and generalized anxiety by comparing three conditions: telling participants either that (a) there was a 60% chance of electric shock if they did not demonstrate adequate levels of physiological (penile) arousal to the presented stimuli, (b) shock may occur and it is unrelated to arousal or (c) no shock will occur. The authors found that both shock conditions increased physiological arousal. Barlow (1986) found non-sexual distractors can cause the opposite patterns, and that sexually dysfunctional men underreport their levels of sexual arousal.

Barlow's and other models of sexual arousal have made considerable contributions to the field of sexual research. These models treat sexual arousal as a unified construct, however, which fails to explain individual differences found in many studies on sexual arousal and interest (Janssen, Everaerd, Spiering and Janssen, 2000). Information processing (IP) approaches to cognition inform many of the current studies on sexual arousal.

INFORMATION PROCESSING

IP approaches consist of various models that focus on quantitative cognitive changes, that is, changes over time in thought patterns, memory recall and attention, rather than quantitative shifts in patterns of thoughts and behaviour characterized by developmental stages (Flavell, Miller and Miller, 2002). IP models view information as cognitive input to be processed, encoded, stored and retrieved. Input is of various types, such as declarative knowledge (knowing 'what'), procedural knowledge (knowing 'how') and conditional knowledge (knowing 'when'), and can be organized into a variety of forms, sizes, levels of complexity and abstraction (Flavell *et al.*, 2002). The overarching goal of IP models is to operationally define elements of the cognitive system, such that the mechanisms of cognitive function and change are detailed in real time and minute detail (Flavell *et al.*, 2002; Geer, Lapour and Jackson, 1993). An area that has received a great deal of consideration in IP is attention or attentional variables because it is through the attentional processes that stimuli first enter the cognitive system (Geer and Janssen, 2000).

IP models of attention focus on how stimulus information is perceived, filtered and then translated into a response. IP models concentrate on three approximate processing phases (with numerous variations in the proposed properties of each stage): first perception and identification, then decision-making and response selection, and finally response execution (Geer *et al.*, 1993; Johnson and Proctor, 2004). Factors known to affect processing within or across each of these phases include (but are not limited to) information previously processed and encoded into implicit or explicit memory, emotions and regulatory processes. These factors can increase or decrease levels of attention to tasks participants are overtly asked to perform, evidenced by a change in speed and/or accuracy in task performance or amount of short-term memory recall. For example, individuals typically take less time to perceive, make decisions and complete a task for which they have established a high level of skill (Flavell *et al.*, 2002). Alternatively, individuals will take more time to complete a task and may make a higher percentage of errors if presented with stimuli that represent emotional concerns or states (Williams, Mathews and MacLeod, 1996). The literature suggests that this occurs because the stimuli occupy attentional resources leaving the task with less attention.

The ability of certain stimuli to distract an individual, which result in delays when performing a particular task, highlights a key assumption of all IP models: the human cognitive system can experience overload. In other words, input and processing can exceed response capacity, which indicates that a maximum capacity exists (Flavell *et al.*, 2002). Maximum capacity is manifested behaviourally when increases in attention to one stimulus or task results in decreases in attention to another, whether or not the individual is aware of the shift in direction of their attention. The notion of system overload does not suggest, however, that all IP is serial; that is, one input is processed at a time. On the contrary, research on IP models of emotion and emotion regulation demonstrate that the brain uses both serial and parallel processing, depending on the information to be processed and the nature of the task (Geer *et al.*, 1993; Lang, 1994). A variety of studies suggest that sexual arousal and interest are, in part, due to emotional reactions and filters. Cognitive models of sexual arousal must, therefore, include both serial and parallel interactions between memory, regulatory and attentional processes (Spiering, Everaerd and Laan, 2004).

IP AND COGNITIVE ATTENTION-BASED MODELS OF SEXUAL AROUSAL AND SEXUAL INTEREST

The IP approach to sexual arousal and interest is an attempt to model cognitive components associated with sexual interest and sexual deviance. The majority of research in this area is built on two suppositions: (a) sexual arousal and interest, in addition to physiological and behavioural aspects, include cognitive and affective components; and (b) stimuli that originate in the environment produce results similar to stimuli that are generated internally (e.g. when visualizing images or engaging in sexual fantasies) (Geer et al., 1993; Janssen et al., 2000).

The appraisal of a stimulus as sexual is the first phase of cognitive models of sexual arousal and interest (Geer et al., 1993). A stimulus requires appraisal and then encoding and/or decoding to determine if the stimulus matches explicit and/or implicit long-term memories for what is 'sexual'. Explicit memories of sexual information include recollections of previous sexual encounters, attitudes towards sex and fantasies (Spiering et al., 2004). This is the type of information gathered by sexual interest questionnaires and interviews (Geer et al., 1993; Janssen et al., 2000). Implicit memories of sexual information include innate sexual reflexes, automatized scripts and classically conditioned sensations. If via implicit memories a stimulus is appraised as 'sexual', the system responds by stimulating genital arousal (Janssen et al., 2000; Morris, 2002). Genital arousal is assessed in research and clinical settings with penile plethysmography (aka phallometry), a measure of penile blood flow through circumferential measurement (or volumetric pressure) of the penis (Freund, 1963; Freund and Watson, 1991; Laws, 2003). If explicit memories corroborate the stimulus as 'sexual', then the system responds by triggering additional attentional and regulation processes.

The trigger of conscious and unconscious regulatory processes is the next step in cognitive models of sexual arousal (Spiering et al., 2004). Conscious regulation processes encode or filter a potentially arousing sexual stimulus through explicit and short-term memories of current societal expectations and the current environment. For example, North American society expects individuals to inhibit their expressions of physical sexual arousal in public places. If conscious information regulation indicates further attention to the sexual stimulus is appropriate, then the system responds by providing more attention. This moves a person closer to a 'complete sexually emotional experience' (Damasio, 2003, p. 86). If the information gathered indicates further attention and processing of the sexual stimulus is inappropriate, then the system responds with conscious inhibitory control (Baars, 1998; Gross, 1998).

Unconscious or automatic regulatory processes use emotional salience to determine the amount of attention given to a potential sexual stimulus (Spiering et al., 2004). Matches between the stimulus and positive explicit and/or implicit long-term memories trigger additional attention to the positive aspects of the stimulus, leading to increases in sexual arousal, while negative implicit and explicit memories indicate a focus on negative information leading to avoidance or a discontinuation of attentional processes (Barlow, 1986; Spiering et al., 2004; Spiering, Everaerd, Karsdorp, Both and Brauer, 2006). A by-product of the increase in attentional processes for a positive match is sexual content-induced delay (SCID), an attentional bias associated with preferred sexual content (images or text), first proposed by Geer and colleagues (Geer and Bellard, 1996; Geer and Melton, 1997). SCID is hypothesized to occur when a salient sexual stimulus triggers attentional processes that then interfere with or limit attentional processes to other tasks causing a delay in task processing. As a special case of attentional bias in general, SCID is subject to the same theoretical assumptions as attentional bias. The assertion that attentional bias is a by-product of an emotional state and is important to the creation and maintenance of that state applies to SCID. In addition, the strength of attentional bias, and therefore SCID, increases as body arousal increases, maintaining arousal and forming a cyclical relationship (Williams *et al.*, 1996). Geer and Melton (1997) examined the effect of priming on lexical decision-making and found erotic text in either the prime or target sentences, when compared to neutral text in both prime and target sentences, caused significant delays in decision-making.

Researchers have investigated the interaction between attentional processes and the emotional salience of explicit and implicit sexual memories by examining the relationship between various sexual behaviours and varying lengths of SCID. These studies present a range of visual sexual information, such as images and/or text, to participants and measure SCID using an assortment of attention-based measures including choice reaction time (CRT) (Giotakis, 2005; Wright and Adams, 1994, 1999), the emotional Stroop (Price, 2006; Smith and Waterman, 2004), eye startle probe reflex (Giargiari, Mahaffey, Craighead and Hutchison, 2005; Hecker, King and Scoular, 2006), rapid serial visual presentation (RSVP; Beech, Kalmus, Tipper, Baudouin and Humphreys, 2006) and viewing time (VT; Abel, Huffman, Warberg and Holland, 1998; Beech *et al.*, 2006; Gress, 2005; Harris, Rice, Quinsey and Chaplin, 1996; Letourneau, 2002).

Some researchers approach the investigation from an IP viewpoint and therefore investigate attentional bias or SCID, while others approach it from an applied or clinical point of view within the context of sexual offender assessment and treatment, and state that they are investigating a measure's ability to quantify and identify sexual interests. Most studies have focused on determining if a particular measure can reliably differentiate adult participants by their sexual orientation and/or sexual age preference (e.g., if individuals who have offended against children demonstrate significantly longer delays to images of children than adults) (Abel, Jordan, Hand, Holland and Phipps, 2001; Gress, 2005; Harris *et al.*, 1996; Worling, 2006).

One particularly intriguing attention-based measure, perhaps due to its simplicity and long and well-established history in cognitive psychology (see Eysenck, 1984 for a thorough review) is CRT.

CRT AND SEXUAL INTEREST

CRT is a simple measure of how quickly and accurately an individual indicates the category to which a presented stimulus belongs. (There must be two or more from which the participant can choose.) Wright and Adams (1994) used CRT to investigate whether a favourable cognitive appraisal and sexual response towards an attractive individual would interfere or compete with other cognitive activity. In general, sexual preference studies using CRT instruct a participant to use specific keys on a keyboard to indicate the position of a white dot superimposed on the image. (There can be multiple positions.) When the participant makes a choice, the software program removes the two stimuli (image and dot) and presents the participant with another image and dot. The location of the white dot, the image content and the apparatus used to indicate location vary from study to study.

Wright and Adams evaluated 80 university undergraduate and local community participants, evenly categorized into four groups by sexual orientation (heterosexual and homosexual) and gender. Their CRT measure contained 60 slides, comprised equally of commercially available nude males, nude females and neutral images from travel magazines and a white dot in any one of five locations (each corner and the middle) counterbalanced by location. The authors found that (a) homosexual males were significant slower at locating the dot on male than female or neutral slides, (b) heterosexual males were significant slower on female than male and neutral slides, (c) heterosexual females were significant slower on male than female slides (but not neutral slides) and (d) homosexual females were significant slower on female and neutral slides. In addition, the male participants made significantly more errors on the CRT task than female participants and both groups made more errors on male images.

Wright and Adams (1999) repeated their experiment using two series of 60 slides (a clothed set with pictures from fashion magazines and a nude set using the same images as the 1994 study) and an additional neutral set consisting of a solid blue background. The results demonstrated that homosexual males had significantly longer latencies when indicating dot location on male nude images than homosexual women (as expected), but not longer than heterosexual men. No significant results were found between groups on clothed imagery.

Heterosexual men demonstrated significantly longer latencies on female nude images than heterosexual women and homosexual men (as expected). When examining within-group latencies, the results were mixed. Each group took significantly longer to complete the task on their respective sexual interest image set than their non-interest group and neutral image set, except for heterosexual women who took longer on male and female images when compared to time taken on neutral images, but their latencies on male images were not significantly longer than the latencies on female images. In addition, heterosexual males had significantly longer latencies on female clothed images than male images but not neutral images. In the learning task, more participants identified novel images and each group demonstrated higher levels of recognition for their preferred category when the images were nude. In summary, these results demonstrate that individuals are distracted from their task when they see images that represent their sexual interest, indicating that a relationship exists between sexual interests and attentional processes.

Giotakis (2005) conducted a similar study of CRT using commercially available clothed images. The author administered 90 photos, 10 photos from nine categories (violence (boxing, war, football), neutral (scenic photos), adult males, adolescent males, boys, adult females, adolescent females, girls and blank) to 135 participants, 58 of whom were sexual offenders (31 convicted for rape, 8 for intra-familial child molestation, 19 for extra-familial child molestation) and 53 males and 24 females as a comparison group (staff from a nearby hospital). The author simplified the CRT task by reducing the number of choices to two possible white dot locations, in either the right or left corner, with a 2-second interval between slides. Two main between-group results emerged: groups convicted for sexual offences demonstrated significantly longer overall reaction times than the comparison group of males and females, and images of boys and girls were viewed significantly less in relation to the other stimuli. There were no significant differences in error analyses. This suggests there is a relationship between SCID and sexual offender status.

Santtila, Mokros and Viljanen (2006) replicated Wright and Adams (1994, 1999), with a few modifications, with 25 male university students (15 heterosexual and 10 homosexual). First, instead of using a plain blue background as the neutral stimulus, Santtila *et al.* used the same pictures in both sexual and neutral sets. The images, obtained from erotic web sites, consisted of 40 nude men and women. The authors modified the images in the neutral set by covering the torso with a solid rectangle. Second, the authors added a priming slide, sexual or neutral, before the target slide using the same images. For statistical analysis, the authors split the trials into three equal phases. In Phase 1, both groups took significantly longer to respond to sexual stimuli matching their sexual interest than all other images. In Phase 2, results were not significant. In Phase 3, the priming slide modified results for heterosexual men. When the prime was sexual, heterosexual men took significantly longer to respond to sexual female images but not when the prime was neutral. Homosexual men responded similarly for all images. An AUC[1] analysis predicting group membership from different scores (latency to female images minus latencies to male images) produced estimates of 0.82 for Phase 1, 0.63 for Phase 2 and 0.60 for Phase 3, demonstrating that the test's performance diminished over trials.

Gress (2007) investigated CRT and VT on the measures' ability to distinguish adult sexual offenders ($n = 22$) from youth non-sexual offenders ($n = 40$) and university students ($n = 59$). The author presented a series of computer-modified clothed male and female images of various ages (Not real people stimuli: Laws and Gress, 2004) separated by a 2-second interval. A white dot was located in one of five locations, each corner and the middle, and counterbalanced so each image was viewed five times (for a total of 200 presentations). Participants indicated dot location by pressing a number on the keypad that matched the Likert scale-like choice presented on screen at all times. Subtests were created by averaging reaction times to specific categories of interest: adult female, adult male, female child and male child. All CRT subtests demonstrated good internal consistency. Unexpectedly, the CRT and VT produced different results. First, CRT results indicated that youth non-sexual offenders and the adult sex offenders viewed female images (on average) significantly longer than male images, but no differences existed (between average times to female and male images) for the university students. VT results demonstrated significant differences for all three groups. Second, for the CRT, all participants viewed the child images significantly longer than the adult images and but only the youth non-sexual offenders viewed the images of female children significantly longer than the images of male children. The VT results showed average times to adult female images significantly longer than all other images. Finally,

---

[1] Area under the curve (AUC) analyses produce receiver operator characteristic (ROC) curves, a graphical plot of the sensitivity versus specificity used to evaluate the binary group prediction.

there were no significant differences between the adult sexual offenders and the youth non-sexual offenders or the university students when overall averages were examined. These results suggest the following: (a) the CRT does not measure the same underlying construct as VT, (b) CRT assesses SCID and the VT assesses a different construct or (c) the CRT measure failed due to poor design.

REACTION TIMES AND SEX RESEARCH: RELATED ISSUES AND POTENTIAL CONFOUNDS

There are a number of variables that affect the measurement and classification accuracy of attention-based response latency measures. Some are characteristics of the data, such as habituation, novelty, outliers and prompt characteristics. Other variables are individual differences, such as psychopathologies, age of participants and volunteer and response biases. This section provides a brief overview of the more common measurement issues.

Habituation

Habituation is the 'decrease in responsiveness to a stimulus when that stimulus is presented repeatedly or for a prolonged time' (Aoyama and McSweeney, 2000, p. 79). Researchers have investigated habituation effects on measures of motivation (Aoyama and McSweeney, 2000), satiation (Aoyama and McSweeney, 2000), anxiety (Barlow, 1986), novelty (Koukounas and Over, 1999) and distraction (Dekker and Everaerd, 1989). Specific to the field of sexual aggression, habituation is 'a reduction in arousal level over the course of repeated stimulation, provided the decrement does not reflect sensory adaptation or effector fatigue' (Koukounas and Over, 1999, p. 542).

Researchers investigating habituation and sexual arousal assessment have demonstrated that repeated exposure to the same or varying stimuli causes a decrease in both physiological (measured by phallometry) and subjective (measured by self-report) arousal (Koukounas and Over, 1999; Meuwissen and Over, 1990; O'Donohue and Greer, 1985; Plaud, Gaither, Henderson and Devitt, 1997). Habituation in the assessment of sexual arousal has been demonstrated in research with both males (Koukounas and Over, 1993, 2000; O'Donohue and Plaud, 1991) and females (Laan and Everaerd, 1995; Meuwissen and Over, 1990). Presentation of varying auditory erotic stimuli may dissuade habituation. For example, Laan and Everaerd (1995) found that women exposed to erotic film excerpts sustained high levels of physical arousal throughout the session. Researchers attributed non-habituation effects to possible attentional and emotional response bias to the stimuli presented (Koukounas and McCabe, 2001; Koukounas and Over, 1999).

Novelty

Research demonstrates an increase in attentional resources to novel stimuli that are either unique or unexpected (Daffner, Scinto, Calvo and Faust, 2000; Suwazono, Machado and Knight, 2000). Daffner *et al.* (2000) examined the effect of stimuli that deviate from contextual expectations by randomly presenting easily recognizable geometric figures and unusual or unfamiliar line drawings. The results demonstrated that participants viewed unfamiliar figures significantly longer than recognizable figures. Koukounas and Over (1993, 1999) investigated the effect of novel film segments on sexual arousal (assessed via penile plethysmography). The authors presented a single film segment depicting heterosexual intercourse over 18 trials: the result was habituation to the film. They then presented a novel (new actors but similar behaviour) film segment for 2 trials and then reintroduced the original film segment for two additional trials. The studies found that novel stimuli counteract habituation in two ways. First, sexual arousal levels for the novel film segment trials matched those from the first six trials of the original film segment, and were significantly higher than the last three trials. Second, sexual arousal levels during the reintroduction of the original film segment were also significantly higher than the last three trials of the original presentation, indicating that stimuli variation and novelty might neutralize habituation. This was in agreement with O'Donohue and Plaud's (1991) results discussed above.

Outliers

The identification and removal of outliers in response time distributions can be challenging for two reasons: response time distributions are skewed (as stated above), and the response times most representative of the research question may indeed be extreme (Miller, 1991). Miller recommends the following methods for outlier identification and removal:

- Elimination of all response times beyond a specific cut-off that is determined either by a combination of the median plus one or more standard deviations, or the mean plus one or more standard deviations computed individually across all participants and conditions.
- Elimination of each participant's longest time in each condition.
- Transformation of the data via the calculation of log or inverse function.
- Windsorizing (replacing observations greater than two standard deviations above the mean with observations at two standard deviations above the mean) and repeat until calculations until all outliers are removed (Miller, 1991).

Prompt Characteristics

Facial characteristics of images and word or sentence length may impact response times regardless of memory, emotional salience or novelty. For example, recent research in evolutionary psychology demonstrated that participants rated features associated with a mate's value, such as physical and biological traits (e.g. youthful and healthy appearances, sexual maturity), status, dominance and a friendly demeanour that females typically value in males, as more likely to attract attention and be rated physically attractive (Ben Hamida, Mineka and Bailey, 1998; Hassebrauck, 1998). In addition, the reading achievement literature suggests individual differences in processing speed exist at lower level word recognition and lexical access, which is the retrieval of individual words for the first few words of the utterance of a first sentence without speaking rather than parallel word retrieval and speech (Meyer, Roelofs and Levelt, 2003) and processes as well as the higher level processes common to reading and listening comprehension (Hannon and Daneman, 2001).

Psychopathologies

As studies use attention-based response latencies to differentiate participants with emotional disorders from non-disordered participants, it makes sense that some psychopathologies, such as depression, affect response latency measurement and classification accuracy. The manifestation and strength of the effect, however, appears to vary depending on the construct and measure used. For example, studies using the dot-probe test to investigate the effects of depression on attentional bias do not differentiate depressed participants from non-depressed participants (Neshat-Doost, Moradi, Taghavi, Yule and Dagleish, 2000).

In the dot-probe test, two words appear on a computer screen for a fixed amount of time. Participants are instructed to read the top word of each pair and in some trials one of the words matches the construct of interest. On the critical trials, a probe dot replaces one of the words. Upon seeing the dot, the participants are to press a button immediately. Shorter times associated with the replacement of the construct of interest word by the dot indicates attentional bias for the construct. On the other hand, the emotional Stroop measure of attentional bias consistently demonstrates that depressed participants take significantly longer than non-depressed participants to name depressive words (Williams et al., 1996).

Age

Cross-sectional research consistently finds that in the third decade of life and onward, age is associated with lower levels of cognitive performance, fluid cognitive processes such as on processing speed, memory and reasoning (Ratcliff, 2006; Salthouse, 2006). Declines appear to begin in for adults in their 20s and 30s and the declines begin accelerating when they reach 50. This is not to say that all individuals experience decline in processing speed or memory; substantial individual variability exists at all ages (Salthouse, 2006).

Volunteer and Response Biases

In addition to regular volunteer bias, that is, participants who tend to find research interesting, are willing to donate their time for a greater cause, or are there for the honorarium or course credit, volunteer bias in studies investigating sexual thoughts and behaviours is considered quite problematic (Trivedi and Sabini, 1998). For example, a study examining pornography use may attract volunteers who are more accepting and/or are more frequent users of pornography, therefore biasing the results and perhaps producing erroneous findings. Strassburg and Lowe (1995) found in their multi-staged study that volunteers in later stages of the study (the participants in the later stages knew they would be volunteering for a study on sexuality) demonstrated a significantly more positive attitude towards sexual thoughts and behaviours than did those who chose not to continue into the later stages of the study.

Trivedi and Sabini (1998) examined volunteer bias by varying the method of volunteer recruitment: a general recruitment for volunteers and a specific recruitment for volunteers in a study on sex. The authors found differences in male and female rates of masturbation dependent upon recruitment. The correlations between masturbation and other sexual activity were positive for females regardless of recruitment technique, although the strength of the relationship varied. For males, the correlation was positive in the general study, but negative in the sex study. Gaither, Sellbom and Meier (2003) investigated whether the content of stimuli used in a response latency study would affect volunteer rates. The authors found that heterosexual males were much more willing to view pictures of females in 'normal', erotic and/or deviant activities. Females, on the other hand, were more interested in viewing images that were less sexually overt or more socially acceptable.

In addition to volunteer bias, research with offenders can suffer from response bias or the effect of impression management or social desirability. Offenders, especially sexual offenders, are prone to intentional and, at times, unintentional, distortions or minimizations of the degree of violence that occurred during their offence (Malcolm, Andrews and Quinsey, 1993).

CONCLUSIONS AND FUTURE CONSIDERATIONS

The studies reviewed above, although limited in number and size, provide strong evidence for the utility of attention-based measures, such as CRT, to assess key aspects of attentional processing and its relationship with sexual interest, in research settings. CRT's history in cognitive psychology is long and distinguished and built upon solid theory and evidence. Its foray into the field of sexual interest has a good beginning. It can reliably differentiate sexual interest for adult females from sexual interest in adult males, with longer latencies associated with sexual interest. Caution is urged, however, when assuming all attention-based measures assess the same variable, as demonstrated by Gress's (2007) comparison of CRT and VT, with results suggesting that the two measures assess different underlying constructs. As a result, the tendency of studies investigating SCID and/or using attention-based measures to cite many of the other methods as evidence of applicability and appropriateness may not be a match to either criterion.

As noted above, future studies should incorporate and address variables that potentially influence response latency assessments of sexual interest, such as age, intellectual capability and other constructs more closely related to sexual behaviours. For example, recent studies demonstrate the influence of high versus low levels of sexual desire on attention-based measures (Conaglen, 2004; Giargiari et al., 2005).

Low levels appear to decrease response latencies and physical arousal. Further investigations in this area, incorporating the work on anxiety and sexual dysfunction by Barlow (1986) and colleagues, will provide further evidence of a cognitive impact on sexual interests, desires, impulses and behaviours.

An interesting set of research and methodological questions would be the investigation of the so far unknown influences or effects of ethnicity, which includes the notions of race as well as cultural influences (Hall, Teten, DeGarmo, Sue and Stephens, 2005; Phinney, 1996), and culture, the interplay between social expectations and individual interpretations of those expectations (Lopez and Guarnaccia, 2000) on attention-based measure of sexual interest. To date, no studies have integrated the resesarch on individual differences associated with culture and ethnicity, sexual behaviours and research on response latency measures of sexual interest. Although differences in actual processing speed between cultures are limited (Naglieri and Ronning, 2000), differences may appear when 'speed and accuracy' are not included in the instructions. Furthermore, we can expect that the connotation of 'viewing' images of males and females of various ages may differ according to culture and ethnicity, potentially affecting the assessment of SCID. This is because, for example, culture 'moderates behaviour as a filter through which the appropriateness of behavior is evaluated' (Hall *et al.*, 2005, p. 830) and viewing an image of the opposite sex, especially if that image represents a person unclothed which may be considered inappropriate or even immoral. Finally, an immediate need is the formulation and testing of a clear and simple scoring method, permitting the use of CRT measures of sexual interest in clinical settings.

REFERENCES

Abel, G.G., Huffman, J., Warberg, B. and Holland, C.L. (1998) Visual reaction time and plethysmography as measures of sexual interest in child molesters. *Sexual Abuse: Journal of Research and Treatment*, **10**, 81–95.

Abel, G.G., Jordan, A., Hand, C.G., Holland, L.A. and Phipps, A. (2001) Classification models of child molesters utilizing the Abel Assessment for Sexual Interest. *Child Abuse and Neglect*, **25**, 703–18.

Aoyama, K. and McSweeney, F.K. (2000) Habituation contributes to within-session changes in free wheel running. *Journal of the Experimental Analysis of Behavior*, **76**, 289–302.

Baars, B.J. (1998) The function of consciousness [reply to a letter of O. G. Cameron]. *Trends in Neurosciences*, **21**, 201.

Barlow, D.H. (1986) Causes of sexual dysfunction: the role of anxiety and cognitive interference. *Journal of Consulting and Clinical Psychology*, **54**, 140–48.

Barlow, D.H., Sakheim, D.K. and Beck, J.G. (1983) Anxiety increases sexual arousal. *Journal of Abnormal Psychology*, **92**, 49–54.

Beech, A., Kalmus, E., Tipper, S.T., Baudouin, J.-Y. and Humphreys, G.W. (2006) Children induce an enhanced attentional blink in child molesters: an objective measure of sexual interest. *Manuscript submitted to Psychological Assessment*.

Ben Hamida, S., Mineka, S. and Bailey, J.M. (1998) Sex differences in perceived controllability of mate value: an evolutionary perspective. *Journal of Personality and Social Psychology*, **75**, 953–66.

Conaglen, H.M. (2004) Sexual content induced delay: a reexamination investigating relation to sexual desire. *Archives of Sexual Behavior*, **33**, 359–67.

Daffner, K.R., Scinto, L.F.M., Calvo, V. and Faust, R. (2000) The influence of stimulus deviance on electrophysiologic and behavioral responses to novel events. *Journal of Cognitive Neuroscience*, **12**, 393–406.

Damasio, A. (2003) *Looking for Spinoza: Joy, Sorrow, and the Feeling Brain*, Harcourt, Orlando, FL.

Dekker, J. and Everaerd, W. (1989) A study suggesting two kinds of information processing of the sexual response. *Archives of Sexual Behavior*, **18**, 435–47.

Eysenck, M.W. (1984) *A Handbook of Cognitive Psychology*, Lawrence Erlbaum Associates, London.

Flavell, J.H., Miller, P.H. and Miller, S.A. (2002) *Cognitive Development*, 4th edn, Prentice Hall, Upper Saddle River, NJ.

Freund, K. (1963) A laboratory method for diagnosing predominance of homo- or heteroerotic interest in the male. *Behaviour Research and Therapy*, **1**, 85–93.

Freund, K. and Watson, R.J. (1991) Assessment of the sensitivity and specificity of a phallometric test: an update of phallometric diagnosis of pedophilia. *Psychological Assessment*, **3**, 254–60.

Gaither, G.A., Sellbom, M. and Meier, B.P. (2003) The effect of stimulus content on volunteering for sexual interest research among college students. *Journal of Sex Research*, **40**, 240–48.

Geer, J.H. and Bellard, H.S. (1996) Sexual content induced delays in unprimed lexical decisions: gender and context effects. *Archives of Sexual Behavior*, **25**, 379–96.

Geer, J.H., Estupinan, L.A. and Manguno-Mire, G.M. (2000) Empathy, social skills, and other relevant cognitive processes in rapists and child molesters. *Aggression and Violent Behavior*, **5**, 99–126.

Geer, J.H. and Janssen, E. (2000) The sexual response system, in *Handbook of Psychophysiology*, 2nd edn (eds J.T. Cacioppo and L.G. Tassinary), Cambridge University Press, New York, pp. 315–41.

Geer, J.H., Lapour, K.J. and Jackson, S.R. (1993) The information processing approach to human sexuality, in *The Structure of Emotion: Psychophysiological, Cognitive, and Clinical Aspects* (eds N. Birbaumer and A. Ohman), Hogrefe-Huber, Toronto, pp. 139–55.

Geer, J.H. and Melton, J.S. (1997) Sexual content-induced delay with double-entendre words. *Archives of Sexual Behavior*, **26**, 295–316.

Giargiari, T.D., Mahaffey, A.L., Craighead, W.E. and Hutchison, K.E. (2005) Appetitive responses to sexual stimuli are attenuated in individuals with low levels of sexual desire. *Archives of Sexual Behavior*, **34**, 547–56.

Giotakis, O. (2005) A combination of viewing reaction time and incidental learning task in child molesters, rapists, and control males and females. *European Journal of Sexology; Sexologies*, **54**, 13–22.

Gress, C.L.Z. (2005) Viewing time measures and sexual interest: another piece of the puzzle. *Journal of Sexual Aggression*, **11**, 117–25.

Gress, C.L.Z. (2007) *Delays in Attentional Processing When Viewing Sexual Imagery: The Development and Comparison of Two Measures*, Unpublished dissertation, University of Victoria, Victoria, BC, Canada.

Gross, J.J. (1998) Antecedent- and response-focused emotion regulation: divergent consequences for experience, expression, and physiology. *Journal of Personality and Social Psychology*, **74**, 224–37.

Hall, G.C.N., Teten, A.L., DeGarmo, D.S., Sue, S. and Stephens, K.A. (2005) Ethnicity, culture, and sexual aggression: risk and protective factors. *Journal of Consulting and Clinical Psychology*, **73**, 830.

Hannon, B. and Daneman, M. (2001) A new tool for measuring and understanding individual differences in the component processes of reading comprehension. *Journal of Educational Psychology*, **93**, 103–28.

Hanson, R.K. and Bussière, M.T. (1998) Predicting relapse: a meta-analysis of sexual offender recidivism studies. *Journal of Consulting and Clinical Psychology*, **66**, 348.

Harris, G.T., Rice, M.E., Quinsey, V.L. and Chaplin, T.C. (1996) Viewing time as a measure of sexual interest among child molesters and normal heterosexual men. *Behaviour Research and Therapy*, **34**, 389–94.

Hassebrauck, M. (1998) The visual process method: a new method to study physical attractiveness. *Evolution and Human Behavior*, **19**, 111–23.

Hecker, J.E., King, M.W. and Scoular, R.J. (2006) *Startle Eye-Blink: Preliminary Support for a Promising Method of Measuring Sexual Interest*. Paper presented at the American Psychology & Law Society, St. Petersburg, FL.

Henson, D.E. and Rubin, H.B. (1971) Voluntary control of eroticism. *Journal of Applied Behavior Analysis*, **4**, 37–44.

Janssen, E., Everaerd, W., Spiering, M. and Janssen, J. (2000) Automatic processes and the appraisal of sexual stimuli: toward an information processing model of sexual arousal. *Journal of Sex Research*, **37**, 8–23.

Johnson, A. and Proctor, R.W. (2004) *Attention: Theory and Practice*, Sage, Thousand Oaks, CA.

Koukounas, E. and McCabe, M.P. (2001) Sexual and emotional variables influencing sexual response to erotica: a psychophysiological investigation. *Archives of Sexual Behavior*, **30**, 393–408.

Koukounas, E. and Over, R. (1993) Habituation and dishabituation of male sexual arousal. *Behavior Research and Therapy*, **31**, 575–85.

Koukounas, E. and Over, R. (1999) Allocation of attentional resources during habituation and dishabituation of male sexual arousal. *Archives of Sexual Behavior*, **28**, 539–52.

Koukounas, E. and Over, R. (2000) Changes in the magnitude of the eyeblink startle response during habituation of sexual arousal. *Behavior Research and Therapy*, **38**, 573–94.

Laan, E. and Everaerd, W. (1995) Habituation of female sexual arousal to slides and film. *Archives of Sexual Behavior*, **24**, 517–41.

Lang, P.J. (1994) The varieties of emotional experience: a meditation on James-Lange theory. *Psychological Review*, **101**, 211–21.

Laws, D.R. (2003) Penile plethysmography: will we ever get it right? in *Sexual Deviance: Issues and Controversies* (eds T. Ward, D.R. Laws and S.M. Hudson), Sage, Thousand Oaks, CA, pp. 82–102.

Laws, D.R. and Gress, C.L.Z. (2004) Seeing things differently: the viewing time alternative to penile plethysmography. *Legal and Criminological Psychology*, **9**, 183–96.

Laws, D.R. and Rubin, H.B. (1969) Instructional control of an autonomic sexual response. *Journal of Applied Behavior Analysis*, **2**, 93–9.

Letourneau, E.J. (2002) A comparison of objective measures of sexual arousal and interest: visual reaction time and penile plethysmography. *Sexual Abuse: Journal of Research and Treatment*, **14**, 207–23.

Lopez, S.R. and Guarnaccia, P.J.J. (2000) Cultural psychopathology: uncovering the social world of mental illness. *Annual Review of Psychology*, **51**, 571–98.

Malcolm, P.B., Andrews, D.A. and Quinsey, V.L. (1993) Discriminant and predictive validity of phallometrically measured sexual age and gender preference. *Journal of Interpersonal Violence*, **8**, 486–501.

Meuwissen, I. and Over, R. (1990) Habituation and dishabituation of female sexual arousal. *Behaviour, Research, and Therapy*, **28**, 217–26.

Meyer, A.S., Roelofs, A. and Levelt, W.J.M. (2003) Word length effects in object naming: the role of a response criterion. *Journal of Memory and Language*, **48**, 131–47.

Miller, J. (1991) Reaction time analysis with outlier exclusion: bias varies with sample size. *The Quarterly Journal of Experimental Psychology A: Human Experimental Psychology*, **43**, 907–12.

Morris, J.S. (2002) How do you feel? *Trends in Cognitive Sciences*, **6**, 317–9.

Naglieri, J.A. and Ronning, M.E. (2000) Comparison of White, African American, Hispanic, and Asian children on the Naglieri Nonverbal Ability Test. *Psychological Assessment*, **12**, 328–34.

Neshat-Doost, H.T., Moradi, A.R., Taghavi, M.R., Yule, W. and Dagleish, T. (2000) Lack of attentional bias for emotional information in clinically depressed children and adolescents on the dot probe task. *Journal of Child Psychology and Psychiatry*, **41**, 363–8.

O'Donohue, W. and Greer, J.H. (1985) The habituation of sexual arousal. *Archives of Sexual Behavior*, **14**, 233–46.

O'Donohue, W. and Plaud, J.J. (1991) The long-term habituation of sexual arousal in the human male. *Journal of Behaviour, Therapy, and Experimental Psychiatry*, **22**, 87–96.

Phinney, J.S. (1996) When we talk about American ethnic groups, what do we mean? *American Psychologist*, **51**, 918–27.

Plaud, J.J., Gaither, G.A., Henderson, S.A. and Devitt, M.K. (1997) The long-term habituation of sexual arousal in human males: a crossover design. *The Psychological Record*, **47**, 385–98.

Price, S. (2006). *A Stroop Replication Study Measuring the Automatic Processing of Sexual Information*. Paper presented at the American Psychology & Law Society, St. Petersburg, FL.

Ratcliff, R. (2006) Modeling response signal and response time data. *Cognitive Psychology*, **53**, 195–237.

Rook, K.S. and Hammen, C.L. (1977) A cognitive perspective on the experience of sexual arousal. *Journal of Social Issues*, **33**, 7–29.

Salthouse, T.A. (2006) Mental exercise and mental aging. *Perspectives on Psychological Science*, **1**, 68–87.

Santtila, P., Mokros, A. and Viljanen, K. (2006) *Using the Choice Reaction Time Task to Detect Sexual Interest: A Feasibility Study Using Gay and Straight Men*. Paper presented at the 2nd International Summer Conference: Research in Forensic Psychiatry, Regensburg, Germany.

Smith, P. and Waterman, M. (2004) Processing bias for sexual material: the Emotional Stroop and sexual offenders. *Sexual Abuse: Journal of Research and Treatment*, **16**, 163–71.

Spiering, M., Everaerd, W., Karsdorp, P., Both, S. and Brauer, M. (2006) Nonconscious processing of sexual information: a generalization to women. *Journal of Sex Research*, **43**, 268–81.

Spiering, M., Everaerd, W. and Laan, E. (2004) Conscious processing of sexual information: mechanisms of appraisal. *Archives of Sexual Behavior*, **33**, 369–80.

Strassburg, D.S. and Lowe, K. (1995) Volunteer bias in sexuality research. *Archives of Sexual Behavior*, **24**, 369–82.

Suwazono, S., Machado, L. and Knight, R.T. (2000) Predictive value of novel stimuli modifies visual event-related potentials and behavior. *Clinical Neurophysiology*, **111**, 29–39.

Trivedi, N. and Sabini, J. (1998) Volunteer bias, sexuality, and personality. *Archives of Sexual Behavior*, **27**, 181–95.

Williams, J.M.G., Mathews, A. and MacLeod, C. (1996) The Emotional Stroop task and psychopathology. *Psychological Bulletin*, **120**, 3–24.

Worling, J. (2006) Assessing sexual arousal with adolescent males who have offended sexually: self-report and unobtrusively measured viewing time. *Sexual Abuse: A Journal of Research and Treatment*, **18**, 383–400.

Wright, L.W. Jr. and Adams, H.E. (1994) Assessment of sexual preference using a choice reaction time task. *Journal of Psychopathology and Behavioral Assessment*, **16**, 221–31.

Wright, L.W. Jr. and Adams, H.E. (1999) The effects of stimuli that vary in erotic content on cognitive processes. *The Journal of Sex Research*, **36**, 145–51.

Chapter 5

THE IMPLICIT ASSOCIATION TEST AS A MEASURE OF SEXUAL INTEREST

NICOLA S. GRAY

Cardiff University, Cardiff, and Caswell Clinic, Bro-Morgannwg NHS Trust, Bridgend, UK

ROBERT J. SNOWDEN

Cardiff University, Cardiff, UK

INTRODUCTION

In many domains of psychology, we wish to measure a person's thoughts, attitudes and emotions to a particular situation or event. By far the most popular way to do this is to simply ask the person to report on these. Whilst we do not doubt that such methods are useful and need to continue, there are three reasons to think that other methods are needed to supplement these explicit statements.

Most of our neural lives are not available for introspection in a conscious form. In vision science, we have learnt that activity in the early stages of visual processing, in the retina, thalamus and primary visual cortex, does not produce a conscious experience available for self-report. A person with severe damage to primary visual cortex may report being blind in certain parts of their visual field, but will flinch if an object appears suddenly in this part of the visual field. This phenomenon of 'blindsight' (Cowey, 2004) is just one of many examples of behaviour being guided by non-conscious mental states (Wilson and Dunn, 2004). Perhaps more surprisingly, even mental states such as 'emotions' can be shown to exist without conscious awareness (Winkielman and Berridge, 2004). Thus, if we are effectively unconscious to many of these influences on our behaviours, we clearly cannot rely on self-report for us to access them. Alternative methods are needed.

Even if I can access my mental state, or indeed reliably report on my overt behaviours, there is still a second problem to overcome. Many self-report questionnaires ask us to comment on how we would react in certain situations – on whether we like going to parties, whether we have a bad temper, etc. To answer such questions, we not only have to speculate and generalize, but also have to 'norm' ourselves to others. So to answer whether I have a bad temper, I have to have some understanding of my temper and to compare it with that of others in order to decide if mine is 'bad' or 'normal'. Of course, *I* believe that I only lose my temper when it is clearly justified; however, others observing me may not agree! This problem is wonderfully illustrated by the finding that most people regard their driving as well above average, indeed over 50% of us think that we are in the top 10%! (Horswill, Waylen and Tofield, 2004; Svenson, 1981). Clearly many individuals regard themselves as good (i.e. above average) as they drive in the way they think is the best way. So someone crawling along the freeway at 30 kmph may regarded this as good safe driving (the people in the cars behind may take a different view), whilst to another executing a handbrake turn on a busy freeway shows their great driving skills (again the cars swerving to avoid this vehicle may beg to differ). There are many other examples of this 'Lake Wobagon' effect (a place where everybody is above average!) (Alicke, Klotz, Breitenbecher, Yurakm and Vrendenburg, 1995).

Finally, in order for self-report to be useful the person reporting needs to be honest. For many reasons this may not be the case, and in the domain of sexual offending there is obvious reason for an offender to minimize, deny or distort their responses (Cooper, 2005).

IMPLICIT MEASURES

Given the limitations of self-report just described, we must look to implicit measures to help us index the mental state of the person under scrutiny. Whilst most of this volume is dedicated to 'new' methods, and in particular methods based on measures of cognitions, using implicit measurement is by no means a new enterprise. For many years, a person's reaction to a stimulus has been indexed by psychophysiological measurements such as heart rate, sweating, brain waves, facial expressions, body language, etc. For example, the pupil of the eye reacts to many situations other than just changes in light. Thus a person's excitement, including sexual interest, can be ascertained by measures of changes in pupil size in response to appropriate stimuli (Hess and Polt, 1960). Indeed, in the domain of sexual offenders (and sexual research in general), measurement of sexual arousal via penile tumescence or vaginal blood flow (see Chapter 4) still remains the 'gold standard' by which the new cognition-based methods will be compared.

More recently, these psychophysiological measurements have been joined by ones based on cognitive methods. Implicit methods have long played a central role in the domain of cognitive psychology. For example, semantic priming experiments have aimed to reveal the nature of how semantic concepts are organized within our minds. In such experiments, a prime is presented (such as the word 'bread') followed by a target word, such as 'butter'. Decisions about the target word (such as 'was it a real word or a made up one') are much faster for the word 'butter' if primed by 'bread' (but not if primed by 'elbow') showing a semantic association between these two concepts. It was not surprising, therefore, that such techniques have been adopted into the domain of social psychology. For example, the priming task was adapted by Fazio, Jackson, Dunton and Williams (1995) to look at associations to different races by presenting pictures of faces that were either white or black, and then following this prime with a word that had to be categorized as a good or bad word. It was hypothesized that if a person has a negative view of a white face then this would prime the response to 'bad' and make such judgments faster. Using this technique, the authors did indeed show that white people are faster when the white face prime occurs before the good words, and a black face prime occurs before the bad words. This shows that there is a bias in the semantic affective associations to pictures of different races. We shall return to whether this is 'racism' in the next section. In the domain of sexual offending, this technique has yet to be employed, though Snowden, Wichter and Gray (2008) show that the technique has exceptional accuracy at identifying sexual orientation in men.

WHAT ARE 'IMPLICIT ATTITUDES'?

There is often great confusion amongst psychology undergraduates when these techniques are first explained to them. The first is the confusion of implicit attitudes with the implicit measurement of attitudes. For example, I am willing to report my support for the England football team (with therefore appropriate anti-support for the German football team) and I would fully expect this pro-English bias to be revealed by an implicit test. Thus, if I was the participant in a priming experiment with primes of English or German footballers and targets of good versus bad words, I expect myself to be fast when good words follow English players and also fast when bad words follow the German footballer primes. The test would have revealed my bias using an implicit technique. In this instance, the implicit technique has revealed a bias, but this bias was clearly also an explicit attitude and would have also been revealed by explicit techniques.

The more interesting case is that these implicit measurement techniques can often disagree with the explicit measurement. Thus, if it were found that I was fast for the good words following German footballers, and also fast when bad words followed English footballers, then this would show that I have some associations that were not tapped by simply asking me for my views. Clearly, years of watching inept displays by England as they underachieved, in contrast to the overachieving German team, combined with heartbreaking defeats in penalty shootouts at their hands, may have led some part of my mind (some might term this my 'sense') to the unquestionable reality that they are indeed 'good' and we are indeed 'bad' despite my desire for the opposite.

This example shows us that any 'attitude' is made from many influences and that we can have dissociations between those that are held implicitly (without our conscious knowledge) and those that are held explicitly (with our conscious knowledge). Hence, we do not believe in the view that implicit measures are simply *only* a 'bona fide pipeline' (Fazio *et al.*, 1995) to measure explicitly held views, rather they offer us a method to probe earlier (and possibly different) automatic associations. These associations may, or may not, be available to consciousness, and may, or may not, be actually endorsed by the person (Olson, Fazio and Hermann, 2007). Nevertheless the presence of such associations influences our behaviours (see also Gawronski, LeBel and Peters, 2007).

So the crucial question becomes 'under what circumstances do these associations have any effect on behaviour'? Indeed, there have been stinging criticisms of the whole endeavour of implicit measurements suggesting that they measure nothing of interest, and that if a person does not endorse the view suggested by the implicit technique then it cannot be called an 'attitude' (Arkes and Tetlock, 2004). To us this is merely a matter of semantics, and we are happy to reserve the term attitude to those that are explicitly endorsed. The most important point, in our opinion, is that the implicit tests can predict future behaviours. The evidence suggests that there are situations where implicit tests can add to that predicted from explicit measurement alone, and in some cases the implicit measurement is by far the greater predictor (Friese, Wänke and Plessner, 2006; McConnell and Leibold, 2001; Phelps, O'Conner, Cunningham, Funayama, Gatenby, Gore and Banaji, 2000; Richeson, Baird, Gordon, Heatherton, Wyland, Trawalter and Shelton, 2003). Given this evidence, it seems that implicit measures have much to offer in many domains of psychology and to dismiss them as 'mere associations' (Arkes and Tetlock, 2004) is to miss the point that these associations are driving forces behind our behaviour (Banaji, Nosek and Greenwald, 2004).

Let us illustrate this in the domain of the implicit measurement of racial bias. Implicit measurements of racial bias (such as priming techniques) have shown that many white Americans appear to have a bias against black people, despite showing no bias on explicit measurements (Nosek, Banaji and Greenwald, 2002). Is an individual with no explicit bias but with an implicitly measured bias a racist? We would argue against this, in that this term should be used for a person that deliberately endorses anti-black (pro-white) sentiments (and vice versa). However, we would argue that such a person is in danger of behaving in a prejudice manner in certain situations (Dovidio, Kawakami, Johnson, Johnson and Howard, 1997). Under situations where they do not have time to consider their decisions, or where decisions are made without the activation of validation processes, then these automatic associations (whether conscious or unconscious) are able to guide behaviour and prejudice may occur (McConnell and Leibold, 2001; Vanman, Saltz, Nathan and Warren, 2004; Strack and Deutsch, 2004; Ziegert and Hanges, 2005; Gawronski and Bodenhausen, 2005; Gawronski et al., 2007).

The issue of the relationship between implicit and explicit attitudes presented here is only a simplified version of a debate that still attracts much attention (and invective), and the interested reader is guided to more detailed discussion in (Gawronski et al., 2007; Nosek, 2007; Olson and Fazio, 2003). We summarize with some simple statements that we think most researchers would agree with:

- Implicit measures capture something different from explicit statements and thus they are not merely another way of measuring the same concept.
- Implicit measures capture automatic associations held by the person (even if they do not explicitly endorse such an association).
- There are conditions under which automatic associations influence behaviour.

- Automatic associations are more likely to guide behaviour when validation processes are not used (either because they cannot be or because the person chooses not to).

Hence, we conclude that implicit measures can bring us information about sex offenders that explicit measures cannot, and that this information might be a guiding influence on the future behaviour of these individuals.

THE IMPLICIT ASSOCIATION TEST

The implicit association test (IAT) is a simultaneous sorting paradigm. We illustrate the technique via an often-used control task (Gray, MacCulloch, Smith, Morris and Snowden, 2003; Greenwald, McGhee and Schwartz, 1998; Snowden, MacCulloch, Smith, Morris and Gray, 2004) that aims to measure the person's relative attitudes to flowers and insects. The target dimension is represented by words that need to be sorted (via pressing one of two buttons) into either flowers (e.g. tulip, rose) or insects (e.g. ant, locust). The affective or evaluative dimension is then represented by words that have to be sorted into either good (e.g. happy, lucky) or bad (e.g. cancer, frown). This second evaluative sort also used the same buttons as the target dimension, hence we can arrange on one block of trials for the concepts of flowers and good to share the same button (and therefore insects and bad the other button), whilst on another block we can reverse this so that flowers and bad share a button (and therefore insects and good the other button). Now imagine the word 'locust' appears on the screen. This should activate the representation of 'insect' within the mind of the person and in turn the impulse to press the 'insect' button. However, the concept 'insect' might also activate the concept 'bad' via the associations held within the mind of this person, and therefore the impulse to press the 'bad' button. Under conditions where bad and insect share the same button, these response impulses should be reinforcing producing fast and accurate performance, but under conditions where they do not share the button this will create response conflict, and performance will slow and accuracy may fall. By comparing speed and accuracy on the two blocks, we can get some idea of whether the person does have associations between insects and bad (and flowers and good) inside their minds. These two test stages are normally presented as stages 3 and 5 in a 5-stage process (see Figure 5.1).

Figure 5.2 illustrates some data from our own experiments. Note that the 'expected' result is found at a group level – most people did indeed perform faster when insects and bad (and flowers and good) shared response buttons. The effect is very large – producing a difference in reaction times of around 300 milliseconds. This difference is also very large when expressed in effect sizes producing a Cohen's $d = 1.72$. Note that a $d = 0.80$ is normally regarded as a 'large effect', so we need new language ('very large') to describe the effects produced. Such very large effect sizes are one of the reasons the IAT has attracted such attention.

The above results demonstrate that at a group level the IAT can be very powerful – but can it really pick up individual differences? When we first started our research on the IAT in forensic settings, we always used the flower/insect IAT as a control task to examine any generalized effects (e.g. IQ, motivation, institutionalization)

Stage	Stage 1	Stage 2	Stage 3	Stage 4	Stage 5
Instructions	● Insect Flower ●	● Good Bad ●	● Insect or Good Flower ● or Bad	● Flower Insect ●	● Flower or Good Insect ● or Bad
Example stimuli	● Locust Tulip ● Rose ● ● Wasp ● Ant Daisy ● . .	● Happy ● Lucky Frown ● Cancer ● Vomit ● ● Smile . .	Daisy ● Cancer ● Rose ● ● Smile ● Ant Frown ● . .	● Rose ● Daisy Locust ● Wasp ● ● Tulip Ant ● . .	Ant ● ● Rose Cancer ● ● Lucky ● Daisy ● Smile . .

Figure 5.1   Illustration of a 5-stage IAT. In stage 1, the participant has to press the left key for insect words and the right key for flower words. In stage 2, they have to press the left key for good words and the right key for bad words. In stage 3, they are instructed to press the left key for insect or good words and the right key for flower or bad words. In stage 4, the flowers and insect key are reversed and they are asked to the left key for flower words and the right key for insect words. Finally, in stage 5, they are instructed to press the left key for flower or good words and the right key for insect or bad words. To calculate the IAT score, we compare average reaction time (and errors) in stage 3 with those in stage 5. For someone who likes flowers and doesn't like insects, we expect them to be faster in stage 5 than in stage 3. Most experiments would also counterbalance whether flowers or insects were presented with the bad words in stage 3 (and therefore stage 5).

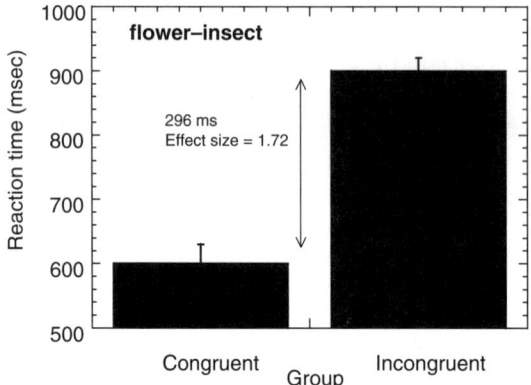

Figure 5.2   Results from a flower–insect IAT in an offender population (from the data of Snowden *et al.*, 2004). Here the term congruent refers to the conditions where flower and good shared the response button (and therefore insect and bad the other button), whilst incongruent is the condition where insect and good shared the response button (and therefore flower and bad the other button).

that might occur. It also served as an introduction to the IAT task and as a form of practice. Our first ever offender participant completed these (and other) IATs, and as we analyzed the results we were very surprised to find that this person was faster to the insect/good combination. Our ethical protocol was to give feedback on the results to the participants and so we attempted to explain the results to him. We were worried that, perhaps, our task was faulty in some way. However, this offender was not surprised by the result and explained to us that when he was a child he was often locked in the cellar. During this time, his only source of creature comforts was to talk to the spiders and insects and so he had always loved them!

This anecdote does not, of course, provide scientific evidence that the IAT can index individual difference in attitude. So what would? This apparently simple question is actually quite hard to answer. After all how do we really know what the individual differences in attitude are? We could explicitly ask the person, but we have already critiqued the limitations of this self-report. When this has been done, the range of correlations between the explicitly and implicitly measured attitudes ranges markedly, with figures anywhere from near 0 (suggesting no relationships) to up to 0.80 (suggesting a close relationship) (Hofman, Gawronski, Gschwendner, Le and Schmitt, 2005). It is not clear to us what figure, if any, would provide evidence that implicit measures can access individual's attitudes. A second method is to use a 'known-groups' technique. Here two groups are defined by some externally defined (and hopefully well agreed) criteria, and then the scores from the IAT are used to examine whether they can differentiate these groups. As we describe later, we have shown (Snowden et al., 2008) that the IAT is capable of near perfect group discrimination under some circumstances.

WHAT ASSOCIATIONS CAN BE MEASURED BY THE IAT?

Greenwald et al. (1998) demonstrated IATs that examined associations between race and valence. Since this time there have been hundreds of different IATs reported in the literature, such that an exhaustive listing would indeed be exhausting. We mention a few here to give an idea of the huge range of areas where the IAT has been used. Attitudes to homosexuals (Banse, Seise and Zerbes, 2001) and the obese (Craeynest, Crombez, De Houwer, Deforche, Tanghe and De Bourdeaudhuij, 2005; Teachman and Brownell, 2001), naughty versus nice foods (Richetin, Perugini, Prestwich and O'Gorman, 2007), consumer choices (Coke vs. Pepsi?) (Karpinski, Steinman and Hilton, 2005), job-hiring decisions (Ziegert and Hanges, 2005) and voting preferences (Karpinski et al., 2005) have all been measured. Of particular interest to our laboratory are the studies that have aimed to measure concepts related to clinical constructs, such as IATs to measure phobias (Teachman, Gregg and Woody, 2001), anxiety (Egloff and Schmukle, 2002; de Jong, 2002), concepts related to eating disorders and body image (Vartanian, Polivy and Herman, 2004), attitudes to alcohol (De Houwer, Crombez, Koster and De Beul, 2004; Wiers, Van Woerden, Smulders and De Jong, 2002) and smoking (De Houwer, Custers and De Clercq, 2006; Huijding, de Jong, Wiers and Verkppijen, 2005), attitudes to violence (Gray et al., 2003; Luo, Nakic, Wheatley, Richell, Martin and Blair, 2006; Snowden et al., 2004), self-harm (Nock and Banaji, 2007) and self-esteem (Greenwald and

Farnham, 2000). It would appear that the ability to measure any association using the IAT is limited only by the experimenter's ingenuity.

METHODOLOGICAL CONSIDERATIONS

Since the first report on the IAT (Greenwald *et al.*, 1998), there have been many attempts to understand if and when variations in the technique produce different results. For instance, is the effect driven by the associations to the exemplars (e.g. locust) or by the category to which they have to be assigned (e.g. insect)? To test these ideas, we can attempt to manipulate the expected valence of the exemplars to be non-congruent with the category. So, for example, what would happen if English participants had to perform a German–English IAT in which the concept of German was represented by much loved Germans (e.g. Beethoven), but the concept of English represented by much hated English (e.g. Thatcher). Surprisingly the results of this type of test (De Houwer, 2001) show that the English participants were still faster under the English-good conditions, and the results differed little from when the concept of English was represented by much-loved English people (e.g. Churchill) and the concept of German by much-hated Germans (e.g. Hitler). Thus these results (and others) (Olson and Fazio, 2003) suggest that the IAT is driven at the categorical level, rather than by the exemplars of this category. This finding is theoretically important in that it tells us about the level of mental representations at which this test operates (note that other implicit tests, such as the priming task may operate at the level of exemplars; see Olson and Fazio, 2003), and also of practical importance as we only need to have sensible representatives of the category and it should therefore be robust against small changes in just how the category is represented. In line with these findings, the IAT appears to be also robust against the number of exemplars used to define the category (Brown, 2006; Nosek, 2005).

Our research in forensic settings has a target population containing many individuals with low cognitive abilities, and/or problems with memory and/or attention. We therefore have performed some experiments to adapt the basic technique to make it more acceptable and easier to administer in such forensic and clinical settings (Brown, 2006). To control for the effects of poor literacy in offender populations, we explored whether substituting pictures for words has an effect. We found that whilst picture versions of the task produced faster reaction times, they did not alter the basic effect, nor the effect sized produced compared to word versions (Brown, 2006). Therefore the use of pictures, or spoken words, may be most useful in applying the IAT to less literate populations such as children (Baron and Banaji, 2006) or those with intellectual disabilities. We now tend to use a hybrid picture–word version in which the target concept (e.g. flowers/insects) is represented by words and the evaluative concept (e.g. good/bad) is represented by words. We have found that the participants regard this task as 'easier' as it appears to demand less memory for just how to classify each stimulus. Whilst the standard 5-stage IAT is quite short (approximately 15 minutes), we found that it was sometimes too long in these applied settings, especially when we required several IATs to be completed. We therefore compared a shortened version in which only the two crucial stages are presented, to the standard 5-stage version using the same stimuli and the same participants. Again, we found no differences in the efficacy of this shortened version (Brown, 2006) and thus can recommend this shortened version for use in such settings (see also Teachman *et al.*, 2001)

Finally, the associations in the mind that produces the IAT effects could be manifest in slower reaction times, or in a greater number of errors, or in some combination of these effects. It would therefore be of great value to somehow combine the two effects into a single score. Greenwald, Nosek and Banaji (2003) have tested several scoring algorithms that attempt to do this and recommend one in which trials on which an error occurs are substituted by a 'punishment' reaction time (for details see their paper), and that the overall IAT score (the difference in the reaction times between the two crucial blocks of trials) is then expressed in terms of the variance in reaction times. This D-score therefore gets round some individual difference problems in overall reaction times (e.g. offenders tend to have slower overall reaction times than non-offenders). We have also found that this method of scoring eliminates a small, but problematic, influence of IQ on the IAT (Brown, 2006; see also Cai, Sriram, Greenwald and McFarland, 2004) and produces greater effect sizes.

In conclusion, the results of many tests seem to show that the IAT is very robust to the exact methodology employed. The scoring method of Greenwald *et al.* (2003) also eliminates 'unwanted' influences of individual differences that are not related to implicit associations *per se* (e.g. IQ). Clearly, these properties are highly desirable in any test that aims to have an applied use.

PSYCHOMETRIC PROPERTIES OF THE IAT

The IAT is still in its infancy and, as mentioned above, there are many method-ological differences between studies that make definitive statements upon the psychometric properties of the IAT impossible. It will also be the case that the subject matter under consideration will play a strong role in determining the psy-chometric properties of the task. Therefore, the properties illustrated in this section are nothing more than illustrative. (For a more comprehensive look at these issues, see Nosek, Greenwald and Banaji, 2007.)

Psychologists normally look for three types of reliability when examining a test – internal reliability (do different parts of the test purporting to measure the same thing give similar results?), inter-rater reliability (do two different raters scoring the same case give similar results?) and test–retest reliability (does the same individual tested at different times give similar results?).

The internal reliability of reaction time tests can be calculated using Cohen and Cohen's (1982) formula which treats each response latency as an item. Using this technique, we found very good internal consistency (Cronbach's alphas = 0.81–0.93) for our flower/insect task (Brown, 2006), a result echoed by others (e.g. Nosek *et al.*, 2007). We also showed the same internal consistency for an IAT designed to look at child and sex associations (Cronbach's alphas = 0.80–0.87; Brown, 2006).

The inter-rater reliability is not an issue for the IAT as it is scored via a computer with no human judgment involved.

The test–retest reliability of the IAT is a more problematic issue. In order to get a sensible figure, we need a mental concept that is not changing between the test sessions. There is no guarantee that this will be the case for the IAT, and what little research there is on this matter certainly does not rule out 'state' influences on the task (Gawronski et al., 2007; Nosek, 2005). Nosek et al. (2007) examined the results from many IATs designed to measure a wide range of concepts and report an average test–retest reliability of $r = 0.60$. This represents a robust and reliable instrument. Of particular relevance to this chapter is that we (Brown, Gray and Snowden, 2009) have measured the test–retest reliability for our child/sex IAT (see below) and found a value of $r = 0.63$.

In conclusion, all measures of the psychometric properties of the IAT, accrued from a diverse range of IATs, methods and population samples, point to an instrument with robust and reliable properties.

FAKING THE IAT

Whilst we have argued that the IAT is more than just a method for measuring the same concepts as those tapped by explicit measures, it is also clear that the IAT hopes to measure attitudes that the person may wish to hide or dissimulate. To this end, there have been several reports of attempts to see if a person can fake the results on an IAT.

Banse et al. (2001) asked participant to fake a positive attitude towards homosexual males. It was found that they were unable to do so, and this lack of ability to fake responses to the IAT when not told how to do so is supported by several studies (Asendorpf, Banse and Mucke, 2002; Egloff and Schmukle, 2002; Kim, 2003), with other studies showing only small effects of attempted faking (Steffens, 2004). However, there is some evidence that if given clear instructions on how to successfully fake an IAT participant can do this (Fiedler and Bluemke, 2005). It should be noted that these deliberate strategies should produce a series of responses that are not the same as someone with the genuine mental association that they are trying to emulate, and efforts are being made to devise algorithms that could detect such deliberate faking strategies (Cvencek and Greenwald, submitted).

In conclusion, it appears that the IAT is hard to fake, but not impossible. Given the possible high stakes for a sex offender, and the possibility that implicit tests could be used to monitor distorted cognitions (thus being tested on multiple occasions), further research is needed so that faking can be minimized, or at least detected when it occurs.

INVESTIGATING SEXUAL ORIENTATION USING THE IAT

As a precursor to testing for distorted cognitions in those with a history of sexual offences, we decided to test the ability of the IAT to successfully detect sexual orientation. We devised an IAT where the target dimension was male versus female (represented by pictures) and the evaluative dimension were words that were sexually attractive versus unattractive. To test the efficacy of this IAT to identify sexual orientation, we tested men who described themselves as either heterosexual or homosexual (Snowden et al., 2008). The results were unremarkable – the IAT for the heterosexual men were consistent with an association between sex and females, whilst those for the homosexual men were consistent with an association between sex and males. What was remarkable was the magnitude of this effect. In terms of effect sizes, this IAT produced an effect size of 2.73 (remember an effect size of 0.80 is regarded as large!).

We then used signal detection theory to examine just how well the IAT could detect a person's sexual orientation. We constructed the receiver operating characteristic (ROC) for the IAT by plotting the percentage of hits (correctly predicting that someone is more attracted to males on the basis of their IAT score) against the false alarms (incorrectly predicting that someone is more attracted to males on the basis of their IAT score) for many possible IAT scores (see Figure 5.2). For a test that cannot distinguish between groups, the probability of the false alarms will equal to that of the hits and the points of the ROC will follow the diagonal line through the middle of the ROC (see dashed line), whilst if we could perfectly detect one group from the other, the data points would fall along the X-axis and then the top of the Y-axis. To quantify the ROC, we can calculate the resulting area under the curve (AUC). If the points fall along the diagonal, the AUC would be half the graph or 0.5. If the points call on the axis, the AUC should be the entire graph or 1.0. The ROC produced by our IAT was 0.97 (which was significantly different from chance levels, $p < 0.0001$).

Armed with this sex IAT, we were able to investigate theories of human sexuality. It has been suggested that women's sexual attractions are far more ambiguous and malleable that those of males (Baumeister, 2000; Bem, 1996; Diamond, 2003). For instance, as male sex drive increases, this is associated with an increased sexual attraction to females, but a decreased sexual attraction to males. For females, increased sex drive is associated with increases in sexual attraction to both males and females (Lippa, 2006; Lippa and Arad, 1997). We (Snowden, Brown and Gray, submitted) therefore predicted that the sex IAT would not show a strong preference for males or females in heterosexual women, despite these women explicitly stating that their sexual preference was for males (and, if we can assume their honesty, that they were involved only in heterosexual relationships). Our results (see Figure 5.3) showed that these heterosexual females showed no strong sex association to either gender, in fact what little bias was found was towards an association between sex and female! Thus, our results suggest that heterosexual women (as a group) have implicit automatic cognitions relating to sex that are quite unlike those of males (be these hetero- or homosexual males), and are quite unlike the ones they explicitly express. The results from the sex IAT mirror those that have used physiological measures of sexual arousal and women (Chivers and Bailey, 2005; Chivers, Rieger, Latty and Bailey, 2004), which also show similar sexual responses to stimuli depicting male erotic and female erotic stimuli in heterosexual women. Again, this differs from the category-specific sexual arousal responses of both heterosexual and homosexual males.

We also tested females who stated that their preferred sexual partners were female (Snowden et al., submitted). These lesbians clearly showed implicit cognitions consistent with an association between sex and female (see Figure 5.4). Thus, the responses of the lesbians on the sex IAT suggest that their sexuality is more like that of a male, with category-specific associations, than those of heterosexual females. Whilst this is clearly a finding in need of replication and exploration using other

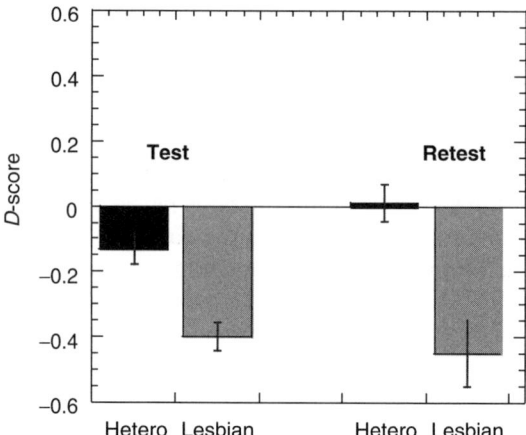

Figure 5.3   Results of the sex–gender IAT in females (from Snowden *et al.* submitted). *D*-scores below 0 indicate faster performance when female and sex are paired (whilst scores above 0 indicate faster performance when male and sex are paired). Participants were tested twice. Error bars represent ±1 SEM.

techniques, it illustrates the power of implicit techniques to explore theories of human sexuality.

CHILD/SEX IAT

Gray, Brown, MacCulloch, Smith and Snowden (2005)

We began our work on the child/sex IAT in 2001 as part of a larger study looking at many different offence-specific IATs (including those related to attitudes to violence, arson, rape as well as control IATs; see Gray *et al.*, 2003; Snowden *et al.*, 2004) in offenders at HMP Grendon (Oxfordshire, UK). One of the advantages of this prison is that it is run as a therapeutic community and all the inmates must not be on psychotropic medication, or take any illegal substances, in order to be admitted and continue to be residence within this community. We designed an IAT that we believed might be able to index associations between sex and children. At this time, only IATs using the affective dimension (good vs. bad) against a target dimension had been published and so our first thoughts were to devise a target dimension of child–sex versus adult–sex and an affective dimension of good versus bad. However, this was not the way forward. Firstly, representing the concept of child–sex is fraught with ethical and moral problems, and the South Wales police service gave us quite unambiguous advice that this was not an area we should explore! Further reflection also suggested that this was not what we wanted to measure. What we would have got from this is a person's view of child–sex (i.e. whether it is a good or bad thing), not whether the person has an association between sex and children. This idea of whether child–sex is bad is not without its own interest in view of evidence that cognitive distortions are prevalent in paedophiles (e.g. Ward, 2000; Ward, Hudson, Johnston and Marshall, 1997; Ward and Keenan, 1999). However, this was not our main area of interest, so we devised an IAT in which the usual affective dimension of good versus bad was replaced by one in which the dimension was sex versus not sex – a radical departure (or so we thought at the time) from the usual IAT. We represented this dimension with words that the offenders at HMP Grendon associated with sex (e. g. cock, pussy) and used words of similar length that we believed were not related to sex to represent the not sex category (e.g. elbow, eye – it actually proved quite hard to find any words related to body parts that no one reported as being related to sex. Our investigations suggest a surprisingly large predilection for toes!). The adult–child dimension was represented by words such as 'beard' and 'mature', and the child dimension by words such as 'infant' and 'school'.

Our results (Gray et al., 2005) showed that the control offenders (no conviction for offending against children under 16) showed faster reaction times when adult and sex concepts shared the same response button, but the sex offender group (any conviction for sexual offending against a child) had faster reaction times when the child and sex concepts shared the response button. The group differences were highly significant ($p < 0.001$) despite the quite small numbers ($N = 18$ for the sex offender group), which reflected a large effect size (Cohen's $d = 0.83$). Construction of the ROC also showed that the child/sex IAT has a moderate ability to distinguish those with a child–sex offence from the other offenders (AUC $= 0.73$). It should be noted that this AUC is likely to be a lower limit of accuracy as we have no means of proving that our control group did not include some people with unconvicted child–sex offences within it. We concluded the paper by suggesting that implicit methods might one day be a useful additions to the armoury of the clinician, as well as a tool for research into offence-related cognitions. Since then there have been four further reports using IATs to explore cognitions in child–sex offenders.

Brown (2006)

Following our initial results, we were keen to replicate and extend the child/sex IAT towards a possible clinical tool. Along with our PhD student, Anthony Brown, we identified a number of factors that were problematic in the original IAT we devised. Amongst these were the long duration of the test(s), memory confusions over what classification was needed (e.g. should they be classifying the word 'beard' according to whether it was adult vs. child or whether it was sex vs. not sex?), and the possible confounds of IQ. In order to get round these problems, we initially tested the effects of changes in the IAT using the control task (flowers and insects) in a sample drawn from the local community, and found that (1) a shortened version of the task (using only the crucial two stages) produced an equivalent IAT effect to the original 5-stage version, (2) using pictures for one dimension (e.g. flowers vs. insects) and words for the other (e.g. good vs. bad) gave the same results as using all words (and indeed all pictures) and (3) there were small effects of IQ on the reaction time scores (such that those with higher IQs had faster reaction times) which in turn should have affected IAT scores (such that those with the higher IQs should have smaller IAT scores). However, as predicted, the use of the D-scoring algorithm (Greenwald *et al.*, 2003) eliminated this IQ confound (Cai *et al.*, 2004).

Given these results, we developed a 2-stage child–sex IAT that used pictures for the dimension of child versus adult, and words for the concepts or sex versus not sex. We then tested this version, and our original 5-stage version on participants drawn from offenders serving community rehabilitation orders, offenders on licence from prison sentences or on remand in bail hostels. The experimental group consisted of 11 men convicted of sexual offences against children. The control group were 15 other offenders without convictions for sexual offences against children. Both versions of the task showed that the experimental group showed an IAT D-score consistent with an association with child and sex, whilst the control group showed an IAT D-score consistent with an association with adult and sex. Thus, the results replicated those of Gray *et al.* (2005), extended them to this to sexual offenders living in the community, and showed that the shortened version of the IAT was also effective.

Brown *et al.* (2009)

It is clear that offenders who have sexually offended against children are not a homogenous group. The motivations to offend are likely to differ between offenders (Beech, 1998; Marziano, Ward, Beech and Pattison, 2006). For instance, distinctions have been drawn between offenders that are 'paedophilic' – defined by being sexually aroused by stimuli of pre-pubertal children, and offenders that are

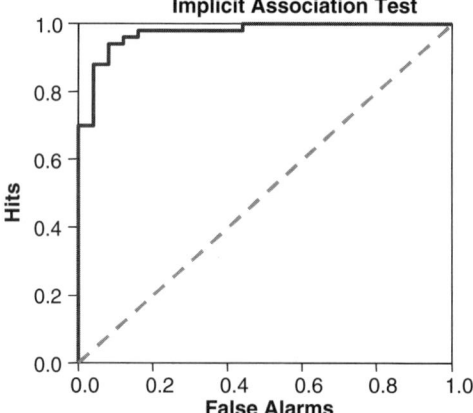

Figure 5.4 Receiver operating characteristic (ROC) analysis of the data from Snowden *et al.* (2008) of the ability of a sex–gender IAT to predict a male's stated sexual preference. The proportion of 'hits' (the correct prediction that someone is a homosexual) is plotted against the proportion of 'false positives' (the incorrect prediction that someone is a homosexual). The dotted line represents the expected result if the test cannot make this prediction. Our line falls a long way from this 'chance' performance revealing the test has exceptional ability to identify sexual orientation in this population.

'hebephilic' – defined as being aroused by stimuli of adolescents (Blanchard, Klassen, Dickey, Kuban and Blak, 2001; Freund and Blanchard, 1989). We therefore hypothesized that it would only be the paedophilic offenders that would show the association between children and sex on the IAT. However, there is the question of how one can identify 'pedophiles' and 'hebephiles' so as to test their implicit cognitions using the IAT. One method might be to use PPG measures of sexual arousal, but this was not available to us, and if PPG and IAT were to be just measuring the same thing using different instruments then the results would only be of interest in the sense that either method could be used. We therefore operationalized the 'pedophile' versus 'hebephile' groups by the nature of the victims of their previous offences. Any sex offender with a victim younger than 12 years was termed a 'pedophile', and those with victims only between 12 and 16 years of age were termed 'hebephiles'. We note that this is a loose approximation of the true meaning of these terms, but any errors in classification caused by this operationalization would work against our hypothesis.

We managed to obtain a much larger sample of sex offenders than our previous studies and our groups contained 54 paedophiles, 21 hebephiles and 49 offender controls that had no convictions for child–sex offences. We used our shortened 2-stage IAT. Our IAT results clearly showed that the paedophile group had implicit cognitive associations between sex and children, whilst the offender controls had implicit cognitive associations between sex and adults – replicating our previous results. However, the results from the child–sex offenders that we termed hebephiles did not show associations between children and sex, instead their implicitly measured associations sexual cognitions appeared similar to the offender controls. This shows that the child/sex IAT appears to have the ability to distinguish between the different sexual cognitions that may characterize individual sex offenders, and therefore strengthens the possible use of implicit measurements in the understanding of sexual offenders at both the group and individual level.

We commenced this chapter by outlining the problems of self-report measures, and that in sex offenders this may be a substantial problem due to deliberate dissimulation. So it was a natural question to consider whether our child/sex IAT would be as effective in a sample of sex offenders who denied or minimized their offences and/or sexual attraction to children, compared to those that admitted their offences. Again 'denial' is a multifaceted term that we cannot hope to cover in such a chapter, so we again used a pragmatic definition that was commensurate with practice within the UK prison service. 'Deniers' and 'admitters' were classed according to the assessments of HM Prison Service sex offender treatment program (SOTP). The theory manual for the SOTP in the United Kingdom lists certain 'not ready criteria'. These are used to classify prisoners who are 'blocked from benefiting from the programme at the present time, but who could potentially overcome the blockage at some point in the future'. Chief among these is 'in total denial of his sexual offending'. This is assessed in two ways. First, clinicians use a structured interview to assess denial and minimization of the offence. Among other questions, the offender is asked what he found attractive about the child and what sexual acts were engaged in. Second, by using scores from the Sex Offence Attitudes Questionnaire (Hogue, 1994), a 50-item self-report questionnaire designed to assess the degree to which the offence is denied, distorted and minimized. In other words, the assessment is made as to the degree the offender denies sexual interest in children in general, and his own offences in particular. On the basis of these criteria, the offender is classed as either a non-denier or a denier and is included or excluded from SOTP by the clinician. Given the results from the hebephiles outlined above, the analysis of denial was confined to those with an offence against a child younger than 12 years.

We found that both groups produce scores that were indicative of an association between sex and children, and that we would not distinguish the scores of the deniers from the non-deniers. Hence, we suggest that the child–sex IAT is able to identify distorted implicit cognitions about sex and children even in offenders who are in denial of their paedophilic tendencies.

Nunes, Firestone and Baldwin (2007)

Nunes *et al.* (2007) tested several IATs relating to possible cognitive distortions in a sample of 27 child molesters (defined by having a victim younger than 14 years) in comparison to offenders without convictions for sexual offences (and who denied ever committing such an offence). In total, they tested six IATs. Each of three concepts (pleasant vs. unpleasant, powerful vs. weak, sexy vs. not sexy) was paired with the attributes of me versus not me, and child versus adult. Only one of these IATs revealed a significant between-group difference – the IAT that examined the concepts of child versus adult against the attribute of sexy versus not sexy. They found that the child molesters were faster when the concepts of child and sexy were on the same response key, and the control offenders were faster when the concepts of adult and sexy shared the same key. The results are therefore in accord with those reported by Gray *et al.* (2005).

Nunes *et al.* (2007) also administered an actuarial measure of future risk of sexual offending to each of the child molester group – the Static-99 (Hanson and Thornton, 2000). They found that the child/sex IAT was correlated ($r = 0.43$) with the Static-99 risk, such that those with IAT scores indicating stronger implicit associations between sex and children have greater risk scores for sexual offending. This is a suggestive finding that the IAT score may have some ability to predict future offending, though direct tests of such a hypothesis are needed.

Mihailides, Devilly and Ward (2004)

Mihailides *et al.* (2004) attempted to test models of implicit cognitions (Ward and Keenan, 1999; Ward, 2000) in sexual offenders using three IATs that related to children as sexual beings, the uncontrollability of sexuality and a sexual-entitlement bias. The first of these IATs is the closest to those so far described. The technique, however, differed to those of our group (and those of Nunes *et al.*, 2007) in that instead of having a child–adult dimension they employed a child–not child dimension (examples of not child words were 'lids', 'rifle' and 'underline'). They found that their experimental group (25 incarcerated male child–sex offenders) showed faster responses to the condition where the child words shared the same button with the sex words, compared to the combination of child and not sex. The difference between conditions was very large (895 milliseconds). However, this difference was also true for the controls (25 incarcerated other offenders) who showed a difference of 513 milliseconds. The groups were distinguishable in that the difference was larger for the sex offenders than the controls. Thus this was interpreted as a greater association of child and sex in the child–sex offender group.

Interpretation of this paradigm is less clear than the previous studies. The results suggest that all groups tested have a greater association with 'child and sex' than between 'not child and sex', though it is hard to really understand what the association between the 'not child' and 'sex' might have meant to the participant given the exemplars under its umbrella include 'lids', 'rifle' and 'underline'.

Discussion and Conclusions

The above review contains five independent data sets of child–sex offenders versus non-sex offender controls in which a child–sex IAT has been tested. All five show the pattern of results that child–sex offenders have a greater association between child and sex than did the other offender controls. This result was consistent across differences in methodologies across the groups (and within the Gray/Snowden group). The finding therefore appears robust. The child/sex IAT appears to be able to identify those offenders who have a sexual offence against children with an AUC on the order of 0.73–0.81 – figures that are comparable with those produced by PPG measurements.

Limitations

Whilst we have done our best to highlight the possible importance of the IAT in the domain of sexual offending, we would be remiss if we did not address its limitations.

First, the IAT is a relational measure. It requires the comparison of two concepts (e.g. flowers vs. insects or child vs. adult) against an evaluative dimension (e.g. good vs. bad or sex vs. not sex). Thus, the current data tell us that child–sex offenders have greater sexual associations with children than with adults. This could, in theory, be because they are attracted to both (but more so to children), or not attracted to either (but less so to adults – if this makes sense). It would be of value to get more data that specifically examines the absolute associations between children and sex, rather than the association relative to that of sex and adult that our IAT produces. There have been attempts to 'rescore' the results from IAT experiments to try and obtain these 'absolute' associations, but the evidence shows that the reaction times from the IAT cannot be rescored to allow this (Nosek, Greenwald and Banaji, 2005). However, there are now techniques with conceptual similarities to the IAT that aim to measure attitudes to a single concept using implicit measurement (e.g. Go–No-Go task – Nosek and Banaji, 2001; Extrinsic Affective Simon

Task – De Houwer, 2003). We (Snowden, Gray, Brown and Power, unpublished report) have collected some preliminary data using the Go–No-Go task (Nosek and Banaji, 2001) that shows that those with a conviction for child–sex offences show a greater association between children and sex than did other offender controls, and than did a group of rapists.

Second, whilst the IAT (and other implicit measurements) may be able to index an association between the concepts of child and sex, it does not tell us why this has arisen. It is feasible that someone undergoing extensive therapy for their sexual offending might well have such associations as they have to discuss their offending behaviour and listen to others discuss such matters. Whilst this is feasible, we are encouraged that this is not the likely explanation of our results as we have also found similar results in those not undergoing treatment programmes (Brown *et al.*, 2009), and in those that are now in the community (Brown, 2006). Nevertheless, any individual might have an association between child and sex for any number of reasons (e.g. an expectant mother!).

Third, we do not yet have any data on the predictive validity of the IAT. The methods used so far are only 'predictive' of past behaviour. Studies are needed to establish the IAT's ability in this domain.

CLINICAL USE OF THE IAT

We have suggested that the IAT may become a valuable addition to the clinician's tool bag in the future. It appears to be able to capture cognitions that are not necessarily accessible to the offender themselves (or, indeed, the assessing clinician), and appears to have a greater robustness against dissimulation than self-report measures. As such, we would like to suggest how it might be used in clinical settings. We fully acknowledge that the IAT is still in its infancy and issues of reliability and dissimulation need to be addressed further before it is actually employed in such a manner.

As a Facilitator to Understanding a Person's Cognitions

As outlined in the introduction, people do not always have conscious access to all their mental processes. IATs could be devised to measure cognitive distortions underpinning their offending behaviour (e.g. Marziano *et al.*, 2006; Ward *et al.*, 1997) in order to understand the cognitions held by each individual offender. The flexibility of the IAT gives it advantages over other physiological techniques that require sexual arousal (e.g. PPG – see Chapter 4) or other specific autonomic responses that are more invasive. Armed with such information, the clinician can make the offender aware of these cognitions, and thus the need for treatment in this area. Of course, we can also rule out the need for specific treatments in some cases and therefore save time, effort and resources providing treatment where none is needed.

As an Indicator of Change

One of the problems faced by those working with sex offenders is how to index the effectiveness of therapy. It is well known that treatment effects are modest in this group (Brooks-Gordon and Bilby, 2006) and currently there is strong reliance on self-report measures to index therapeutic change. What is commonly found is that treatment programmes show large effects on self-report measures, but limited, if any, effects on reoffending rates (leaning some to question the validity of treatment effectiveness as indexed via self-report).

Of interest here is whether the IAT could ever index clinical change. The answer appears to be positive in that Teachman and Woody (2003) show that an IAT designed to measure specific phobias (e.g. spider phobia) showed change as treatment for this phobia progressed, and that this change in the IAT was mirrored by behavioural change in approach to the phobic object. Thus, in at least one domain, the IAT has been shown to index treatment effects. Studies are now required that monitor these cognitions via implicit (and explicit) measures during the course of treatment, and consider the long-term outcome (including sexual recidivism) in such offenders.

CONCLUSIONS

The IAT appears to hold great promise as a tool for investigating cognitions related to sexual offending. It is flexible and can be adapted to measure a variety of concepts. It returns large effect sizes, has good psychometric properties and is relatively hard to dissimulate. It can measure associations that the offender may not be aware of, or ones that they are not willing to explicitly report. We believe, therefore, that the IAT will continue to be a most valuable instrument for research into sexual offending, and we can envisage that it may eventually provide the clinician with a instrument that will help them understand the motivations and sexual interest profile of the offender, inform treatment and management regimes, and monitor the effectiveness of such treatment.

REFERENCES

Alicke, M.D., Klotz, M.L., Breitenbecher, D.L., Yurakm T.J. and Vrendenburg, D.S. (1995) Personal contact, individuation, and the better-than-average effect. *Journal of Personality and Social Psychology*, **68**, 804–25.

Arkes, H.R. and Tetlock, P.E. (2004) Attributions of implicit prejudice, or 'would Jesse Jackson "fail" the implicit association test?' *Psychological Inquiry*, **15**, 257–78.

Asendorpf, J.B., Banse, R. and Mucke, D. (2002) Double dissociation between implicit and explicit personality self-concept: the case of shy behavior. *Journal of Personality and Social Psychology*, **83**, 380–93.

Banaji, M.R., Nosek, B.A. and Greenwald, A.G. (2004) No place for nostalgia in science: a response to Arkes and Tetlock. *Psychological Inquiry*, **15**, 279–89.

Banse, R., Seise, J. and Zerbes, N. (2001) Implicit attitudes towards homosexuality: reliability, validity, and controllability of the IAT. *Zeitschrift fur Experimentelle Psychologie*, **48**, 145–60.

Baron, A.S. and Banaji, M.R. (2006) The development of implicit attitudes: evidence of race evaluations from ages 6 and 10 and adulthood. *Psychological Science*, **17**, 53–8.

Baumeister, R.F. (2000) Gender differences in erotic plasticity: the female sex drive as socially flexible and responsive. *Psychological Bulletin*, **126**, 347–74.

Beech, A.R. (1998) A psychometric typology of child abusers. *International Journal of Sex Offender Therapy and Comparative Criminology*, **42**, 319–39.

Bem, D.J. (1996) Exotic becomes erotic: a developmental theory of sexual orientation. *Psychological Review*, **103**, 320–35.

Blanchard, R., Klassen, P., Dickey, R., Kuban, M.E. and Blak, T. (2001) Sensitivity and specificity of the phallometric test for pedophilia in nonadmitting sex offenders. *Psychological Assessment*, **13**, 118–26.

Brooks-Gordon, B. and Bilby, C. (2006) Psychological interventions for treatment of adult sex offenders. *British Medical Journal*, **333**, 5–6.

Brown, A., Gray, N.S. and Snowden, R.J. (2009) Implicit measurement of sexual association in child sex abusers: role of victim type and denial. Sexual Abuse: *A Journal of Research and Treatment*, **21**, 166–180.

Brown, A.S. (2006) *Developing an Implicit Association Test for Forensic Use: Discriminating Paedophiles from Other Offenders*. Cardiff University, Wales, UK.

Cai, H.J., Sriram, N., Greenwald, A.G. and McFarland, S.G. (2004) The implicit association test's D measure can minimize a cognitive skill confound: comment on McFarland and Crouch (2002). *Social Cognition*, **22**, 673–84.

Chivers, M.L. and Bailey, J.M. (2005) A sex difference in features that elicit genital response. *Biological Psychology*, **70**, 115–20.

Chivers, M.L., Rieger, G., Latty, E. and Bailey, J.M. (2004) A sex difference in the specificity of sexual arousal. *Psychological Science*, **15**, 736–44.

Cohen, J. and Cohen, P. (1982) *Applied Multiple Regression/Correlation Analysis for the Behavioral Sciences*, 2nd edn, Erlbaum, Hillsdale, NJ.

Cooper, S. (2005) Understanding treating and managing sex offenders who deny their offence. *Journal of Sexual Aggression*, **11**, 85–94.

Cowey, A. (2004) The 30th Sir Frederick Bartlett lecture: fact, artefact, and myth about blindsight. *Quarterly Journal of Experimental Psychology. Section A – Human Experimental Psychology*, **57**, 577–609.

Craeynest, M., Crombez, G., De Houwer, J., Deforche, B., Tanghe, A. and De Bourdeaudhuij, I. (2005) Explicit and implicit attitudes towards food and physical activity in childhood obesity. *Behaviour Research and Therapy*, **43**, 1111–20.

Cvencek, D. and Greenwald, A.G. (submitted) Faking of the Implicit Association Test is statistically detectable and partly correctable.

De Houwer, J. (2001) A structural and process analysis of the implicit association test. *Journal of Experimental Social Psychology*, **37**, 443–51.

De Houwer, J. (2003) The extrinsic affective Simon task. *Experimental Psychology*, **50**, 77–85.

De Houwer, J., Crombez, G., Koster, E.H.W. and De Beul, N. (2004) Implicit alcohol-related cognitions in a clinical sample of heavy drinkers. *Journal of Behavior Therapy and Experimental Psychiatry*, **35**, 275–86.

De Houwer, J., Custers, R. and De Clercq, A. (2006) Do smokers have a negative implicit attitude toward smoking? *Cognition & Emotion*, **20**, 1274–84.

de Jong, P.J. (2002) Implicit self-esteem and social anxiety: differential self-favouring effects in high and low anxious individuals. *Behaviour Research and Therapy*, **40**, 501–8.

Diamond, L.M. (2003) What does sexual orientation orient? A biobehavioral model distinguishing romantic love and sexual desire. *Psychological Review*, **110**, 173–92.

Dovidio, J.F., Kawakami, K., Johnson, C., Johnson, B. and Howard, A. (1997) On the nature of prejudice: automatic and controlled processes. *Journal of Experimental Social Psychology*, **33**, 510–40.

Egloff, B. and Schmukle, S.C. (2002) Predictive validity of an implicit association test for assessing anxiety. *Journal of Personality and Social Psychology*, **83**, 1441–55.

Fazio, R.H., Jackson, J.R., Dunton, B.C. and Williams, C.J. (1995) Variability in automatic activation as an unobtrusive measure of racial attitudes: a bona fide pipeline? *Journal of Personality and Social Psychology*, **69**, 1013–27.

Fiedler, K. and Bluemke, M. (2005) Faking the IAT: aided and unaided response control on the Implicit Association Tests. *Basic and Applied Social Psychology*, **27**, 307–16.

Freund, K. and Blanchard, R. (1989) Phallometric diagnosis of pedeophilia. *Journal of Consulting and Clinical Psychology*, **57**, 100–105.

Friese, M., Wänke, M. and Plessner, H. (2006) Implicit consumer preferences and their influence on product choice. *Psychology & Marketing*, **23**, 727–40.

Gawronski, B. and Bodenhausen, G.V. (2005) Accessibility effects on implicit social cognitions: the role of knowledge activation versus retrieval processes. *Journal of Personality and Social Psychology*, **89**, 672–85.

Gawronski, B., LeBel, E.P. and Peters, K.R. (2007) What do implicit measures tell us? *Perspectives on Psychological Science*, **2**, 181–93.

Gray, N.S., Brown, A.S., MacCulloch, M.J., Smith, J. and Snowden, R.J. (2005) An implicit test of the associations between children and sex in pedophiles. *Journal of Abnormal Psychology*, **114**, 304–8.

Gray, N.S., MacCulloch, M.J., Smith, J., Morris, M. and Snowden, R.J. (2003) Violence viewed by psychopathic murderers. *Nature*, **423**, 497–8.

Greenwald, A.G. and Farnham, S.D. (2000) Using the Implicit Association Test to measure self-esteem and self-concept. *Journal of Personality and Social Psychology*, **79**, 1022–38.

Greenwald, A.G., McGhee, J.L. and Schwartz, J.L. (1998) Measuring individual differences in implicit cognition: the implicit association test. *Journal of Personality and Social Psychology*, **74**, 1464–80.

Greenwald, A.G., Nosek, B.A. and Banaji, M.R. (2003) Understanding and using the implicit association test: I. An improved scoring algorithm. *Journal of Personality and Social Psychology*, **85**, 197–216.

Hanson, R.K. and Thornton, D. (2000) Improving risk assessments for sex offenders: a comparison of three actuarial scales. *Law and Human Behavior*, **24**, 119–36.

Hess, E.H. and Polt, J.M. (1960) Pupil size related to interest value of visual stimuli. *Science*, **132**, 349–50.

Hofman, W., Gawronski, B., Gschwendner, T., Le, H. and Schmitt, M. (2005) A meta-analysis on the correlation between the Implicit Association Test and the explicit self-report measures. *Personality and Social Psychology Bulletin*, **31**, 1369–85.

Hogue, T.E. (1994) Sex offence information questionnaire: assessment of sexual offenders' perceptions of responsibility, empathy and control. *Issues in Criminology and Legal Psychology*, **21**, 68–75.

Horswill, M.S., Waylen, A.E. and Tofield, M.I. (2004) Driver's rating of different components for their own driving skill: a greater illusion of superiority for skills that relate to accident involvement. *Journal of Applied Social Psychology*, **34**, 177–95.

Huijding, J., de Jong, P.J., Wiers, R.W. and Verkppijen, K. (2005) Implicit and explicit attitudes toward smoking in a smoking and non-smoking setting. *Addictive Behaviors*, **30**, 949–61.

Karpinski, A., Steinman, R.B. and Hilton, J.L. (2005) Attitude importance as a moderator of the relationship between implicit and explicit attitude measures. *Personality and Social Psychology Bulletin*, **31**, 949–62.

Kim, D.Y. (2003) Voluntary controllability of the Implicit Association Test (IAT). *Social Psychology Quarterly*, **66**, 83–96.

Lippa, R.A. (2006) Is high sex drive associated with increased sexual attraction to both sexes? *Psychological Science*, **17**, 46–52.

Lippa, R.A. and Arad, S. (1997) The structure of sexual orientation and its relation to masculinity, femininity, and gender diagnosticity: different for men and women. *Sex Roles*, **37**, 187–208.

Luo, Q., Nakic, M., Wheatley, T., Richell, R., Martin, A. and Blair, R.J.R. (2006) The neural basis of implicit moral attitude – an IAT study using event-related fMRI. *NeuroImage*, **30**, 1449–57.

Marziano, V., Ward, T., Beech, A.R. and Pattison, P. (2006) Identification of five fundamental implicit theories underlying cognitive distortions in child abusers: a preliminary study. *Psychology Crime & Law*, **12**, 97–105.

McConnell, A.R. and Leibold, J.M. (2001) Relations among the implicit association test, discriminatory behavior, and explicit measures of racial attributes. *Journal of Experimental Social Psychology*, **37**, 435–42.

Mihailides, S., Devilly, G.J. and Ward, T. (2004) Implicit cognitive distortions and sexual offending. *Sexual Abuse: A Journal of Research and Treatment*, **16**, 333–50.

Nock, M.K. and Banaji, M.R. (2007) Assessment of self-injurious thoughts using a behavioral test. *American Journal of Psychiatry*, **164**, 820–23.

Nosek, B.A. (2005) Moderators of the relationship between implicit and explicit evaluation. *Journal of Experimental Psychology: General*, **134**, 565–84.

Nosek, B.A. (2007) Implicit–explicit relations. *Current Directions in Psychological Science*, **16**, 65–9.

Nosek, B.A. and Banaji, M.R. (2001) The go/no-go association task. *Social Cognition*, **19**, 625–64.

Nosek, B.A., Banaji, M.R. and Greenwald, A.G. (2002) Harvesting implicit group attitudes and beliefs from a demonstration web site. *Group Dynamics: Theory, Research, and Practice*, **6**, 101–15.

Nosek, B.A., Greenwald, A.G. and Banaji, M.R. (2005) Understanding and using the implicit association test: II. Method variables and construct validity. *Personality and Social Psychology Bulletin*, **31**, 166–80.

Nosek, B.A., Greenwald, A.G. and Banaji, M.R. (2007) The implicit association test at age 7: a methodological and conceptual review, in *Automatic Processes in Social Thinking and Behavior* (ed. J.A. Bargh), Psychology Press, New York, pp. 265–92.

Nunes, K.L., Firestone, P. and Baldwin, M.W. (2007) Indirect assessment of cognitions of child sexual abusers with the implicit association test. *Criminal Justice and Behavior*, **34**, 454–75.

Olson, M.A. and Fazio, R.H. (2003) Relations between implicit measures of prejudice: what are we measuring? *Psychological Science*, **14**, 636–9.

Olson, M.A., Fazio, R.H. and Hermann, A.D. (2007) Reporting tendencies underlie discrepancies between implicit and explicit measures of self-esteem. *Psychological Science*, **18**, 287–291.

Phelps, E.A., O'Conner, K.J., Cunningham, W.A., Funayama, E.S., Gatenby, J.C., Gore, J.C. and Banaji, M.R. (2000) Performance on indirect measures of race evaluation predicts amygdala activation. *Journal of Cognitive Neuroscience*, **12**, 729–38.

Richeson, J.A., Baird, A.A., Gordon, H.L., Heatherton, T.F., Wyland, C.L., Trawalter, S. and Shelton, J.N. (2003) An fMRI investigation of the impact of interracial contact on executive function. *Nature Neuroscience*, **6**, 1323–8.

Richetin, J., Perugini, M., Prestwich, A. and O'Gorman, R. (2007) The IAT as a predictor of food choice: the case of fruits versus snacks. *International Journal of Psychology*, **42**, 166–73.

Snowden, R.J., Brown, A.S. and Gray, N.S. (submitted) Implicit sexual associations in heterosexual women and lesbians.

Snowden, R.J., MacCulloch, M.J., Smith, J., Morris, M. and Gray, N.S. (2004) Implicit affective associations to violence in psychopathic murderers. *Journal of Forensic Psychiatry and Psychology*, **15**, 620–41.

Snowden, R.J., Wichter, J. and Gray, N.S. (2008) Implicit and explicit measurements of sexual preference in gay and heterosexual men: a comparison of priming techniques and the implicit association task. *Archives of Sexual Behavior*, **37** (4), 558–65.

Steffens, M.C. (2004) Is the implicit association test immune to faking? *Experimental Psychology*, **51**, 165–79.

Strack, F. and Deutsch, R. (2004) Reflective and impulsive determinants of social behavior. *Personality and Social Psychology Review*, **8**, 220–47.

Svenson, O. (1981) Are we all less risky and more skillful than our fellow drivers? *Acta Psychologica*, **47**, 143–8.

Teachman, B.A. and Brownell, K.D. (2001) Implicit anti-fat bias among health professionals: is anyone immune? *International Journal of Obesity*, **25**, 1525–31.

Teachman, B.A., Gregg, A.P. and Woody, S.R. (2001) Implicit associations for fear-relevant stimuli among individuals with snake and spider fears. *Journal of Abnormal Psychology*, **110**, 226–35.

Teachman, B.A. and Woody, S.R. (2003) Automatic processing in spider phobia: implicit fear associations over the course of treatment. *Journal of Abnormal Psychology*, **112**, 100–109.

Vanman, E.J., Saltz, J.L., Nathan, L.R., and Warren, J.A. (2004) Racial discrimination by low-prejudiced whites – facial movements as implicit measures of attitudes related to behavior. *Psychological Science*, **15**, 711–4.

Vartanian, L.R., Polivy, J. and Herman, C.P. (2004) Implicit cognitions and eating disorders: their application in research and treatment. *Cognitive and Behavioral Practice*, **11**, 160–67.

Ward, T. (2000) Sexual offenders' cognitive distortions as implicit theories. *Aggression and Violent Behavior*, **5**, 491–507.

Ward, T., Hudson, S.M., Johnston, L. and Marshall, W.L. (1997) Cognitive distortions in sex offenders: an integrative review. *Clinical Psychology Review*, **17**, 479–507.

Ward, T. and Keenan, T. (1999) Child molesters' implicit theories. *Journal of Interpersonal Violence*, **14**, 821–38.

Wiers, R.W., Van Woerden, N., Smulders, F.T.Y. and De Jong, P.J. (2002) Implicit and explicit alcohol-related cognitions in heavy and light drinkers. *Journal of Abnormal Psychology*, **111**, 648–58.

Wilson, T.D. and Dunn, E.W. (2004) Self-knowledge: its limits, value, and potential for improvement. *Annual Review of Psychology*, **55**, 493–518.

Winkielman, P. and Berridge, K.C. (2004) Unconscious emotion. *Current Directions in Psychological Science*, **13**, 120–23.

Ziegert, J.C. and Hanges, P.J. (2005) Employment discrimination: the role of implicit attitudes, motivation, and a climate for racial bias. *Journal of Applied Psychology*, **90**, 553–62.

Chapter 6

MEASURING CHILD MOLESTERS' IMPLICIT COGNITIONS ABOUT SELF AND CHILDREN

KEVIN L. NUNES

Department of Psychology, Carleton University, Ottawa, Ontario, Canada

Many theorists have posited that child molesters' cognitions concerning themselves, their victims and other adults play a central role in the initiation and persistence of child sexual abuse. Such cognitions are also considered important in practice, as evidenced by their inclusion as items in risk assessment instruments (Hanson, Harris, Scott and Helmus, 2007; Wong, Olver, Nicholaichuk and Gordon 2004) and targets in treatment programs (Marshall, Anderson and Fernandez, 1999; Yates, Goguen, Nicholaichuk, Williams and Long, 2000). Despite the importance attributed to these constructs in both research and practice, knowledge in the area remains incomplete due, in part, to reliance on self-report measures, which are generally restricted to consciously accessible thoughts and are susceptible to presentation bias. In contrast to some of the assessment procedures commonly used with sex offenders, there is a procedure called the implicit association test (IAT; Greenwald, McGhee and Schwartz, 1998), which is relatively easy to administer, inexpensive and unaffected by attempts at dissimulation (Nosek, Greenwald and Banaji, 2007). In the study summarized here (Nunes, Firestone and Baldwin, 2007), a series of IATs were designed to measure the domains of evaluation (positive vs. negative), social power (interpersonal dominance vs. submissiveness) and sexual attractiveness of self (relative to others) and children (relative to adults). Child molesters were compared to non-sex offenders on these IAT measures and, among the child molesters, the relationship between the IAT measures and risk of sexual recidivism was examined. The purpose of this chapter is to introduce the IAT procedure, summarize our study, integrate the findings into the larger body of research on the IAT and sex offenders and propose future directions for research.

Cognitive Approaches to the Assessment of Sexual Interest in Sexual Offenders   Edited by D. Thornton and D. R. Laws
© 2009 John Wiley & Sons, Ltd

IMPLICIT COGNITION

Implicit cognition is generally described as automatic associations that are not accessible through introspection (i.e. outside of conscious awareness; Greenwald and Banaji, 1995; but see Fazio and Olson, 2003 for a slightly different perspective). Explicit cognition, in contrast, is accessible through introspection and can be self-reported. This distinction between implicit and explicit cognition generally corresponds to distinctions between automatic versus controlled, unconscious versus conscious and procedural versus declarative processes, as well as indirect versus direct measurement (Greenwald and Banaji, 1995). Implicit cognition is typically assessed with response latency (or reaction time) measures, whereas explicit cognition is usually assessed with self-report measures (Hofmann, Gawronski, Gschwendner, Le and Schmitt, 2005). 'The term *implicit* has come to be applied to measurement methods that avoid requiring introspective access, decrease the mental control available to produce the response, reduce the role of conscious intention, and reduce the role of self-reflective, deliberative processes' (Nosek *et al.*, 2007, p. 267).

IMPLICIT ASSOCIATION TEST

A promising and relatively simple procedure for measuring implicit cognitions is the IAT. In the IAT procedure, the relative strength of automatic associations in memory between concepts (e.g. *me* and *pleasant*) is inferred from the speed with which one sorts stimulus words into categories. Respondents must sort each stimulus word into one of four categories by pressing one of two keys on a computer keyboard. Thus, two categories are indicated by one key while the remaining two categories are indicated by the other key. Response speed is expected to depend on the extent to which the categories that share one key are associated in one's memory. An illustration of the IAT procedure is presented in Figure 6.1 (self-esteem IAT from Greenwald and Farnham, 2000). The main task was to sort words into one of the following categories: me, not me, pleasant or unpleasant. On the first trial shown in Figure 6.1a, the stimulus word *THEM* is presented. The task is to indicate whether *THEM* belongs in the *ME* or *NOT ME* category by pressing, respectively, *d* on the computer keyboard with the index finger of the left hand or *k* with the index finger of the right hand. In this case, *k* would be pressed to indicate that *THEM* belongs in the *NOT ME* category. Each categorization of a stimulus word constitutes one trial. The response latency for each trial is recorded. In the second trial shown in Figure 6.1a, the task is to indicate whether *paradise* belongs in the *pleasant* or *unpleasant* category. The participant would indicate *paradise* belongs in the *pleasant* category by pressing *d* with the index finger of left hand. To make the category pairs distinct from one another, one pair (e.g. *ME* vs. *NOT ME*) and its stimulus words (e.g. *SELF, THEM*) are usually presented in uppercase letters, whereas the other pair (e.g. *pleasant* vs. *unpleasant*) and its stimulus words are presented in lowercase letters (e.g. *paradise, vomit*).

As noted above, response latencies for the various categorization tasks of the IAT should reflect the degree to which the configuration of the categories is congruent

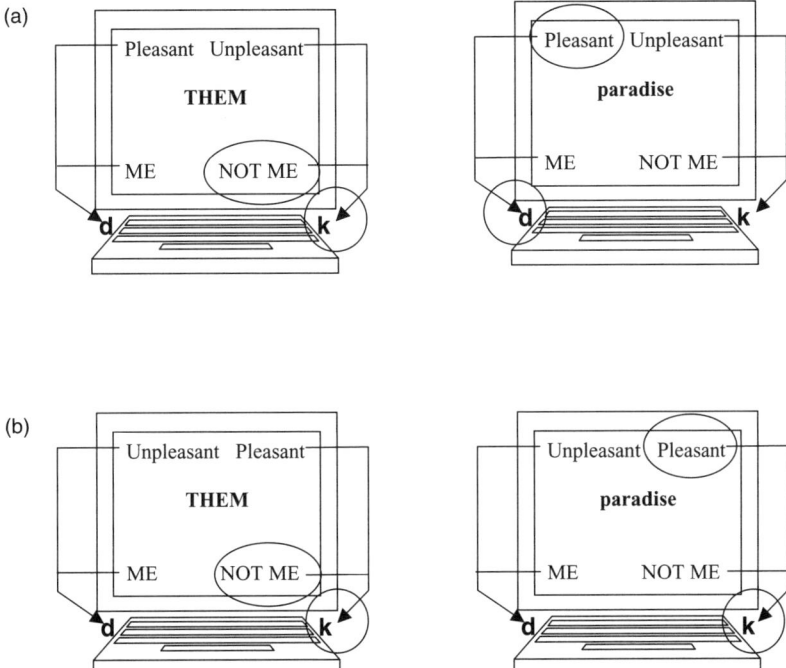

Figure 6.1   (a) Example of trials from one critical phase of a self-esteem IAT. In these trials, *pleasant* and *ME* are both indicated by the same key (*d*) and *unpleasant* and *NOT ME* are both indicated by the same key (*k*). (b) Example of trials from another critical phase of a self-esteem IAT. In these trials, *unpleasant* and *ME* are both indicated by the same key (*d*) and *pleasant* and *NOT ME* are both indicated by the same key (*k*). If one has a positive implicit view of self (i.e. high implicit self-esteem), one should categorize the words presented in the center of the screen more quickly in the first critical phase (part a) than in this one.

with the configuration of one's associations in memory. For someone with high implicit self-esteem, the configuration of categories shown in Figure 6.1a would be congruent with the configuration of associations in his or her memory. More specifically, just as *ME* and *pleasant* are associated with the same response key, they would also be associated in the memory of someone with high implicit self-esteem. This categorization task should be relatively easy for someone with high implicit self-esteem. In contrast, the categorization task in Figure 6.1b should be more difficult for someone with high implicit self-esteem because the configuration of the categories would not be congruent with his or her implicit associations in memory. Pairing *ME* and *unpleasant* and pairing *NOT ME* and *pleasant* would be at odds with the pairings stored in the memory of someone with high implicit self-esteem. Accordingly, response speed should be quicker when *ME* and *pleasant* share the same response key than when *ME* and *unpleasant* share the same response key for someone with high implicit self-esteem. Conversely, the opposite pattern would be expected for someone with low implicit self-esteem. A difference score called the *IAT effect* is typically computed by subtracting the average response latency in one critical phase (e.g. *ME* and *pleasant*/*NOT ME* and *unpleasant*) from that in the other critical phase (e.g. *ME* and *unpleasant*/*NOT ME* and *pleasant*).

Psychometric Properties

Since its introduction (Greenwald *et al.*, 1998), the IAT procedure has been used to measure an impressively wide variety of implicit cognitions, such as self-esteem (Greenwald and Farnham, 2000), gender stereotypes (Nosek, Banaji and Greenwald, 2002), racial attitudes (Rudman, Greenwald and McGhee, 2001), voting attitudes (Nosek *et al.*, 2002), brand attitudes (Maison, Greenwald and Bruin, 2004), sexual orientation attitudes (Jellison, McConnell and Gabriel, 2004), erotic preference (Snowden, Wichter and Gray, 2008), attitudes towards smoking (Swanson, Rudman and Greenwald, 2001), attitudes towards alcohol (Wiers, Van Woerden, Smulders and De Jong, 2002), shyness (Asendorpf, Banse and Mücke, 2002), anxiety (Egloff and Schmukle, 2002), phobias (Teachman, Gregg and Woody, 2001), aggressive self-concept (Uhlmann and Swanson, 2004) and attitudes towards violence (Gray, MacCulloch, Smith, Morris and Snowden, 2003; Snowden, Gray, Smith, Morris and MacCulloch, 2004). The flexibility of the IAT is undoubtedly one of the reasons for its popularity.

The proliferation of the IAT is also attributable to the procedure's good psychometric properties. In non-offender samples, the IAT has shown adequate internal consistency and test–retest reliability (Asendorpf *et al.*, 2002; Bosson, Swann and Pennebaker, 2000; Cunningham, Preacher and Banaji, 2001). IAT measures have also demonstrated good predictive validity. Across a wide range of constructs, both IAT (average $r = .27$) and self-report measures (average $r = .33$) predict criterion measures (Greenwald, Poehlman, Uhlmann, and Banaji, in press). However, IAT measures are much less vulnerable to deliberate attempts at dissimulation than self-report measures (Asendorpf *et al.*, 2002; Greenwald and Farnham, 2000; Greenwald *et al.*, in press; Steffens, 2004). Although there is much support for the IAT procedure, it should be noted that it is not without its critics. A number of researchers have raised concerns about the validity of IAT measures (e.g. Fiedler, Messner and Bluemke, 2006).

Implicit and explicit cognition appear to be correlated but distinct constructs (Cunningham *et al.*, 2001; Greenwald and Farnham, 2000; Nosek and Smyth, 2007). A recent meta-analysis (Hofmann *et al.*, 2005) found a medium-sized relationship between IAT and explicit measures (average $r = .24$; 126 studies). Greenwald and Farnham (2000) administered IAT and explicit measures of self-esteem to samples of university students and, through confirmatory factor analysis, found that they formed correlated but distinct factors. Interestingly, Hofmann *et al.* (2005) found that stronger correlations between IAT and explicit measures were observed for self-report measures that rely on more spontaneous responses ('gut reactions'). Similarly, Greenwald *et al.* (in press) found that the relationship between the self-report measures and outcome criteria was reduced when the outcome was in a socially sensitive area (e.g. racial attitudes) and consisted of spontaneous behaviour (e.g. eye contact); however, this was not the case for IAT measures, which performed similarly well regardless of the nature of the outcome in terms of its social desirability or degree of conscious controllability. Thus, IAT measures may tap aspects of cognitive representations that cannot be assessed with self-report measures and, of special importance in forensic assessment, IAT measures appear to be less susceptible to attempts at dissimulation.

Using the IAT with Sex Offenders

The largest source of data about the role of cognitions in child sexual abuse has been provided by self-report measures. Despite the strengths of many self-report measures (Tafarodi and Ho, 2006; Westen and Weinberger, 2004), this body of research has yielded, with few exceptions (e.g. Thornton, Beech and Marshall, 2004), small effect sizes (Cohen, 1988; Rice and Harris, 2005) in conflicting directions (e.g. Fisher, Beech and Browne, 1999; Hanson and Morton-Bourgon, 2004, 2005; Horley and Quinsey, 1994; Katz, 1990; Overholser and Beck, 1986; Segal and Marshall, 1985; Ward, McCormack and Hudson, 1997). The validity of such self-report measures with offenders has been called into question by many researchers (e.g. Andrews and Bonta, 2003; Beech, 1998; Horley, 2000; Marshall *et al.*, 1999; Ward, Hudson, Johnston and Marshall, 1997). As noted above, these measures require respondents to access their cognitions through introspection and to report them accurately. However, some or all aspects of the cognitions of interest may not be consciously accessible or, if they are accessible, may not be accurately articulated or reported honestly (Fazio and Olson, 2003; Nosek and Smyth, 2007; Ward, Hudson *et al.*, 1997). Although many self-report measures have not demonstrated adequate validity with sex offenders, it should be noted that there is evidence that some self-report measures are predictive of recidivism among sex offenders (Firestone, Nunes, Moulden, Broom and Bradford, 2005) and non-sex offenders (Walters, 2006).

Even when valid self-report measures are available, assessments would be strengthened by incorporating multiple methods to provide complementary information. IAT and self-report measures can provide independent information (Nosek and Smyth, 2007), and interactions between IAT and self-report measures may provide important information beyond either one alone or the sum of their contributions (Jordan, Spencer, Zanna, Hoshino-Browne and Correll, 2003). The validity of research and clinical assessment is generally improved through multi-method measurement of the construct of interest (Kazdin, 2003). Thus, complementing more commonly used measures with implicit measures, such as the IAT, may fill some important gaps in knowledge about sex offenders (e.g. Hanson and Morton-Bourgon, 2004; Ward, Hudson *et al.*, 1997).

The IAT procedure has recently been used to study the cognitions of sex offenders. Gray, Brown, MacCulloch, Smith and Snowden (2005; also see Chapter 5 by Gray and Snowden) created an IAT to assess the degree to which children (relative to adults) are associated with sex and administered it to 18 men who had committed sexual offences against children and 60 men who had never been convicted of sexual offences against children. The IAT categories were *adult* versus *child* and *sex* versus *not sex*. Examples of their stimulus words for each of the categories were *beard* for adult, *infant* for child, *breasts* for sex and *elbow* for not sex. Gray *et al.*

(2005) found that the child molesters' response latencies were slower on the trials in which *adult* and *sex* shared the same response key than on the trials in which *child* and *sex* shared the same response key, whereas the non-molesters showed the opposite pattern. The magnitude of the difference between the child molesters and non-molesters was large ($d = 0.84$) with child molesters showing a stronger association between children and sex than non-molesters.

Gray *et al.*'s (2005) findings are consistent with theory and research. Sexual attraction to children has been identified as an important factor in the initiation of child sexual abuse by many theorists (Finkelhor, 1984; Finkelhor and Araji, 1986; Hall and Hirschman, 1992; Marshall and Barbaree, 1990; Ward and Siegert, 2002). When sexual interest is measured with penile plethysmography (PPG; see Chapter 2 by Laws) or viewing time (VT) measures (see Chapter 5 by Glasgow; Chapter 3 by Gress; Chapter 4 by Gress and Laws), child molesters generally have shown greater sexual interest in children than men who have not sexually abused children (e.g. Barsetti, Earls, Lalumière and Bélanger, 1998; Baxter, Marshall, Barbaree, Davidson and Malcolm, 1984; Harris, Rice, Quinsey and Chaplin, 1996; Looman and Marshall, 2001; Marshall, Barbaree and Christophe, 1986; Quinsey and Chaplin, 1988).

Mihailides, Devilly and Ward (2004) used the IAT to examine a broader range of implicit cognitions in child molesters. They compared 25 child molesters, 25 non-sex offenders, 25 male university students and 25 female university students on IAT measures designed to tap implicit cognitions in three domains: (a) children as sexual beings, (b) uncontrollability of sexuality and (c) sexual entitlement. To estimate the magnitude of the difference between the groups on the IAT measures, effect sizes have been obtained by calculating point-biserial correlation coefficients (r_{pb}) from the t-test results reported by Mihailides *et al.* Point-biserial correlations around .10 are small, .24 are medium and .37 are large (Cohen, 1988; Rice and Harris, 2005). Generally, large-sized effects were found, with child molesters viewing children as more sexual than non-sex offenders ($r_{pb} = .31$), male non-offenders ($r_{pb} = .44$) and female non-offenders ($r_{pb} = .45$). Similarly, child molesters viewed sexuality as more uncontrollable than non-sex offenders ($r_{pb} = .27$), male non-offenders ($r_{pb} = .42$) and female non-offenders ($r_{pb} = .40$). Child molesters also exhibited greater sexual entitlement than non-sex offenders ($r_{pb} = .17$, but not statistically significant), male non-offenders ($r_{pb} = .37$) and female non-offenders ($r_{pb} = .39$). Although little research has examined the utility of the IAT with sex offenders, these initial studies suggest that it may be a useful tool with which to study a variety of implicit cognitions that may play a role in the aetiology of child sexual abuse.

In addition to sexual interest in children and the other cognitions examined above, some fundamental cognitive representations of self, children and adults have been implicated in the aetiology and maintenance of child sexual abuse. In many theories, child molesters are thought to begin and persist in offending not only because they are sexually attracted to children, but also because they (a) have low self-esteem, (b) lack self-confidence, (c) prefer the company of children over adults and (d) view children as a safe and non-threatening alternative to adults (Finkelhor, 1984; Finkelhor and Araji, 1986; Hall and Hirschman, 1992; Marshall and Barbaree, 1990; Ward and Siegert, 2002). Thus, viewing self (relative to others) as negative, socially weak and sexually unattractive and viewing children (relative to adults) as positive, socially weak and sexually attractive may play a role in the initiation as well as persistence of child sexual abuse.

The purpose of our study (Nunes *et al.*, 2007) was to examine differences that may exist between child molesters and non-sexual offenders in their implicit views of self and children (relative to adults) along evaluative, power and sexual attractiveness dimensions. We also examined the association between these constructs and risk of sexual recidivism. Twenty-seven child molesters and a comparison group of 29 non-sex offenders completed six computer-administered IATs: the *pleasant self IAT*, *powerful self IAT*, *sexy self IAT*, *pleasant child IAT*, *powerful child IAT* and *sexy child IAT*. Each IAT consisted of one of two concept pairs (i.e. *me* vs. *not me* or *child* vs. *adult*) combined with one of three other concept pairs (i.e. *pleasant* vs. *unpleasant*, *powerful* vs. *weak* or *sexy* vs. *not sexy*). Selection of the stimulus words was rationally and empirically guided on the basis of previous research (Asendorpf *et al.*, 2002; Greenwald *et al.*, 1998; Greenwald and Farnham, 2000; Haines, 1999; Rudman *et al.*, 2001) and pre-testing. The IAT procedure used followed that of Greenwald *et al.*, (1998) and is described in detail in the study by Nunes *et al.*, (2007).

Risk was assessed with the Rapid Risk Assessment for Sexual Offense Recidivism (RRASOR; Hanson, 1997) and the Static-99 (Hanson and Thornton, 2000). Higher scores on the RRASOR and Static-99 are indicative of greater risk for sexual recidivism. Given the sensitive nature of many of the cognitions examined (e.g. Harris *et al.*, 1996), we also administered the Impression Management scale of the Balanced Inventory of Desirable Responding (BIDR-IM; Paulhus, 1988, 1991). Higher BIDR-IM scores are indicative of greater response bias due to a deliberate attempt to present oneself in a favorable light. Once participants had completed all measures, their official files were reviewed. For the child molesters, gender of victims in the index and past sexual offences was recorded. Among the child molesters, 6 (22.2%) had exclusively victimized girls, 13 (48.1%) had exclusively victimized boys and 8 (29.6%) had victimized both girls and boys. The child molesters had an average of 1.74 (SD = 2.63) prior sexual offence convictions and 7.56 (SD = 11.09) index sexual offence convictions. In terms of treatment exposure, file review indicated that 8 (29.6%) of the child molesters had completed a sexual offender treatment program while under the supervision of Correctional Service Canada (CSC). The Static-99 ($M = 5.52$, SD = 2.10) and RRASOR ($M = 3.26$, SD = 1.46) were taken from the child molesters' intake assessments or, if unavailable, they were scored from file information.

Comparing Child Molesters and Non-Sex Offenders

The primary hypotheses involve differences between child molesters and non-sex offenders on the IATs. It was expected that, compared to non-sex offenders, child molesters would view themselves as less positive, less powerful and less sexually attractive. It was also predicted that, compared to non-sex offenders, child molesters would view children as more positive, less powerful and more sexually attractive. The IAT data were transformed by taking the natural log (ln) of the raw response latencies (Greenwald *et al.*, 1998; see Nunes *et al.*, 2007 for more detailed description of treatment of the data). Larger positive values on the

Table 6.1 IAT Effects

IAT effect (ln)	Non-sex offenders		Child molesters				
	n	M (SD)	n	M (SD)	df	F	r_{pb}
Self							
Pleasant	28	0.26 (0.15)	25	0.33 (0.18)	1, 51	1.83	.19
Powerful	28	0.01 (0.18)	26	0.01 (0.16)	1, 52	0.02	.02
Sexy	27	0.31 (0.15)	21	0.24 (0.23)	1, 46	1.27	−.16
Child							
Pleasant	29	0.00 (0.20)	27	0.08 (0.18)	1, 54	2.49	.21
Powerful	28	−0.29 (0.15)	25	−0.27 (0.17)	1, 51	0.30	.08
Sexy	29	−0.05 (0.20)	24	0.07 (0.16)	1, 51	6.01[a]	.33

Note: Point-biserial correlation coefficients (r_{pb}) were reported as effect size estimates indicating the magnitude of the difference between groups. ln = natural log.
[a] $p < .05$.

pleasant self IAT effect reflect a more positive view of self. Larger positive values on the powerful self IAT and the sexy self IAT effects suggest a view of self as, respectively, more powerful and more sexually attractive. With regard to the child IATs, larger positive values on the pleasant, powerful and sexy child IAT effects imply a view of children as, respectively, more pleasant, more powerful and more sexually attractive.

One-way ANOVAs were performed to compare the child molesters and non-sex offenders on the IAT effects (ln). In addition to significance tests, effect size estimates (r_{pb}) were reported for each IAT effect (ln) to provide an indication of the magnitude of the differences between groups. As shown in Table 6.1, only one of the six comparisons reached statistical significance. The groups differed significantly in their sexy child IAT effects, suggesting that the child molesters viewed children as more sexually attractive than did the non-sex offenders. Follow-up analyses revealed that among the child molesters, mean log response latencies were significantly faster on the trials in which *child* and *sexy* shared the same response key (M = 6.72) than on the trials in which *adult* and *sexy* shared the same response key (M = 6.80), F(1, 23) = 4.90, p < .05, r_{pb} = .42. In contrast, for the non-sex offenders, the difference was in the opposite direction, but did not reach statistical significance. On the trials in which *child* and *sexy* shared the same response key, the non-sexual offenders' mean log response latency was 6.75 and on the trials in which *adult* and *sexy* shared the same response key, the mean log latency was 6.70, F(1, 28) = 1.70, p > .05, r_{pb} = −.26. As illustrated in Figure 6.2, the child molesters viewed children as more sexually attractive than adults, whereas the non-sex offenders viewed children as less sexually attractive than adults, although this difference was not significant for the non-sex offenders.

Four potentially confounding variables in our study were age, race, sexual orientation and impression management (BIDR-IM). Compared to the non-sex offenders, the child molesters were significantly older, less likely to be *Aboriginal*, more likely to be bisexual or homosexual and scored higher on impression management.

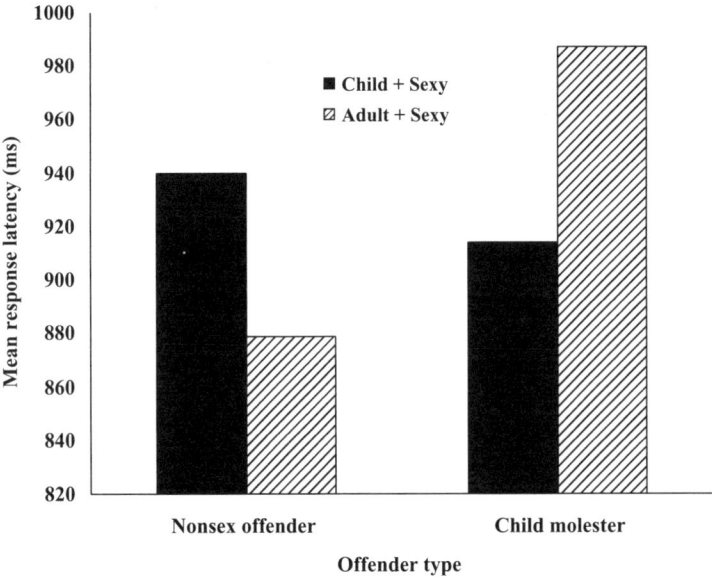

Figure 6.2   Sexy child IAT (untransformed response latencies).

The results found for the IAT measures could be attributable to these extraneous factors. However, a number of *post hoc* analyses controlling for these factors suggest that differences in age, race, sexual orientation or impression management do not account for the differences, or lack thereof, between child molesters and non-sex offenders on the IAT measures.

Relationship between IAT Measures and Risk of Sexual Recidivism

The secondary hypotheses concerned correlations between the IAT measures and risk of sexual recidivism. It was hypothesized that greater risk would be associated with an implicit view of self as less pleasant, less powerful and less sexually attractive. In addition, greater risk was expected to be associated with an implicit view of children as more pleasant, less powerful and more sexually attractive. Intercorrelations between the IAT effects (ln), the Static-99 and the RRASOR are presented in Table 6.2. For correlations between continuous variables, coefficients of 0.10, 0.30 and 0.50 are generally considered to be, respectively, small, medium and large effect sizes (Cohen, 1988). As hypothesized, greater risk on the Static-99 was significantly associated with higher sexy child IAT effects (ln), which reflect a view of children as more sexually attractive. Contrary to expectations, however, greater risk on the RRASOR was significantly associated with higher powerful child IAT effects (ln), which reflect a view of children as *more* powerful. Thus, offenders who viewed children as more sexually attractive and *more* powerful were at greater risk for sexual recidivism.

Table 6.2 Intercorrelations between the Static-99, RRASOR, BIDR-IM and IAT Effects (ln) in child molesters

	1	2	3	4	5	6	7	8	9
1. Static-99	—	.78**	−.40*	−.32	.28	.15	.05	.17	.43*
		(27)	(27)	(25)	(26)	(21)	(27)	(25)	(24)
2. RRASOR			−.36†	−.31	.12	.23	.33†	.40*	.27
			(27)	(25)	(26)	(21)	(27)	(25)	(24)
3. BIDR-IM				.38†	.09	−.16	.30	.08	−.22
				(25)	(26)	(21)	(27)	(25)	(24)
4. Pleasant self IAT					.33	.35	.42*	−.08	.27
					(24)	(20)	(25)	(24)	(23)
5. Powerful self IAT						.52*	.16	−.26	.33
						(21)	(26)	(24)	(23)
6. Sexy self IAT							.52*	−.30	.12
							(21)	(20)	(20)
7. Pleasant child IAT								.19	.20
								(25)	(24)
8. Powerful child IAT									.33
									(23)
9. Sexy child IAT									—

Note: Sample size is in parentheses. ln = natural log.
†$p < .10$, *$p < .05$, **$p < .001$.

Integrating the Results into the Literature

Contrary to expectations, none of the self IATs significantly differed between child molesters and non-sex offenders, nor did they correlate significantly with risk of sexual recidivism as measured by the Static-99 or the RRASOR. The results were not particularly supportive of theorists' suggestions that a view of self as negative, socially weak or unattractive plays a role in the aetiology or maintenance of child sexual abuse. Results for the child IATs were only partially consistent with expectations. The findings did not support theoreticians' suggestions that viewing children as pleasant and socially weak is involved in the aetiology of child molestation. Partial support was found, however, for the suggested link between a more positive view of children and risk of sexual recidivism as evidenced by a medium correlation with the RRASOR ($r = .33$) that tended towards significance ($p < .10$). Although this association was weakened when the BIDR-IM was taken into account, a cogent argument has been made against the common practice of controlling for offenders' BIDR scores to eliminate the influence of social desirability (Mills and Kroner, 2005, 2006; Mills, Loza and Kroner, 2003). Consistent with this argument, the BIDR-IM itself was correlated with the RRASOR and Static-99.

  With regard to the powerful child IAT, no significant relationship was found with the Static-99. Greater risk on the RRASOR, however, was significantly associated with viewing children as *more* powerful, which was contrary to our hypothesis. Whereas it has been suggested that viewing children as non-threatening and socially weak is associated with persistence of sexual offending, our results suggest that, at least on an implicit level, the reverse may be the case. Perhaps greater risk of sexual recidivism may be associated with imbuing children with greater social power, such as believing that they are capable of giving informed consent to sexual activity with adults (Abel, Becker and Cunningham-Rathner, 1984; Abel, Gore, Holland, Camp, Becker and Rathner, 1989; Bumby, 1996; Hanson, Gizzarelli and Scott, 1994; Ward and Keenan, 1999). Explicit cognitive distortions regarding child sexual abuse, however, are often only weakly associated with risk assessment instruments (Nunes and Cortoni, 2007) and sexual recidivism (Hanson and Morton-Bourgon, 2004). Additional research is required to clarify the meaning of the correlation observed between the powerful child IAT and the RRASOR.

For the sexy child IAT, the hypotheses received almost complete support. As expected, compared to the non-sex offenders, child molesters viewed children as significantly more sexually attractive. The sexy child IAT was also significantly associated with greater risk of sexual recidivism on the Static-99 ($r = .43$). These findings concur with theory in which sexual attraction to children has been identified as playing a role in the aetiology and maintenance of child sexual abuse. The correlation with the RRASOR, however, did not reach statistical significance. It was unexpected that the sexy child IAT was not more strongly correlated with the RRASOR than the Static-99 because the RRASOR has been conceptualized as a more focused measure of sexual deviance than the Static-99 (Doren, 2004; Roberts, Doren and Thornton, 2002).

Assuming that the sexy child IAT does measure sexual interest in children, our findings fit well with previous PPG, VT and other IAT research. As noted above, greater sexual attraction to children (relative to adults) has been found among child molesters compared to men who have not sexually abused children on PPG and VT measures. In addition, researchers who have used the IAT have found that child molesters more strongly associate children with sex (Gray et al., 2005) and view children as more sexual (Mihailides et al., 2004) than do men who have not sexually abused children. Similarly, there is convergence between the current and past findings regarding maintenance of sexual offending. We found that the sexy child IAT effect was significantly associated with the risk of sexual recidivism and there is considerable evidence that PPG-assessed sexual attraction to children is predictive of persistence in sexual offending (Hanson and Morton-Bourgon, 2004, 2005). There is an impressive degree of convergence across samples and methods, which justifies optimism regarding the construct validity of the sexy child IAT and makes a strong case for the involvement of sexual attraction to children in child molestation.

Limitations

Although there were some interesting and novel findings, we did not find most of the expected between-group differences. This is open to at least three different interpretations. First, the average child molester may simply not be very different from other criminals on many of the cognitions that were examined. For example, it has been argued and demonstrated that personal distress variables, such as low self-esteem, are not predictive of general criminal behaviour (Andrews and Bonta,

2003; Gendreau, Little and Goggin, 1996). Second, the IAT measures may have failed to adequately capture the cognitions of interest. A third possibility is that few between-group differences were found because there are multiple etiological pathways to child sexual abuse that create different types of child molesters characterized by different cognitions (e.g. Ward and Siegert, 2002). Some or all of these groups may have been present within the sample. Additional research is required to evaluate the validity of these, and other, interpretations.

Cautious interpretation of our results is also warranted by certain issues, such as the correlational retrospective design, small sample size and treatment of the IAT data. Although ideally our study would contribute to knowledge about the aetiology and maintenance of child sexual abuse, the extent to which it does so is unclear because of the research design. Confidence in the validity of our results, however, was increased, by collecting and statistically controlling for several potential confounding variables. More difficult to address are the limitations of the design for evaluating the predictive validity of the IAT measures. Although some of the IAT measures were significantly correlated with the Static-99 or RRASOR, the inference that these implicit cognitions play a causal role in (or even simply predict) sexual recidivism is premature. The findings are certainly encouraging, but it must be acknowledged that a correlation with a risk assessment instrument will not necessarily translate into a similar correlation with recidivism because the instrument itself is not perfectly correlated with recidivism.

Because of the small sample size, only medium to large effect sizes reached statistical significance. For example, the correlation between the RRASOR and the pleasant self IAT was .31, but with a sample size of 25 it did not reach statistical significance ($p > .05$). Clearly, this is not a negligible association (Cohen, 1988; Rosenthal, 1991), but a larger sample would have permitted greater confidence in the degree to which a similar association exists in the larger population of incarcerated child molesters. The current study was lacking in statistical power and a non-significant result does not necessarily indicate the absence of an effect.

In addition, the scoring method we used for the IATs is somewhat outdated. A new algorithm has been developed and shown to have advantages over the older method (e.g. yields slightly larger effect sizes) in a large sample of non-offenders (Greenwald, Nosek and Banaji, 2003). However, research with child molesters (Gray et al., 2005) and a meta-analysis with non-offenders (Greenwald et al., in press) suggest that the specific treatment of the IAT data would not have dramatically changed our findings; that is, both scoring procedures would be expected to yield very similar results. Nevertheless, in our current projects, the latest procedures and algorithm are being used (Greenwald et al., 2003; Nosek, Greenwald and Banaji, 2005).

Implications for Assessment and Treatment

Our results have implications for assessment and treatment of child molesters. The finding that greater risk of sexual recidivism was moderately associated, although not always significantly, with an implicit view of children as more pleasant, powerful and sexually attractive as measured by the IATs suggests the possibility that these implicit cognitions may also be predictive of sexual recidivism. With the exception of sexual interest, cognitive predictors of sexual recidivism have often been assessed with self-report measures with generally poor predictive validity (Hanson and Morton-Bourgon, 2004, 2005). In contrast, our findings are very encouraging because they identify implicit cognitions that may be associated with sexual recidivism and they offer viable measures for assessing these cognitions. If future research were to demonstrate a relationship between these measures and sexual recidivism, they may become valuable additions to existing assessment batteries. As such, the IAT measures could potentially contribute to increasing the breadth and predictive accuracy of risk assessments.

Ideally, risk assessments not only provide an estimate of risk, but also identify treatment targets (Andrews and Bonta, 2003; Beech, Fisher and Thornton, 2003; Hanson et al., 2007). Administering IAT measures could potentially identify areas to address in treatment. Our findings suggest that, for those child molesters who view children as more positive, powerful and sexually attractive, targeting these cognitions in treatment (as is the current practice in many programs) may reduce their risk of reoffending. Given that IAT measures appear to be sensitive to change (e.g. Rudman, Ashmore and Gary, 2001; Rudman and Lee, 2002; Teachman and Woody, 2003), they may be useful for assessing treatment progress. Of course, application of the IAT to clinical work would be contingent upon further encouraging results from a larger body of research (Gray et al., 2005; Nosek et al., 2007).

Future Research

There are many important directions for research given that investigators have only recently begun to adapt implicit measures to study sex offenders' cognitions. As noted above, a high priority would be to establish the construct validity of the IAT. In this context, construct validity 'refers to the extent to which a measure has been shown to assess the construct (e.g., intelligence) of interest' (Kazdin, 2003, p. 573). It seems reasonable to believe that well designed IAT measures can assess the constructs for which they were designed. Recent research has demonstrated the ability of a sexual orientation IAT to classify men as homosexual or heterosexual with an impressively high degree of accuracy (Snowden et al., 2008) and there is ample evidence for the construct validity of a variety of other IAT measures with non-offender samples (Greenwald et al., in press). However, researchers have not yet convincingly demonstrated that the novel IAT measures that have been used with sex offenders are actually measuring the constructs of interest. Confidence that the sexy child IAT, for example, is truly tapping sexual interest would be increased by demonstrating convergence with established measures of sexual interest, such as PPG and VT (Gray et al., 2005).

If IAT measures do demonstrate adequate construct validity with sex offenders, evaluation of the incremental validity of IAT measures would be an important next step. Given that IAT and self-report measures are related but distinct factors, it would be interesting to examine whether IAT measures provide information about sex offenders' cognitions that complements information obtained from self-report measures. Interactions of IAT and self-report measures may also yield additional important information. For example, in research on non-offenders, Jordan *et al.* (2003) found that implicit and explicit self-esteem interacted to predict defensiveness. More specifically, low implicit self-esteem combined with high explicit self-esteem was associated with greater defensiveness than other combinations of implicit and explicit self-esteem. It may be fruitful to consider possible interactions between self-report and IAT measures of various cognitions in sex offenders. It would also be interesting to examine whether interactions between IAT and PPG measures of sexual interest would provide more information about sexual interests than they would individually or additively. More onerous research questions concern the extent to which IAT measures are predictive of sexual recidivism and, if so, whether they are tapping criminogenic needs, such that change on the measures is associated with corresponding change in the likelihood of recidivism (Andrews and Bonta, 2003).

Another interesting avenue of research would be to compare the validity of IAT and other implicit measures, such as the Stroop (see Chapter 8 by Smith) and rapid serial visual presentation (see Chapter 7 by Flak and Beech). It is expected that different implicit measures would contribute independent information about cognitions associated with sexual offending. Research on non-offenders suggests that there may be little overlap between the IAT and many other implicit measures (e.g. Bosson *et al.*, 2000; but see Snowden *et al.*, 2008). IAT measures would also be expected to be among the most valid implicit measures for assessing sex offenders' cognitions. For example, in research with non-offenders, IAT measures are generally found to be more internally consistent than many other implicit measures (e.g. Bosson *et al.*, 2000; see Nosek *et al.*, 2007, for a review). Poor internal consistency would be expected to place an upper limit on validity; reliability is necessary but not sufficient for validity (Nunnally and Bernstein, 1994). Another advantage of the IAT is its flexibility. As noted above, the IAT procedure can be easily adapted to measure diverse constructs, ranging from self-esteem to sexual interest in children. For example, we are currently using IAT measures to assess sexually coercive men's implicit cognitions about women in terms of evaluation and submissiveness.

CONCLUSION

Although in our research many of the hypotheses were not supported, our findings suggest that (a) an implicit view of children as sexually attractive may be a distinctive characteristic of child molesters compared to other criminals and (b) an implicit view of children as more powerful and more sexually attractive may be associated with greater risk of sexual recidivism. Combined with findings from Gray *et al.* (2005) and Mihailides *et al.* (2004), the evidence suggests that the IAT is a very promising tool for studying child molesters' offence-related implicit cognitions. Implicit measures like the IAT make it possible to examine many intriguing hypotheses (e.g. Hanson, 1999; Mann and Beech, 2003; Ward *et al.*, 1997; Ward and Keenan, 1999) that have, as yet, received little empirical attention. Given the relatively strong psychometric properties and flexibility of IAT measures, it is anticipated that they will become an important component of multimethod research and, eventually, assessment of sexual offenders.

ACKNOWLEDGEMENTS

The research presented in this chapter was facilitated by a Social Sciences and Humanities Research Council of Canada Doctoral Fellowship and Ontario Graduate Scholarships (OGS). Thanks go to Mark Baldwin, Drew Kingston and Heather Moulden for helpful comments on an earlier draft of this chapter.

REFERENCES

Abel, G.G., Becker, J.V. and Cunningham-Rathner, J. (1984) Complications, consent, and cognitions in sex between children and adults. *International Journal of Law and Psychiatry*, **7**, 89–103.

Abel, G.G., Gore, D.K., Holland, C.L., Camp, N., Becker, J.V. and Rathner, J. (1989) The measurement of the cognitive distortions of child molesters. *Annals of Sex Research*, **2**, 135–53.

Andrews, D.A. and Bonta, J. (2003) *The Psychology of Criminal Conduct*, 3rd edn, Anderson, Cincinnati, OH.

Asendorpf, J.B., Banse, R. and Mücke, D. (2002) Double dissociation between implicit and explicit personality self-concept: the case of shy behavior. *Journal of Personality and Social Psychology*, **83**, 380–93.

Barsetti, I., Earls, C.M., Lalumière, M.L. and Bélanger, N. (1998) The differentiation of intrafamilial and extrafamilial heterosexual child molesters. Journal of Interpersonal Violence, **13**, 275–86.

Baxter, D.J., Marshall, W.L., Barbaree, H.E., Davidson, P.R. and Malcolm, P.B. (1984) Deviant sexual behavior: differentiating sex offenders by criminal and personal history, psychometric measures, and sexual responses. *Criminal Justice and Behavior*, **11**, 477–501.

Beech, A.R. (1998) A psychometric typology of child abusers. *International Journal of Offender Therapy and Comparative Criminology*, **42**, 319–39.

Beech, A.R., Fisher, D.D. and Thornton, D. (2003) Risk assessment of sex offenders. *Professional Psychology and Practice*, **34**, 339–52.

Bosson, J.K., Swann, W.B. and Pennebaker, J.W. (2000) Stalking the perfect measure of self-esteem: the blind men and the elephant revisited? *Journal of Personality and Social Psychology*, **70**, 631–43.

Bumby, K.M. (1996) Assessing the cognitive distortions of child molesters and rapists: development and validation of the MOLEST and RAPE scales. *Sexual Abuse: A Journal of Research and Treatment*, **8**, 37–54.

Cohen, J. (1988) *Statistical Power Analysis for the Behavioral Sciences*, 2nd edn, Erlbaum, Hillsdale, NJ.

Cunningham, W.A., Preacher, K.J. and Banaji, M.R. (2001) Implicit attitude measures: consistency, stability, and convergent validity. *Psychological Science*, **121**, 163–70.

Doren, D.M. (2004) Toward a multidimensional model for sexual recidivism risk. *Journal of Interpersonal Violence*, **19**, 835–56.

Egloff, B. and Schmukle, S.C. (2002) Predictive validity of an Implicit Association Test for assessing anxiety. Journal of Personality and Social Psychology, **83**, 1441–55.

Fazio, R.H. and Olson, M.A. (2003) Implicit measures in social cognition research: their meaning and use. *Annual Review of Psychology*, **54**, 297–327.

Fiedler, K., Messner, C. and Bluemke, M. (2006) Unresolved problems with the 'I', the 'A', and the 'T': a logical and psychometric critique of the Implicit Association Test (IAT). *European Review of Social Psychology*, **17**, 74–147.

Finkelhor, D. (1984) *Child Sexual Abuse: New Theory and Research*. Free Press, New York.

Finkelhor, D. and Araji, S. (1986) Explanations of pedophilia: a four factor model. *The Journal of Sex Research*, **22**, 145–61.

Firestone, P., Nunes, K.L., Moulden, H., Broom, I. and Bradford, J.M. (2005) Hostility and recidivism in sexual offenders. *Archives of Sexual Behavior*, **34**, 277–83.

Fisher, D., Beech, A. and Browne, K. (1999) Comparison of sex offenders to nonoffenders on selected psychological measures. *International Journal of Offender Therapy and Comparative Criminology*, **43**, 473–91.

Gendreau, P., Little, T. and Goggin, C. (1996) A meta-analysis of the predictors of adult offender recidivism: What works! *Criminology*, **34**, 575–607.

Gray, N.S., Brown, A.S., MacCulloch, M.J., Smith, J. and Snowden, R.J. (2005) An implicit association test of the associations between children and sex in pedophiles. *Journal of Abnormal Psychology*, **114**, 304–8

Gray, N.S., MacCulloch, M.J., Smith, J., Morris, M. and Snowden, R.J. (2003) Violence viewed by psychopathic murderers. *Nature*, **423**, 497–8.

Greenwald, A.G. and Banaji, M.R. (1995) Implicit social cognition: attitudes, self-esteem, and stereotypes. *Psychological Review*, **102**, 4–27.

Greenwald, A.G. and Farnham, S.D. (2000) Using the Implicit Association Test to measure self-esteem and self-concept. *Journal of Personality and Social Psychology*, **79**, 1022–38.

Greenwald, A.G., McGhee, D.E. and Schwartz, J.L.K. (1998) Measuring individual differences in implicit cognition: the Implicit Association Test. *Journal of Personality and Social Psychology*, **74**, 1464–80.

Greenwald, A.G., Nosek, B.A. and Banaji, M.R. (2003) Understanding and using the Implicit Association Test: I. An improved scoring algorithm. *Journal of Personality and Social Psychology*, **85**, 197–216.

Greenwald, A.G., Poehlman, T.A., Uhlmann, E. and Banaji, M.R. (in press). Understanding and using the Implicit Association Test: III. Meta-analysis of predictive validity. *Journal of Personality and Social Psychology*.

Haines, E.L. (1999) *Elements of a Social Power Schema: Gender Stand-Point, Self-Concept, and Experience*. Unpublished doctoral dissertation, City University of New York.

Hall, G.C.N. and Hirschman, R. (1992) Sexual aggression against children: a conceptual perspective of etiology. *Criminal Justice and Behavior*, **19**, 8–23.

Hanson, R.K. (1997) *The Development of a Brief Actuarial Risk Scale for Sexual Offense Recidivism*. Ministry of Public Safety and Emergency Preparedness Canada, Ottawa.

Hanson, R.K. (1999) Working with sex offenders: a personal view. *The Journal of Sexual Aggression*, **4**, 81–93.

Hanson, R.K., Gizzarelli, R. and Scott, H. (1994) The attitudes of incest offenders: sexual entitlement and acceptance of sex with children. *Criminal Justice and Behavior*, **21**, 187–202.

Hanson, R.K., Harris, A.J.R., Scott, T.-L. and Helmus, L. (2007) *Assessing the Risk of Sexual Offenders on Community Supervision: The Dynamic Supervision Project*. Public Safety Canada, Ottawa.

Hanson, R.K. and Morton-Bourgon, K. (2004) *Predictors of Sexual Recidivism: An Updated Meta-Analysis*. Public Safety and Emergency Preparedness Canada, Ottawa.

Hanson, R.K. and Morton-Bourgon, K.E. (2005) The characteristics of persistent sexual offenders: a meta-analysis of recidivism studies. *Journal of Consulting and Clinical Psychology*, **73**, 1154–63.

Hanson, R.K. and Thornton, D. (2000) Improving risk assessments for sex offenders: a comparison of three actuarial scales. *Law and Human Behavior*, **24**, 119–36.

Harris, G.T., Rice, M.E., Quinsey, V.L. and Chaplin, T.C. (1996) Viewing time as a measure of sexual interest among child molesters and normal heterosexual men. *Behavior Research and Therapy*, **34**, 389–94.

Hofmann, W., Gawronski, B., Gschwendner, T., Le, H. and Schmitt, M. (2005) A meta-analysis on the correlation between the Implicit Association Test and explicit self-report measures. *Personality and Social Psychology Bulletin*, **31**, 1369–85.

Horley, J. (2000) Cognitions supportive of child molestation. *Aggression and Violent Behavior*, **5**, 551–64.

Horley, J. and Quinsey, V.L. (1994) Assessing the cognitions of child molesters: use of the semantic differential with incarcerated offenders. *Journal of Sex Research*, **31**, 187–95.

Jellison, W.A., McConnell, A.R. and Gabriel, S. (2004) Implicit and explicit measures of sexual orientation attitudes: ingroup preferences and overt behaviours among gay and straight men. *Personality and Social Psychology Bulletin*, **30**, 629–42.

Jordan, C.H., Spencer, S.J., Zanna, M.P., Hoshino-Browne, E. and Correll, J. (2003) Secure and defensive high self-esteem. *Journal of Personality and Social Psychology*, **85**, 969–78.

Katz, R.C. (1990) Psychosocial adjustment in adolescent child molesters. *Child Abuse and Neglect*, **14**, 567–75.

Kazdin, A.E. (2003) *Research Design in Clinical Psychology*, 4th edn, Allyn and Bacon, Boston, MA.

Looman, J. and Marshall, W.L. (2001) Phallometric assessments designed to detect arousal to children: the responses of rapists and child molesters. *Sexual Abuse: A Journal of Research and Treatment*, **13**, 3–13.

Maison, D., Greenwald, A.G. and Bruin, R.H. (2004) Predictive validity of the Implicit Association Test in studies of brands, consumer attitudes, and behavior. *Journal of Consumer Psychology*, **14**, 405–15.

Mann, R.E. and Beech, A.R. (2003) Cognitive distortions, schemas and implicit theories, in *Sexual Deviance: Issues and Controversies* (eds T. Ward, D.R. Laws and S.M. Hudson), Sage, Thousand Oaks, CA, pp. 135–53.

Marshall, W.L., Anderson, D. and Fernandez, Y. (1999) *Cognitive Behavioural Treatment of Sexual Offenders*. John Wiley & Sons, Inc., New York.

Marshall, W.L. and Barbaree, H.E. (1990) An integrated theory of the etiology of sexual offending, in *Handbook of Sexual Assault: Issues, Theories, and Treatment of the Offender* (eds W.L. Marshall, D.R. Laws and H.E. Barbaree), Plenum, New York, pp. 257–75.

Marshall, W.L., Barbaree, H.E. and Christophe, D. (1986) Sexual offenders against female children: sexual preferences for age of victims and type of behaviour. *Canadian Journal of Behavioural Science*, **18**, 424–39.

Mihailides, S., Devilly, G.J. and Ward, T. (2004) Implicit cognitive distortions and sexual offending. *Sexual Abuse: A Journal of Research and Treatment*, **16**, 333–50.

Mills, J.F. and Kroner, D.G. (2005) An investigation into the relationship between socially desirable responding and offender self-report. *Psychological Services*, **2**, 70–80.

Mills, J.F. and Kroner, D.G. (2006) Impression management and self-report among violent offenders. *Journal of Interpersonal Violence*, **21**, 178–92.

Mills, J.F., Loza, W. and Kroner, D.G. (2003) Predictive validity despite social desirability: evidence for the robustness of self-report among offenders. *Criminal Behaviour and Mental Health*, **13**, 140–50.

Nosek, B.A., Banaji, M.R. and Greenwald, A.G. (2002) Harvesting implicit group attitudes and beliefs from a demonstration web site. *Group Dynamics: Theory, Research, and Practice*, **6**, 101–15.

Nosek, B.A., Greenwald, A.G. and Banaji, M.R. (2005) Understanding and using the Implicit Association Test: II. Method variables and construct validity. *and Social Psychology Bulletin*, **31**, 166–80.

Nosek, B.A., Greenwald, A.G. and Banaji, M.R. (2007) The Implicit Association Test at age 7: a methodological and conceptual review, in *Automatic Processes in Social Thinking and Behavior* (ed. J.A. Bargh), Psychology Press, pp. 265–292.

Nosek, B.A. and Smyth, F.L. (2007) A multitrait–multimethod validation of the Implicit Association Test. *Experimental Psychology*, **54**, 14–29.

Nunes, K.L. and Cortoni, F. (2007) *Assessing Treatment Change in Sexual Offenders* (Research Report No. R-184). Correctional Service Canada, Ottawa, Canada.

Nunes, K.L., Firestone, P. and Baldwin, M.W. (2007) Indirect assessment of cognitions of child sexual abusers with the Implicit Association Test. *Criminal Justice and Behavior*, **34**, 454–75.

Nunnally, J.C. and Bernstein, I.H. (1994) *Psychometric Theory*, 3rd edn, McGraw-Hill, New York.

Overholser, J.C. and Beck, S. (1986) Multimethod assessment of rapists, child molesters, and three control groups on behavioral and psychological measures. *Journal of Consulting and Clinical Psychology*, **54**, 682–7.

Paulhus, D.L. (1988) *Assessing Self-Deception and Impression Management in Self-Reports: The Balanced Inventory of Desirable Responding*. Unpublished manual, University of British Columbia, Vancouver, Canada.

Paulhus, D.L. (1991) Measurement and control of response bias, in *Measures of Personality and Social Psychological Attitudes*, vol. 1 (eds J.P. Robinson, P.R. Shaver and L.S. Wrightsman), Academic Press, San Diego, CA, pp. 17–59.

Quinsey, V.L. and Chaplin, T.C. (1988) Penile responses of child molesters and normals to descriptions of encounters with children involving sex and violence. *Journal of Interpersonal Violence*, **3**, 259–74.

Rice, M.E. and Harris, G.T. (2005) Comparing effect sizes in follow-up studies: ROC area, Cohen's *d*, and *r*. *Law and Human Behavior*, **29**, 615–20.

Roberts, C.F., Doren, D.M. and Thornton, D. (2002) Dimensions associated with assessments of sex offender recidivism risk. *Criminal Justice and Behavior*, **29**, 569–89.

Rosenthal, R. (1991) *Meta-Analytic Procedures for Social Research*, rev. edn, Sage, Newbury Park, CA.

Rudman, L.A., Ashmore, R.D. and Gary, M. (2001) 'Unlearning' automatic biases: the malleability of implicit prejudice and stereotypes. *Journal of Personality and Social Psychology*, **81**, 856–68.

Rudman, L.A., Greenwald, A.G. and McGhee, D.E. (2001) Implicit self-concept and evaluative implicit gender stereotypes: self and ingroup share desirable traits. *Personality and Social Psychology Bulletin*, **27**, 1164–78.

Rudman, L.A. and Lee, M.R. (2002) Implicit and explicit consequences of exposure to violent and misogynistic rap music. *Group Processes and Intergroup Relations*, **5**, 133–50.

Segal, Z.V. and Marshall, W.L. (1985). Heterosexual social skills in a population of rapists and child molesters. *Journal of Consulting and Clinical Psychology*, **53**, 55–63.

Snowden, R.J., Gray, N.S., Smith, J., Morris, M. and MacCulloch, M.J. (2004) Implicit affective associations to violence in psychopathic murderers. *The Journal of Forensic Psychiatry and Psychology*, **15**, 620–41.

Snowden, R.J., Wichter, J. and Gray, N.S. (2008) Implicit and explicit measurements of sexual preference in gay and heterosexual men: a comparison of priming techniques and the Implicit Association Task. *Archives of Sexual Behavior*, **37**, 558–65.

Steffens, M.C. (2004) Is the implicit association test immune to faking? *Experimental Psychology*, **51**, 165–79.

Swanson, J.E., Rudman, L.A. and Greenwald, A.G. (2001) Using the Implicit Association Test to investigate attitude–behavior consistency for stigmatized behavior. *Cognition and Emotion*, **15**, 207–30.

Tafarodi, R.W. and Ho, C. (2006) Implicit and explicit self-esteem: What are we measuring? *Canadian Psychology*, **47**, 195–202.

Teachman, B.A., Gregg, A.P. and Woody, S.R. (2001) Implicit associations for fear-relevant stimuli among individuals with snake and spider fears. *Journal of Abnormal Psychology*, **110**, 226–35.

Teachman, B.A. and Woody, S.R. (2003) Automatic processing in spider phobia: implicit fear associations over the course of treatment. *Journal of Abnormal Psychology*, **112**, 100–109.

Thornton, D., Beech, A. and Marshall, W.L. (2004) Pretreatment self-esteem and posttreatment sexual recidivism. *International Journal of Offender Therapy and Comparative Criminology*, **48**, 587–99.

Uhlmann, E. and Swanson, J. (2004) Exposure to violent video games increases automatic aggressiveness. *Journal of Adolescence*, **27**, 41–52.

Walters, G.D. (2006) Risk-appraisal versus self-report in the prediction of criminal justice outcomes. *Criminal Justice and Behavior*, **33**, 279–304.

Ward, T., Hudson, S.M., Johnston, L. and Marshall, W.L. (1997) Cognitive distortions in sex offenders: an integrative review. *Clinical Psychology Review*, **17**, 479–507.

Ward, T. and Keenan, T. (1999) Child molesters' implicit theories. *Journal of Interpersonal Violence*, **14**, 821–38.

Ward, T., McCormack, J. and Hudson, S.M. (1997) Sexual offenders' perceptions of their intimate relationships. *Sexual Abuse: A Journal of Research and Treatment*, **9**, 57–73.

Ward, T. and Siegert, R.J. (2002) Toward a comprehensive theory of child sexual abuse: a theory knitting perspective. *Psychology, Crime, and Law*, **8**, 319–51.

Westen, D. and Weinberger, J. (2004) When clinical description becomes statistical prediction. *American Psychologist*, **59**, 595–613.

Wiers, R.W., Van Woerden, N., Smulders, F.T.Y. and De Jong, P.J. (2002) Implicit and explicit alcohol related cognitions in heavy and light drinkers. *Journal of Abnormal Psychology*, **111**, 648–58.

Wong, S., Olver, M.E., Nicholaichuk, T.P. and Gordon, A. (2004) *The Violence Risk Scale: Sexual Offender version (VRS:SO)*. Regional Psychiatric Centre and University of Saskatchewan, Saskatoon, Saskatchewan, Canada.

Yates, P.M., Goguen, B.C., Nicholaichuk, T.P., Williams, S.M. and Long, C.A. (2000) *National Sex Offender Programs (Volume II: Moderate Intensity)*, Correctional Service of Canada, Ottawa, ON.

Chapter 7

THE RAPID SERIAL VISUAL PRESENTATION TEST OF SEXUAL INTEREST IN CHILD MOLESTERS

VANJA E. FLAK AND ANTHONY R. BEECH

Centre for Forensic and Criminological Psychology, School of Psychology, University of Birmingham, Birmingham, UK

GLYN W. HUMPHREYS

Behavioural Brain Sciences Centre, School of Psychology, University of Birmingham, Birmingham, UK

INTRODUCTION

Sexual preference is an important predictor of sexual recidivism in child molesters (Hanson and Bussière, 1998; Hanson and Morton-Bourgon, 2004). Measuring sexual preference is considered an essential part of clinical evaluation (Fisher, 1994; Freund, 1978) with an important aspect of sexual interest being the erotic response (Kalmus and Beech, 2005). Rempel and Serafini's (1995) definition of the erotic response is that sexual desire is a psychological process and the physical response is 'sexual arousal'. Singer (1984) proposed a theory of sexual arousal separating the erotic response into three independent chronological stages which can be independently experienced. The first stage, the *aesthetic response*, is the emotional affective reaction aroused by seeing an attractive face or figure leading to increased attention towards the individual. The second stage, the *approach response*, is more of a physical reaction, such as approaching the object of interest. The final (third) stage, the *genital response*, is a physiological response reflected as genital tumescence in males and is often the result of close proximity to the object of attraction.

Singer (1984) notes that although a range of differing physiological responses arise in sexual arousal, the research literature argues that the most dependable, and most available to measure in males, is the genital response. As such, sexual offenders' sexual preferences have typically been measured by their penile response to visual stimuli using the penile plethysmograph (PPG; see Chapter 2 by

Sachsenmaier and Gress). However, a number of reported problems associated with the use of phallometry have been observed in the literature such as difficulty in its practical application, difficulty in interpretation, severe methodological problems and the invasiveness of this instrument (Marshall and Fernandez, 2000).

The need for a measurement tool which does not have the problems mentioned above is therefore in demand, and thus researchers have started to focus on computer-based measures such as viewing time and information-processing procedures for assessing attentional allocation to stimuli (Flak, Beech and Fisher, 2007; Kalmus and Beech, 2005). Unfortunately, there has been little research applying these procedures to sex offenders. Tasks that have been used are the implicit association test (IAT), the emotional Stroop task, choice reaction time tasks and the Gress paradigm. The IAT (Gray, Brown, MacCulloch, Smith and Snowdon, 2005; Mihailides, Devilly and Ward, 2004) is a test most often employed in social psychology to measure social beliefs (e.g. racism) implicitly and indirectly. Whether this can be used as a measure of sexual interest is discussed in Chapter 5 and Chapter 6 and Flak et al. (2007). The emotional Stroop task (Smith and Waterman, 2004; see Chapter 8 by Smith, and Flak et al., 2007) has been used to test information-processing biases in sexual offenders. This is a measure of socio-affective responses to irrelevant stimuli. Whether it is capable of measuring true sexual interest has yet to be established. Choice reaction time measures (Giotakis, 2005; Santtila, Mokros and Viljanen, 2006; Wright and Adams, 1994; see Chapter 4 by Gress and Laws) reflect the time taken to indicate which category out of two or more a stimulus belongs to. This paradigm has some promising findings and appears to be able to measure sexual interest (Santtila et al., 2006). Finally, the Gress paradigm (2001; 2006a; 2006b; see Chapter 4 by Gress and Laws) employs both choice reaction time and viewing time combined and has been successfully applied to measure sexual interest in child sex offenders and other normative groups.

Viewing time is based on the simple assumption that individuals will look at images found attractive longer than images found unattractive. This is validated by Rosenzweig's (1942) observations that differential viewing times of sexual images correlate with sexual interest. Similarly, Zamansky (1956) observed that homosexual men viewed images of naked men longer than images of naked women, while heterosexual men viewed images of naked women for longer. Kalmus and Beech (2005) note that recent studies using explicit stimulus sets to combine phallometry with measurements of viewing time, found viewing time to correlate well with measurements of sexual arousal and, in addition, there were strong test–retest reliabilities (e.g. Abel, Huffman, Warberg and Holland, 1998; Harris, Rice, Quinsey and Chaplin, 1996). Two assessments using viewing time procedures are the *Abel Assessment for sexual interest* (Abel et al., 1998) and *affinity* (Glasgow, Osbourne and Croxen, 2003). For more details on these measures and other methodologies of assessing sexual interest, see the study by Kalmus and Beech (2005) and Flak et al. (2007).

In information-processing terms, enhanced attention towards attractive images may have a number of measurable consequences (Flak et al., 2007; Kalmus and Beech, 2005). For example, Kalmus and Beech (2005, p. 210) commented that the 'increase in viewing time was not only the amount of time it took the viewer to look at the pictures but also a product of the degree of interference that each image produced on this easy reaction task'. Findings that measure viewing time and choice reaction time change across objects of differential sexual interest fits with Singer's (1984) first stage of sexual arousal. However, to understand the specific factors that might be influenced by sexual interest, and how such factors might differ in sexual offenders, we need to utilize cognitive tasks where the particular underlying factors can be decomposed and assessed.

One potential procedure that may be useful here is the rapid serial visual presentation (RSVP)[1] technique, which induces a so-called attentional blink (AB) reflecting attentional limitations on the processing of rapidly presented images (Raymond, Shapiro and Arnell, 1992). By looking at whether stimuli that attract sexual interest may induce an AB in participants, it may be possible to measure the automatic capture of attention by the stimulus. Also, since the effect of the AB is on the report of a different, second stimulus (see below), the effect may not easily be contaminated by the demand characteristics of the task (e.g. deliberately slowing responses to a sexually arousing image). Here we review the RSVP procedure as a tool to assess sexual interest in child sex offenders.

In order to understand how the RSVP procedure can be utilized with sexual offenders, it is important to understand some of the theoretical background concerning the AB and recent research using the paradigm.

RSVP AND THE 'ATTENTIONAL BLINK'

Our sensory system is at all times bombarded with information attempting to gain access to our consciousness. In order for us to make sense of the input, we need to select information on the basis of its level of importance. The consequences of selection, and particularly the time course over which selection may be influencing processing, can be examined through the AB. Typically the AB is revealed when participants make two or more predefined responses to stimuli in the rapid serial stream. If two images, target 1 and target 2 (T1 and T2), are presented within or below half a second (500 ms) of each other, detection of the second image (T2) is often delayed such that the stimulus may not be reported at all (Shapiro, 2001). This is the AB. The effect is not due to low-level visual masking of the second target. If participants are asked not to report T1 but simply to report T2, then T2's identification is greatly improved, indicating that the effect is induced when participants attend to T1 for perceptual identification.

Several theories of the AB have been developed. Here we review three of the major contenders (see Shapiro, 2001, for a more extensive discussion), and consider their implications for developing the AB as a tool to assess sexual interest.

THEORIES OF ATTENTIONAL BLINK

The Inhibitory Model

Broadbent and Broadbent (1987) were the first to report the AB using an RSVP procedure. In their task, participants were instructed to detect a target and a probe

---

[1]RSVP is also used as an abbreviation of a forensic risk assessment tool (Hart, Kropp, Laws, Klaver, Logan, and Watt, 2003); however, it is also commonly used as the abbreviation for the rapid serial visual presentation procedure within cognitive psychology literature which is what we are referring to in this chapter.

word located at differing serial positions amongst a series of (not related) lowercase words. The number of items appearing between the target and the probe differed from trial to trial. Broadbent and Broadbent (1987) reported that if the target and the probe were presented consecutively, participants correctly responded to either the target or the probe but never to both. Interestingly, when time between target and probe decreased, the likelihood of identifying the probe word accurately on target-correct trials substantially improved; in contrast, when probe was presented within 400 milliseconds post-target, the participants frequently reported that they had not seen the probe at all. Similar findings were also reported by Reeves and Sperling (1986) and Weichselgartner and Sperling (1987). Broadbent and Broadbent (1987) concluded that this deficit in reporting both items was related to an inhibitory process operating at an initial stage when the targets were identified. This account lay at the heart of one of the first influential models of the AB, the *inhibition model* (Raymond *et al.*, 1992). According to this model, identification of first target led to the inhibition of attentional and identification processes for some subsequent period, so that the second stimulus could not be identified (e.g. Shapiro and Raymond, 1994; Shapiro, Caldwell and Sørensen, 1997a; Shapiro, Driver, Ward and Sørensen, 1997b). In an attempt to test the inhibition model, Shapiro, Raymond and Arnell (1994) conducted several experiments looking at the effects of a range of target manipulations where the difficulty of the first target varied whilst the second target did not vary. The reasoning behind this was the difficulty of processing the first target should influence the degree of inhibition. The findings showed that task difficulty only correlated very slightly with the magnitude of the blink which was interpreted by the authors to not support the predictions of the inhibition model. Therefore, the inhibition model was perceived as being an inadequate explanation of the AB effect. However, the research did give rise to a different 'inhibitory' model, the *interference model*, which we will now briefly outline.

The Interference Model

Many models of human selective attention assume that there are two broad stages of processing. At the *first stage*, sensory processing takes place in parallel. For example, in vision, features may be processed at various spatial scales, and these features may also be mapped onto stored representations. Subsequently, the stimuli may be consolidated into a representation in short-term memory, to enable the item to be reported (e.g. see Duncan and Humphreys, 1989). The process of consolidating an item into short-term memory may consume resources, and so is limited to just a few items at a time and also it may be limited across a given time period. Ward and colleagues (Ward, Duncan and Shapiro, 1996) termed this the *attentional dwell time*. In the RSVP procedure, a T2 item appearing shortly after T1 has been presented may suffer because of the attentional dwell time consumed by T1, and this may induce an AB because there are not sufficient resources available to consolidate the representation of T2. This account differs from the inhibition account on at least one critical point, which relates to the amount of processing conducted on T2. While the *inhibition account* assumes that there should be minimal process-ing of stimuli subject to an AB, the account in terms of the *attentional dwell time* does allow stimuli subject to the blink to be processed, at least to the extent that stimuli can activate stored representations during the first stage of processing (see above). Shapiro *et al.* (1997b) carried out a study providing evidence in favour of the *interference account* by the use of a priming measure. They proposed that 'if the attentional blink prevents processing of further stimuli at very early levels of the visual system, then targets missed during the attentional blink should be unable to prime subsequent targets. If, however, priming can be observed, some degree of processing must take place during the attentional blink' (Shapiro *et al.*, 1997b, p. 95). In line with their reasoning, priming effects for missed target letters were observed. In further support of this finding, Maki, Frigen and Paulson (1997) established that non-critical items in the RSVP did in fact prime a semantically associated T2 which were present either during or after the AB. Maki *et al.* (1997) concluded that word meaning does in fact survive the AB.

The Two-Stage Model

A somewhat different model of the AB was offered by Chun and Potter (1995). Here, the identification of targets in the RSVP procedure is held to occur in two chronological stages. In *Stage 1*, there is an immediate detection of the item, but the representation that is encoded can be easily forgotten or erased as subsequent RSVP stimuli are presented. In *Stage 2* (a capacity-limited operation), a complete report of the target must be processed and consolidated further. When Stage 2 is busy with a target, a second target cannot be consolidated (Chun and Potter, 1995; Jolicaeur, 1998). Consequently, the AB happens due to decay of T2 representation occurring while T1's processing is finished, so if an individual takes longer on T1 then the blink will increase resulting in a great delay imposed on T2. In contrast, the *inhibition* model suggests that there is a competition between the items in both perceptual and semantic processing resources, while the *interference model* proposes that the stimuli is processed and identified before selection, the theory suggests that participants select between possible targets from the succeeding presentation in the RSVP stream with the help of preset filters, where items presented during the AB are highly processed and compete in VSTM for identification (Shapiro *et al.*, 1994). The AB reflects the competition of several items in the RSVP stream resulting in a delay in reporting T2 (Isaak, Shapiro and Martin, 1999).

Event-Related Potentials and Functional Magnetic Resonance Imaging Research

As mentioned above, experiments have produced evidence that there is indeed a semantic processing of items presented during the AB (e.g. Luck, Vogel and Shapiro, 1996; Maki *et al.*, 1997; Shapiro *et al.*, 1997b). Recent research of the AB has now utilized more advanced electrophysiological techniques such as event-related potentials (ERPs) and functional magnetic resonance imaging (fMRI). We will briefly go through some of the most recent findings adding support to assumptions made by the *interference theory*.

ERPs (for more detail on ERP, see Luck and Vogel, 2001) are a useful tool when looking at processing of stimuli in the RSVP paradigm. Resent research have been interested in looking at ERP waves in paradigms where stimuli is processed but not overtly reported by the participant (see Hillyard and Picton, 1987; Luck and Girelli, 1998 for more details). In these types of paradigms (RSVP), a comparison is made between ERP waveforms of stimuli detection versus no detection of stimuli. ERP waveforms are measured in positive and negative deflections termed 'peaks' 'waves' or 'components', they are often abbreviated with an 'N' or a 'P' (as a sign of positive or negative) followed by a number (signifying timing, for example 'P1' for the first positive peak or 'P110' signifying exact timed latency of 100 milliseconds; Vogel, Luck and Shapiro, 1998). Vogel *et al.* (1998) conducted multiple experiments employing ERP providing additional weight to the *interference theory*. In one experiment, they looked at whether AB is a result of 'suppression of sensory processing' (Vogel *et al.*, 1998. p. 1659). The findings suggested that the AB is a reflection of a late processing procedure of the stimuli (i.e. that AB occurs after identification of a stimulus has been accomplished). Further experiments by Vogel *et al.* (1998) looked at the N400[2] component, as this has the ability to look at whether a word presented during the AB is in fact identified, although not overtly reported (Besson *et al.*, 1992), which is precisely what they found. The results suggest T2 words presented for the duration of the AB was 'identified to the point of meaning extraction' (Vogel *et al.*, 1998. p. 1664). In light of their findings mentioned above suggesting that stimuli is fully identified during the AB and that it is processed at least to a stage of word recognition during the AB, a final experiment looking at the P300[3] component (suggested to indicate whether a stimulus is processed in working memory; Donchin, 1981; Donchin and Coles, 1988) was conducted. The aim of this experiment was to investigate whether there is a specified time within the processing of stimuli where processing seizes during the AB interval. The result confirmed their hypothesis where the P300 component was fully suppressed throughout the AB interval. Vogel *et al.* (1998) suggest that this indicates the AB defect arises at the stage of working memory. They concluded, 'our experiments provide strong evidence that the AB reflects an impairment that arises after stimulus processing has been completed, probably at the stage of working memory' (Vogel *et al.*, 1998. p. 1668).

The notion of working memory has also been suggested in previous RSVP research by Potter (1976) using pictures as stimuli. Potter (1976) reported that if participants had to both perceive images and store them in working memory when presented at high speed, an elevated rate of inaccuracy was observed. Potter (1976) suggested that this may be due to overload in working memory during the RSVP which might be an indication that attentional selection is important in relation to deciding which information is encoded or consolidated in working memory.

---

[2]N400 is used to determine whether a stimulus has been identified even though it is not reported (Vogel *et al.*, 1998). N400 is extremely sensitive to the level of mismatch between, for example, a word and a previously already established semantic context (e.g. Besson, Kutas and Van Petten, 1992).

[3]P300 component is believed to be related to updating of working memory (Donchin, 1981; Donchin and Coles, 1988). If P300 wave is high, it indicates that working memory is active, if it is low or non-existent, it indicates that working memory is not active.

Resent research by Kranczioch, Debener and Engel (2003) confirm the findings of Vogel *et al.* (1998). They compared ERP pattern of detected and missed T2s presented within the AB interval. The result showed that detected T2 produced a P3 component, while missed T2 did not. Similarly to Vogel *et al.* (1998), this indicates that detected T2 does enter 'awareness' (Vogel *et al.*, 1998).

As mentioned, fMRI studies have also been conducted investigating the AB. Marois, Yi and Chun (2004) examined the AB by looking at consciously versus non-consciously perceived T2 items. Stimuli used included faces (T1), scenes (T2) and scrambled scenes (distractors). One of their findings suggested that dependent on whether T2 was overtly reported or not elicited differential activation in lateral frontal cortex where correctly detected T2 compared with missed T2 and control (T2 not present) increased the hemodynamic response. Another recent fMRI study by Kranczioch, Debener, Schwarzbach, Goebel and Engel (2005) produced slightly differential results than did the study by Marois *et al.* (2004). Kranczioch *et al.* (2005) looked at letters presented successively where T2 was either presented within the AB span, outside the AB span or not at all. The results revealed a substantial activation within the frontal and parietal cortices when T2 was detected relative to when it is missed. In contrast, when T2 was missed, a substantial increase in occipitotemporal regions was found compared to detected T2. Furthermore, increased activity was also found in several frontal and parietal areas when T2 was missed as opposed to when no target was presented. Interestingly, when T2 was detected, there was a decrease in areas known to be involved in emotional processing. These findings were interpreted to reflect the predominant role of the frontal cortex in selecting consciously perceived items. Similar finding were also reported by Marois, Chun and Gore (2000).

Attentional Capture and the Attentional Blink

Whichever account is put forward for the AB, the procedure provides a means of examining attentional limitations on visual information processing, either on the processing of T1 or on T2. Interestingly, there is some work indicating that an AB can be induced when T1 stimuli capture attention and are processed automatically. If there is capture of a T1 stimulus based on its sexual interest to a participant, then it is possible that a sexually interesting stimulus can induce an AB, and this might provide a measure of sexual interest. If this is truly an attentional capture effect, then an AB may be induced by a critical stimulus even when that item does not have to be reported – providing a way of examining attentional capture unmediated by demand characteristics of having to respond to T1.

There is evidence that automatic attentional capture can occur in a variety of experimental paradigms, and under these conditions, an irrelevant stimulus can affect report of stimuli relevant for the actual response. Many studies have examined effects of bottom-up salience – e.g. when a distractor is unique colour in a display (Theeuwes, 1992). However, capture effects may be based not only on bottom-up stimulus salience but also on other factors such as the emotional context of the stimulus, whether the stimulus is part of the observer's 'set' and whether people have been used to responding to that stimulus. For example, Harris and

Pashler (2004) showed that emotional words, when occasionally presented in visual displays, attracted attention and prevented participants from reporting other target stimuli. Folk, Leber and Egeth (2002) examined the effects of attentional set on the AB. They had participants reporting a red letter in an RSVP stream of grey letters. A grey letter preceding the red target could be surrounded by four small dots, which were either red or green in colour. Folk *et al.* (2002) found that report of the red target decreased if the dots appearing earlier were red compared with when they were green (these results reversed for green target letters, indicating that it was not the bottom-up saliency of either the red or green dots that captures attention). These results suggest that an AB was induced by a first stimulus capturing attention, and this occurred when the first stimulus matched the 'set' the participants had for the task (attend to red or attend to green). Kyllingsbæk, Schneider and Bundesen (2001) also showed similar capture effects from stimuli that people had frequently responded to as targets in a search task. If, as these results suggest, attention can be captured by stimuli that are emotionally salient, part of an attentional set or frequently responded to as target, then it is possible that attentional capture in an AB procedure may provide one way to examine abnormal sexual interest in individuals. For example, people with an abnormal sexual interest in a particular type of person (e.g. young children) might find pictures of such individuals emotionally charged, and so allocate attention to such stimuli even if they are irrelevant to a given task. Similarly, the strong sexual interest may form part of an individual's long-term 'set' for attending to the world, tuning in the individual to attend to these stimuli rather than others. Or, the strong sexual interest may lead to particular stimuli being viewed regularly, and, due to this, the stimuli may then capture attention. Whichever is the case, it can be predicted that a stimulus linked to abnormal sexual interest may trigger a relatively strong AB in individuals. Also, judging from the study of Folk *et al.* (2002), this may even occur when the stimulus itself does not have to be responded to, though the effects might be enhanced when responses to the stimulus are required (e.g. when the stimulus of sexual interest is T1 in an AB procedure).

On the other hand, Shapiro *et al.* (1997a) failed to find strong effects from an emotionally salient stimulus as T1 (the participant's own name) in an AB procedure, but they did when that stimulus appeared as T2. In the latter case, there was a reduced AB (i.e. better report of T2) when participants saw their own names relative to when they saw the name of another person. This suggests that an alternative way to use the blink paradigm to examine sexual interest would be to examine recovery from the blink as a function of whether T2 is of sexual interest or not – though this might be affected by demand characteristics of reporting T2. Anderson (2005) conducted an experiment employing the RSVP with sexually arousing words as T2. He found sexually arousing words elicited a smaller AB effect compared to neutral T2 words (i.e. higher accuracy reporting sexually arousing words compared to neutral words).

The converse of the idea that stimuli which capture attention induce a large AB is that stimuli who require minimal resources to process should generate only a weak AB (Anderson, 2005). Results consistent with this have been reported by Olivers and Nieuwenhuis (2005). These authors demonstrated that the AB was reduced when participants were encouraged into a relaxed mood state, for example by listening to music that they liked. They suggest that being in a relaxed state enabled participants to adopt a broader span of attention, so that more resources were available for stimulus processing. According to this idea a stimulus of sexual interest could have a different effect on a participant, with a reduced AB being generated if a sexually interesting picture induces a good mood. Nevertheless, the task may still provide an indirect index of sexual interest. This effect of mood may reflect a modulation at a neural level by activity in the locus coeruleus, as suggested by Nieuwenhuis, Gilzenrat, Holmes and Cohen (2005) and simulated in recent computational models of the blink (e.g. Bowman and Wyble, 2007; Nieuwenhuis *et al.*, 2005; Dehaene, Sergent and Changeux, 2003).

ASSESSING SEXUAL OFFENDERS USING THE RSVP PARADIGM

Can the blink be applied to measure abnormal sexual interest? Beech, Kalmus, Tipper, Baudouin, Humphreys and Flak (2008) examined the AB with sexual offenders, contrasting pictures of children with pictures of animals as T1. If there was sexual interest to the picture of the child, then an AB may be induced, due to greater attentional engagement on the child T1 than the animal T1. The data matched this proposal. When T1 was a picture of a child, a greater deficit in reporting of T2 was detected for the sexual offenders. This effect was not found in a normal control group of non-sexual offenders.

In order to further establish the RSVP procedure as being sensitive to sexual interest, a few other unpublished studies have been conducted using normative samples of heterosexual males and females comparing whether images of males and females induce a larger AB compared with animals. For example, if males have stronger attraction to images of females compared with images of males and animals, then male participants should show a greater AB when images of the females are T1 as opposed to males and animals; the opposite may apply for female participants.

Grace (2005) examined the RSVP procedure with T1 images of clothed and unclothed males/females on a sample of heterosexual male and female college students. There was an overall significant difference in the AB induced by clothed and unclothed images, with images of nude females eliciting a particularly large blink in males (in contrast, images of nude males did not elicit a greater AB than images of nude females in female participants). Hudson (2005), in contrast, failed to establish differences between images of clothed males and females as T1, on male and female participants, suggesting that the images need to be potent cues for sexual interest to be effective.

PROBLEMS WITH THE RSVP PARADIGM

Anxiety

One concern raised with the RSVP paradigm is the potential issue of anxiety that child molesters may exhibit while viewing images of children – perhaps because for these individuals sexual interest is associated with punishment and imprisonment. Anxiety, cued by the pictures, may even have an effect independent of the individual's direct sexual interest in a particular image, making interpretation of any positive result difficult (is a given individual showing increased sexual interest or increased anxiety, associated with the images?). To test this, we are currently measuring anxiety alongside measuring the AB in offenders. We will ask whether anxiety levels predict any enhancement of the AB to pictures of children, in these individuals.

Faking

Another important issue in relation to assessment tools for child sex offenders is the problem of faking. For example, it has been argued that faking can affect the PPG measures of sexual interest (e.g. Henson and Rubin, 1971; Laws and Rubin, 1969; Laws and Gress, 2004; Laws and Holmen, 1978), and an important question is whether the same may hold for the AB. The AB is revealed by worse identification of the T2 stimulus after a T1 that draws sexual interest. To fake the effect of the test, participants would have to realize this and not report the T2 after the 'control' T1 stimulus (the animal). This is possible. However, we are also interested in whether an AB could be induced by a sexually interesting T1 stimulus even when only T2 has to be reported (see Beech et al., 2008). Here participants do not have to make a response to T1, reducing the possibility that they could alter their responses to T2 based on noticing consciously what T1 was. Further work is needed to verify this. It would also be interesting to examine whether sexually arousing T1 images could induce an AB even when they are not correctly/consciously identified – it is possible that the image could draw attention to itself unconsciously, even if it is not available for perceptual report (e.g. when participants miss-classify the T1 item). This should be tested under conditions in which T1 report is made difficult.

Procedural Problems

One other concern in relation to the RSVP procedure is the problem of fatigue and tiredness associated with conducting the experiment. The rapid visual presentation conditions make the task quite demanding on an individual's attentional span. This could add noise to any measurement, making it less diagnostic of abnormal sexual interest. Work here is required to examine whether the effect of sexual images on the AB is found with the stimuli presented in short blocks of trials, to maximize the participant's attention throughout.

CLINICAL IMPLICATIONS

The preliminary research conducted to date indicates that the RSVP procedure could potentially be a useful tool in assessing sexual preference in child molesters. It is also possible that this paradigm could be used as an alternative to PPG due to the problems inherent in the latter procedure. The benefit of the RSVP procedure is that it can be implemented in any setting with access to a computer and it is very easy for the researcher to comprehend and use. This makes it very useful, particularly as it is relatively simple for the participant to complete and may cause less stress or upset than the PPG, whilst at the same time being more difficult to fake.

CONCLUSIONS

Previous research has looked into benefits and downfalls of the PPG, and researchers have identified a need for an easy accessible assessment tool without the problems inherent in the PPG. The RSVP procedure is a new way of assessing deviant sexual interest in child sex offenders, linked to the consolidation of information in short-term memory (Beech *et al.*, 2008) and/or to interference from the time taken for attention to be disengaged from T1 (the attentional dwell time). Thus, if there is an effect of sexual interest in relation to the image shown as the T1 stimulus, then it becomes possible to link it to an explicit theory of visual selection. Further work is now required both to establish the robustness of the effect and to evaluate the conditions under which it occurs.

REFERENCES

Abel, G.G., Huffman, J., Warberg, B. and Holland, C.L. (1998) Visual reaction time and plethysmography as measures of sexual interest in child molesters. *Sexual Abuse: A Journal of Research and Treatment*, **10**, 81–95.

Anderson, A. (2005) Affective influences on the attentional dynamics supporting awareness. *Journal of Experimental Psychology: General*, **134**, 258–81.

Beech, A.R., Kalmus, E., Tipper, S.P., Baudouin, J.-Y., Humphreys, G.W. and Flak, V.E. (2008) Children induce an enhanced attentional blink in child molesters. *Psychological Assessment*, **20**, 397–402.

Besson, M., Kutas, M. and Van Petten, C. (1992) An event-related potential (ERP) analysis of semantic congruity and repetition effects. *Journal of Cognitive Neuroscience*, **4**, 132–49.

Bowman, H. and Wyble, B. (2007) The simultaneous type, serial token model of temporal attention and working memory. *Psychological Review*, **40**, 38–70.

Broadbent, D.E. and Broadbent, M.H. (1987) From detection to identification: response to multiple targets in rapid serial visual presentation. *Perception and Psychophysics*, **42**, 105–13.

Chun, M.M. and Potter, M.C. (1995) A two-stage model for multiple target detection in rapid serial visual presentation. *Journal of Experimental Psychology: Human Perception and Performance*, **21**, 109–27.

Dehaene, S., Sergent, C. and Changeux, J.-P. (2003) A neuronal network model linking subjective reports and objective physiological data during conscious perception. *Proceedings of the National Academy of Sciences, USA*, **100**, 8520–25.

Donchin, E. (1981) Surprise! . . . Surprise? *Psychophysiology*, **18**, 493–513.

Donchin, E. and Coles, M.G.H. (1988) Is the P300 component a manifestation of context updating. *Behavioral Brain Science*, **11**, 357–74.

Duncan, J. and Humphreys, G.W. (1989) Visual search and stimulus similarity. *Psychological Review*, **96**, 433–58.

Fisher, D. (1994) Adult sex offenders: who are they? Why and how do they do it? in *Sexual Offending Against Children: Assessment and Treatment of Male Abusers* (eds T. Morrison, M. Erooga and R.C. Beckett), Routledge, London, pp. 1–24.

Flak, V., Beech, A. and Fisher, D. (2007) Forensic assessment of sexual interests: the current position. *Issues in Forensic Psychology*, **6**, 70–83.

Folk, C.L., Leber, A.B. and Egeth, H.E. (2002) Made you blink! Contingent attentional capture produces a spatial blink. *Perception & Psychophysics*, **64**, 741–53.

Freund, K. (1978) A conceptual framework for the study of anomalous erotic preferences. *Journal of Sex and Marital Therapy*, **4**, 3–10.

Glasgow, D., Osbourne, A. and Croxon, J. (2003) An assessment tool for investigating paedophile sexual interest using viewing time: an application of single case research methodology. *British Journal of Learning Disabilities*, **31**, 96–102.

Giotakis, O. (2005) A combination of viewing reaction time and incidental learning task in child molesters, rapists, and control males and females. *European Journal of Sexology, Sexologies*, **54**, 13–22.

Grace, J. (2005) Measure of sexual interest in a student sample by the use of Rapid Serial Visual Presentation procedure. Unpublished undergraduate thesis, University College Cork, Ireland.

Gray, N.S., Brown, A.S., MacCulloch, M.J., Smith, J. and Snowden, R.J. (2005) An implicit test of the associations between children and sex in pedophiles. *Journal of Abnormal Psychology*, **114**, 304–8.

Gress, C. (2006a) *Delays in Cognitive Processing When Viewing Sexual Material: An Investigation of Two Response Latency Measures*. Paper presented at the 2nd International Summer Conference: Research in Forensic Psychiatry, Regensburg, Germany.

Gress, C. (2006b) *Delays in cognitive processing when viewing sexual material: An investigation of two response latency measures*. Unpublished doctoral thesis, University of Victoria, Victoria, BC.

Gress, C.L.Z. (2001) *An Evaluation of a Sexual Interest Assessment Tool*. Unpublished manuscript, University of Victoria, Canada.

Hanson, R.K. and Bussière, M.T. (1998) Predicting recidivism: a meta-analysis of sexual offender recidivism studies. *Journal of Consulting and Clinical Psychology*, **66**, 348–62.

Hanson, R.K. and Morton-Bourgon, K.E. (2004) *Predictors of Sexual Recidivism: An Updated Meta-Analysis* (Research Rep. No. 2004-02) Public Safety and Emergency Preparedness Canada, Ottawa, Canada.

Harris, C.R. and Pashler, H. (2004) Attention and the processing of emotional words and names – not so special after all. *Psychological Science*, **15**, 171–8.

Harris, G.T. Rice, M.E., Quinsey, V.L. and Chaplin, T.C. (1996) Viewing time as a measure of sexual interest among child molesters and heterosexual men. *Behaviour Research and Therapy*, **34**, 389–94.

Hart, S.D., Kropp, P.R., Laws, D.R., Klaver, J., Logan, C. and Watt, K.A. (2003) *The Risk for Sexual Violence Protocol (RSVP): Structured Professional Guidelines for Assessing Risk of Sexual Violence*. The Mental Health, Law & Policy Institute, Simon Fraser University, Burnaby, BC.

Henson, D.E. and Rubin, H.B. (1971) Voluntary control of eroticism. *Journal of Applied Behavior Analysis*, **4**, 38–44.

Hillyard, S.A. and Picton, T.W. (1987) Electrophysiology of cognition, in *Handbook of Physiology: Section 1. The Nervous System: Volume 5. Higher Functions of the Brain. Part 2* (ed. F. Plum), Waverly Press, Bethesda, MD, pp. 519–84.

Hudson, T. (2005) Further development of an information processing assessment of sexual interest. Unpublished undergraduate thesis, University of Birmingham, UK.

Isaak, M.I., Shapiro, K.L. and Martin, J. (1999) The attentional blink reflects retrieval competition among multiple RSVP items: tests of the interference model. *Journal of Experimental Psychology: Human Perception and Performance*, **25**, 1774–92.

Jolicaeur, P. (1998) Modulation of the attentional blink by on-line response selection: evidence from speeded and unspeeded Task-sub-1 decisions. *Memory and Cognition*, **2**, 1014–32.

Kalmus, E. and Beech, A.R. (2005) Forensic assessments of sexual interest: a review. *Aggression and Violent Behavior*, **10**, 193–217.

Kranczioch, C., Debener, S. and Engel, A.K. (2003) Event-related potential correlates of the attentional blink phenomenon. *Cognitive Brain Research*, **17**, 177–87.

Kranczioch, C., Debener, S., Schwarzbach, J., Goebel, R. and Engel, A.K. (2005) Neural correlates of conscious perception in the attentional blink. *NeuroImage*, **24**, 704–14.

Kyllingsbæk, S., Schneider, W.X. and Bundesen, C. (2001) Automatic attraction of attention to former targets in visual displays of letters. *Perception and Psychophysics*, **63**, 85–98.

Laws, D.R. and Gress, L.Z.C (2004) Seeing things differently: the viewing time alternative to penile plethysmography. *Legal and Criminological Psychology*, **9**, 183–96.

Laws, D.R. and Holmen, M.L. (1978) Sexual response faking by pedophiles. *Criminal Justice and Behavior*, **5**, 343–56.

Laws, D.R. and Rubin, H.B. (1969) Instructional control of an autonomic response. *Journal of Applied Behavior Analysis*, **2**, 93–9.

Luck, S.J. and Girelli, M. (1998) Electrophysiological approaches to the study of selective attention in the human brain, in *The Attentive Brain* (ed. R. Parasuraman), MIT Press, Cambridge, MA, pp. 71–94.

Luck, S.J. and Vogel, E.K. (2001) Multiple sources of interference in dual-task performance, in *The Limits of Attention. Temporal Constraints in Human Information Processing* (ed. K.L. Shapiro), New York, Oxford, pp. 124–40.

Luck, S.J., Vogel, E.K. and Shapiro, K.L. (1996) Word meanings can be accessed but not reported during the attentional blink. *Nature*, **382**, 616–8.

Maki, W.S., Frigen, K. and Paulson, K. (1997) Associative priming by targets and distractors during rapid serial visual presentation: does word meaning survive the attentional blink? *Journal of Experimental Psychology: Human Perception and Performance*, **23**, 1014–34.

Marois, R., Chun, M.M. and Gore, J.C. (2000) Neural correlates of the attentional blink. *Neuron*, **28**, 299–308.

Marois, R., Yi, D.J. and Chun, M.M. (2004) The neural fate of consciously perceived and missed events in the attentional blink. *Neuron* **41**, 465–72.

Marshall, W.L. and Fernandez, Y.M. (2000) Phallometric testing with sexual offenders: limits to its value. *Clinical Psychology Review*, **20**, 807–22.

Mihailides, S., Devilly, G. and Ward, T. (2004) Implicit theories in sexual offenders: an experimental study. *Sexual Abuse: Journal of Research and Treatment*, **16**, 333–50.

Nieuwenhuis, S., Gilzenrat, M.S., Holmes, B.D. and Cohen, J.D. (2005) The role of the locus coeruleus in mediating the attentional blink: a neurocomputational theory. *Journal of Experimental Psychology: General*, **134**, 291–307.

Olivers, C.N.L. and Nieuwenhuis, S. (2005) The beneficial effect of concurrent task-irrelevant mental activity on temporal attention. *Psychological Science*, **16**, 265–9.

Potter, M.C. (1976) Short-term conceptual memory for pictures. *Journal of Experimental Psychology: Human Learning and Memory*, **2**, 509–22.

Raymond, J.E., Shapiro, K.L. and Arnell, K.M. (1992) Temporary suppression of visual processing in an RSVP task; An attentional blink? *Journal of Experimental Psychology: Human Perception and Performance*, **18**, 849–60.

Reeves, A. and Sperling, G. (1986) Attention gating in short term visual memory. *Psychological Review*, **93**, 180–206.

Rempel, J. and Serafini, T. (1995) Factors influencing the activities that people experience as sexually arousing: a theoretical model. *Canadian Journal of Human Sexuality*, **4**, 3–14.

Rosenzweig, S. (1942) The photoscope as an objective devise for evaluating sexual interest. *Psychosomatic Medicine*, **4**, 150–7.

Santtila, P., Mokros, A. and Viljanen, K. (2006) *Using the Choice Reaction Time Task to Detect Sexual Interest: A Feasibility Study Using Gay and Straight Men*. Paper presented at the 2nd International Summer Conference: Research in Forensic Psychiatry, Regensburg, Germany.

Shapiro, K.L. (2001) *The Limits of Attention. Temporal Constraints in Human Information Processing*, Oxford, New York.

Shapiro, K.L. Caldwell, J. and Sørensen, R.E. (1997a) Personal names and the attentional blink: a visual 'cocktail party' effect. *Journal of Experimental Psychology: Human Perception and Performance*, **23**, 504–14.

Shapiro, K.L., Driver, J., Ward, R. and Sørensen, R.E. (1997b) Priming from the attentional blink: a failure to extract visual tokens but not visual types. *Psychological Science*, **8**, 95–100.

Shapiro, K.L. and Raymond, J.E. (1994) Temporal allocation of visual attention: inhibition or interference? in *Inhibitory Processes in Attention, Memory, and Language* (eds D. Dagenbach and T.H. Carr), Academic Press, San Diego, CA, pp. 151–88.

Shapiro, K.L., Raymond, J.E. and Arnell, K.M. (1994) Attention to visual pattern information produces the attentional blink in rapid serial visual presentation. *Journal of Experimental Psychology: Human Perception and Performance*, **20**, 357–71.

Singer, B. (1984) Conceptualizing sexual arousal and attraction. *The Journal of Sex Research*, **20**, 230–40.

Smith, P. and Waterman, M. (2004) Processing bias for sexual material: the Emotional Stroop and sexual offenders. *Sexual Abuse: A Journal of Research and Treatment*, **16**, 163–71.

Theeuwes, J. (1992) Perceptual selectivity for color and form. *Perception & Psychophysics*, **51**, 599–606.

Vogel, E.K., Luck, S.J. and Shapiro, K.L. (1998) Electrophysiological evidence for a postperceptual locus of suppression during the attentional blink. *Journal of Experimental Psychology: Human Perception and Performance*, **24**, 1656–74.

Ward, R., Duncan, J. and Shapiro, K. (1996) The slow time-course of visual attention. *Cognitive Psychology*, **30**, 79–109.

Weichselgartner, E. and Sperling, G. (1987) Dynamics of automatic and controlled visual attention. *Cognitive Psychology*, **30**, 79–109.

Wright, L. and Adams, H. (1994) Assessment of sexual preference using choice reaction time task. *Journal of Psychopathology and Behavioural Assessment*, **16**, 221–31.

Zamansky, H.S. (1956) A technique for measuring homosexual tendencies. *Journal of Personality*, **24**, 436–48.

Chapter 8

ASSESSING SEXUAL INTEREST WITH THE EMOTIONAL STROOP TEST

PAUL SMITH

Department of Psychology, Leeds Trinity and All Saints, Leeds, UK

The Stroop colour-naming task (Stroop, 1935) is one of the most robust experimental tasks in the psychology laboratory. There can be few psychology graduates in the world today who were not introduced to the Stroop as a cognitive laboratory practical due to its remarkable ability to identify information-processing differences between groups of participants. Given a careful and considered choice of stimulus materials which are based on sound theoretical reasons, and with the appropriate experimental controls almost invariably a Stroop 'effect' is generated. There are currently in the region of 1000 published peer-reviewed articles on the Stroop effect with around 425 of them being articles focusing on the use of the Stroop task to study individual differences, and John Ridley Stroop's original paper published in *The Journal of Experimental Psychology* in 1935 is one of the most cited papers in the history of psychology.

The Stroop test requires participants to be shown words printed in a variety of colours (originally the word were presented in blocks but more recently single word presentations are the norm), and they are instructed to name the colour of the word (and not name the word itself). Participants are instructed to respond as quickly as possible whilst ignoring the word meaning. As word reading is an automatic process, the latency of the naming response is seen to reflect the extent to which the processing of word meaning takes place. Stroop interference occurs when respondents are slower to colour name a stimulus class; conversely, Stroop facilitation occurs when respondents are quicker to colour name a stimulus class. In the Stroop task, participants might be presented with the following series of stimuli. First, 'XXXXX', followed by the word 'TABLE' followed by the word 'GREEN' in a variety of colours. As 'XXXXX' has no meaning (i.e. there is no reading process), the participant should be able to name the colour of this presentation quickly. The word TABLE, of course, does have a meaning and the participant will read this word, hence a slightly slower time to name the colour of this presentation. Finally, the word GREEN which has a meaning and furthermore it is a colour. The participant is normally slowest to colour name this presentation due to the increased sophistication of the target. Researchers do not present colour words in the matching colour, as they are unable to determine whether the participant has simply read the word or named the colour! An easy way to think about this is to compare the two processes involved in the Stroop. One is reading of the words and the other is the colour naming of the words. For most of us, reading is a completely non-conscious automatic process as we go about our daily lives; conversely, colour naming is not.

WHAT IS THE STROOP EFFECT?

There are several alternate explanations for the Stroop effect, and without careful inspection many of them can appear to be essentially arguing the same thing. Stroop (1935) felt that relative speed-of-processing accounted for the phenomenon. On the basis of the notion that words are read faster than colours are named the Stroop effect is the consequence of the competition between these two processes. Automaticity explanations focus on the idea that the processing of one dimension requires more attention than the processing of the other dimension. Colour naming being seen as more demanding of attentional resources than reading (MacLeod and Dunbar, 1988). Stage of perceptual encoding explanations differs in focus in that rather than seeing interference occurring at the late selection stage (i.e. competing processes), they postulate that the interference is actually happening at the perceptual encoding stage (Hock and Egeth, 1970). The perceptual encoding of stimuli is slowed by conflicting/incompatible information for the colour word (which is of course not present in the control). Parallel processing models eliminate the sequential processing of early models and argue that cumulative weights (a stable automatic weight and a flexible attentional weight) contribute to a response threshold being reached for the dimension of interest (Logan, 1980). However, none of the explanations can successfully account for all the data to date (MacLeod, 1991; William et al., 1997). Later in the chapter, an information-processing model of offending behaviour that seeks to explain the Stroop effect in more clinical terms and which encompasses these explanations will be outlined.

STROOP VARIANTS

The Stroop task has generated a wide range of variants (see MacLeod, 1991, for a comprehensive review of the literature). Whilst it is beyond the remit of this chapter to cover these variants in detail, given the focus on the emotional Stroop, it is important to at least mention this diversity as this is one of the strengths of the task (the MacLeod article is an excellent starting point for interested readers). The range includes the classic colour–word Stroop, the picture–word Stroop (where the words are embedded in line drawings and the experimental task is to name the picture), auditory analogues (e.g. high or low or left and right for tones), flanker variants (with irrelevant words or letters placed adjacent to the target), global–local Stroop (e.g. the number five made up of smaller letter sevens). In essence, the number of cognitive assessments of competing processes is limited only by the ingenuity of the researcher and there seems no reason why sexual interest should not generate its own novel measures of attentional bias in the future. Crucially, some variants have been found to be especially suitable for use with children and adults with learning difficulties and this may point to methods for the assessment of bias within these groups in forensic settings.

THE EMOTIONAL STROOP

Around a quarter of a century ago, investigators started to use the Stroop and analogous tasks to study information-processing deficits in clinical and community samples as a consequence of emotional disturbance (Williams, Watts, Macleod and Matthews, 1997). The emotional Stroop (Ray, 1979) is based on the notion that participants are further distracted by 'emotional' words. In essence, the emotional valence of the stimuli further increases interference effects when compared to non-emotional (i.e. neutral) words. Pathologies with affective elements such as depression (Gotlib and McCann, 1984), anxiety (MacLeod, Matthews and Tata, 1986), post-traumatic stress disorder (Foa, Feske, Murdock, Kozak and McCarthy, 1991), panic disorder (Ehlers, Margraf, Davies and Roth, 1988), obsessive–compulsive disorder (Foa, Ilal, McCarthy, Shoyer and Murodock, 1993), social phobia (Hope, Rapee, Heimberg and Dombeck, 1990) and specific phobia (Watts, 1986) have been investigated. Participants with affective disorders generally take longer to identify the colour of words with threatening or salient themes than control words when compared with normal participants (Williams, Matthews and MacLeod, 1996; Williams et al., 1997).

Given this robust relationship, some researchers also started looking at individual differences in processing of anger related stimuli. Studies focused on trait and state manipulations of anger. (Trait levels are inferred from self-report questionnaires and state levels are manipulated by experimental procedure such as induction.) High trait anger individuals have been shown to demonstrate Stroop interference in responding to anger words (Eckhardt and Cohen, 1997), threat words (van Honk Tuiten, van den Hout, Putman, de Haan and Stam, 2001a) and angry faces (van Honk, Tuiten, de Haan, Van den Hout and Stam, 2001b). Similar interference was also observed using visual search tasks (Cohen, Eckhardt and Schagat, 1998). Whilst this research was promising, there were some problems. It could not be assumed that the relationship between trait levels of anger and bias performance is identical to that observed in respect of trait levels of anxiety in clinical samples. Firstly, the anger disorders are somewhat nebulous at present with no official diagnostic criteria. Secondly, anger does not underpin aggression in the way that anxiety underpins the anxiety disorders, because we are sure that not all acts of human aggression are accompanied by elevated levels of anger. Furthermore, the non-unitary nature of anxiety (Evenden, 1999) and the complexity of interactions between anxiety and anger (van Honk et al., 2001a, b) also caution against substituting trait anger for trait anxiety in any explanations of bias performance. It would seem clinically unwise to attempt to pathologize anger in all cases and theoretically misleading. Our theoretical understanding of both anger and aggression needs to be substantially advanced before definitive explanations are likely to emerge (Smith and Waterman, 2003).

AGGRESSION AND THE STROOP

In the process of developing a representational model of offending behaviour (Smith, 2003), a series of information-processing studies were carried out by the author to explore relationships between anger, impulsivity and aggression. A variety of cognitive tasks including the dot-probe, themed dot-probes and visual search tasks were utilized in addition to the emotional Stroop. In the initial research (Smith and Waterman, 2003), two studies (a dot-probe and emotional Stroop) examined the effect of presenting aggressively themed words to a group of offenders and undergraduates. Violent offenders (as classified by their index offence) demonstrated significant response biases to aggression words in both tests. This effect was also found in the aggressive undergraduates (as classified by their self-reported anger scores). An important distinction in cognitive performance is that between content-dependent and content-independent tasks (McNally, 1998). Abnormalities in content-dependent performance arise when the participant is presented with information that is salient to their current concerns; abnormalities in content-independent performance arise irrespective of the valence of the information presented. The observation that the violent offenders also demonstrated Stroop interference in naming negative emotion words was consistent with the evidence that anxiety reliably correlates with performance in the emotional Stroop for negatively valenced stimuli (Williams *et al.*, 1997) due to the large number of highly anxious individuals in this group. This was a useful finding as it provides some evidence that the results were not an artefact of the experimental design. Furthermore, the violent and non-violent offenders showed different bias performance dependent on the nature of the target word, again suggesting effects were content-dependent and did not reflect a general retardation of response latency irrespective of stimulus type (a major concern when using forensic samples), this was also supported by the finding that all three groups demonstrated similar levels of interference when presented with colour themed words). This data confirmed the saliency of aggression words to aggressive individuals and suggested that these simple cognitive tests may offer a potential objective measure of assessment in forensic populations.

A follow-up study using a visual search task and a themed dot-probe (Smith and Waterman, 2004a) explored the role of experience and impulsivity within aggression bias using violent and non-violent offenders and a community sample. Violent offenders demonstrated significant response biases to aggression words in both tests. This effect was also found in the aggressive undergraduates (as classified by their self-reports on an aggression scale). These data confirmed the saliency of aggression words to aggressive individuals across populations and emphasized the role of experience in cognitive bias for this type of material. Finally, to explore the role of gender differences, another study was conducted (Smith and Waterman, 2005) to explore sex differences in processing words relating to acts of direct and indirect aggression. This was a response to findings that gender differences in violent populations appeared to be minimized in both subjective self-report and objective cognitive task measures in the previous studies. Using direct and indirect aggression words as targets, it was observed that males demonstrated a perceptual bias for words relating to acts of direct aggression, taking significantly longer to correctly colour name direct aggression words. Females were slower to correctly colour name indirect aggression words but not significantly so. Verbal aggression, as expected, predicted bias performance for indirect aggression words but anger rather than physical aggression was the best predictor of bias for direct aggression words. Gender was a predictor for bias with both sets of words. It was observed that a high level of physical aggression was the best predictor of bias in both males and females.

Taken together these studies suggested that levels of anger, impulsivity and aggression were reflected in bias performance in cognitive tests of attention and that these bias effects were present in both forensic and general populations. This evidence led to consideration of more specific offending behaviours and it was during conversations with psychologists working in HM Prison Service that the idea of extending the research to sexual offenders first emerged.

SEXUAL BEHAVIOUR AND THE STROOP

In comparison to the extensive theoretical work on information-processing deficits in the emotional disorders, there has been comparatively little work in respect of sexual behaviour. Attention, arousal and expectancies have been explored using the dot-probe and emotional Stroop paradigms in normal and sexually dysfunctional males (van den Hout and Barlow, 2000) but until recently not in sexual offenders. It appears that both sexually functional and dysfunctional males demonstrate vigilance for sexual material but that this vigilance is greatest in the functional males. In addition, evidence of processing effects for sexual material has been shown using priming paradigms to introduce sexual content-induced delay (SCID) (Spiering, Everaerd and Elzinga, 2002). These data were interpreted in terms of an information-processing model of sexual arousal (Janssen, Everaerd, Spiering and Janssen, 2000) which conceptualizes sexual response as an interaction of controlled and automatic processing. In terms of information processing or representation activation, there are certain key associations that we can legitimately expect to be present in the neocortex of the sexually aggressive individuals. A person with an extended history of offending behaviour would presumably have many representations that were thematically (cognitively), affectively (emotionally) and behaviourally (physiologically) associated. This relationship between components may well differ depending on the targets of interest and type of offending behaviour. Theoretically, there are clear reasons to expect very real differences to emerge in the cognitive processes of sex offenders as a function of their interests (Abel, Gore, Holland, Camp, Becker and Rathner, 1989; Ward, Hudson, Johnston and Marshall, 1997; Geer, Estupinan and Manguno-Mire, 2000). The learning history would therefore predispose them to perceive, interpret and act upon stimulus configurations on the basis of these experiences. We would then expect such people to demonstrate attentional biases similar to those seen in clinical groups presenting with anxiety and depression if we were to present them with stimuli that were salient to their concerns or interests (McNally, 1998).

Whilst the emotional Stroop can be broadly classified as an attentional methodology in respect of its application to the assessment of deviant interest, there is actually a little more to it. The emotional Stroop is more accurately described as an information-processing measure of sexual interest as the response latency is a function of the processing of the stimuli presented. This processing is not just at the unconscious or perceptual level; due to the distributed nature of cognition and the polymodal nature of sexual representations, representational activation is likely to have both cognitive and affective components very quickly in sexual offenders (much more so than in community controls). The automaticity reflected in the Stroop effect may have important implications for our understanding of offending behaviour. When the participants read the word presented, it activates the representations associated with that word that are based on that individuals previous learning history and is also influenced by their current emotional state. The greater the meaning ascribed to that stimulus word, the greater the interference that will be manifest in the colour-naming task. This information-processing approach is consistent with the role of stimuli in the environment as automatic sources of aggression (Todorov and Bargh, 2002), as representational activity is of course not restricted to activation by simple word presentations. The evidence from current information-processing models of sexual interest also argues for an automatic non-conscious processing of sexual material (Wright and Adams, 1998; Janssen et al., 2000). Trigger stimuli have been argued to increase the chances of aggressive behaviour emerging by chronic accessibility (Dodge and Crick, 1990) and automatic effects on behaviour (Berkowitz, 1990). There seems little reason to suppose that sexual stimuli do not share this quality. This is not to suggest that the words themselves act as primes for offending behaviour but simply that the bias elicited by their presentation reflects the strength and potency of representations associated with the words.

THE PROBLEM OF SEXUAL INTEREST AND VALENCE

In early studies, response latency in the emotional Stroop was calculated by comparing response times to target (affectively valenced) words with neutral words (Williams et al., 1997). However, this is a relatively gross measure of attentional bias as it fails to address the fact that the words differ both semantically and affectively. Consequently, researchers now tend to use affectively similar words as controls for the comparisons to create content-specific bias scores. One might expect a patient with an anxiety disorder to demonstrate negative valence for negative emotional words and also for anxiety- or threat-related words. The content-specific bias scores are calculated by subtracting either the mean reaction time (RT) to emotion (positive or negative) word presentations from the mean RTs to the target word conditions (e.g. adult or child victims). A positive bias score indicated a longer response latency to identify the colour of the word in the target condition when compared to the time taken to identify the colour of the word in the paired emotion condition (positive or negative emotion word). In effect, the researcher can infer how positively or negatively the participant views the word.

However, whilst this is easily implemented in clinical samples (e.g. negative emotion words acting as controls for depression or anxiety words), it is more difficult to address this issue when using words relating to aggressive and/or sexual behaviour. It has been argued that sexual interest is, at the level of the individual, a positive emotional process (Wright and Adams, 1998). However, this is not likely to be the case for all stimulus materials with the victims of sexual crime. Participants can attribute either positive or negative valence to aggression/sexual words and we cannot always identify in advance the direction of this interest. For some individuals the very nature of their crimes may give us a clue as to the directionality we would anticipate for the target stimuli. The attention of a sadist is captured by the word 'hit' because they gain pleasure from the act; the attention of the sadist's victim is also captured by the word 'hit' because they were distressed by the act. Both participants are slowed in the colour-naming task, but we cannot identify the emotional content of the representation activated by the exposure to the word simply the interference it causes. Conversely, if we had a masochistic participant, they also would demonstrate a link between a positive emotional state and the target word. The valence properties of a target word are specific to that individual. Yet it would hold salience for both victim and protagonist in this instance (Riemann and McNally, 1995). Similarly, the child sex offender will find salience in the word 'child' but so will the new parent. Consequently, it is important to stress that the presence of a bias is not a measure of behaviour *per se*, but rather an indicator of meaning ascribed to the target word. The salience of the word is a function of that individuals learning history and a careful consideration of that learning history is essential prior to testing. This also introduces another potential difficulty in that we cannot assume negative or positive valence from the offender undergoing treatment. If, as is hoped, the treatment is having a positive impact on the offender, we might expect some form of affective element (e.g. remorse, guilt or shame) or cognitive restructuring (e.g. availability and rights of women) to now become embedded into that unique representational structure (or more precisely for those representations to change in their potency). Indeed, simply the length of time incarcerated, independent of any treatment programme experience, may change these cognitive associations. Consequently, data analysis needs to consider the response patterns across all target categories if the researcher is to accurately interpret the results of testing on an idiographic basis.

RUNNING AN EMOTIONAL STROOP IN A FORENSIC ENVIRONMENT

It is important to be consistent in the use of computers for running the task. Different models may introduce timing errors, and if using keyboards for motor responses, particular care needs to be taken as some keyboards will also introduce timing errors. Given the reduction in Stroop interference typically observed with manual responses, verbal responses are preferred (MacLeod, 1991). Typically, one specifies the processor, software, screen size, resolution and refresh rate (e.g. stimuli were presented on a Pentium II (233 MHz) laptop computer with a VGA (11.4-inch screen) display and 60-Hz refresh rate). The programs ran under the DOS operating system and the screen resolution was 16 bit (800×600 pixels). Font type and size should also be controlled. Programmes can be easily written using most commercial laboratory software systems such as SuperLab or E-Prime. Participants need to be seated a consistent distance from the screen (normally 70 cm from the screen). Response selection is typically by means of microphone connected to a voice-activated relay key linked to the RS232 or USB port of the laptop computer for verbal responses. The computer will record participants' response time, stimulus configuration (word and colour) and whether their response was correct. Inter-trial intervals should be varied randomly between 500 and 1000 milliseconds and stimulus order should be randomized. (Normally this can be achieved easily by a random seed generator taking timings from the internal clock of the computer.) Stimulus sets should be sufficiently small to minimize participant boredom effects and reduce running time. Normally, between 12 and 25 words per category will suffice.

Given the capacity for elevated levels of depression and anxiety in community samples to impact on Stroop performance, measures of affective functioning should always be administered. It has been estimated that as many as 37% of sentenced prisoners in UK prisons are suffering some form of mental disorder (Gunn, Maden and Swinton, 1991; Birmingham, Gray, Mason and Grubin, 2000) and a study of female remand offenders found nearly 60% with a mental disorder and 11% suffering psychosis (Parsons, Walker and Grubin, 2001). Consequently, these tests need to be used to identify participants for any potential confounding clinical or social biases (i.e. anxiety, depression and social desirability) that may alter response profiles independently of any hypothesized representational bias for the stimulus material. Recommended measures would include the State–Trait Anxiety Inventory (STAI, Spielburger, Gorsuch, Lushene, Vagg and Jacobs, 1983), the Social Desirability Scale (SDS, Crowne and Marlowe, 1964) and the Beck Depression Inventory (BDI, Beck, Ward, Mendelson, Mock and Erbaugh, 1961). These questionnaire measures should be counterbalanced to avoid potential priming of Stroop responses.

Data from trials with errors should be discarded prior to analysis. Using box and whisker plots, you can identify outliers (typically RTs less than 300 ms and greater than 1750–2000 ms) and remove them from the data set. After this, the content-specific bias scores can be calculated and then a full analysis using the depression and anxiety scores as covariates can be run.

THE EMOTIONAL STROOP AND SEX OFFENDERS – PRELIMINARY STUDIES

Smith and Waterman (2004b) conducted a preliminary study in a forensic sample of 10 sex offenders and 10 violent offenders in the United Kingdom. A computerized version of the emotional Stroop task revealed a significant interaction between group membership and word type ($F(4, 72) = 2.41, p = 0.026, \omega^2 = 0.429$).

The large effect size (Kirk, 1996) generated by this small sample was particularly encouraging, as effect size indicates the magnitude of treatment effect independent of sample size.

The sample consisted of five paedophiles (indecent assault) and five rapists (including two serial offenders). The violent sex offenders showed greater Stroop interference for aggressive words ($t[8] = 2.13$, $p < 0.05$, $d = 0.893$). There was no significant difference in the bias scores ($t[8] = 0.134$, $p = 0.21$, $d = 0.814$) for the sexually themed material. This finding was consistent with differential PPG findings for these groups in terms of use of force as an arousing influence. Crucially, it was at odds with their self-reported levels of anger and aggression.

Violent offenders were consistently slower than sexual offenders in colour-naming words across all categories and significantly so for the aggression stimuli. This was consistent with previous research (Smith and Waterman, 2003) in which violent and non-violent offenders consistently demonstrated increased latencies across word classes compared to undergraduate samples. Intriguingly, this effect was much weakened in the sexual offenders, though they in turn were slower than an undergraduate sample tested with the same stimuli. Colour words are usually the stimuli for which participants show the greatest Stroop interference, yet violent offenders were still marginally slower with the aggression words. Again, this was consistent with research using a sample of extremely violent offenders (Smith and Waterman, 2003). With offender samples, there may be interactions between the effects of stimulus salience and subtle neuropsychological impairments (e.g. distractibility and impulsivity). Self-reported levels of impulsivity positively correlated with error rates for the aggression words but not for the sexual words. The majority of aggressive acts can be conceptualized as impulsive, but it is highly unlikely that all deviant sexual behaviour is impulsive. Indeed, some sexual offences clearly require extended planning and delayed gratification.

As both violent and sexual offenders demonstrated some bias for both stimuli, the most parsimonious explanation was that the stimuli were unable to differentiate between the groups. However, as differences had previously emerged for violent material within similar groups (Smith and Waterman, 2003), this seemed unlikely. It had to be considered that the violent offenders were also sexually aggressive, but it seemed more likely that the sexual words also had violent connotations, which recruited attention in the violent offenders. Word selection is fundamental to the strength and direction of any observed bias effects (Williams *et al.*, 1997); although words were independently rated for sexual and aggressive content for this preliminary study, some of the sexual words also had aggressive connotations (e.g. force, slap, penetrate).

This study was replicated using the same stimuli and procedures (Smith, 2006) with another group of 10 offenders (matched as closely as possible to the original group) and a significant main effect of word type ($F(4, 72) = 8.27$, $p = 0.001$, $\omega^2 = 0.315$), and an interaction effect between group and word type ($F(4, 72) = 1.99$, $p = 0.050$, $\omega^2 = 0.100$) was found. Whilst the effect size diminished, it remained significant and moderately large (Kirk, 1996).

A further replication together with a further study including enhancements to address some of the shortcomings of the original was also conducted independently in Canada (Price, 2006). Limitations addressed included collecting more comprehensive sexual histories of participants, the use of a revised word list in the second study to differentiate sexual words into child and adult targets, increased sample size and a vocabulary test. Rapists were significantly slower than the community sample to colour name sexual words and slower, but not significantly slower, compared with the child molesters, violent and non-violent offenders. Unfortunately, using the new word list, there were no significant group differences. In terms of effect size for the replication, the averaged effect size across the two studies was $d = 0.375$, with no significant variability across the two studies. Unfortunately, participant levels of anxiety and depression were not controlled for in these studies and this may account for some of the findings. Nevertheless, the results, although weaker than those found in the Smith and Waterman (2004a) study, were broadly consistent and similar patterns were evident and it was concluded that there are differences in cognitive processing between sexual offenders and non-offenders (Price, 2006).

STRENGTHS OF THE EMOTIONAL STROOP

The millisecond timing measures involved in Stroop responses mean that it is incredibly resilient to faking. A human being cannot consistently control verbal or motor responses over an extended period of stimulus exposures without generating a data set that looks unusual to the administrator of the test. Personal experience within the laboratory and out in the field has shown that neither offenders wishing to 'beat the system' nor community participants instructed to fake good or bad can generate data sets sufficiently consistent across 60 or more trials to remain undetected. Data sets that are unnaturally uniform are generated. Research using trained professional actors attempting to mirror responses for post-traumatic stress disorder (PTSD) patients (Buckley, Galovski, Blanchard and Hickling, 2003) showed an ability to slow responses across all word categories but an inability to mirror response latencies in the illness-specific word classes expected for the PTSD sufferers. As most participants are naïve to the aims of the emotional Stroop task, they are actually ignorant as to how to fake; and even if they deduce it is a response-time focused task, they are likely to be unsure as to whether they need to respond quickly or slowly for the target stimuli. Consequently, when standardized response profiles are established, this makes deception very difficult. There is also physiological and neurological evidence to suggest that autobiographical stimuli actually introduce more disruption when participants attempt deception (Gronau, Ben-Shakhar and Cohen, 2005; Nunez, Casey, Egner, Hare and Hirsch, 1995). It is, of course, possible to produce unusual data sets by the participants attempting the defocusing of their eyes (in an attempt to reduce/remove the automatic response of word reading leaving the colour-naming response unimpaired), but normally this is picked up by inspecting the timings of the data or by casual observation of the participants whilst testing. Again, the timing consistency required by the participant makes it extremely unlikely that such strategies would go undetected. However, in cases where such behaviour is observed or anticipated in advance of testing, the incorporation of some form of ocular monitoring would address this concern.

The emotional Stroop does have one unique property compared with the other measures of attention that can be utilized to assess sexual interest. There is

literature that shows that clinical patients who receive treatment for their pathologies show a reduction in Stroop interference post-treatment for illnesses including
depression (Gotlib and Crane, 1987) and generalized anxiety disorder (Matthews,
Mogg, Kentish and Eysenck, 1995). Whilst it is by no means certain that sexual
interest can be pathologized in all cases, this does raise an interesting possibility
for assessing some elements of treatment effects. Representational restructuring
achieved during treatment interventions may reduce bias effects by changing associations and in effect reducing the saliency of the materials. Now whilst the merit
of attempting to alter saliency (taken as a reflection of sexual preference) is still a
matter of debate (Marshall and Fenandez, 2003), evidence of (1) a transition from
a positive to negative valence for the target materials or (2) a diminished level of
interference from Stroop testing may be of value to clinicians working in the field.
Indeed, as the majority of intervention programmes explicitly see the addressing
of cognitive distortions and the introduction of new schema as a consequence of
treatment, representational change is a de facto result of the treatment. One note of
caution that needs to be stressed is that the research has shown that victims of childhood sexual abuse who have recently been re-victimized showed greater Stroop
interference when presented with sexual threat words compared with other childhood sexual abuse victims (Field, Classen, Butler, Koopman, Zarcome and Spiegel,
2001). Whilst one would not expect incarcerated offenders to have the opportunity to re-offend whilst in prison (and consequently re-instantiate the potency of
the deviant representational structures), there is the chance that extensive use of
deviant fantasy in some offenders may make any cognitive restructuring difficult
to achieve and could actually increase the strength of the pre-existing schema. As
the Stroop measures salience and not behaviour *per se*, it may even be that salience
does not change, but the associated valence does. A final strength, in common with
all the cognitive assessments of deviant interest, is that the same test can be used
with men and women.

POTENTIAL PROBLEMS WITH THE EMOTIONAL STROOP

Picture and word sets do exist for clinical and undergraduate populations (but
only in respect of pathologies such as anxiety, depression, PTSD and phobias), but
there are currently no validated word stimuli sets for use with offenders in respect
of sexual and violent crimes. Word selection may be fundamental to the success
of the tests (Smith and Waterman, 2003; Price, 2006). Poor selection may result
in words that do not discriminate between offenders and community samples,
or are not sensitive enough to discriminate between offender subgroups. Sexual
words are particularly problematic as many of the acts are not unique to offenders
(i.e. it is the context rather than the act which is deviant) and so the words may
not discriminate. Furthermore, one might anticipate age effects given changing
patterns in sexual behaviour over time and some colloquialisms or slang terms
may not be understood across samples.

   To address these concerns, words should be generated during consultations with
forensic psychologists working in the treatment programmes with the offenders
who are to participate. The stimuli should be based on case histories, offence characteristics and clinical interviews with the offender groups of interest. In addition,

focus groups could be held within the prisons with other prisoners undergoing treatment programmes to generate material pertinent to particular subtypes of offenders and to examine patterns and common themes in offender's interest and fantasy. The stimulus word categories should always include deviant and normal sexual behaviours, and positive, negative and neutral valenced material to allow comparisons between bias performances in the tests. The negative and positive affect stimulus words are best taken from a theoretically sound source such as the empirical taxonomy of the affective lexicon derived by Clore, Ortony and Foss (1987). Response latencies for exposure to simple word stimuli are not generally affected by reading levels/intelligence of participants in community populations. Furthermore, the diversity of incarcerated sex offenders means that they are often more similar to the general population than violent offenders in respect of levels of educational ability. Nevertheless, reading levels do need to be carefully identified in all participants prior to testing, and offenders with diagnosed learning difficulties should be excluded from any word-based studies. It seems prudent to suggest that standardized word sets need to be generated for adult and juvenile offenders in respect of both the targeted sexual offending behaviours and the associated counterbalance and filler word conditions.

Words need to be matched for both length and frequency of occurrence (the simplest way is by using reference sources such as Carroll, Davies and Richman, 1971). However, an excellent resource is the Medical Research Council Psycholinguistic database (the interface for which is available from a variety of Internet sites such as www.psych.rl.ac.uk/MRC_Psych_Db.html). This database allows the user to match stimulus words across a wide variety of dimensions including number of letters, phonemes, syllables, written and verbal frequencies, norms, concreteness, imagibility, meaningfulness and age of acquisition. It is also recommended that prior to any pilot studies, researchers present all the stimulus words to a separate panel for additional rating to establish measure of inter-observer rating agreement. This can be measured using either Cohen's (Cohen, 1960) or Fleiss's (1981) kappa, depending on the numbers involved in rating the words. Careful piloting is fundamental to the creation of a robust stimulus set.

There is some evidence to indicate practice effects in Stroop interference (MacLeod, 1991), but due to differing definitions of the level and type of practice employed being studied across a variety of Stroop, tasks results have been inconsistent. Exposure can be seen as a means of developing expertise in the less automatic response; however, repeated exposure to salient offence-related stimuli may not have the same effect. It is therefore important to distinguish at this stage between clinical Stroops and standard individual difference Stroops. This situation is further complicated because comparatively little research has focused on clinical samples with the emotional Stroop. One of the few reported studies using social phobics found that treatment responders show reduced interference and non-responders show increased interference (Mattia, Heimberg and Hope, 1993). One possible explanation is that in non-responders repeat testing increases the association and potency of stimuli. To date, no test–retest studies have been published in respect of offender samples so any comments are speculative. In light of this, the sensible advice is to test infrequently (3–6 months) and closely monitor performance.

EXPLAINING THE STROOP EFFECT FOR SEXUAL INTEREST – RACE

Perception and memory can be seen as embedded overlapping cortical systems (Fuster, 1997). Representations can be seen as the building blocks from which an individual's personality traits emerge, being reflected in their behaviours. A cognitive-representational model of sexual interest would suggest that the representational organization/activation in the trait 'strong' would lead to a restricted choice and uneven prioritization of the available behavioural options in response to stimulus configurations that are deemed potentially of interest in real time and encourage the inappropriate designation of events as arousing and requiring an overtly sexual response. This is a viewpoint similar to the information-processing model of schemas and scripts (Huesmann, 1988, 1998). However, there are differences to the traditional information-processing account. Spreading representational activation is sufficient to drive the system and the levels of activation in themselves are sufficient to elicit behavioural activity and conscious experience. From this perspective, attention becomes the activation of the representational nodes and clusters rather than a discrete cognitive process or component. The greater the level of activation of any particular representation, the greater the level of 'attention' directed at the stimulus. A cognitive-representational model of sexual interest would therefore see both bias performance and self-report as consequences of the same existing representational structures. However, cognitive bias is a relatively pure measure of representational activation due to the automatic non-conscious nature of the response (although of course the colour-naming component must be considered as an integral part of the process being explored).

The initial representation activation is perceptually focused but spreading activation and feedback mechanisms (inter-personal, intra-personal, intra-cognitive and consciousness) facilitate representational divergence. Appraisals are actually reflections of the diversity of representational activation. As more sophisticated representations become active so the apparent complexity of 'appraisal' increases. Distinctions between primary and secondary appraisal (Frijda, 1986) merely reflect levels of activation across representations. At its simplest level, primary appraisal may be seen as the initial perceptual–attentional processing of a stimulus and secondary appraisal as the processing that occurs in the presence of multiple associated activations. This accounts for the temporal sequence often reported in emotion theory. The representation with the strongest level of activation at any one particular moment in time is expressed in behaviour that may or may not be conscious and/or overt. Representational activity is perhaps best compared with an analogy of the light-emitting diode readouts on consumer electronics equipment. Multiple channels are active at any one time and only when the output level on any one channel reaches a critical threshold level does behaviour (potentially) change, and this change can be independent of any conscious experience. More importantly, the dominant channel can switch in a fraction of a second. This is the concatenation process of representational activity. Consciousness is an output not a mediator (i.e. it does not function as a decision maker *per se* but influences representational activity by feedback mechanisms and the subjective experience of events). Representations have both perceptual and processing dimensions.

The RACE model (representation–activation–concatenation–execution), based in part on the data obtained from the emotional Stroop used with sexual and violent offenders, can accommodate the predictions of previous information-processing models of sexual interest and also explain the difference between high and low 'recognizers' of sexual primes more parsimoniously. Representational activity is seen as sufficient to account for all aspects of the individual sexual interest response. In comparison, Speiring, Evereard and Laan (2004) draw a distinction between the role of explicit and implicit memory systems for evaluation and arousal respectively. Transitional states of non-conscious and conscious processing in the arousal process (Speiring *et al.*, 2004) can be subsumed into the representation activation concatenation and execution process (Smith, 2003; Smith and Waterman, under review). Even allowing for the problems in identifying the source of any salience, and discriminating between positive and negative valence associated with salience (McNally, 1998; Spiering *et al.*, 2002) and our current limited understanding of any changes in stimulus salience as a consequence of either treatment or time, there may be great potential in this research – the Stroop task being seen as tapping directly into the perception–representation–activation stage of the model.

CLINICAL IMPLICATIONS OF THE EMOTIONAL STROOP

As the representations themselves are envisaged as comprising of cognitive, physiological and behavioural components, there are clear implications for interventions aimed at reducing sexual offending behaviour. Already researchers have speculated about the existence of discrete cognitive and non-cognitive routes for information in a variety of pathologies (Williams *et al.*, 1997; Power and Dalgliesh, 1997) which interestingly bears a resemblance to some of the ideas from current information-processing models of sexual interest (Speiring *et al.*, 2004, 2006). The representational model of sexual interest presented here would indicate that clinical and therapeutic interventions need to be considered that address all three components involved in the target behaviour; however, this does not negate the possibility that in some instances one particular element may be dominant. One problem with cognitive-based interventions is that it is almost impossible to identify why they work with some patients and not with others. The model identifies that if the dominant component in a cluster of representations associated with a deviant behaviour (e.g. sexual offending) is physiological or behavioural then cognitive interventions will only impact insofar as they exert an indirect effect upon the physiological and behavioural components. Furthermore, interventions would need to discriminate as to whether the representational drivers for the behaviour were operating principally at the perceptual level or at a later level of activation.

That is not to say that for the majority of individuals the behaviour probably originates from all three components; nevertheless, if the individual's antisocial activities are principally driven by physiological arousal then any treatment that effectively ignores this component is unlikely to prove successful. Given this framework, cross-validation with PPG studies is a matter of some interest and may help drive our understanding of the cognitive structures that underpin the offending behaviour forward.

Accepting the apparent differences between violent offenders and sex offenders (Gudjonsson and Sigurdsson, 2000), it may be that tests like these can be used to explore affective responses more directly, without the influence of social desirability inherent to self-report measures. Additionally, given sufficient biographical information on a patient, it might prove possible to identify elements that can be introduced as word stimuli to enable testing for specific dysfunctions or deviances, and to any monitor changes related to cognitive restructuring during therapy. This work could be carried out across cohorts or on an individual level. For example, Smith (2003) tested several female arsonists using stimulus words selected by the senior psychologist from case histories and interviews (which were idiographically matched to their individual crimes) at the prison in which the women were serving their sentences. Very strong Stroop interference was observed in the emotional Stroop task for the offence-related words when compared to other stimuli and words relating to their specific offences produced greater interference than words relating to arson crimes in general. Obviously, further research is needed for idiographic applications of the emotional Stroop, but given the extensive clinical literature, there seems little reason to suppose its use cannot be extended to forensic populations.

CONCLUSION/SUMMARY

The preliminary evidence presented here suggests that the emotional Stroop consistently differentiates between sexual offenders and non-offenders. It also suggests a trend for non-significant differences between sexual offenders and violent offenders and that there is potential to differentiate the response profiles of rapists and child sex offenders with further work. It is important to remember that compared to the vast body of research already published in respect of other clinical samples, we are still at a very early stage. Standardized stimulus sets generated by clinicians working in the field are urgently required and research is also needed to develop a picture–word Stroop which may facilitate the demonstration of differences between sub-types of sexual offenders. However, the objective nature of the test, the ease of application and interpretation of results, the inherent resistance to deception of the task itself, the capacity for group and idiographic assessments and ease and low cost of testing mean that there is much to commend the emotional Stroop test as a measure of sexual interest for both clinicians and researchers. Stroop applications might include initial assessment of deviant interest, monitoring of clinical efficacy, monitoring of the use of deviant fantasy and follow-up testing on release back into the community as part of an integrated treatment and rehabilitation package. The Stroop should not, however, be seen as a stand-alone assessment tool, as indicated in the RACE information-processing explanation of its operation, it should form part of a toolkit of objective measures that address all the components (cognitive, behavioural and physiological) of sexual interest. The strength of the Stroop is in its relatively pure measurement of the perceptual stage of cognition component of the interest process. The simplicity of the Stroop makes it an attractive prospect if the research base continues to show evidence consistent with the findings to date. It would be unrealistic to suggest the emotional Stroop is a panacea to the problem of the objective measurement of sexual interest but given its heritage there is much to suggest its potential.

REFERENCES

Abel, G.G., Gore, D.K., Holland, C.L., Camp, N., Becker, I.V. and Rathner, J. (1989) The measurement of the cognitive distortions of child molesters. *Annals of Sex Research*, **2**, 135–52.

Beck, A.T., Ward, C.H., Mendelson, H., Mock, J. and Erbaugh, J. (1961) An inventory for measuring depression. *Archives of General Psychiatry*, **4**, 561–71.

Berkowitz, L. (1990) On the formation and regulation of anger and aggression: a cognitive-neoassociationistic analysis. *American Psychologist*, **45** (4), 494–503.

Birmingham, L., Gray, J., Mason, D. and Grubin, D. (2000) Mental illness at reception into prison. *Criminal Behaviour and Mental Health*, **10**, 77–87.

Buckley, T.C., Galovski, T., Blanchard, E.B. and Hickling, E.J. (2003) Is the Emotional Stroop paradigm sensitive to malingering? A between-groups study with professional actors and actual trauma survivors. *Journal of Traumatic Stress*, **16** (1), 59–66.

Carroll, J.B., Davies, P. and Richman, B. (1971) *Word Frequency Book*. American Heritage, New York.

Clore, G.L., Ortony, A. and Foss, M.A. (1987) The psychological foundations of the affective lexicon. *Journal of Personality and Social Psychology*, **53** (4), 751–66.

Cohen, J. (1960) A coefficient of agreement for nominal scales. *Educational and Psychological Measurement*, **20**, 37–46.

Cohen, D.J., Eckhardt, C.I. and Schagat, K.D. (1998) Attention allocation and habituation to anger-related stimuli during a visual search task. *Aggressive Behavior*, **24**, 399–409.

Crowne, D.P. and Marlowe, D. (1964) *The Approval Motive: Studies in Evaluative Dependence*. John Wiley & Sons, Inc., New York.

Dodge, K.A. and Crick, N.R. (1990) Social information processing bases of aggressive behaviour in children. *Personality and Social Psychology Bulletin*, **16**, 8–22.

Eckhardt, C.I. and Cohen, D.J. (1997) Attention to anger-relevant and irrelevant stimuli following naturalistic insult. *Personality and Individual Differences*, **23** (4), 619–29.

Ehlers, A., Margraf, J., Davies, S. and Roth, W.T. (1988) Selective processing of threat cues in subjects with panic attack. *Cognition and Emotion*, **2**, 201–19.

Evenden, J.L. (1999) Varieties of impulsivity. *Psychopharmacology*, **146**, 348–61.

Field, N.P., Classen, C., Butler, L.D., Koopman, C., Zarcone, J. and Speigel, D. (2001) Revictimization and information processing in women survivors of childhood sexual abuse. *Anxiety Disorders*, **15**, 459–69.

Fleiss, J.L. (1981) *Statistical Methods for Rates and Proportions*, 2nd edn, John Wiley & Sons, Inc., New York, pp. 38–46.

Foa, E.B., Feske, U., Murdock, T.B., Kozak, M.J. and McCarthy, P.R. (1991) Processing of threat related information in rape victims. *Journal of Abnormal Psychology*, **100**, 156–62.

Foa, E.B., Ilal, D., McCarthy, P.R., Shoyer, B. and Murodock, T. (1993) Information processing in obsessive-compulsive disorder. *Cognitive Therapy Research*, **17**, 173–89.

Frijda, N.J. (1986) *The Emotions*, Cambridge University Press, Cambridge.

Fuster, J.M. (1997) Network memory. *Trends in Neurosciences*, **20** (10), 451–9.

Geer, J.H., Estupinan, L.A. and Manguno-Mire, G.M. (2000) Empathy, social skills and relevant cognitive processes in rapists and child molesters. *Aggression and Violent Behavior*, **5** (1), 99–126.

Gotlib, I.H. and Cane, D.B. (1987) Construct accessibility and clinical depression: a longitudinal investigation. *Journal of Abnormal Psychology*, **96**, 199–204.

Gotlib, I.H. and McCann, C.D. (1984) Construct accessibility and depression: an examination of cognitive and affective factors. *Journal of Personality and Social Psychology*, **47**, 427–39.

Gronau, N., Ben-Shakhar, G. and Cohen, A. (2005) Behavioral and physiological measures in the detection of concealed information. *Journal of Applied Psychology*, **90** (1), 147–58.

Gudjonsson, G.H. and Sigurdsson, J.F. (2000) Differences and similarities between violent offenders and sexual offenders. *Child Abuse and Neglect*, **24** (3), 363–72.

Gunn, J., Maden, A. and Swinton, M. (1991) Treatment needs of patients with psychiatric disorders. *British Medical Journal*, **303**, 338–41.

Hock, H.S. and Egeth, H. (1970) Verbal interference with encoding in a perceptual classification task. *Journal of Experimental Psychology*, **83**, 299–303.

Hope, D.S., Rapee, R.M., Heimberg, R.G. and Dombeck, M.J. (1990) Representations of the self in social phobia: vulnerability to social threat. *Cognitive Research Therapy*, **14**, 477–85.

Huesmann, L.R. (1988) An information processing model for the development of aggression. *Aggressive Behavior*, **14**, 13–24.

Huesmann, L.R. (1998) The role of social information processing and cognitive schema in the acquisition and maintenance of habitual aggressive behavior, in *Human Aggression: Theories, Research and Implications for Social Policy* (eds R.G. Geen and E. Donnerstein), Academic Press, London, pp. 73–109.

Janssen, E., Everaerd, W., Spiering, M. and Janssen, J. (2000) Automatic cognitive processes and the appraisal of sexual stimuli: towards an information-processing model of sexual arousal. *Journal of Sex Research*, **37**, 8–23.

Kirk, R.E. (1996) Practical significance: a concept whose time has come. *Educational and Psychological Measurement*, **56**, 746–59.

Logan, G.D. (1980) Attention and automaticity in Stroop and priming tasks: theory and data. *Cognitive Psychology*, **12**, 523–53.

MacLeod, C.M. (1991) Half a century of research on the Stroop effect: an integrative review. *Psychological Bulletin*, **109** (2), 163–203.

MacLeod, C.M. and Dunbar, K. (1988) Training and Stroop-like interference: evidence for a continuum of automaticity. *Journal of Experimental Psychology: Learning, Memory and Cognition*, **14**, 126–35.

MacLeod, C., Matthews, A. and Tata, P. (1986) Attentional bias in emotional disorders. *Journal of Abnormal Psychology*, **95**, 15–20.

Marshall, W.L. and Fernadnez, Y.M. (2003) Sexual preferences: are they useful in the assessment and treatment of sexual offenders? *Aggression and Violent Behavior*, **8**, 131–43.

Matthews, A.M., Mogg, K., Kentish, J. and Eysenck, M. (1995) Effect of psychological treatment on cognitive bias in generalised anxiety disorder. *Behavior Research and Therapy*, **33**, 293–303.

Mattia, J.I., Heimberg, R.G. and Hope, D.A. (1993) The revised Stroop color-naming task in social phobics. *Behavior Research and Therapy*, **31**, 305–13.

McNally, R.J. (1998) Information processing abnormalities in anxiety disorders: implications for cognitive neuroscience. *Cognition and Emotion*, **12**, 479–95.

Nunez, J.M., Casey, B.J., Egner, T., Hare, T. and Hirsch, J. (1995) Intentional false responding shares neural substrates with response conflict and cognitive control. *Neuroimage*, **25**, 267–77.

Parsons, S., Walker, L. and Grubin, D. (2001) Prevalence of mental disorder in female remand prisons. *The Journal of Forensic Psychiatry*, **12** (1), 194–202.

Power, M.J. and Dalgleish, T. (1997) *Cognition and Emotion: From Order to Disorder*, Psychology Press, Hove, UK.

Price, S.A. (2006) *A Modified Stroop Task with Sexual Offenders: Replication of a Study*. Unpublished Masters Thesis. Carleton University, Ottawa, Ontario, Canada.

Ray, C. (1979) Examination stress and performance on a colour-word interference test. *Perceptual and Motor Skills*, **49**, 400–402.

Riemann, B.C. and McNally, R.J. (1995) Cognitive processing of personally relevant information. *Cognition and Emotion*, **9**, 325–40.

Smith, P. (2006) *Cognitive Bias in Sexual Offenders*. Paper presented at the Association for the Treatment of Sexual Abusers 25th Annual Research and Treatment Conference, 27–30 October 2006, Chicago, IL.

Smith, P. (2003) *Cognitive, Psychophysiological and Self-Reported Correlates of Aggression: Towards a Representational Model*. Unpublished PhD Manuscript, Department of Psychology, University of Leeds, UK.

Smith, P. and Waterman, M. (2003) Processing bias for aggression words in forensic and non-forensic samples. *Cognition and Emotion*, **17** (5), 681–701.

Smith, P. and Waterman, M. (2004a) The role of experience in processing bias for aggressive words in forensic and non-forensic populations. *Aggressive Behavior*, **30** (2), 105–22.

Smith, P. and Waterman, M. (2004b) Processing bias for sexual material: the emotional Stroop and sex offenders. *Sexual Abuse: A Journal of Research and Treatment*, **16** (2), 163–71.

Smith, P. and Waterman, M. (2005) Gender differences in direct and indirect aggression: a cognitive test of information processing bias for salient words. *Aggressive Behavior*, **31**, 271–82.

Smith, P. and Waterman, M. (Under review). RACE (representation activation concatenation and execution) an information-processing model of offending behaviour.

Speiring, M., Evereard, W. and Laan, E. (2004) Conscious processing of sexual information: mechanisms of appraisal. *Archives of Sexual Behaviour*, **33** (4), 369–80.

Spielburger, C.D., Gorsuch, R.L., Lushene, R., Vagg, P.R. and Jacobs, G.A. (1983) *Manual for the State-Trait Anxiety Inventory*. Consulting Psychologists Press, Palo Alto, CA.

Spiering, M., Everaerd, W. and Elzinga, B. (2002) Conscious processing of sexual information: interference caused by sexual primes. *Archives of Sexual Behavior*, **31** (2), 159–164.

Stroop, J.R. (1935) Studies of interference in serial verbal reactions. *Journal of Experimental Psychology*, **18**, 643–62.

Todorov, A. and Bargh, J.A. (2002) Automatic sources of aggression. *Aggression and Violent Behavior*, **7**, 53–68.

Van Den Hout, M. and Barlow, D. (2000) Attention, arousal and expectancies in anxiety and sexual disorders. *Journal of Affective Disorders*, **61**, 241–56.

van Honk, J., Tuiten, A., de Haan, E., Van den Hout M. and Stam, H. (2001b) Attentional biases for angry faces: relationships to trait anger and anxiety. *Cognition and Emotion*, **15** (3), 279–97.

van Honk, J., Tuiten, A., van den Hout, M., Putman, P., de Haan, E. and Stam, H. (2001a) Selective attention to unmasked and masked threatening words: relationships to trait anger and anxiety. *Personality and Individual Differences*, **30**, 711–20.

Ward, T., Hudson, S.M., Johnston, L. and Marshall, W.L. (1997) Cognitive distortions in sex offenders: an integrative review. *Clinical Psychology Review*, **17** (5), 479–507.

Watts, F.N. (1986) Cognitive processing in phobias. *Behavioral Psychotherapy*, **14**, 295–301.

Williams, J.M.G., Matthews, A. and MacLeod, C. (1996) The emotional Stroop task and psychopathology. *Psychological Bulletin*, **120**, 3–24.

Williams, J.M.G., Watts, F.N., MacLeod, C. and Mathews, A. (1997) *Cognitive Psychology and the Emotional Disorders*, 2nd edn. John Wiley & Sons, Ltd, Chichester.

Wright, L.W. and Adams, H.E. (1998) The effects of stimuli that vary in erotic content on emotional process. *The Journal of Sex Research*, **36** (2), 145–51.

Chapter 9

COMPARING TWO IMPLICIT COGNITIVE MEASURES OF SEXUAL INTEREST: A PICTORIAL MODIFIED STROOP TASK AND THE IMPLICIT ASSOCIATION TEST

CAOILTE Ó CIARDHA AND MICHAEL GORMLEY

School of Psychology, University of Dublin, Trinity College, Dublin, Ireland

That cognitive methods have the potential to offer alternatives to penile plethysmography has been well established in this book. However, ambiguity remains regarding the positive and negative aspects of each of these alternatives. Also unclear is the relationship between these different measures. The measurement of sexual interest is complicated by the fact that many elements impact on that measurement. It is likely that our sexual histories, sexual associations, cultural and societal influences, not to mention our perception of our own sexual orientation, all interact to contribute to our physiological, cognitive and behavioural reactions to sexually salient stimuli. It is also likely that these varied influences contribute to sexual interest at different times and with different levels of awareness. Parts of this process may be instantaneous and automatic while others may take longer and be under our conscious control. Physiological, cognitive or self-report measures of sexual interest are an attempt to take a snapshot of the interaction between these processes at a given point in time. Whether different methods are better predictors of sexual behaviour remains to be seen. The study outlined in this chapter looks at the utility of two implicit cognitive measures of sexual interest in differentiating between gay and straight men and explores the implications of these results for the assessment of sexual offenders.

Understanding the heterogeneity that exists among those who have sexually offended against children must be a primary concern for professionals working with such men and women, as the 'type' of offender a person is has implications for risk assessment, treatment and child protection (Prentky, Knight and Lee, 1997). Establishing whether an individual has a preferential sexual interest in children and determining whether the individual experiences an underlying association of children with sex are two possible dimensions upon which this group may vary. Methods of implicit measurement provide us with an opportunity to assess associations, attitudes, compulsions and so on that may not be accessible through self-report, perhaps because the offender is not explicitly aware of them (Ward, 2000) or because he/she is motivated to disguise or minimize them (e.g. Marshall and Serran, 2000). Such implicit methods may provide an alternative or an adjunct to physiological measures such as penile plethysmography.

Implicit measurement is an umbrella term applied to various measurement methods that make it difficult to influence responses through conscious control. Viewing time tasks, currently in use with offenders, adopt this principle (see Chapter 2 by Sachsenmaier and Gress and Chapter 3 by Glasgow). However, other implicit measurement tasks have also been used in research with samples of sex offenders and have shown potential for further application. One of these, the modified Stroop task, allows us to explore the extent to which the offender is able to ignore stimuli relating to his/her offence while trying to carry out a colour-naming task. Three studies have found that sexual offenders against children show a greater attentional bias towards words relating to sexual offending when compared with violent non-sexual offenders and non-offending controls (Price, 2005; Smith, 2006; Smith and Waterman, 2004). Choice reaction time (CRT; see Chapter 4 by Gress and Laws) tasks, which are similar tasks to the modified Stroop, in which to-be-attended-to stimuli competed with to-be-ignored stimuli for attention, found sexual orientation to be predictive of an attentional bias towards either male or female stimuli (Wright and Adams, 1994, 1999). The existence of an attentional bias within the sexual offending population may allow us to examine the relationships between this bias and the offence behaviour and also the risk assigned to the individual by clinicians and actuarial tools and so on. The study outlined in this chapter departs from previous research by developing a modified Stroop paradigm for use with sexual offenders that uses images instead of words. Data presented in this chapter are from the piloting of this procedure with non-offenders.

The second implicit task we discuss in detail in this chapter, the implicit association test (IAT, Greenwald, McGhee and Schwartz, 1998), allows us to explore the participant's attitudes, schemas and cognitive distortions by comparing reaction times to concept pairs that the participant may implicitly identify as incongruous with concept pairs that they may identify as congruous. Mihailides, Devilly and Ward (2004), Gray, Brown, MacCulloch, Smith and Snowden (2005) along with Nunes, Firestone and Baldwin (2007) have all found group differences between sexual offenders against children and non-offenders using versions of the IAT (see also Chapter 6 by Nunes and Chapter 5 by Gray and Snowden). Furthermore, Gray *et al.* (2005) reported that their 'child–sex association' IAT was able not only to identify group differences between offenders and controls, but also showed promise in being able to discriminate between offenders and controls on an individual level. Results of two IAT versions are outlined in this chapter. As with the modified pictorial Stroop tasks, both IATs were piloted with non-offenders. The first IAT compared responses when the concepts of child and sex are paired relative to adult and sex (child–sex IAT). The second looked at male versus female names paired with sex words (gender–sex IAT).

THE MODIFIED STROOP TASK

The word version of the modified Stroop task is a common implicit task used to explore a wide variety of topics. The terms emotional Stroop and modified Stroop are used interchangeably, even by the same authors (e.g. Cox, Fadardi and Klinger, 2006). Strictly speaking, while any adaptation of the Stroop design may be a modified Stroop task, the label of emotional Stroop suggests that it is the emotional content of any potentially salient stimuli that is responsible for any attentional bias. To avoid this assumption, we use the more general term of modified Stroop task. The modified Stroop task, as with the traditional Stroop task, presents a to-be-ignored stimulus concurrently with a to-be-attended-to stimulus. The to-be-attended-to stimulus is always a colour, be it the colour of the font in which a word is written (word Stroop) or the colour of a picture (pictorial Stroop). Participants are asked to name the colour as quickly as they can. Any systematic difficulty in doing this is interpreted as demonstrating that the to-be-ignored stimuli hold some salience for the participant. This type of content-induced delay can be used to investigate many research questions, from responses of cocaine addicts towards images related to cocaine use (Hester, Dixon and Garavan, 2006) to the reaction of violent offenders to words relating to aggression (Smith and Waterman, 2003). An attractive feature of any Stroop task is its simplicity. The participant needs only to name out loud or press the button that corresponds to the colour[1] of the image or word. In the case of the pictorial modified Stroop, the participant does not even need to be able to read as all instructions can be read to him/her, if necessary.

The word version of the modified Stroop task is far more commonly used than the newer pictorial adaptation. The word-modified Stroop has been mostly used in looking for attentional biases related to the perception of potentially threatening stimuli, often among anxious, phobic or post-traumatic stress disorder participants (e.g. Bradley, Mogg, Millar and White, 1995; Egloff and Schmukle, 2004; Holle, Neely and Heimberg, 1997; McNally, Riemann, Louro and Lukach, 1992; Mogg, Bradley, Dixon, Fisher, Twelftree and McWilliams, 2000; Wikström, Lundh and Westerlund, 2003). However, the technique has also been used widely to investigate attention to addiction-related stimuli including alcohol (e.g. Carrigan, Drobes and Randall, 2004; Cox, Yeates and Regan, 1999; Kramer and Goldman, 2003; Ryan, 2002; Sharma, Albery and Cook, 2001), smoking (e.g. Mogg and Bradley, 2002; Munafò, Mogg, Roberts, Bradley and Murphy, 2003; Powell, Tait and Lessiter, 2002; Waters and Feyerabend, 2000; Waters, Shiffman, Sayette, Paty, Gwaltney and Balabanis, 2003; Wertz and Sayette, 2001), gambling (e.g. Boyer and Dickerson, 2003; McCusker and Gettings, 1997) as well as heroin, cocaine and marijuana abuse (e.g. Carpenter, Schreiber, Church and McDowell, 2006; Field, 2005; Hester *et al.*, 2006). Other applications of the method have included investigating attention to stimuli related to food, eating disorders, body image and appearance (e.g. Braet and Crombez, 2003; Formea and Burns, 1996; Green, Elliman and Rogers,

---

[1]Clearly, if the participants were colour-blind, they may not be able to differentiate between the colours, which would void their results. Between approximately 3 and 8%, depending on ethnicity, of males have some form of colour-blindness with the prevalence among women being much lower (Sekuler and Blake, 1994).

1996; Labarge, Cash and Brown, 1998; Mahamedi and Heatherton, 1993; Perpiña, Leonard, Treasure, Bond and Baños, 1998), as well as disease, fear of illness and malingering (e.g. Cannon, 2003; Erblich, Montgomery, Valdimarsdottir, Cloitre and Bovbjerg, 2003; Fortune, Richards, Corrin, Taylor, Griffiths and Main, 2003; Jessop, Rutter, Sharma and Albery, 2004; Lecci and Cohen, 2002; Zeitlin, Bradburn and Lawson-Kerr, 1995). Attention to disorder-related material has been investigated in depressed and hypomanic participants (e.g. Dalgleish, Taghavi, Neshat-Doost, Moradi, Canterbury and Yule, 2003; French, Richards and Scholfield, 1996; Gotlib and Cane, 1987) as well as for suicide-related words in suicide attempters (Becker, Strohbach and Rinck, 1999). Processing for aggression words has also been investigated (e.g. Smith and Waterman, 2003, 2005) as has attention to salient stimuli among perpetrators and victims of sexual violence (e.g. Dubner and Motta, 1999; Foa, Feske, Murdock, Kozak and McCarthy, 1991; Freeman and Beck, 2000; Smith and Waterman, 2004). The methodology adopted across the studies cited above and other modified Stroop studies varies quite considerably but most consistently finds evidence of attentional bias towards their target stimuli.

The ability of certain stimuli to divert or compete with the individual's attention allows the experimenter to interpret the salience of those stimuli for that individual. One must be cautious in extrapolating meaning from what is essentially a momentary increase in attentional demands. For example, two modified Stroop studies have shown victims of sexual violence to show attentional bias towards words relating to the abuse/assault that they suffered. (Post-traumatic stress disorder was an additional factor in both; Dubner and Motta, 1999; Foa *et al.*, 1991.) These studies, taken with the studies that demonstrate an attentional bias towards offence-related words among perpetrators of sexual violence (Price, 2005; Smith, 2006; Smith and Waterman, 2004), demonstrate that the interpretation of any bias must be tentative and viewed in the context of how the stimuli have come to be salient. It has been shown that performance on a Stroop task *can* be predictive of behaviour: Waters *et al.* (2003) found that smokers trying to quit who showed the strongest attentional bias towards smoking-related words were more likely to lapse within the follow-up period, even when years smoking and self-reported urges were controlled for. Some studies have shown promise in demonstrating that an attentional bias demonstrated by the Stroop task may be malleable through treatment (e.g. Lundh and Öst, 2001; Mattia, Heimberg and Hope, 1993). While such studies suggest that the modified Stroop task is capable of tapping into dynamic and predictive cognitive processes, the mechanism by which the task does this is still unclear. Smith (Chapter 8) explores this question in more detail. The inclusion of pictorial stimuli to the modified Stroop task may facilitate a better understanding of the manner in which this task interferes with the attentive process as well as providing new avenues for the types of potentially salient stimuli that can be utilized.

THE PICTORIAL MODIFIED STROOP TASK

Some research questions may be best addressed by eliciting a concept using words. Consider the offender whose sexual interest involves committing sadistic acts with specific victims. Images may not be useful with this individual; either because researchers are unprepared or unable to include images depicting sadistic acts, because such an image may become too multi-featured for practical use in a rapid-response task or because too many specific features may be necessary to produce a response from this individual (child age, gender, hair colour, ethnicity, type of sadism). In cases such as these, it may be preferable to use words such as 'hit', 'beat', 'gag' and so on over images so that the stimulus does not become too specific to produce a response. On the other hand, the use of images as stimuli in the Stroop task has certain advantages over words. Using images, we can manipulate the age of the individual depicted, their gender, their pose, their ethnicity and the emotion they portray. When trying to assess sexual interest towards children generally, the use of pictures affords a greater scope and flexibility to present potentially sexually salient stimuli to the participant. In order to do the same with words, one would have to come up with many words that suggest the concept of 'sex with children' to the participant, which would be more difficult. As with any measure of reaction time to salient stimuli, the interpretation of such an attentional bias is potentially problematic. One could propose several reasons why a participant would have a slowed response to a given image. It is the consistency of response across stimulus category that we may interpret, in this case, as indicative of sexual interest.

The pictorial version of the modified Stroop task has been used in many of the same fields of research where the word-modified Stroop task has been used, albeit in a limited way. Studies include the assessment of attention to facial emotion (Ashwin, Wheelwright and Baron-Cohen, 2006; Heim-Dreger, Kohlmann, Eschenbeck and Burkhardt, 2006; van Honk, Tuiten, de Haan, van den Hout and Stam, 2001; van Honk, Tuiten, van den Hout, Koppeschaar, Thijssen, de Haan and Verbaten, 1998; van Honk, Tuiten, van den Hout, Koppeschaar, Thijssen, de Haan and Verbaten, 1999; van Honk, Tuiten, van den Hout, Koppeschaar, Thijssen, de Haan and Verbaten, 2000) to cocaine-related images (Hester *et al.*, 2006) to phobia-related material (Constantine, McNally and Hornig, 2001; Elsesser, Heuschen, Pundt and Sartory 2006; Kindt and Brosschot, 1997, 1999; Kolassa, Musial, Mohr, Trippe and Miltner, 2005; Lavy and Van den Hout, 1993), as well as towards images related to eating disorders (Stormark and Torkildsen, 2004; Walker, Ben-Tovim, Paddick and McNamara, 1995). The methodology used has varied across studies. Most adopt an unblocked design, where all stimuli are presented randomly as opposed to being presented in groups of matching stimuli (except Hester *et al.*, 2006; Stormark and Torkildsen, 2004). Some studies use pictorial stimuli where the image and the colour are not integrated, with the colour forming a border around the image (e.g. Elsesser *et al.*, 2006), instead of having a coloured version of the image (e.g. Constantine *et al.*, 2001; Côté and Bouchard, 2005).

Two of the studies cited above found similar or reduced bias for pictorial Stroop compared with word Stroop (Kindt and Brosschot, 1997; Lavy and Van den Hout, 1993), whereas further two studies were unable to find a Stroop effect at all (Kindt and Brosschot, 1999; Kolassa *et al.*, 2005). In the case of Kindt and Broschott (1997), the researchers did find an attentional bias for pictorial and word stimuli among their spider-phobic participants compared with controls but they found that linguistic stimuli performed better than pictorial stimuli. Interestingly, they also compared non-integrated linguistic stimuli (which were words placed on a coloured circle) which also performed worse than the integrated words. The picture stimuli in this study were created by placing images of spiders on coloured circles. The lack of integration of picture and colour may have been a factor in the relative weakness of the pictorial stimuli to produce results. In their 1999 study, Kindt and Broschott again used non-integrated images. Interestingly, three of the four null or poor findings with the pictorial Stroop used the same images in their studies (Kindt and Brosschot, 1997, 1999; Lavy and Van den Hout, 1993). Some possible explanations for their own null finding were put forward by Kolassa *et al.* (2005) and included the fact that they had used only two colours in their version of the Stroop task, that their design was not blocked and that response modality was manual, whereas oral responses are considered optimal in producing effects (MacLeod, 1991). Since all four studies were with spider-phobics, a phenomenon specific to attention for phobia-related material may underlie these findings (possibly with spider images there might be a conflict of aversion and attention involved). Despite these particular studies, it is apparent that a pictorial Stroop design can, with certain methodological considerations, identify attentional bias towards salient stimuli.

The study outlined in this chapter adopted a blocked design where each category of stimulus was grouped together as recommended by Cox, Fadardi and Pothos (2006). Several modified Stroop studies have shown a blocked design to elicit stronger attentional biases than non-blocked designs (Ballesteros, Reales and Manga, 2000; Cox *et al.*, 2006; Holle *et al.*, 1997; Richards, French, Johnson and Naparstek, 1992; Waters and Feyerabend, 2000). Cox *et al.*, (2006) recommend that matching stimuli are grouped together in order that any carry-over effect (further processing of a given stimulus, after the participant has moved onto another trial, which might interfere with attention on the new trial) would be carried over onto similar trials as opposed to unrelated trials. This means that any additional cognitive interference caused by a stimulus will contribute to the overall reaction time for the correct stimulus category. Although not in keeping with best practices in Stroop design (MacLeod, 1991), a manual response modality was chosen for this study for practical reasons. It was hypothesized that the pictorial modified Stroop task would show group differences between gay and straight men. It was further hypothesized that, within the Stroop task, responses to orientation-consistent stimuli would produce longer reaction times than responses to orientation-inconsistent stimuli (i.e. gay men would take longer to identify the colour when the images were of men and vice versa for straight men).

STIMULI USED IN THE STROOP TASK – NOT REAL PEOPLE

Stimuli used in the pictorial modified Stroop task consisted of images of adult males, adult females, female children, male children and control images of large cats (lions, tigers etc.). All images of people were clothed in bathing suits or shorts. Child images were taken from the Not Real People (NRP) image set created by Laws and Gress (2004). Some of the adult images were also taken from the NRP. The NRP is a set of images of males and females that have been computer modified for use in the assessment of and research involving sexual offenders (Laws and Gress, 2004). 'Each finished image was produced by compiling and morphing three or more images, plus additional modifications such as hair, eye and body colour, simple pose modifications and clothing' (Laws and Gress, 2004, p. 188). Images in the NRP are classified according to their secondary sexual characteristics, using

Tanner stages (Tanner, 1973). Three male and three female images from Tanner stages 1–4 were included in the child stimulus category of the pictorial modified Stroop task, yielding a total of 12 images of each gender. Several of the Tanner stage 5 images were included in the adult category. It was necessary to create a further 6 adult male images and 9 adult female images for several reasons. First, it was necessary to have 12 unique adult images in each of the gender categories. Second, it was deemed that a few of the NRP Tanner 5 images were not of a high enough quality for inclusion. Unique adult images were created by the authors using a similar technique to those adopted by Laws and Gress. It was decided to attempt to mirror the process by which the NRP images were created as closely as was possible since morphed images are likely to vary systematically from non-morphed images in eliciting reaction times.

Images were created using Adobe Photoshop Elements 3.1 and two image-morphing programmes.[2] Morphed images were composed of two faces morphed together onto one body. The backgrounds of all images (NRP and novel morphs) were removed and the images coloured using the 'Colour Replacement Brush' tool in Photoshop. It was found that using this technique to alter the colour of the images instead of simply placing a coloured filter over the image produced images that were much clearer, since the colour-replaced images retained a greater deal of shading, thus minimizing the changes to the original pictures. The removal of the background ensured that in order to respond to the image participants would have to attend to the image itself and not be able to rely on any area of tinted background. Large cats were chosen as control images, as it was important that the control images form a coherent category and also that these controls should be animate. Cats were chosen over other potential animate controls, apes for example, mainly for the reason that the colour replacement method used worked better with images containing a good amount of contrasting colours. Unfortunately, in the clothed version of the NRP, the clothing worn by the female images varies depending on the Tanner stage of the image with Tanner stages 1–3 wearing one-piece bathing suits, while the 4 and 5 Tanner stage images are wearing two-piece bathing suits. To compensate for this lack of uniformity, it was ensured that the adult female stimuli would have the same ratio of two-piece to one-piece bathing suits as was present in the child female images. Since all the images had different amounts of light areas versus dark (due to the amount of skin showing, skin tone, darkness of clothing and differences in the on-screen size of the person or cat), there was some concern that there would be a systematic difference across the image types in the level of the target colours present. To address this, a version of the pictorial modified Stroop task, where all our experimental images were scrambled, was conducted which yielded uniform response times to image categories.

CARRYING OUT THE STROOP TASK

A mixed factorial design was used, with gay and straight participants completing all experimental tasks: the pictorial modified Stroop task, the gender–sex IAT, the age–sex IAT as well as a version of the traditional Stroop task. The traditional

[2]Morpher and WinMorph (Fujimiya, 2001; Kumar, 2002).

Stroop compares reaction times to word font colour when the words used are congruent with word colour (e.g. the word 'red' with a red font), incongruent with the word colour (e.g. the word 'blue' in a yellow font) or have no relationship ('house' written in a green font). This task was included as it is intended to compare offender and non-offender performance in future studies. If offenders and non-offenders performed differently on the traditional Stroop task, any differences found using the pictorial modified Stoop task would have to be interpreted in the light of these differences. No analyses of these data are included in this chapter. Participants were recruited through university and community Internet noticeboards along with university postering. Recruitment materials called for 'males of all sexual orientations'. A total of 21 males were recruited, 8 of whom classified themselves as having an exclusive sexual preference towards males, while 11 stated an exclusive sexual preference towards females. One participant identified himself as having a preference for males with some sexual interest in females, while another stated that he had a preference for females with some sexual interest towards males. In the absence of a large amount of individuals with non-exclusive sexual preferences, these two participants were included in the gay and straight categories, respectively, yielding an overall sample of 9 gay and 12 straight participants. All participants were college educated and had fluent English; however, 3 gay and 3 straight participants were not native Anglophones. Mean age for the sample was 26.7 years (gay 25.2, straight 27.8). Computerized tasks were presented on a Gateway Pentium III computer with a Gateway EV9108 19" CRT monitor. Participant responses were made via a Cedrus response pad (model RB-620) with four coloured buttons (red, green, blue and yellow). Tasks were run using the SuperLab4 stimulus presentation software. A two-item questionnaire was also administered, asking the participants about their age and sexual orientation. Stimuli included images of male and female children and adults in bathing suits along with control images of large cats. As already mentioned, all images of children and some of the adults were taken from the NRP image set (Laws and Gress, 2004).

   Participants first filled in the questionnaire and then carried out the Stroop section. Responses were given via the response pad. All instructions for the task were presented on the computer screen. The Stroop section contained several subsections. First, participants completed a practice trial where words were presented in the different colours. Feedback was given in the form of a red X appearing if the wrong colour was selected. Participants could not continue to the next word until they gave the correct answer. This was to ensure that participants properly understood the procedure; no feedback was given on the subsequent sections and participants had no opportunity to correct mistakes. Second, participants completed a traditional Stroop task with congruent, control and incongruent font colour to word pairings. In the final part of the Stroop section, participants were presented with the modified pictorial Stroop condition. Stimuli were grouped according to stimulus type; therefore, there were five blocks: adult males, adult females, child males, child females and large cats (controls). As with the previous tasks, participants had to identify, using a button box, the colour with which each image had been tinted. Block order was randomized across participants and trials were randomized within blocks. For each participant, mean reaction times of correct responses were calculated for each block within the Stroop task after excluding trials that were more than 1.5 times the interquartile range beyond the 25th or 75th percentile.

THE IMPLICIT ASSOCIATION TEST

In this book, Gray and Snowden (Chapter 5) along with Nunes (Chapter 6) have introduced the concept and history of the implicit association test (IAT) and its potential in the assessment of sexual interest. To avoid repetition, this chapter will focus on some methodological issues in the use of the IAT to investigate sexual interests and associations. Gray and Snowden (Chapter 5) have highlighted the methodological inconsistencies across all of the IATs used to investigate sexual associations. The study outlined in this chapter adopts a different methodology again in that, instead of assigning word lists based on sex versus not-sex categorization as adopted by most of the previous authors, we have opted for sex versus a neutral category. This approach ensures that categorizing words into one of the two options is not made more difficult by virtue of the fact that the words do not form a consistent category in the case of the not-sex words.

When developing stimuli to assess sexual interest in children using the IAT, there can be an accumulative difficulty in attempting to satisfy two of the principles of good IAT constructions: that stimuli should be easily classifiable into one of the four coherent categories and that categories are formed as contrasting pairs (Nosek, Greenwald, Banaji and Bargh, 2007). To illustrate this, we consider the following cognitions that might be held by sexual offenders against children:

1) Children are sexual beings.
2) Children are associated with sex or sexual activity.
3) Children are sexually attractive.

Researchers may be interested in investigating whether these cognitions are held by offenders and, if so, whether they are held by all offenders or just a subset of offenders and how common such cognitions are among the non-offending population. While each of these three cognitions are very similar, the nuances of each would suggest using slightly different IATs to assess them. First of all each of these cognitions would most likely be investigated by comparing speed of child–sex associations to adult–sex associations. Child versus adult are opposite and mutually exclusive concepts, and the picking of stimuli that are easily classifiable as one or the other would cause little difficulty. The task becomes more difficult when choosing contrasting sex/not-sex categories. For the first association mentioned above, 'children as sexual beings', a contrasting pair of category labels might be 'sexual' and 'non-sexual'. Virtually anything can be non-sexual, but there are very few words that would satisfactorily form a coherent 'non-sexual' category. Mihailides *et al.* (2004) used words that were phonetically similar to their sexual words to form their non-sexual words (e.g. orgasm and sarcasm) resulting in a non-sexual category lacking coherency and a lack of contrast between the two categories. In addition, instead of an adult–sex versus child–sex comparison, Mihailides *et al.* (2004) also used a 'child' versus 'not-child' comparison with words that were phonetically similar to the child words forming the 'not-child' words (e.g. kids and lids). The lack of coherent contrasting categories makes the interpretation of what exactly was being measured by this task unclear.

Looking at the second association one might want to measure, that of 'children being associated with sex or sexual activity', the creation of 'sex' versus 'not-sex' categories again causes difficulty. Gray *et al.* (2005) deal with this association by creating a coherent set of words not commonly considered sexual and that are all related to the body as their 'not-sex' category. It could be argued that this does not constitute a contrasting category so much as an unrelated category with a contrasting label. Of the three studies looking at offenders against children, possibly the most successful in their creation of categories to assess the third association mentioned above (children as sexually attractive) is that of Nunes *et al.* (2007). They chose 'sexy' and 'not-sexy' as the titles of their categories and were able to create a coherent category of 'not-sexy' words that provide a real contrast to the 'sexy' words. 'Sexy' versus 'not-sexy' was chosen instead of 'sexually attractive' and 'sexually unattractive'. However, it could be argued that 'sexy' captures a different association than 'sexually attractive' with 'sexually attractive' being more passive compared to the slightly more active role the target stimuli (adult or child) may take in being 'sexy'. This distinction is not necessarily a criticism of the method used, as the inclusion of 'sexy' may incorporate some of the 'child as sexual being' cognitive distortion into the 'children as sexually attractive' association that Nunes *et al.* (2007) set out to explore. Nunes *et al.* chose 'sexy'/'not-sexy' as they felt this was clearer, more concise as well as being easier to differentiate between categories compared to 'sexually attractive'/'sexually unattractive' (K.L. Nunes, personal communication, 13 December 2007).

Any study involving offenders against children must take into account that some of their participants may suffer from intellectual and/or learning difficulties (Langevin and Curnoe, 2007). This necessitates that researchers ensure that instructions, stimuli and categories are as clear as possible when designing experimental procedures. However, without this constraint, Snowden, Wichter and Gray (2008) were able to carry out an IAT that had an excellent ability to discriminate gay men from straight men using 'sexually attractive' versus 'sexually unattractive' as their contrasting pair labels. As the study was interested in sexual interest towards adults only, they were also able to use images of adult males and females as their male and female stimuli. It is worth noting that the images used in this study were of nude adults. While the study outlined in this chapter was also investigating sexual interest in non-offenders, it was designed so that the exact same procedure could be administered to an offending population. Therefore, a design such as that used by Snowden *et al.* (2008; i.e. using images instead of words) was not adopted so that our male and female categories would have the potential to elicit the concept of males and females of any age in our participants and also that our category labels would be as clear as possible. It should be noted that the results of the Snowden *et al.* (2008) study were unknown to us at the time of design.

The present study departed from the previous studies by using a control category instead of a contrasting category. In both versions of the IAT reported here, that category consisted of furniture items. Obviously, this decision was at the expense of having an 'opposite to sex' category, though in the case of Mihailides *et al.* (2004)

and Gray *et al.* (2005), we would argue that the opposite category was opposite in name only. It should be stressed that all three of the published studies, using the IAT with offenders against children, were able to identify group differences using their respective methodologies, suggesting that and the effect is robust enough to transcend methodological variations. On the other hand, movement towards a consistent methodology when conducting sexual interest IATs would allow for a better understanding of what exactly is being measured by this task and would also allow direct comparisons of studies carried out by different researchers. Given the success of the Snowden *et al.* (2008) study and the appeal of its simplicity, future IATs for the assessment of sexual interest may follow their method. Whether or not it is necessary to present nude images and whether 'sexually attractive' versus 'sexually unattractive' are suitable labels for participants of different abilities should be addressed by future research. Another possibility is to do away with the not-sex category completely and to adopt a method like the Go/No-Go association task (Nosek and Banaji, 2001).

The IAT is an instruction-heavy procedure that is quite straightforward to carry out but is somewhat difficult to explain to the participants. With that in mind, along with the fact that some offenders will have below-average intellectual abilities or reading capabilities, the two IATs used in our study had instructions that were as simple as possible. The instructions, therefore, deviated in wording but not in content, to any great degree, from those typically used by Greenwald and colleagues. It is worth mentioning that the IAT has been used with children as young as 6 years, albeit using a computer game-like version of the task (Baron and Banaji, 2006). A feedback version of the IAT was used here, where participants were not able to continue on to the next stimulus until they answered correctly. This design was chosen to ensure that participants were completing the task correctly. Both time-to-first-response and time-to-correct-response were recorded. As with the Stroop task, it was hypothesized that the gender–sex IAT would show group differences between gay and straight men, whereas the age–sex IAT would show no between-group differences in sexual associations of children and sex compared with adults and sex. With regard to the gender–sex IAT, it was hypothesized that male–sex word pairings would facilitate faster responding in gay men and that female–sex word pairings would facilitate faster responses in straight men.

ISSUES WITH IAT SCORING ALGORITHMS

Treatment of extreme data proposed by Greenwald and his colleagues (e.g. Greenwald, Nosek and Banaji, 2003) involves the removal or replacement of data if certain thresholds are passed. Depending on which algorithm is used, this may involve the removal of trials if reaction time is greater than 10 seconds (new D algorithm) or the replacement of reaction times with 3 seconds if actual reaction time is over that (conventional algorithm). Since participants could have short average responses (in the present study, some participants had block mean times that were lower than 500 ms with standard deviations less than 300 ms), it seems inadvisable to potentially include reaction times of 10 seconds (or even 3 s, if one was using the conventional scoring algorithm) in the data set. A method of removing outliers based on the interquartile range of responses of each participant seems much more prudent.[3] Additionally, since the goal of research using the cognitive methods outlined in this volume is to identify procedures with clinical uses, we must consider how these tests perform on an individual level. Extreme value treatment must attempt to best capture the individuals true typical response while minimizing the noise introduced into the data by distraction, lapses of attention, cognitive impairments, fatigue and loss of interest. Selecting arbitrary cut-points beyond which data are removed or recoded is a method that may suit the improvement of global data but should not be applied when attempting to best interpret the results of an individual. Blanton and Jaccard (2006) raise several criticisms of the IAT, including questions about the meaningfulness and arbitrariness of the scoring method used. Questions raised include issues surrounding the potential of distorted results for individuals with small standard deviations in their reaction times and also the danger of interpreting effect sizes using Cohen's (1988) definitions, without also looking at unstandardized scores. For both sides of the debate, see Blanton and Jaccard, 2006; Blanton, Jaccard, Gonzales and Christie, 2006; Blanton, Jaccard, Christie and Gonzales, 2007; Greenwald, Nosek and Sriram, 2006; Nosek and Sriram, 2007. Given the concerns raised by Blanton and colleagues and also our own feelings on the extreme value treatment included in the different algorithms recommended by Greenwald and his colleagues, it was decided to adopt a different strategy in scoring the test. Since this study is, in the main, a piloting of a new method and is initially concerned with identifying group differences, the simplest method of analysis was desired. Interestingly, the three previous published studies that looked at sexual interest/sexual cognitions among offenders using the IAT (Gray et al., 2005; Mihailides et al., 2004; Nunes et al., 2007) each used different methods of data assessment, again suggesting that the phenomenon may be robust enough to materialize despite differences in consensus regarding the best methodology.

CARRYING OUT THE IMPLICIT ASSOCIATION TESTS

All participants completed the Stroop task first and had a short break before proceeding to the first IAT. Order of IAT-type (gender–sex, age–sex) presentation was randomized across participants with the procedure for both IATs being exactly the same. All instructions were presented on the computer screen. Participants were instructed to use the two outer buttons (left and right) on the response pad. Over seven blocks, participants first categorized words that appeared on the screen one by one into one of two categories (e.g. male names vs. female names in the gender–sex IAT, child words vs. adult words in the age–sex IAT) using the left and right buttons. Participants then classified words as being sex words or furniture

---

[3]In the present study (gender-sex IAT), a comparison between using scoring algorithm D (Greenwald et al., 2003) and using a modified version of the same algorithm, which uses conventional methods of outlier removal, results in very different overall scores, suggesting that further investigation is required. Using ROC curves to see which of these two scores best predicted sexual orientation, the D algorithm yielded an AUC of 0.648, whereas the modified version yielded an AUC of 0.778. Neither one of these methods of scoring was used in any further analysis.

words in the same way. Once this had been practiced, categories were combined so that categories were paired with each other (e.g. push the left button if the word that appears on the screen is either a sex word *or* a child word; push the right button if the word is either a furniture word *or* an adult word). In later trials, this order was reversed, thus creating a new word pairing. Child was now paired with furniture words, while sex and adult were paired. For both IATs, participants could only move on to the next word once they answered correctly. Time to initial response was recorded as well as timing of every subsequent response until the correct answer was given. All participants completed the gender–sex IAT and the age–sex IAT.

As discussed, the scoring involved an alternative method to that commonly used for the IAT. In the case of the gender–sex IAT, average reaction times were calculated for each participant on trials in which sex was paired with a male or a female name. Trials that were over 1.5 times the interquartile range beyond the 25th and 75th percentiles (within each block) were not included in the analysis. Trials which were answered incorrectly were also excluded. Since the control (furniture) association in each block was somewhat redundant (from an analysis point of view) given the fact that contrasting pairs of target category were not used, a mean value of sex associations only was calculated for each block. Since there were two blocks where female and sex were associated and two blocks where male and sex were associated, total average male–sex reaction times and female–sex reaction times were calculated. A difference score was also calculated by subtracting the average female–sex reaction times from the average male–sex reaction times for each participant. The age–sex IAT was treated in the exact same way, with trials in which child and sex were associated and adult and sex were associated being the trials of interest.

RESULTS OF THE STROOP TASK

A $2 \times 2 \times 2$ mixed factorial ANOVA was carried out on the results of the modified Stroop task with sexual orientation as the between-subjects factor and gender of stimulus images as the first within-group factor and age of stimulus images (child vs. adults) the second. There were significant main effects of age of stimulus as well as for gender of stimulus along with a significant interaction of gender of stimulus with sexual orientation. However, since there was a significant three-way interaction of gender of stimulus, age of stimulus and sexual orientation of participant all findings were interpreted in light of this; $F(1, 19) = 8.616, p = 0.008$, partial $\eta^2 = 0.312$. In order to identify the source of the interaction, further analyses were conducted. First, separate 2×2 mixed factorial ANOVAs were carried out, looking at child and adult stimuli separately (see Figures 9.1 and 9.2). A Bonferroni conversion was applied to these results to reduce familywise error. For child stimuli, no interaction was found between gender of stimulus and sexual orientation; however, there was a main effect of gender of stimulus with participants, regardless of sexual orientation, typically taking longer to react to images of male children (mean $= 728.4$ ms, SD $= 111.2$) than images of female children (mean $= 680.4$, SD $= 82.9$); $F(1, 19) = 7.25, p = 0.014$. For adult stimuli, there was a significant interaction of gender of stimuli and sexual orientation; $F(1, 19) = 8.067, p = 0.01$. Pairwise

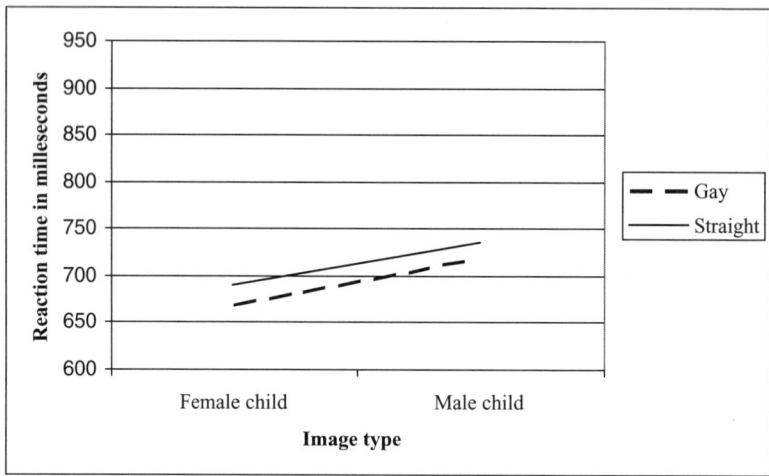

Figure 9.1 Mean reaction times of gay and straight men to images of male and female children from the pictorial modified Stroop task.

comparisons were carried out in order to investigate the source of the interaction. Four t-tests (two independent samples and two paired samples) showed a significant difference only between reaction times for adult female images between gay and straight men with straight men taking longer to respond: $t(19) = -2.153$, $p = 0.044$, two-tailed. The difference between adult female and adult male images was approaching significance among gay men: $t(8) = -2.079, p = 0.071$, two-tailed. The same comparison among straight men yielded a non-significant t. However, when a further Bonferroni conversion was applied to allow for familywise error,

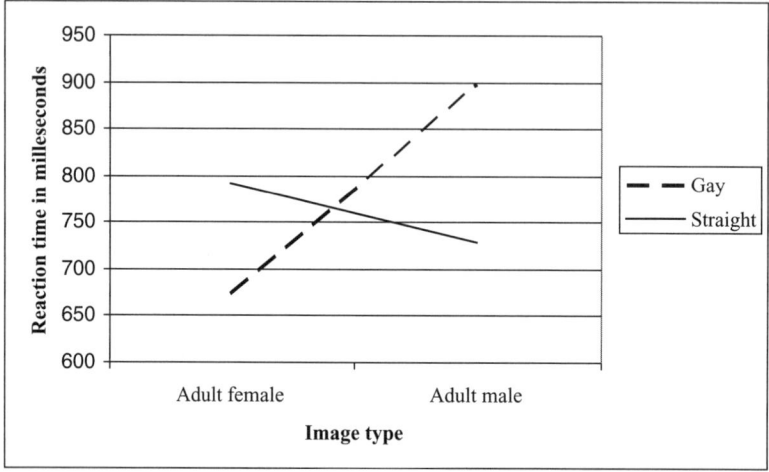

Figure 9.2 Mean reaction times of gay and straight men to adult male and female images using the pictorial modified Stroop task.

none of the results from these t-tests were significant. Reaction times to control stimuli (large cats) were consistent across gay and straight participants (mean for gay participants was 671.8, SD = 97.8; mean for straight participants was 679.4, SD = 113.9) with no significant differences found between them.

A receiver operating characteristic (ROC) curve was plotted to assess how well a score based on the difference between mean reaction time to adult female stimuli and mean reaction time to adult male images was capable of predicting self-reported sexual orientation. An ROC curve is a 'function that relates hit and false-alarm rates to each other' (Macmillan and Creelman, 1990, pp. 62–63). This analysis shows an area under the ROC curve (AUC) of 0.898. Chance alone should yield an AUC of 0.5, while a task that predicted sexual orientation correctly all the time would have an AUC of 1. An ROC of 0.898 represents a predictive ability that differs significantly ($p = 0.002$; SE $= 0.073$) from 0.5. As mentioned, difference scores were based on reaction times where outliers beyond 1.5 times the interquartile range were removed. For the sake of completeness, a second (less conservative) score was also calculated where only reaction times that were more than three times the interquartile range beyond the 25th and 75th percentiles were removed. If you base the calculation on Stroop scores using this approach to outlier removal, the AUC increases to 0.926 ($p = 0.001$, SE $= 0.061$). An examination of the coordinate points generated to draw the ROC curve indicated that the optimum cut-off point (if one were looking for a point on the Stroop difference scores that sees the best trade-off between correct classification of participants into one or other of the sexual orientation groupings) for either Stroop difference score is very close to zero. This suggests that the practice of subtracting an adult male mean from an adult female mean produces a score with a meaningful zero point. Put another way, we would expect the cut-off point to be zero since a score greater than zero indicates a bias for female images compared with male images and that a score below zero indicates the opposite. Using this cut-off point for the less conservative Stroop difference score (actual value = 0.53 ms), gay participants were correctly identified 83% of the time, while straight participants were identified correctly 89% of the time.

RESULTS OF THE IMPLICIT ASSOCIATION TEST

A 2 × 2 mixed factorial ANOVA was carried out on the results of the age–sex IAT with responses to child–sex concept pairings versus adult–sex pairings as the within-subjects factor and sexual orientation as the between-subjects factor. No significant main effects or interactions were found. A 2 × 2 mixed factorial ANOVA was carried out on the results of the gender–sex IAT with responses to the pairing of male names with sex words versus female names with sex words as the within groups factor and sexual orientation as the between-subjects factor. No significant main effect was found. However, there was a significant interaction between gender of name–sex pairing with sexual orientation: $F(1, 19) = 5.876$, $p = 0.025$, partial $\eta^2 = 0.236$. Pairwise comparisons were carried out in order to find the source of the interaction. Four t-tests (two independent samples and two paired samples) showed a significant difference only between reaction times for

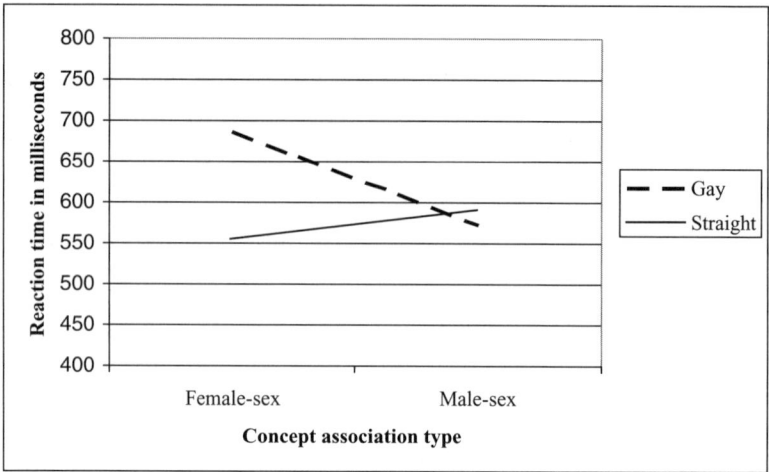

Figure 9.3   Mean reaction times to female–sex and male–sex associations for gay and straight participants in gender–sex IAT.

female–sex word pairings between gay and straight men with gay men taking longer to respond: $t(19) = 2.341, p = 0.03$, two-tailed. However, when a Bonferroni conversion was applied to allow for familywise error, no results were significant. Although non-significant, results were in the direction expected, with gay men taking longer to respond to female–sex pairings than they did to male–sex pairings, which was the inverse of the pattern for straight men (see Figure 9.3). An ROC curve was plotted to determine how well the gender–sex IAT difference score (difference in mean reaction times between male–sex pairings and female–sex pairings) predicted sexual orientation. The AUC was 0.806 ($p = 0.019$, SE $= 0.098$). As with the Stroop difference score, an inspection of the coordinates of the ROC curve reveals that the optimum cut-off point, if one is looking for the best trade-off between sensitivity and specificity, is again very close to zero. At this score (actual value $= -0.6$ ms), gay participants were correctly identified 75% of the time, while straight participants were identified correctly 78% of the time. A value close to zero, like the Stroop difference score, is as we would predict, given that theoretically a score greater than zero indicates a facilitatory effect when the concepts of sex and female are paired and that a score of less than zero indicates a facilitatory effect when male and sex are paired.

COMPARING THE PICTORIAL MODIFIED STROOP TASK AND THE IAT

While on the face of it many of the implicit tasks seem to be measuring similar if not identical constructs, this may not be strictly true. Indeed, in Chapter 4, Gress and Laws find very little to suggest a relationship between their CRT and viewing time measures, while Snowden *et al.* (2008; see also Chapter 5 by Gray and Snowden) found significant agreement between their priming task and their IAT ($r = 0.59$, $p < 0.001$) as well as with their explicit measure when it came to assessing sexual orientation in gay and straight men. It is likely that agreement of implicit measures is contingent on the methodology as well as the measures used. It is also likely that small differences in stimuli may affect the ability of measures to agree. While finding implicit tasks of sexual interest whose results co-vary may go some way towards strengthening the construct validity of these tests, it is also interesting to explore what underlies those measures that do not agree. It is potentially interesting to see whether sexy–child associations yield the same response as sexually attractive–child associations or children–sex associations, and whether these match reactions for stimuli that include images of children or words related to the perpetration of abuse. The ability of these tasks to tap into subtle nuances of sexual interest would be potentially very interesting. However, it may be that many of the tasks will measure the same associations. To investigate the relationship between the Stroop and IAT tasks conducted, the results of both were compared. It was expected that the two measures would show some shared variance but that they were unlikely to be highly correlated given the difference in stimuli. Unlike Snowden *et al.* (2008) the stimulus materials were not the same for both tasks. While the Stroop used images of males and females, the IAT used names of males and females to illicit the different categories.

Among our data, a comparison between the Stroop and the IAT shows limited evidence for a correlation between the two. A Pearson's correlation between the Stroop difference score (less conservative method of outlier removal using three times the interquartile range as the removal criteria) and the IAT difference score was approaching significance and in the direction expected $r = -0.401$, $p = 0.076$, two-tailed. These results do not allow us to draw any conclusions about the relationship between these two tasks other than that any relationship that exists between these two variables is not a strong one. An increased sample size would have allowed us to be more definitive about any relationships that exist. Despite the lack of a clear relationship between the IAT and the Stroop task we know that scores on both show group differences between gay and straight participants. Both can also categorize participants with a sensitivity and specificity that is between good and excellent[4] according to ROC analysis. It may be that both tasks are tapping into separate components of sexual interest. If this was the case, both together might better predict sexual orientation. With this in mind, two forced entry binary logistic regressions were carried out to assess whether a combination of both the IAT and Stroop scores yielded a better categorization of participants as either gay or straight than either did individually. The less conservative Stroop score was again used as it was shown by the ROC curve analysis to have a better trade-off

---

[4]Tape (1999) describes a heuristic for interpreting AUCs with over 0.9 being excellent, 0.8–0.9 good, 0.7–0.8 fair, 0.6-0.7 poor and AUCs of 0.5–0.6 being described as fails. Rice and Harris (2005), on the other hand, equate AUCs to common measurements of effect size, including Cohen's *d*, equating AUCs of 0.556, 0.639 and 0.714 to effect sizes that Cohen (1988) would consider small, medium and large effects, respectively. It is probably best to interpret AUCs not by these conventions but rather by the trade-off of specificity versus sensitivity that best suits the research in question. Whereas tests designed to diagnose illness may be considered too inaccurate at an AUC of 0.8, such a value would be considered very useful when performing exploratory investigations such as this one.

between hit and false-alarm rate than the more conservative score. In the first regression analysis, the IAT difference score served as the predictor variable in the first block and the Stroop difference score was the predictor variable in the second block. This order of inclusion in the analysis was reversed in the second regression. The analysis was conducted in both directions to see how each score performed on their own and then when the other was included. Taken together, both scores yielded an overall classification rate of 90.5% with 88.9% (8/9) of gay and 91.7% (11/12) of straight participants being correctly classified. Individually, the Stroop score outperformed the IAT score in terms of categorization (85.7% compared with 71.4%). Both scores explained large amounts of the variance, with the Stroop model ($R^2 = 0.68$) being higher than the IAT ($R^2 = 0.41$). The combination of both predictor variables yielded an 8% increase in total variance explained ($R^2 = 0.76$). The Stroop score accounted for 35% of unique variance, while the IAT accounted only for 8%. Thirty-three per cent of the variance in categorization was attributable to overlapping variance between the IAT and Stroop. The addition of the IAT score to the regression model including the Stroop score increased the classification rate by 6% which corresponded to the correct classification of one additional gay participant. From a practical perspective, an increase of 6% of correct classification is noteworthy, given the implications for large samples. This increase also suggests the utilization of both IAT and Stroop in combination is a fruitful research strategy.

THE INFLUENCE OF ORDER ON THE OBSERVED DATA

The pictorial modified Stroop task used here incorporated a blocked design to maximize group differences when reacting to potentially sexually salient stimuli. However, the disadvantage of this technique is that it also may introduce order effects. This does not cause a problem for between-group comparisons, as any order effects should be counterbalanced by the random presentation of blocks across participants. However, if one takes the next step and analyzes data at the individual level, the resultant confounding variance may reduce the sensitivity of identifying sexual orientation. Therefore, statistical consideration was given to the effect of block presentation order on results. Mean scores with outliers removed (1.5 times the interquartile range) were calculated for blocks on the basis of presentation order across each participant. On inspection of boxplots, one block mean for one participant was removed from analysis as it was considered an extreme outlier (6.44 times the interquartile range). Less extreme outliers (less than three times the interquartile range) were not removed as their removal would involve too great a loss of data. This was also deemed acceptable since these values were not single observations but block means (with outliers already removed) for each participant. A repeated measures ANOVA was carried out on these presentation order block means, which found a significant effect of block order; $F(4,76) = 4.826$, $p = 0.002$. Pairwise comparisons show significant differences between block 1 and each of blocks 3, 4 and 5 and also between blocks 2 and 5 and between blocks 3 and 5. All differences are in a direction that shows a decrease in reaction times across successive blocks. However, when a Bonferroni correction is applied, only one of these differences continues to be significant, that between block 1 and 5;

$t(19) = 3.785, p = 0.001$, two-tailed.[5] When between-group differences between gay and straight participants were investigated, no significant interaction was found between sexual orientation and block order.

Given the presence of an order effect in the data, it seems likely that the removal of that order effect would have produced data with an even better ability to discriminate the sexual interest of participants. The presence of this effect may have impacted on our ability to detect correlations between IAT results and Stroop results and would necessarily have impacted on our ability to see whether Stroop results were on a continuum that might allow us to measure strength of interest. These two issues are important research questions that should be addressed by future research. To this end, we suggest two methods that may reduce the impact of order. The first, quite obviously, is to do away with the blocked design, and completely randomize all stimuli. This would insure that any effects of order would be randomly distributed across all trial types. The cost of this design may be to reduce the impact of our experimental manipulation as argued earlier in the chapter. The second method is an attempt to strike a balance between the fully random and the blocked design: in a 'clustered' design, matching stimuli would be presented in small blocks or clusters with several clusters of each trial type being spread across the task. One could even adopt a pseudorandom presentation that would ensure that a cluster of each trial type must be presented in random order before moving on to a second cluster of any trial type and so on. This design should go some way to removing the impact of order and, therefore, improving classification at the individual level.

CONCLUSIONS

Results of the analysis on the pictorial modified Stroop task showed an interaction of gender of adult stimuli and sexual orientation in line with the hypothesis that gay and straight men would have different reaction times to adult male and female images. Although the directions of the group differences were as predicted, the analysis lacked sufficient statistical power, due to a small sample size, to reach definitive conclusions about the full nature of the interaction. Results supported the prediction that there would be no significant differences in reactions to child images. Examination of the differences between reaction times to male and female adult images suggests that the task has the potential to discriminate between gay and straight participants at an individual level. As hypothesized and in line with the Stroop findings, the age–sex IAT found no significant differences between gay and straight participants in their reaction times to child–sex associations versus adult–sex associations. Furthermore, results of the gender–sex IAT were in line with the stated hypothesis that gay and straight men would perform differently on the task. As with the Stroop, a significant interaction was found between gender of name–sex association and orientation of participant. When this interaction was investigated further, differences were in the directions predicted, but again the analysis suffered from a lack of power. The IAT did not appear to be as good as

---

[5]Using the Bonferroni correction critical alpha is set at 0.005.

the Stroop at predicting orientation based on comparisons of the area under the ROC curve. Results of the Stroop and the gender–sex IAT were in the direction expected with reaction times to orientation-consistent stimuli in the Stroop being longer (demonstrating an attentional bias) than orientation-inconsistent stimuli. The IAT on the other hand showed a facilitative effect when orientation-consistent stimuli were associated with sex compared to when the association was between orientation-inconsistent stimuli. Results suggested that, within the modified Stroop task, reaction times to child male stimuli were significantly longer than child female stimuli across participants. The reason for this is unclear and should be addressed in future studies. Results supported the conclusion that these two implicit tasks have the potential to tap into sexual interest and associations. Correlations between the measures were not significant, though a larger study would be required to explore the presence of a relationship between the two. Logistic regression analysis did indicate that the inclusion of both measures in the model did improve its ability to correctly categorize participants as either gay or straight. The relationship between both these measures still remains unclear, but this study does justify the inclusion of both types of task as a usual research approach, since combined they improved the correct classification of sexual orientation. The findings justify the next step of the process, which is to use the techniques within an offending population. The end goal of this vein of research is to examine the utility of these measures as potential new tools to add to the arsenal of clinicians involved in the assessment of people who sexually abuse. To that end, group differences are not sufficient to establish utility. One way in which the Stroop may be improved is to reduce the potential for order effects. As mentioned, the blocking technique is the current best practice (i.e. related stimuli are presented together instead of randomly) in terms of producing the biggest effect size. However, this comes at the expense of risking an effect of order on results. Future research may minimize this order effect while maintaining the increased sensitivity to differences by presenting stimuli in smaller blocks or 'clusters'. In terms of the IAT, more work on the best method to collate the results may prove to increase the utility of the task on an individual assessment level.

In this chapter and other chapters in this book, the authors report areas under the ROC curve as indicators of the ability of our tasks to predict group membership or to discriminate between offenders and non-offenders and so on. We advise a note of caution in the use of this analysis. ROCs originated from signal detection theory and are widely used in medical studies. In the medical literature, they are used to examine how well a given measure predicts the presence or absence of a given pathology or illness. Using them to asses the validity of implicit tasks is slightly different. We are developing tasks that may identify the presence or absence of certain implicit or explicit cognitions, namely sexual interest in children. But we are testing the utility of our tasks by seeing whether they correctly predict membership of the offender and non-offender groups. We usually say that a 'perfect test' would have an AUC of 1. However, by using offender versus non-offender as the variable, we would like to predict that a test which has an AUC of 1 would be telling us what we already know: which of our participants have offended against children. While such a test would undoubtedly have its use in the detection of abuse, it would not shed any light on the heterogeneity that exists within offenders. Given that we would not expect all offenders to have sexual cognitions that were different to those of non-offenders, it would be unlikely that this 'perfect test' would be truly measuring sexual interest. A perfect test of sexual interest (or any other test of deviant cognitive schema) would yield an AUC of less than 1 as it would have correctly identified some of the offending group as not having the deviant interest or association in question (and possibly correctly identifying the cognition to be also present to some degree in the non-offending population). This is not to say that the ROC analysis should not be used but merely to exercise caution in its interpretation. When the Stroop design outlined in this chapter is used with sexual offenders against children, the AUC value will not be as high as it was in discriminating gay men from straight men. The challenge will be to ascertain how much of this 'imperfection' is due to testing error and how much is due to the true prevalence of the cognitions in question. In other words, if using offender versus non-offender as the variable we would like to predict, we must be conscious of what a false positive on our implicit task means: that our offender has abused a child but does not have the deviant cognition we expected *or* that the task was unable to identify the presence of the cognition due to error. Likewise, false negatives could indicate task error *or* the presence of the deviant cognition in someone who has not abused a child.

One of the benefits of the current interest in cognitive methods of the assessment of sexual interest is the potential for the advancement of one method on the back of progress with another. For example, if a blocked or clustered method of stimulus presentation proves to be the most useful in a modified Stroop paradigm, it might be worth investigating whether such an approach might improve outcomes with CRT tasks. We already see such developments with the migration of the NRP image set from viewing time tasks to CRT and now Stroop tasks. A next step may be the development of a pictorial IAT for use with offenders against children. The widening field of cognitive psychology will undoubtedly provide further inspiration for tasks such as those utilizing the subliminal presentation of stimuli. Advances in computer science have already produced realistic computer animations of children for use with tasks (Chartier, Renaud, Bouchard, Proulx, Rouleau, Fedoroff and Bradford, 2006). Neuroscience may also provide an avenue for research where brain-imaging techniques could be used while participants engage in these cognitive tasks.

REFERENCES

Ashwin, C., Wheelwright, S. and Baron-Cohen, S. (2006) Attention bias to faces in Asperger Syndrome: a pictorial emotion Stroop study. *Psychological Medicine*, **36** (6), 835–43.
Ballesteros, S., Reales, J.M. and Manga, D. (2000) Effects of type of design (blocked vs. randomized) on Stroop and emotional Stroop tasks. *Psicothema*, **12**, 60–63.
Baron, A.S. and Banaji, M.R. (2006) The development of implicit attitudes: evidence of race evaluations from ages 6 and 10 and adulthood. *Psychological Science*, **17** (1), 53–8.
Becker, E.S., Strohbach, D. and Rinck, M. (1999) A specific attentional bias in suicide attempters. *Journal of Nervous and Mental Disease*, **187** (12), 730–35.
Blanton, H. and Jaccard, J. (2006) Arbitrary metrics in psychology. *American Psychologist*, **61** (1), 27–41.
Blanton, H., Jaccard, J., Christie, C. and Gonzales, P.M. (2007) Plausible assumptions, questionable assumptions and post hoc rationalizations: will the real IAT, please stand up? *Journal of Experimental Social Psychology*, **43** (3), 399–409.

Blanton, H., Jaccard, J., Gonzales, P.M. and Christie, C. (2006) Decoding the implicit association test: implications for criterion prediction. *Journal of Experimental Social Psychology*, **42** (2), 192–212.

Boyer, M. and Dickerson, M. (2003) Attentional bias and addictive behaviour: automaticity in a gambling-specific modified Stroop task. *Addiction*, **98** (1), 61.

Bradley, B.P., Mogg, K., Millar, N. and White, J. (1995) Selective processing of negative information: effects of clinical anxiety, concurrent depression, and awareness. *Journal of Abnormal Psychology*, **104** (3), 532–6.

Braet, C. and Crombez, G. (2003) Cognitive interference due to food cues in childhood obesity. *Journal of Clinical Child and Adolescent Psychology*, **32** (1), 32–9.

Cannon, B.J. (2003) An emotional Stroop effect to malingering-related words. *Perceptual and Motor Skills*, **96** (3), 827–34.

Carpenter, K.M., Schreiber, E., Church, S. and McDowell, D. (2006) Drug Stroop performance: relationships with primary substance of use and treatment outcome in a drug-dependent outpatient sample. *Addictive Behaviors*, **31** (1), 174–181.

Carrigan, M.H., Drobes, D.J. and Randall, C.L. (2004) Attentional bias and drinking to cope with social anxiety. *Psychology of Addictive Behaviors*, **18** (4), 374–80.

Chartier, S., Renaud, P., Bouchard, S., Proulx, J., Rouleau, J.L., Fedoroff, P. and Bradford, J. (2006) Sexual preference classification from gaze behavior data using a multilayer perceptron. *Annual Review of CyberTherapy and Telemedicine*, **4**, 149–57.

Cohen, J. (1988) *Statistical Power Analysis for the Behavioral Sciences*, 2nd edn. L. Erlbaum Associates, Hillsdale, NJ.

Constantine, R., McNally, R.J. and Hornig, C.D. (2001) Snake fear and the pictorial emotional Stroop paradigm. *Cognitive Therapy and Research*, **25** (6), 757.

Côté, S. and Bouchard, S. (2005) Documenting the efficacy of virtual reality exposure with psychophysiological and information processing measures. *Applied Psychophysiology and Biofeedback*, **30** (3), 217–32.

Cox, W.M., Fadardi, J.S. and Klinger, E. (2006) Motivational processes underlying implicit cognition in addiction, in *The Handbook of Implicit Cognition and Addiction* (eds R.W. Wiers and A.W. Stacy), Sage Publishers, Thousand Oaks, CA, pp. 253–66.

Cox, W.M., Fadardi, J.S. and Pothos, E.M. (2006) The addiction-Stroop test: theoretical considerations and procedural recommendations. *Psychological Bulletin*, **132** (3), 443–76.

Cox, W.M., Yeates, G.N. and Regan, C.N. (1999) Effects of alcohol cues on cognitive processing in heavy and light drinkers. *Drug and Alcohol Dependence*, **55** (1), 58–89.

Dalgleish, T., Taghavi, R., Neshat-Doost, H., Moradi, A., Canterbury, R. and Yule, W. (2003) Patterns of processing bias for emotional information across clinical disorders: a comparison of attention, memory, and prospective cognition in children and adolescents with depression, generalized anxiety, and posttraumatic stress disorder. *Journal of Clinical Child and Adolescent Psychology*, **32** (1), 10–21.

Dubner, A.E. and Motta, R.W. (1999) Sexually and physically abused foster care children and posttraumatic stress disorder. *Journal of Consulting and Clinical Psychology*, **67** (3), 367–73.

Egloff, B. and Schmukle, S.C. (2004) Gender differences in implicit and explicit anxiety measures. *Personality and Individual Differences*, **36** (8), 1807–15.

Elsesser, K., Heuschen, I., Pundt, I. and Sartory, G. (2006) Attentional bias and evoked heart-rate response in specific phobia. *Cognition and Emotion*, **20** (8), 1092–1107.

Erblich, J., Montgomery, G.H., Valdimarsdottir, H.B., Cloitre, M. and Bovbjerg, D.H. (2003) Biased cognitive processing of cancer-related information among women with family histories of breast cancer: evidence from a cancer Stroop task. *Health Psychology*, **22** (3), 235–44.

Field, M. (2005) Cannabis 'dependence' and attentional bias for cannabis-related words. *Behavioural Pharmacology*, **16** (5), 473–6.

Foa, E.B., Feske, U., Murdock, T.B., Kozak, M.J. and McCarthy, P.R. (1991) Processing of threat-related information in rape victims. *Journal of Abnormal Psychology*, **100** (2), 156–62.

Formea, G.M. and Burns, G.L. (1996) Selective processing of food, weight, and body-shape words in nonpatient women with bulimia nervosa: interference on the Stroop task. *Journal of Psychopathology and Behavioral Assessment*, **18** (2), 105–118.

Fortune, D.G., Richards, H.L., Corrin, A., Taylor, R.J., Griffiths, C.E.M. and Main, C.J. (2003) Attentional bias for psoriasis-specific and psychosocial threat in patients with psoriasis. *Journal of Behavioral Medicine*, **26** (3), 211.

Freeman, J.B. and Beck, J.G. (2000) Cognitive interference for trauma cues in sexually abused adolescent girls with posttraumatic stress disorder. *Journal of Clinical Child Psychology*, **29** (2), 245–56.

French, C.C., Richards, A. and Scholfield, E.J.C. (1996) Hypomania, anxiety and the emotional Stroop. *British Journal of Clinical Psychology*, **35** (4), 617–26.

Fujimiya, M. (2001) Morpher (Version 3.1) [Computer software], http://www.asahi-net.or.jp/~FX6M-FJMY/mop00e.html (retrieved 10 May 2006).

Gotlib, I.H. and Cane, D.B. (1987) Construct accessibility and clinical depression: a longitudinal investigation. *Journal of Abnormal Psychology*, **96** (3), 199–204.

Gray, N.S., Brown, A.S., MacCulloch, M.J., Smith, J. and Snowden, R.J. (2005) An implicit test of the associations between children and sex in pedophiles. *Journal of Abnormal Psychology*, **114** (2), 304–8.

Green, M.W., Elliman, N.A. and Rogers, P.J. (1996) Hunger, caloric preloading and the selective processing of food and body shape words. *British Journal of Clinical Psychology*, **35** (1), 143–51.

Greenwald, A.G., McGhee, D.E. and Schwartz, J.L.K. (1998) Measuring individual differences in implicit cognition: the implicit association test. *Journal of Personality and Social Psychology*, **74** (6), 1464–80.

Greenwald, A.G., Nosek, B.A. and Banaji, M.R. (2003) Understanding and using the implicit association test: I. An improved scoring algorithm. *Journal of Personality and Social Psychology*, **85** (2), 197–216.

Greenwald, A.G., Nosek, B.A. and Sriram, N. (2006) Consequential validity of the implicit association test: comment on Blanton and Jaccard (2006). *American Psychologist*, **61** (1), 56–61.

Heim-Dreger, U., Kohlmann, C.-W., Eschenbeck, H. and Burkhardt, U. (2006) Attentional biases for threatening faces in children: vigilant and avoidant processes. *Emotion*, **6** (2), 320–5.

Hester, R., Dixon, V. and Garavan, H. (2006) A consistent attentional bias for drug-related material in active cocaine users across word and picture versions of the emotional Stroop task. *Drug and Alcohol Dependence*, **81** (3), 251–7.

Holle, C., Neely, J.H. and Heimberg, R.G. (1997) The effects of blocked versus random presentation and semantic relatedness of stimulus words on response to a modified Stroop task among social phobics. *Cognitive Therapy and Research*, **21** (6), 681–97.

Jessop, D.C., Rutter, D.R., Sharma, D. and Albery, I.P. (2004) Emotion and adherence to treatment in people with asthma: an application of the emotional Stroop paradigm. *British Journal of Psychology*, **95** (2), 127–47.

Kindt, M. and Brosschot, J.F. (1997) Phobia-related cognitive bias for pictorial and linguistic stimuli. *Journal of Abnormal Psychology*, **106** (4), 644–8.

Kindt, M. and Brosschot, J.F. (1999) Cognitive bias in spider-phobic children: comparison of a pictorial and a linguistic spider Stroop. *Journal of Psychopathology and Behavioral Assessment*, **21** (3), 207–20.

Kolassa, I.-T., Musial, F., Mohr, A., Trippe, R.H. and Miltner, W.H.R. (2005) Electrophysiological correlates of threat processing in spider phobics. *Psychophysiology*, **42** (5), 520–30.

Kramer, D.A. and Goldman, M.S. (2003) Using a modified Stroop task to implicitly discern the cognitive organization of alcohol expectancies. *Journal of Abnormal Psychology*, **112** (1), 171–5.

Kumar, S. (2002) WinMorph (Version 3. *01*). [Computer software].

Labarge, A.S., Cash, T.F. and Brown, T.A. (1998) Use of a modified Stroop task to examine appearance-schematic information processing in college women. *Cognitive Therapy and Research*, **22** (2), 179–90.

Langevin, R. and Curnoe, S. (2007) The therapeutic challenge of the learning impaired sex offender [Electronic Version]. *Sexual Offender Treatment*, **2**, http://www.sexual-offender-treatment.org/56.0.html (accessed 17 December 2007).

Lavy, E. and Van den Hout, M. (1993) Selective attention evidenced by pictorial and linguistic Stroop tasks. *Behavior Therapy*, **24** (4), 645–57.

Laws, D.R. and Gress, C.L.Z. (2004) Seeing things differently: the viewing time alternative to penile plethysmography. *Legal and Criminological Psychology*, **9**, 183–96.

Lecci, L. and Cohen, D.J. (2002) Perceptual consequences of an illness-concern induction and its relation to hypochondriacal tendencies. *Health Psychology*, **21** (2), 147–56.

Lundh, L.-G. and Öst, L.-G. (2001) Attentional bias, self-consciousness and perfectionism in social phobia before and after cognitive-behaviour therapy. *Scandinavian Journal of Behaviour Therapy*, **30** (1), 4–16.

MacLeod, C.M. (1991) Half a century of research on the Stroop effect: an integrative review. *Psychological Bulletin*, **109** (2), 163–203.

Macmillan, N.A. and Creelman, C.D. (1990) *Detection Theory: A User's Guide*. Cambridge University Press, Cambridge.

Mahamedi, F. and Heatherton, T.F. (1993) Effects of high calorie preloads on selective processing of food and body shape stimuli among dieters and nondieters. *International Journal of Eating Disorders*, **13** (3), 305–14.

Marshall, W.L. and Serran, G.A. (2000) Current issues in the assessment and treatment of sexual offenders. *Clinical Psychology and Psychotherapy*, **7** (2), 85–96.

Mattia, J.I., Heimberg, R.G. and Hope, D.A. (1993) The revised Stroop color-naming task in social phobics. *Behaviour Research and Therapy*, **31** (3), 305–13.

McCusker, C.G. and Gettings, B. (1997) Automaticity of cognitive biases in addictive behaviours: further evidence with gamblers. *British Journal of Clinical Psychology*, **36** (4), 543–54.

McNally, R.J., Riemann, B.C., Louro, C.E. and Lukach, B.M. (1992) Cognitive processing of emotional information in panic disorder. *Behaviour Research and Therapy*, **30** (2), 143–9.

Mihailides, S., Devilly, G.J. and Ward, T. (2004) Implicit cognitive distortions and sexual offending. *Sexual Abuse: Journal of Research and Treatment*, **16** (4), 333–50.

Mogg, K. and Bradley, B.P. (2002) Selective processing of smoking-related cues in smokers: manipulation of deprivation level and comparison of three measures of processing bias. *Journal of Psychopharmacology*, **16** (4), 385–92.

Mogg, K., Bradley, B.P., Dixon, C., Fisher, S., Twelftree, H. and McWilliams, A. (2000) Trait anxiety, defensiveness and selective processing of threat: an investigation using two measures of attentional bias. *Personality and Individual Differences*, **28** (6), 1063–77.

Munafò, M., Mogg, K., Roberts, S. *et al.* (2003) Selective processing of smoking-related cues in current smokers, ex-smokers and never-smokers on the modified Stroop task. *Journal of Psychopharmacology*, **17** (3), 310–16.

Nosek, B.A. and Banaji, M.R. (2001) The Go/No-go association task. *Social Cognition*, **19** (6), 625–66.

Nosek, B.A., Greenwald, A.G., Banaji, M.R. and Bargh, J.A. (2007) *The Implicit Association Test at Age 7: A Methodological and Conceptual Review*. Psychology Press, New York.

Nosek, B.A. and Sriram, N. (2007) Faulty assumptions: a comment on Blanton, Jaccard, Gonzales, and Christie (2006). *Journal of Experimental Social Psychology*, **43** (3), 393–8.

Nunes, K.L., Firestone, P. and Baldwin, M.W. (2007) Indirect assessment of cognitions of child sexual abusers with the Implicit Association Test. *Criminal Justice and Behavior*, **34** (4), 454–75.

Perpiña, C., Leonard, T., Treasure, J., Bond, A. and Baños, R. (1998) Selective processing of food- and body-related information and autonomic arousal in patients with eating disorders. *The Spanish Journal of Psychology*, **1** (1), 3–10.

Powell, J., Tait, S. and Lessiter, J. (2002) Cigarette smoking and attention to signals of reward and threat in the Stroop paradigm. *Addiction*, **97** (9), 1163.

Prentky, R.A., Knight, R.A. and Lee, A.F.S. (1997) *Child Sexual Molestation: Research Issues* (No. NCJ-163390). U.S. Department of Justice, Washington DC.

Price, S. (2005) *Measuring the Deviant Schema of Sexual Offenders: A Stroop Replication Study*. Unpublished Masters, Carleton University.

Rice, M. and Harris, G. (2005) Comparing effect sizes in follow-up studies: ROC area, Cohen's *d*, and *r*. *Law and Human Behavior*, **29** (5), 615–20.

Richards, A., French, C.C., Johnson, W. and Naparstek, J. (1992) Effects of mood manipulation and anxiety on performance of an emotional Stroop task. *British Journal of Psychology*, **83** (4), 479–91.

Ryan, F. (2002) Attentional bias and alcohol dependence: a controlled study using the modified Stroop paradigm. *Addictive Behaviors*, **27** (4), 471–82.

Sekuler, R. and Blake, R. (1994) *Perception*, 3rd edn. McGraw-Hill, New York, London.

Sharma, D., Albery, I.P. and Cook, C. (2001) Selective attentional bias to alcohol related stimuli in problem drinkers and non-problem drinkers. *Addiction*, **96** (2), 285–95.

Smith, P. (2006) *Cognitive Bias in Sexual Offenders*. Paper presented at the 25th Annual Research and Treatment Conference of the Association for the Treatment of Sexual Abusers, 27–30 October 2006, Chicago, IL.

Smith, P. and Waterman, M. (2003) Processing bias for aggression words in forensic and nonforensic samples. *Cognition and Emotion*, **17** (5), 681.

Smith, P. and Waterman, M. (2004) Processing bias for sexual material: the emotional Stroop and sexual offenders. *Sexual Abuse: Journal of Research and Treatment*, **16** (2), 163–71.

Smith, P. and Waterman, M. (2005) Sex differences in processing aggression words using the emotional Stroop task. *Aggressive Behavior*, **31** (3), 271–82.

Snowden, R., Wichter, J. and Gray, N. (2008) Implicit and explicit measurements of sexual preference in gay and heterosexual men: a comparison of priming techniques and the implicit association task. *Archives of Sexual Behavior*, **37**, 558–65.

Stormark, K.M. and Torkildsen, O. (2004) Selective processing of linguistic and pictorial food stimuli in females with anorexia and bulimia nervosa. *Eating Behaviors*, **5** (1), 27–33.

Tanner, J.M. (1973) Growing up. *Scientific American*, **229** (3), 34–43.

Tape, T.G. (1999). *Interpreting Diagnostic Tests*. University of Nebraska Medical Center, http://gim.unmc.edu/dxtests/roc3.htm (retrieved 7 December 2007).

van Honk, J., Tuiten, A., de Haan, E., van den Hout, M. and Stam, H. (2001) Attentional biases for angry faces: relationships to trait anger and anxiety. *Cognition and Emotion*, **15** (3), 279–97.

van Honk, J., Tuiten, A., van den Hout, M., Koppeschaar, H., Thijssen, J., de Haan, E. and Verbaten, R. (1998) Baseline salivary cortisol levels and preconscious selective attention for threat: a pilot study. *Psychoneuroendocrinology*, **23** (7), 741–7.

van Honk, J., Tuiten, A., van den Hout, M., Koppeschaar, H., Thijssen, J., de Haan, E. and Verbaten, R. (2000) Conscious and preconscious selective attention to social threat: different neuroendocrine response patterns. *Psychoneuroendocrinology*, **25** (6), 577–91.

van Honk, J., Tuiten, A., Verbaten, R., van den Hout, M., Koppeschaar, H., Thijssen, J. and de Haan, E. (1999) Correlations among salivary testosterone, mood, and selective attention to threat in humans. *Hormones and Behavior*, **36** (1), 17–24.

Walker, M.K., Ben-Tovim, D.I., Paddick, S. and McNamara, J. (1995) Pictorial adaptation of Stroop measures of body-related concerns in eating disorders. *International Journal of Eating Disorders*, **17** (3), 309–11.

Ward, T. (2000) Sexual offenders' cognitive distortions as implicit theories. *Aggression and Violent Behavior*, **5** (5), 491–507.

Waters, A.J. and Feyerabend, C. (2000) Determinants and effects of attentional bias in smokers. *Psychology of Addictive Behaviors*, **14** (2), 111–20.

Waters, A.J., Shiffman, S., Sayette, M.A., Paty, J.A., Gwaltney, C.J. and Balabanis, M.H. (2003) Attentional bias predicts outcome in smoking cessation. *Health Psychology*, **22** (4), 378–87.

Wertz, J.M. and Sayette, M.A. (2001) Effects of smoking opportunity on attentional bias in smokers. *Psychology of Addictive Behaviors*, **15** (3), 268–71.

Wikström, J., Lundh, L.-G. and Westerlund, J. (2003) Stroop effects for masked threat words: pre-attentive bias or selective awareness? *Cognition & Emotion*, **17** (6), 827–42.

Wright, L.W. Jr. and Adams, H.E. (1994) Assessment of sexual preference using a choice reaction time task. *Journal of Psychopathology and Behavioral Assessment*, **16** (3), 221–31.

Wright, L.W. Jr. and Adams, H.E. (1999) The effects of stimuli that vary in erotic content on cognitive processes. *Journal of Sex Research*, **36** (2), 145–51.

Zeitlin, S.B., Bradburn, D.O. and Lawson-Kerr, K. (1995) Selective processing of epilepsy-related cues in patients with high fear of seizures. *Journal of Epilepsy*, **8** (1), 16–22.

Chapter 10

THE STARTLE PROBE REFLEX: AN ALTERNATIVE APPROACH TO THE MEASUREMENT OF SEXUAL INTEREST

Jeffrey E. Hecker and Matthew W. King

Department of Psychology, University of Maine, Orono, ME, USA

R. Jamie Scoular

Highlands Behavioral Health Systems, Denver, CO, USA

Our basic argument is that the strength of a man's eyeblink reflex in response to a startling stimulus recorded while he is observing visual images can inform us about whether or not he is sexually interested in those images. When men are unexpectedly startled, they show a decreased startle reaction if they are attending to images they find sexually appealing as compared to when they are observing neutral or emotionally aversive images (Bradley, Codispoti, Sabatinelli and Lang, 2001b; Hecker, King and Scoular, 2006; Jansen and Frijda, 1994; Janssen, Vorst, Finn and Bancroft, 2002; Koukounas and McCabe, 2001; Koukounas and Over, 2000). This basic finding may prove to have significant implications for the assessment of sexual interests in men who have committed sexual offences.

In order to understand the implications of eyeblink intensity for the measurement of sexual interests, it is important to first understand the significance of the startle reflex in the context of a broad theory of emotion and motivation. Emotions can be viewed as dispositional states that incline the organism to behave in certain ways that have survival value (Lang, 1995). While the array of emotions experienced by human beings can seem strikingly complex, emotional states can be organized along two dimensions: hedonic valence (pleasant vs. aversive) and arousal (the strength of the motivational activation) (Lang, 1995; Lang, Bradley and Cuthbert, 1998). This organizational structure is supported by evidence indicating that emotions originate from one of two neurological systems: one defensive and the other appetitive. The appetitive system is activated when organisms are stimulated by cues that require an approach response to facilitate survival – for example food motivates consumption, nurturance cues motivate care-giving behaviour and sexual stimuli motivate copulation. This appetitive motivation gives rise to subjectively pleasant emotions such as lust, passion and affection. In contrast, the defensive system is activated when environmental cues suggest threat and require a harm avoidance response, such as withdrawal, escape or attack. Defensive motivation is experienced subjectively as unpleasant emotions such as fear and disgust (Bradley, Codispoti, Cuthbert and Lang, 2001a). Thus hedonic valence reflects which of the two systems are engaged, while arousal reflects the intensity of the attracted or repulsed emotional reaction.

Defensive reflexes provide valuable information about the activation of an organism's motivational systems and thus its emotional state. When an organism is aversively motivated, its autonomic defensive reflexes are exacerbated or stronger in magnitude. In contrast, when appetitively motivated, defensive reflexes are muted or reduced in magnitude (Lang, 1995). The eyeblink reflex is the most commonly studied exemplar of this affective modulation in humans. The eyeblink is part of a more general defensive startle response that presumably evolved because it serves to protect the organism by avoiding injury to the eye (Graham, 1979). Any abrupt, unexpected sensory stimulation can elicit a defensive eyeblink.

The human startle eyeblink can be measured rather easily by recording electromyographic (EMG) activity in the muscle surrounding the eye. This can be accomplished with two passive electrodes placed over the orbicularis oculi muscle (just below the eye) and an isolated ground electrode placed on an electrically neutral site, such as the forehead (Blumenthal, Cuthbert, Filion, Hackley, Lipp and vanBoxtel, 2005). In research studies, the blink reflex usually is elicited by acoustic stimulation, although other means of stimulation can be used (Blumenthal *et al.*, 2005). Typically, a white noise generator is used to present a brief (e.g. 50 ms) burst of broadband noise (95 db) over a set of headphones at unexpected intervals during stimuli presentation (see, for example, Bradley *et al.*, 2001a). Blumenthal *et al.* (2005) provide a review of the technical issues and alternative approaches associated with startle measurement and quantification.

There is a large body of research which has shown a consistent relationship between the magnitude of participants' eyeblink responses and the affective quality of stimuli to which they are attending. In a prototypical study of emotion-modulated startle, participants are presented with a series of pictures that vary in emotionality. Many of these studies use pictures from the International Affective Picture System (IAPS; Lang, Bradley and Cuthbert, 2005) – a set of several hundred pictures normatively rated on the dimensions of valence (unpleasant–pleasant) and arousal. While observing these pictures, participants are periodically startled (e.g. by a white noise probe). The magnitude of the EMG response of the orbicularis oculi muscle is measured. Quite consistently across studies, it has been found that the magnitude of the participants' startle eyeblink is smallest when they are observing pleasant slides, larger when observing neutral slides and largest when observing unpleasant slide. Figure 10.1 provides an illustration of the typical pattern of findings. A sample of studies which have shown this effect using variations of the paradigm described above include Bradley *et al.* (2001a), Lang *et al.* (1998),

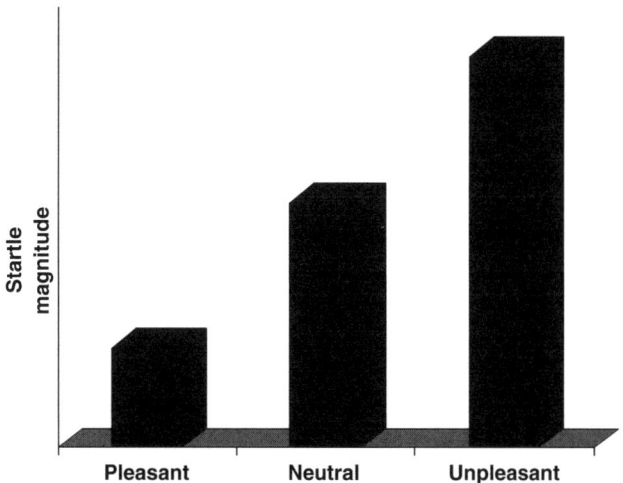

Figure 10.1 Typical pattern of startle reflex magnitude while participants view pleasant, neutral and unpleasant slides.

Smith, Löw, Bradley and Lang, (2006), Smith and O'Connor (2003) and Stanley and Knight (2004).

The relationship between magnitude of startle eyeblink and emotional experience is robust. A consistent relationship between the emotional properties of pictures and the magnitude of startle eyeblink has been found when the startle probe is delivered shortly after the onset of the picture stimuli (e.g. 300 ms) and later in picture viewing (e.g. 2–5 s from the time picture is presented) (Stanley and Knight, 2004). Emotion modulation of the startle response has been found when pictures are presented for very brief periods (e.g. 300 ms-duration) (Larson, Ruffalo, Nietert and Davidson, 2005) and when pictures are presented rapidly in a contiguous stream (Smith *et al.*, 2006). The same relationship is found whether participants are resting or physically active when they observe pictures (Smith and O'Connor, 2003). The relationship between eyeblink startle magnitude and emotionality is present when participants look at still pictures, listen to audio clips (Bradley and Lang, 2000) or watch video clips (Koukounas and McCabe, 2001).

Emotion-modulated startle reactions have been observed across species and in humans across the lifespan. Rats classically conditioned to fear a neutral stimulus show an augmented startle reflex when presented with an auditory startle stimulus while in the presence of the conditioned cue (Davis, 2006). In a classic study, Brown, Kalish and Farber (1951, described in Davis, 2006) conditioned rats to fear a light by pairing the light with shock. Later the rats showed an exaggerated startle reaction when startled in the presence of the light. Balaban (1995) showed 5-month-old infants pictures of happy, neutral and angry faces and measured their startle eyeblink to a brief acoustic noise. Blink size was largest when viewing angry faces and smallest when viewing happy faces.

The brain systems involved in the appetitive and aversive motivation systems underlying emotions are believed to be largely subcortical (Lang, 1995). The neural substrates of the defensive motivational system are better understood than are the appetitive system. Animal studies that utilize neural ablation, neuropharmacology and neural stimulation point to the amygdala as the mediator of defensive behaviour (Lang, 1995).

SEX AND THE STARTLE REFLEX

Sexual arousal in most circumstances is accompanied by a positive emotional state. Stimuli that elicit sexual arousal tend also to elicit positive feelings, or in the language of Lang's two-dimensional model of emotions, an appetitive emotional state. It follows, therefore, that the eyeblink startle reflex should be diminished when people are startled while attending to stimuli they find sexually arousing. There are several published studies that have demonstrated this effect with consistency.

Jansen and Frijda (1994) provoked eyeblink startle reactions as their participants watched brief film clips of sexual scenarios, fearful scenarios (i.e. horror movie clips) and neutral scenarios. Nine brief film segments of each type were shown in a mixed order. Startle reactions during sexual films were significantly reduced compared to fearful films, and also as compared to neutral films amongst those participants who rated the sexual films as subjectively pleasant. Koukounas and McCabe (2001) showed male participants five 2-minute clips from commercially available erotic videos and five clips from videos of nature scenes depicting flowers and trees. They found smaller eyeblink startle responses when participants were watching the erotic compared to the neutral films.

Similar findings have been reported in studies that used still images of nudes or erotic images. Bradley *et al.* (2001b) showed 72 pictures drawn from the IAPS collection to 45 male undergraduates. There were 4 pictures in each of 18 categories including 8 pleasant (nature, families, food, sports, adventure, male erotic, female erotic, erotic couples), 2 neutral (household objects, mushrooms) and 8 unpleasant (pollution, illness, loss, accidents, contamination, attacking animals, attacking humans, mutilated bodies). Males showed the smallest eyeblink startle reactions to images of erotic couples and erotic females. In our laboratory, we examined undergraduate males' eyeblink startle responses to pictures of nude adult females, neutral images (i.e. nature scenes) and unpleasant images (i.e. mutilated bodies). As Figure 10.2 illustrates, the smallest blinks were recorded when participants looked at the nude females and the largest while they looked at pictures of mutilated bodies with the neutral scenes falling in the middle (Hecker, King and Scoular, 2006).

Support for the convergent validity of the eyeblink startle reflex has been demonstrated in a number of studies that found relationships between startle blink magnitude and both subjective and physiological measures of sexual arousal and emotional experiences. Koukounas and McCabe (2001) found significant negative correlations between the size of participants' eyeblinks and their subjective ratings of feelings of sexual arousal as they observed erotic and neutral film clips. Similarly, they found significant negative correlations between startle response and participants' ratings of positive feelings (not at all – extremely) while watching the film clips. Phallometric responses were also measured during the film clip viewings,

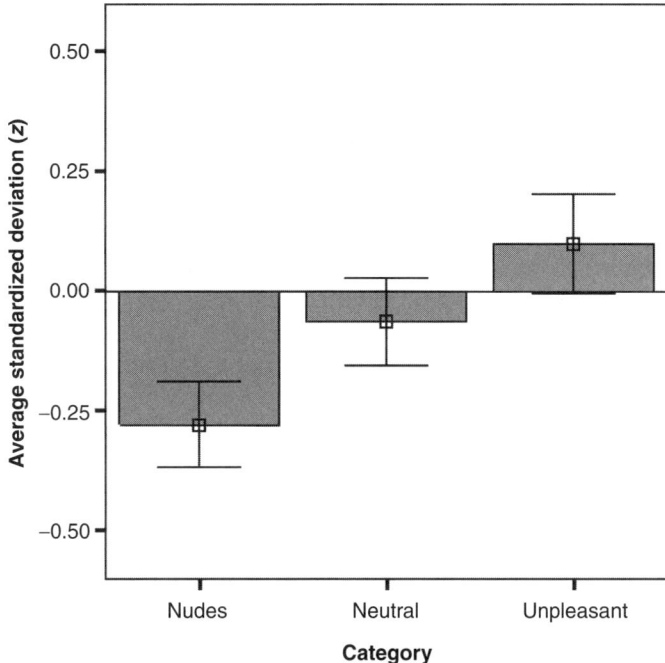

Figure 10.2   Mean standardized startle reflex magnitudes while participants viewed images of nude female, neutral and unpleasant images. Error bars reflect ±1 standard error.

and although the correlation between magnitude of startle and penile tumescence was not significant, it was fairly strong and in the predicted direction (−0.65). Janssen *et al.* (2002) similarly examined self-rated and phallometrically measured sexual arousal and self-rated emotionality along with startle response during the viewing of film clips depicting consensual or coercive sexual interactions. They found general agreement amongst the four measures: penile tumescence and self-ratings of sexual arousal and positive affect were higher, and startle responses smaller, during the consensual sex stimuli compared to the coercive sex stimuli. These findings support the ideas that the magnitude of startle reflex assessed while participants view sexual stimuli is measuring something important about the human sexual response.

Further support for the validity of startle eyeblink magnitude as a measure of a component of men's sexual interest response can be taken from research which shows that eyeblink startle magnitude become larger as men's sexual arousal habituates to repeated presentation of the same sexual stimuli. Koukounas and Over (2000) measured change in startle responses, penile tumescence and self-rated sexual arousal over several trials in which men were repeatedly shown the same 60-second film clip depicting heterosexual intercourse. As expected, physiological and subjective sexual arousal decreased in a steady linear fashion over repetitions of the film clip. Startle responses showed a generally similar rate of change, increasing in magnitude as interest in the film waned. All measures reflected a rapid rise in interest during two subsequent trials in which a novel film clip was shown, followed by a partial return to their maximally habituated level when the original clip was re-introduced.

Clearly, the eyeblink startle reaction measures a meaningful component of the sexual response. Small startle responses are found when men are viewing sexually provocative images whether these are in the form of still pictures or brief film clips. The magnitude of eyeblink startle correlates with sexual arousal and subjective ratings of viewers' emotional experience while viewing the images. The strength of the startle reaction follows the same pattern as sexual arousal over repeated presentations of the same stimuli. The startle reaction 'habituates' by getting larger with repeated presentations. Magnitude of startle eyeblink is correlated with physiological measures of sexual arousal but the startle reaction is measuring something different. Diminished eyeblinks are found in response to other forms of pleasant stimuli that presumably do not elicit penile tumescence (Bradley *et al.*, 2001; Lang, 1995).

THE STARTLE REFLEX AND MEASUREMENT OF DEVIANT SEXUAL INTERESTS

Men who have committed sexual offences and who are sexually aroused by deviant sexual stimuli present a higher risk for sexual re-offending than do men without deviant sexual interests (Hanson and Bussière, 1998; Hanson and Morton-Bourgon, 2005) and the presence of deviant sexual interests has implication for treatment planning with male sexual offenders. Undoubtedly, therefore, there is a need for reliable and valid methods of measuring deviant sexual interests.

The 'gold standard' for measuring sexual interests is the penile plethysmography, sometimes referred to as phallometric testing. This approach to assessment measures penile erection response to stimuli depicting various sexual behaviours or partners. There is an extensive research literature on phallometric testing and the strengths and limitations of plethysmography are well known (Marshall, 2006). Briefly, problems with reliability, validity and faking limit the usefulness of phallometry in clinical settings.

An alternative method of measuring sexual interests in sexual offenders is to surreptitiously measure viewing time as the subject looks at models of different ages and genders and portrayals of different sexual acts. The examinee controls the progression of images as he engages in some overt task such as rating interest in the stimuli, the length of time he spends viewing each image is recorded. A commercially available viewing time measure is the Abel Assessment for Sexual Interest (AASI; Abel Screening, Inc., 2004). The AASI is popular among clinicians working with sexual offenders (King, Patten, Hecker and Parisot, 2005a). While popular, the AASI has limitations in clinical use. The fact that viewing time assessment requires deception (i.e. examinees do not know that the time they spend viewing the images is being recorded) may limit its utility since once the deception is known respondents may be able to consciously control their viewing times.

Clearly, therefore, there is a need for alternative methods of measuring sexual interests. It is our contention that characteristics of eyeblink startle reflex magnitude make it a viable paradigm for measuring sexual interests.

First, it is theoretically plausible that eyeblink startle response may be resistant to conscious efforts by the examinee to distort the measurement of his sexual interests. The relationship between the size of an eyeblink and interest in a particular sex partner or act is not obvious. Even if an informed examinee is aware of the behaviour of interest, he would likely have difficulty exerting voluntary motor control over this rapid autonomic reflex, and in all likelihood would not be able to do so as covertly as, for example using abdominal muscles to fake penile reactions (i.e. 'pumping'), which is a tactic used to distort phallometric readings (Freund, Watson and Rienzo, 1988). Eyeblink startle reflexes that are being intentionally distorted by physical means (e.g. looking away, squeezing the eyes shut, etc.) should be relatively easy to identify and invalidate.

Another reason for this theoretical resistance is related to the nature of the appetitive and defensive motivational systems. Lang (1995) suggests that these systems are mutually inhibitory when activated. Thus it is reasonable to hypothesize that an examinee would have limited success in dissimulating a reaction on the other end of the valence spectrum from their instinctive response. For example, if an examinee experiences a spontaneous appetitive reaction to the suggestion of sex with a child, a decreased eyeblink response to a startle probe would be expected. Even if he attempts to manipulate his thoughts to simulate a disgust reaction, concurrent inhibition of the defensive system should prevent the eyeblink response from increasing to the level of a genuine aversive reaction. This is an empirical question that has yet to be tested, but there is related evidence that suggests it is plausible. Dillon and LaBar (2005) showed erotic pictures, amongst a larger set of positive, neutral and negative valence pictures all drawn from the IAPS, to a sample of young men and women, and prompted them while viewing the pictures either to enhance, maintain or suppress their natural emotional reaction using whatever cognitive strategy they felt would be effective. Startle probes were presented during and after picture presentation to assess the effects of the emotional regulation attempts. They found for all positive pictures, erotica included, that efforts to suppress natural emotional reactions did not produce eyeblink reflexes that differed significantly in magnitude from those observed during efforts to maintain the natural reaction. Although the suppression efforts in this study were targeted towards general emotional reactions and not specifically sexual interest, the finding does provide tentative support for the notion that cognitive efforts to suppress spontaneous appetitive reactions are not effective in altering the physiological activation that moderates blink reflex magnitude.

A second advantage of eyeblink startle reflex is that it appears able to provide information on a different aspect of sexual response behaviour than is measured by current technologies. Singer (1984) proposed a fruitful model of sexual arousal that suggested that the arousal response can involve three stages: an aesthetic response, where interest in a sexual stimulus elicits increased attention and orienting behaviour; an approach response, which encompasses behaviour intended to move oneself towards the object of interest; and finally the genital response, in preparation for copulation. From the perspective of this model, phallometry obviously provides a measure of the genital response, while viewing time has been conceptualized as a measure of the aesthetic response (Abel Screening, Inc., 2004). Eyeblink startle reflex, on the other hand, may be a useful measure of the approach response component, in that the affective state indexed by the reflex is an indicator of an examinee's motivation to engage in approach behaviour, which theoretically could be a more discriminating measure of sexual interest than either the aesthetic or arousal response.

Startle eyeblink magnitude is a measure of emotional response to stimuli. Emotional response is distinct from interest and from arousal. Humans may be very interested in highly arousing stimuli but have a negative emotional reaction to those stimuli (e.g. horror movies, car accidents). For instance, Lang, Greenwald, Bradley and Hamm (1993) found that individuals tend to view unpleasant but interesting pictures just as long as pleasant and interesting pictures. Their factor analysis of physiological correlates of picture viewing revealed that viewing time and interest ratings are strongly associated with the arousal dimension and much less so with the valence dimension. This could help to explain why some in the field have found that phallometry and viewing time frequently have difficulty, for instance, discriminating rapists from non-rapists (see Marshall and Fernandez, 2000; Letourneau, 2002), in that these measures may have limited ability to distinguish between pleasantly aroused and unpleasantly aroused reactions. In contrast, startle eyeblink, as a measure of valence, may be able to distinguish a rapist's aroused appeal to a sadistic portrayal from a normal control's aroused aversion. This question also awaits determination, but the potential is there for a significant gain in sex offender assessment capabilities. Understanding sexual offenders' emotional reactions to various sexual stimuli may help us develop more sophisticated models of sexual offending.

In our research laboratory, we are beginning to explore the application of the startle eyeblink reflex to issues relevant to sexual offending. In one line of research, we are exploring emotional reactions to slide materials depicting various sexual partners using the startle eyeblink (Scoular, 2006). In a second line of research, we are beginning to test the extent to which the eyeblink startle reaction is resistant to dissimulation or faking (King, Scoular and Hecker, 2005b).

STARTLE EYEBLINK WHILE VIEWING NORMAL AND DEVIANT SEXUAL STIMULI

All of our startle reflex studies to date have used 'normal' adult males as participants. These are male college students who have never been convicted of a sexual offence and who self-select as heterosexual. There is an extant literature showing that men have a diminished eyeblink startle reaction when viewing sexual stimuli. In these studies, men were shown either video clips of male–female adult pairs engaged in consenting sexual activity (e.g. Koukounas and McCabe, 2001; Koukounas and Over, 2000) or still images of heterosexual couples engaged in erotic activities or female nudes (e.g. Bradley et al., 2001b). We sought to examine men's eyeblink startle responses while viewing images of potential sexual partners who varied in age and gender. We were interested in how men would respond to images of a variety of potential sexual partners including partners who would be considered deviant.

In the first phase of this research, we developed a set of slide stimuli that depicted males and females at ages varying from toddler through adult. Each slide depicted one model clothed in a bathing suit and viewed frontally. The photos were obtained from several public Internet domains but primarily swimsuit retailers. The slide set adhered to the guidelines of the Association for the Treatment of Sexual Abusers (ATSA) for stimulus materials (ATSA, 1997). Each photo was categorized on the basis of the judged age of the model. There were four categories: toddler (0–3 years old), prepubescent (4–9 years old), pubescent (11–16 years old) and adult (18 years old and older). There were 20 photos in each category, 10 of male and 10 of female. A pilot sample of heterosexual male undergraduate students were shown the slides and asked to rate their sexual interest in the model depicted in each slide on a scale from 1 (sexually aversive) to 7 (highly sexually interested). As expected, adult and pubescent females elicited high to moderate sexual interest, while all other models were generally rated sexually aversive.

In the second phase of this research, we examined startle eyeblink magnitude while a second group of participants looked at the images of male and female bathing suit models from the four age categories described above. In order to provoke participants into viewing the models depicted in the slides as potential sexual partners, each photo was accompanied by one of a number of brief text phrases, and participants were instructed to interpret the phrases as being spoken to them by the models. The phrases were stored in a separate data file from the photos, and were paired randomly with the photos during each presentation. An example phrase was 'I want to have sex with you'. In addition to the eight categories of potential sexual partners, participants were shown 13 unpleasant slides (e.g. mutilated bodies) taken from the IAPS collection. These slides had all been rated as highly arousing and highly aversive in the IAPS norming process. We included these unpleasant slides as a standard comparison. The slides were presented in a pseudorandom order that was the same for each participant. Participants in this study were 19 undergraduate males between the ages of 21 and 23.

Following data collection, in order to assess whether our age and gender categorizations had successfully elicited consistent patterns of blink modulation as anticipated, reliability alphas were computed for each picture category. All categories demonstrated acceptable reliability with the exception of male toddlers. Hypothesizing that the inconsistent responses may have been a result of difficulty with the instructional task (i.e. imagining the captions as being spoken to them by toddlers), responses to toddler images, both male and female, were excluded from comparisons between the categories.

Startle eyeblink findings are depicted in Figure 10.3. Participants' mean blink magnitude while viewing each picture category was transformed into an ipsative z-score that reflects the deviation from his overall mean blink magnitude across all categories. The average deviation across the sample for each category is shown. Not unexpectedly, initial comparisons revealed no significant differences between responses to adult and pubescent females, and to responses between adult and pubescent males. Therefore these categories were combined in order to improve

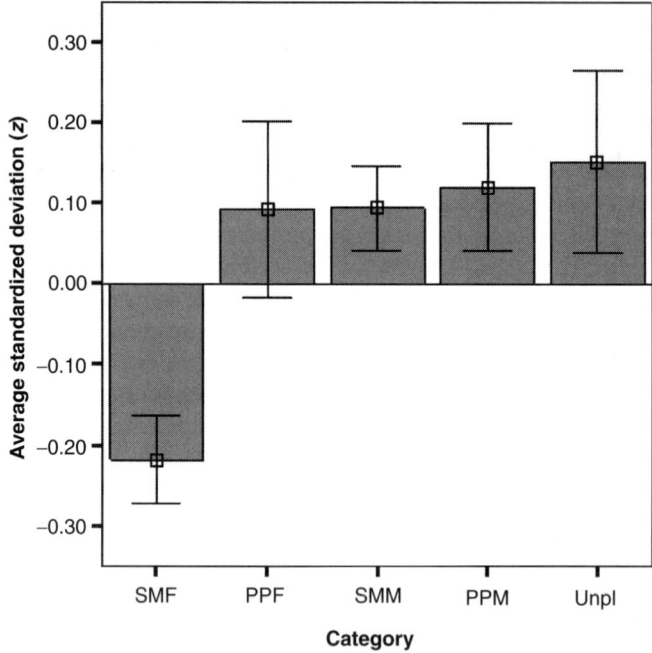

Figure 10.3   Mean standardized startle reflex magnitudes while participants viewed images of sexually mature females (SMF), prepubescent females (PPF), sexually mature males (SMM), prepubescent males (PPM) and unpleasant scenes (Unpl). Error bars reflect ±1 standard error.

the reliability of the category means, and the figure shows the combined categories. Participants demonstrated the smallest relative startle eyeblinks while viewing images of sexually mature females. Significantly larger startle eyeblinks were recorded when participants were looking at prepubescent females and males of any age. The average relative magnitudes of these latter categories were comparable to the blinks recorded while participants viewed the unpleasant IAPS images (Scoular, 2006).

The findings from this first study are encouraging. The startle eyeblink response magnitudes were smaller when men viewed images that had been rated as sexually attractive. Men reported that they found the images of pubescent and adult females sexually attractive and men showed smaller startle eyeblinks while viewing these images when cued to view them as potential sexual partners. Men reported no interest in males of any age or in prepubescent age females and men showed larger eyeblinks when looking at corresponding images and cued to think of them as potential sexual partners. The finding that heterosexual males showed a relatively large eyeblink when looking at non-preferred potential sexual partners (i.e. males and prepubescent-age females) is intriguing. It suggests that the participants had negative emotional reactions when cued to think of the models depicted in these images as potential sexual partners.

Our research to date has looked at men's startle responses to still images of normal and deviant potential sexual partners. There is also some existing evidence that startle response is a valid measure of interest in normal versus deviant choices of sexual activity. Janssen *et al.* (2002) have examined eyeblink responses while men are looking at video clips of consensual, explicit sexual activity and film clips of coercive but non-explicit sexual interactions. In the consensual clips, male–female partners are equally involved in petting, foreplay and intercourse. In contrast, the coercive clips were taken from commercially available films and depicted 'coercive sexual interaction with no explicit sexual activity being shown' (p. 129). Male undergraduates showed reduced startle responses to the consensual scenes compared to the coercive scenes. The findings of Janssen *et al.* are intriguing in that they suggest that normal males have a less positive, or perhaps negative, emotional response to scenes depicting coercive sexual encounters. Unfortunately, the coercion versus consensual difference between the video clips used in this study was confounded by a difference in explicit sex as well. The consensual scenes included explicit sexual activity and the coercive scenes did not.

DECEPTION AND THE STARTLE EYEBLINK

For work with sexual offenders, the practical value of any measure of sexual interest is related to the degree to which the measurement is resistant to faking. An omnipresent threat to the reliability and validity of measures of sexual interest is the tendency for sexual offenders to deny deviant sexual interests and attempt dissimulation of those interests in order to evade detection of their true interest pattern (Sewell and Salekin, 1997). There would be no need for books such as the present volume if one could rely on the personal honesty of sexual offenders when interviewed about their sexual interests. Dissimulation is an issue for any measure of sexual interest including penile plethysmography and viewing time.

The eyeblink startle is an unlearned response that is thought to be largely under the control of subcortical brain structures. It is possible, therefore, that the eyeblink startle reaction may be resistant to efforts to consciously suppress sexual interest. We examined what impact instructing men to suppress their sexual interest in attractive nude women depicted in slide images would have upon the size of their startle eyeblink (King *et al.*, 2005b).

Participants were 16 undergraduate males. Once again, these men reported that they had never been arrested for a sexual crime and that their sexual orientation was heterosexual. In this study, three types of slide images were used: nude adult females, viewed frontally standing in non-sexual poses; affectively neutral (nature scenes drawn from the IAPS); and unpleasant (highly aversive IAPS images). There were eight slide images in each category. Men viewed the entire set of slides twice in a pseudorandom order that was the same for each participant. During the first viewing, participants were instructed to attend to the images, and when viewing one of the nudes, to consider her as a potential sexual partner. Prior to the second viewing, they were advised that most heterosexual men would find the images of nude women sexually attractive, but that when viewing one of these slides for the second time, they were to attempt to suppress their natural sexual interest. They were instructed to do so using only their thoughts, and not to look away from the pictures. The intent behind this instruction was to simulate a forensic setting,

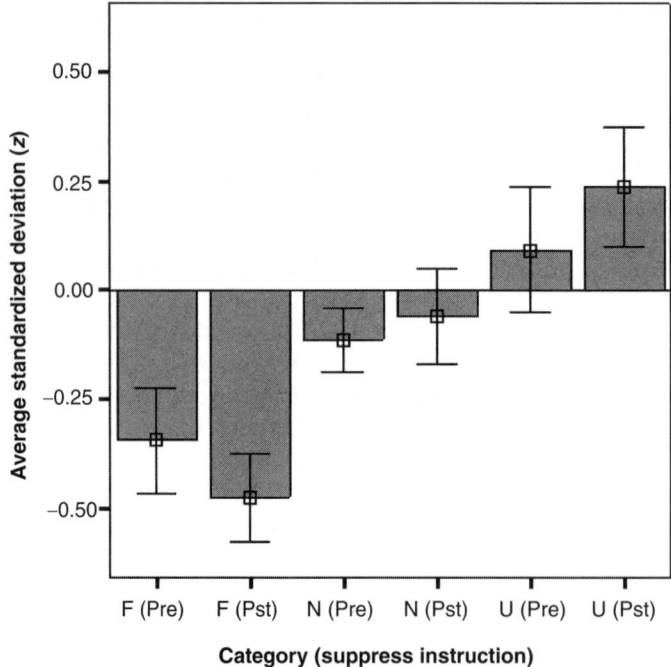

Figure 10.4   Mean standardized startle reflex magnitudes while participants viewed nude females (F), neutral scenes (N) and unpleasant images (U) before instructions to suppress sexual interest (Pre) and after receiving suppression instructions (Pst). Error bars reflect ±1 standard error.

where an examinee might be motivated to suppress any display of interest but would not want that effort to be apparent to the examiner.

Findings are depicted in Figure 10.4. When the men viewed the slides for the first time (Pre), the pattern of startle eyeblink responses was consistent with published literature: smaller relative eyeblink magnitude to the nude females, larger relative blinks to the neutral scenes and largest relative blinks to the unpleasant slides. The ordering of average eyeblink magnitudes did not change with the second viewing (Pst), despite the instruction to suppress sexual interest. These findings suggest that cognitive efforts to suppress sexual interest in the nude female images did not appreciably alter their spontaneous emotional reactions as measured by their startle eyeblink reflexes.

STARTLE EYEBLINK: ISSUES AND FUTURE DIRECTIONS

The startle eyeblink response has several strengths which suggest that a useful technology for assessing sexual interests in sex offenders can be developed with a paradigm based on the startle reflex. First, there are now several published studies which consistently show that men demonstrate a reduced magnitude eyeblink startle reflex when they are looking at images they find sexually attractive. This is a robust phenomenon. Second, the fact that there is no obvious relationship between eyeblink startle magnitude and sexual interest is an advantage. It is not clear how one should alter the eyeblink to disguise interest in deviant sexual stimuli or to simulate an interest in acceptable stimuli. Third, while additional work on resistance to dissimulation needs to be done, our findings suggest that men attempting to suppress their sexual interest cannot alter their affect modulated startle reflex. Fourth, the relationship between startle intensity and emotion has been found when emotional reactions are elicited through auditory and visual stimuli (Lang, 1995). Being able to use auditory scripts of sexual encounters will allow for the assessment of eyeblink startle reaction to a variety of types of sexual interactions including some that are not easily conveyed via visual stimuli (e.g. exposing oneself). Fifth, startle eyeblink magnitude is associated with one's emotional state and is not a direct measure of sexual arousal. Examining startle reactions while simultaneously measuring sexual arousal will allow for the exploration of the interaction between emotional reactions and sexual arousal to varying types of stimuli. Finally, while our work to date has involved only male subjects, the startle eyeblink paradigm is suitable for evaluating women's responses to sexual stimuli (Bradley *et al.*, 2001b).

While a startle eyeblink-based paradigm for assessing sexual interests has much to offer, there is a great deal of work that needs to be done before a valid system for evaluation of sex offenders is available. We conclude this chapter by discussing some of the issues that need additional explication.

ANTICIPATORY ANXIETY

Identification of potential issues which will need to be addressed before a valid technology for assessing sexual interest in sexual offenders can be facilitated by imagining the circumstances under which the assessment of sexual interest might be used. If we were to imagine a prototypical case example, it might be a man who has been convicted of a sexual offence against a prepubescent child. While not all men who sexually molest prepubescent children are sexually aroused by images of young children (Blanchard, Klassen, Dickey, Kuban and Blak, 2001; Seto and Lalumiere, 2001), for the sake of our prototype example we will assume that our sex offender has a paedophilic sexual orientation. This man would be shown images of children and adults as well as some neutral stimuli. He would be cued in some way to think about the people depicted in the images as potential sexual partners. At random points while he is looking at the images and during intertrial intervals, he will be startled by a brief blast of white noise. The magnitude of the startle reactions will be measured and recorded. Our hypothesis is that the magnitude of the average startle reactions while viewing the various stimulus categories will provide information about his sexual interests. In this case, we would predict smaller startle reactions when he is looking at images of prepubescent children, compared to when he is looking at adults or neutral slides.

To broaden our prototypical example, we should consider what might be the circumstances under which the emotion-modulated startle reflex would be applied to measure sexual interest. Our hypothetical sex offender might undergo an evaluation that would include startle probe measurement of sexual interest as part of a presentence evaluation in which risk assessment is a central concern. Or he might be evaluated before or after court-mandated treatment. Or our hypothetical offender might be required to participate in an evaluation as part of an assessment to determine whether or not he is a 'sexual predator' who should be required to remain incarcerated beyond his sentence. In each of these circumstances, the sexual offender might be motivated to disguise or dissimulate his true sexual interests. However, it is also true that in any of these circumstances images of young children could be viewed as threatening, since the detection of his interest in these images would have negative consequences for the offender.

In the prototype example described above, the meaning of a stimulus that would normally be viewed as pleasant (e.g. a picture of a child in a bathing suit) may be altered such that the stimulus now cues danger (i.e. detection of deviant interest). In research with humans, when a neutral stimulus is given threat value, participants show an enhanced startle reflex in the presence of that stimulus. For example, when research participants are told that they could receive an electric shock when a red light is on, but that they will not receive a shock when a green light is on, they show a larger reaction when startled in the presence of the red light compared to the green light (Grillon, Ameli, Woods, Merikangas and Davis, 1991). Anticipatory anxiety potentiates the startle reflex.

Bradley, Moulder and Lang (2005) examined whether the threat of receiving an electric shock would change the magnitude of the startle reflex when participants were instructed that either pleasant or unpleasant slides indicated the possibility that an electric shock could occur. Participants who were told that they might receive an electric shock when they viewed pleasant slides showed a much larger startle reaction while viewing those slide than did participants who believed that they were safe from the threat of shock when viewing pleasant slides. When pleasant pictures cued shock threat, participants showed potentiated startle reflexes to those pictures. In the study of Bradley et al. one of the 18 pleasant images depicted a heterosexual couple engaged in an erotic interaction.

The research showing that anticipatory anxiety leads to exacerbated startle reactions suggests a potential problem for the application of this paradigm to studying men convicted of sexual offences. If images of deviant sexual partners signals threat than a larger startle reflex is expected. The study of Bradley et al. (2005) suggests that anticipatory anxiety potentiates the startle reflex even when the threat cue would normally be viewed positively. There are at least two empirical questions that require investigation before it can be concluded that the problem of anticipatory anxiety will nullify the value of the startle probe assessment of sexual interest. First, it is an empirical question whether sex offenders respond with anxiety to images of deviant sexual partners. Or, more precisely, under what circumstances do men convicted of sexual offences react to images of deviant sexual partners with anticipatory anxiety. The complementary question is what are the characteristics of men who show anticipatory anxiety to deviant sexual stimuli versus those who do not. Second, will anticipatory anxiety lead to enhanced startle reactions to sexual stimuli? In the study of Bradley et al., most of the pleasant images were not sexual. Men show the smallest startle reactions when viewing images of erotic couples and erotic nude females compared to other types of pleasant images (e.g. sports, food, families, nature) (Bradley *et al.*, 2001b). It is possible that the anticipatory anxiety may not impact startle reactions to sexual stimuli as strongly.

PSYCHOPATHY

The magnitude of the startle reflex is modulated by the person's emotional experience at the time that the person is startled (Lang, 1995). As a measure of sexual interest, therefore, the startle probe reflex provides information about people's emotional reactions as they attend to sexual stimuli. The bulk of the research on emotion-modulated startle is based on the work with normal human subjects whose emotional functioning is presumably not disturbed. A legitimate concern about the startle probe as a measure of sexual interest is whether or not the paradigm would be applicable with men whose emotional functioning is known to be atypical.

One of the hallmark features of psychopathy is a disturbance in emotional functioning. Impulsivity, lack of anxiety, guilt or remorse and inability to form loving relationships are hallmark features of the psychopathic personality (Cleckley, 1955). Contemporary thinking about psychopathy has been strongly influenced by Robert Hare who developed the Psychopathy Checklist – Revised (PCL-R) (Hare, 1991) to measure psychopathy and identify individuals with psychopathic personality disorder. Factor analysis of the PCL-R suggests that it measures two important aspects of the psychopathic personality: Factor 1 captures the emotional detachment of the psychopath and Factor 2 the criminal and antisocial behaviour (Harpur, Hare and Hakstian, 1989).

A minority of men who are convicted of sexual offences are psychopaths (Langevin, 2003; Over and Wong, 2006). However, the presence of psychopathy is a risk factor for both sexual and violent recidivism (Over and Wong, 2006; Quinsey, Harris, Rice and Cormier, 1998). Deviant sexual interests and antisocial orientation are the two factors which appear most strongly associated with sexual re-offending in male sexual offenders (Hanson and Bussière, 1998; Hanson and Morton-Bourgon, 2005). While these two factors are each associated with sexual recidivism, when both are present there is an interaction which inflates the risk for sexual re-offending (Over and Wong, 2006). The validity of a measure of deviant sexual interests when applied to psychopathic men, therefore, is an important consideration.

Psychopathic men show an unusual pattern of startle responses when looking at pleasant, neutral and unpleasant visual stimuli. Patrick, Bradley and Lang (1993) carefully evaluated psychopathy in 54 male sexual offenders in a forensic treatment facility. Using their scores on the PCL-R, the men were divided into three groups: non-psychopathic, psychopathic features and clearly psychopathic. The men were shown pleasant, neutral and unpleasant slides. The non-psychopathic men, as well as the men with only some psychopathic features, showed the pattern of responding seen in normal subjects: small blinks to pleasant slides, larger blinks to neutral slides and still larger blinks to unpleasant slides. The psychopathic men, in contrast, showed a different pattern. Their startle eyeblinks to the pleasant and unpleasant stimuli were similar and smaller than to neutral stimuli. The pattern of responding suggested that the psychopathic men were interested in both the pleasant and unpleasant slides and had a similar emotional reaction to each. When Patrick *et al.* examined the PCL-R factor scores for their participants, they were able to look at men who had high and low Factor 1 (emotional detachment) scores and high Factor 2 (antisocial behaviour) scores. Men who had low Factor 1 scores showed the largest startle responses to unpleasant slides, moderate responses to neutral slides and smallest responses while viewing pleasant slides. However, the high Factor 1 men (high emotional detachment) showed a relatively small startle reaction while viewing pleasant and unpleasant slides compared to their startle reactions while viewing the neutral slides. Men who show the emotional detachment that is a central feature of psychopathy showed the aberrant pattern of startle eyeblinks – they showed a similar interest in the pleasant and unpleasant slides.

The findings of Patrick *et al.* (1993) have been replicated by Benning, Patrick and Iacono (2005) in a study of men who participated in the Minnesota Twin Family Study (Iacono, Carlson, Taylor, Elkins and McGue, 1999). The dimensions of psychopathy were measured using the Multidimensional Personality Questionnaire (MPQ) (Benning, Patrick, Hicks, Blonigen and Krueger, 2003). When men are selected for being at the extremely high (top 10%) end of the continuum of scores on the fearless dominance factor of the MPQ, their pattern of startle eyeblinks matches that seen in psychopaths: low startle reaction to the pleasant and unpleasant slides and higher to the neutral slides.

What are the implications of the unusual pattern of responses seen in psychopaths for the startle eyeblink as a measure of sexual interest? Psychopaths show an unusual response to aversive slide images. Fortunately, it will be men's startle eyeblink responses to potentially positive images that will be of greatest interest when the paradigm is applied to sex offenders. The research with psychopaths to date suggests that they show a diminished eyeblink startle reflex when looking at pleasant images. However, our findings with normal males suggest that they show an enhanced startle reaction when viewing images of inappropriate sexual targets and are encouraged to view them as potential sexual partners (see Figure 10.3). It may be that psychopaths will not show this exacerbated startle reaction while looking at deviant sexual partners. This lack of startle enhancement would as likely be due to the lack of anxiety generated by the task as it is to sexual attraction to the slide images. We would still predict, however, that they would show the reduced startle response to stimuli they find sexually attractive. Obviously, there is startle probe research work to be done with male psychopaths. Specifically, their startle reactions while viewing appropriate potential sexual partners (e.g. adult female) and inappropriate potential sexual partners (e.g. prepubescent children) merit investigation.

HABITUATION AND NOVELTY

Habituation of the eyeblink magnitude over repeated trials is an interesting and challenging issue. When considering changes in startle eyeblink magnitude over repeated presentations of sexual and non-sexual stimuli, two forms of habituation need to be considered. First, the absolute size of the startle eyeblink decreases over repeated presentations of the startle probe (Blumenthal *et al.*, 2005). Therefore, care needs to be taken in the arrangement of neutral, normal-sexual and deviant-sexual stimuli across trials. Blink magnitude will be relatively smaller during later, as compared to earlier, trials.

There are at least two solutions to the habituation problem. The most straight-forward solution would be to assure that examples of each type of stimuli are distributed throughout the trials, with some of each stimuli-type appearing early and later in the trial sequence. The other approach is to account for the order of stimuli presentation effect statistically by using order as a covariate. The z-score distributions are calculated by comparing the magnitude of each startle response to the residualized mean score for each participant.

The second way in which habituation is a concern when measuring sexual inter-ests using the eyeblink startle reflex has to do with men's diminishing interest in sexual stimuli across repeated presentations. Men's interest in, and arousal to, sex-ual stimuli habituates over repeated presentations of the same stimuli (Koukounas and Over, 2000; O'Donohue and Plaud, 1991). When interest is measured with the startle eyeblink, habituation is evidenced by increasing eyeblink magnitudes over repeated trials (Koukounas and Over, 2000).

There is an interesting interaction between the two ways that habituation may be an issue for startle probe measurement of sexual interest. Repeated presentation of the startle probe results in habituation of the startle magnitude, defined as smaller blinks over time, and repeated presentation of the same sexual stimuli results in habituation of interest in the stimuli, defined as larger eyeblinks over time. It will be important to explicate the parameters of these two forms of habituation, and their interaction, before the startle eyeblink assessment of sexual interest can be put to practical use.

STIMULUS AROUSAL LEVELS

Basic research on human emotion suggests that there is an interesting relationship between arousal and valence. Stimuli that elicit low levels of arousal are experi-enced as neither strongly pleasant nor unpleasant (Bradley *et al.*, 2001a). However, as arousal increases, the valence of our emotional experience becomes positive or negative. Stimuli that arouse us strongly are experienced as pleasant or unpleas-ant but never neutral. When research participants are asked to rate the hedonic value (i.e. pleasure) and arousal of stimuli their ratings form a boomerang-shaped distribution. At lower levels of arousal, pleasure ratings converge at a mid-level but as arousal ratings increase, pleasure ratings separate so that highly arousing images are viewed as either very unpleasant or very pleasant. The same distri-bution is found regardless of whether people rate words or pictures (Bradley *et al.*, 2001a). Not surprisingly, therefore, there is a similar relationship between the arousal ratings and startle eyeblink magnitude. Humans show eyeblink reflexes of similar magnitude to pleasant and unpleasant stimuli when the stimuli provoke low levels of arousal. However, for stimuli rated as moderately to highly arousing, startle blink magnitudes diverge so that small blinks are observed when subjects are looking at pleasant images and are large when they are looking at unpleasant images (Dawson, Schell and Böhmet, 1999; Lang, 1995).

The need to use stimuli that provoke at least a moderate level of arousal has implications for the startle eyeblink as a measure of sexual interest. In our pilot work with the startle reflex, we found that male college students produced startle eyeblinks similar to those produced while looking at neutral images when startled while looking at pictures of young children. We hypothesized that the images of young children clad in bathing suits elicited minimal arousal and that was why blink magnitudes while looking at these images were no smaller than for neutral images. We predicted that provoking participants to consider the child in the image as a potential sexual partner would raise the arousal level elicited by the slide. Consistent with our hypothesis, participants' blink magnitudes when looking at pictures of young children were large and indicated a negative emotional response when they were told to consider the child a potential sexual partner (Scoular, 2006).

There are ethical and legal issues that need to be considered when developing visual and auditory stimuli to be used in the assessment of deviant sexual interests regardless of the method. The challenge for the eyeblink methodology is that the stimuli must be moderately arousing at the same time morally and legal defensible. For example, in developing stimuli that might be useful in detecting whether or not men are sexually attracted to prepubescent children, still images of children (or auditory stimuli describing encounters with children) must be arousing enough to impact the size of the startle magnitude without violating child pornography laws or ethical standards.

SEXUAL OFFENDERS

At this point in time, only one study has examined the startle reflex in men convicted of sexual offences and the focus of this study was on psychopathy. In the study of Patrick *et al.* (1993) described above, 54 male residents of a forensic treatment facility for sexual offenders were studied. Unfortunately, very little descriptive information about these men was included in the Patrick *et al.* publication. We know that they were convicted felons who had been transferred to the sexual offender facility from state prisons in Florida. We do not know what types of sexual crimes they committed or if the sample included men with paedophilia. These men were shown three types of picture slides: positive slides that included images of female nudes as well as food, sports scenes and children; neutral slides (e.g. household objects, neutral faces) and unpleasant (e.g. mutilated bodies, aimed guns) slides. Non-psychopathic men showed the normal pattern of eyeblink responses with small blink magnitudes to pleasant slides and large to unpleasant slides with blinks while viewing neutral slides falling in between, which is re-assuring and indicates that the paradigm is applicable to sexual offenders. Unfortunately, we do not know about their blink magnitudes in response to the sexual (female nudes) as opposed to non-sexual pleasant stimuli.

Clearly, there is much research on the startle reflex with sexual offenders to be done. Some pressing empirical questions include the following:

1) Will paedophiles show the predicted pattern of startle eyeblinks while looking at images of young children? That is, will their blink magnitudes be smaller when looking at images of prepubescent children compared to their blink magnitudes to neutral or normative sexually arousing images?

2) Can eyeblink startle response be used to differentiate men who have a positive emotional reaction to coercive sexual scenes from those who respond negatively to such scenes? The findings of Janssen *et al.* (2002) suggest that normal males have larger eyeblinks to coercive sexual scenes than to scenes of consensual sexual encounters. It remains to be seen whether or not rapists will respond differently to the different scene types. There is controversy in the plethysmography literature about whether or not rapists have a stronger erectile response to rape scenes than to scenes of consenting sex (see Lalumiére and Rice, 2007; Looman and Marshall, 2005; Looman, 2007). The startle eyeblink paradigm may shed some light on this controversy by providing information about rapists' emotional, as opposed to their purely erectile, responses to various types of sexual activity.

3) If reliable group differences between non-offending men and various subtypes of sexual offenders can be found, can decision rules be developed to categorize men on the basis of their eyeblink startle reactions? What will be the sensitivity and specificity of these decision rules?

CONCLUSIONS

Men show a diminished startle eyeblink reflex when they are engaged with stimuli they find sexually arousing. This is a well-established empirical finding that can be exploited to develop a measurement system for use with men who have engaged in criminal sexual behaviour. Our preliminary findings suggest that normal men have a negative emotional reaction when they are looking at images of children and cued to think about them as sexual partners. In addition, we have found that men are unable to disguise their interest in images of nude females when instructed to do so, when interest is measured by relative magnitude of startle eyeblink. While there are many empirical issues that remain to be addressed, the eyeblink startle reaction shows great potential as a measure of deviant sexual interest.

REFERENCES

Abel Screening, Inc. (2004) Review of the empirical support for the Abel Assessment for Sexual Interest™, http://abelscreening.com/ (retrieved 27 March 2005).

Association for the Treatment of Sexual Abusers (1997) *The ATSA Practitioner's Handbook.* Author, Beaverton, OR.

Balaban, M.T. (1995) Affective influences on startle in five-month-old infants: reactions to facial expressions and emotion. *Child Development,* **66**, 28–36.

Benning, S.D., Patrick, C.J. and Iacono, W.G. (2005) Psychopathy, startle blink modulation, and electrodermal reactivity in twin men. *Psychophysiology,* **42**, 753–62.

Benning, S.D., Patrick, C.J., Hicks, B.M., Blonigen, D.M. and Krueger, R.F. (2003) Factor structure of the psychopathic inventory: validity and implications for clinical assessment. *Psychological Assessment*, **15**, 340–50.

Blanchard, R., Klassen, P., Dickey, R., Kuban, M.E. and Blak, T. (2001) Sensitivity and specificity of the phallometric test for pedophilia in nonadmitting sex offenders. *Psychological Assessment*, **13**, 118–26.

Blumenthal, T.D., Cuthbert, B.N., Filion, D.L., Hackley, S., Lipp, O.V. and van Boxtel, A. (2005) Committee report: guidelines for human startle eyeblink electromyographic studies. *Psychophysiology*, **42**, 1–15.

Bradley, M.M., Codispoti, M., Cuthbert, B.N. and Lang, P.J. (2001a) Emotion and motivation I: defensive and appetitive reactions in picture processing. *Emotion*, **1**, 276–98.

Bradley, M.M., Codispoti, M., Sabatinelli, D. and Lang, P.J. (2001b) Emotion and motivation I: sex differences in picture processing. *Emotion*, **1**, 300–19.

Bradley, M.M. and Lang, P.J. (2000) Affective reactions to acoustic stimuli. *Psychophysiology*, **37**, 204–15

Bradley, M.M., Moulder, B. and Lang, P.J. (2005) When good things go bad: the reflex physiology of defense. *Psychological Science*, **16**, 468–73.

Cleckley, H., (1955) *The Mask of Sanity*, 3rd edn. Mosby, St. Louis, MO.

Dawson, M.E., Schell, A.M. and Böhmelt, A.H. (1999) *Startle Modification: Implication for Neuroscience, Cognitive Science, and Clinical Science*. University of Cambridge Press, New York.

Davis, M. (2006) Neural systems involved in fear and anxiety measured with fear-potentiated startle. *American Psychologist*, **62**, 741–56.

Dillon, D.G. and LaBar, K.S. (2005) Startle modulation during conscious emotion regulation is arousal-dependent. *Behavioral Neuroscience*, **119**, 1118–24.

Freund, K. Watson, R. and Rienzo, D. (1988) Signs of feigning in the phallometric test. *Behaviour Research and Therapy*, **26**, 105–12.

Graham, F.K. (1979) Distinguishing among orienting, defense, and startle reflexes, in *The Orienting Reflex in Humans: An International Conference Sponsored by the Scientific Affairs Division of the North Atlantic Treaty Organization* (eds H.D. Kimmel, E.H. van Olst and J.F. Orlebeke), Erlbaum, Hillsdale, NJ, pp. 137–67.

Grillon, C., Ameli, R., Woods, S.W., Meikangas, K. and Davis, M. (1991) Fear potentiated startle in humans: effects of anticipatory anxiety on the acoustic blink reflex. *Psychophysiology*, **28**, 588–95.

Hanson, R.K. and Bussière, M.T. (1998) Predicting relapse: a meta-analysis of sexual offender recidivism studies. *Journal of Consulting and Clinical Psychology*, **66** (2), 348–62.

Hanson, R.K. and Morton-Bourgon, K. (2005) The characteristics of persistent sexual offenders: a meta-analysis of recidivism studies. *Journal of Consulting and Clinical Psychology*, **73**, 1154–63.

Hare, R.D. (1991) *The Hare Psychopathy Checklist – Revised*. Multi-Health Systems, Toronto.

Harpur, T.J., Hare, R.D. and Hakstian, A.R. (1989) Tow-factor conceptualization of psychopathy: construct validity and assessment implications. *Psychological Assessment: A Journal of Consulting and Clinical Psychology*, **2**, 338–41.

Hecker, J.E., King, M.W. and Scoular, R.J. (2006) Startle eye blink: preliminary support for a promising method of measuring sexual interest, in *Cognitive Approaches to the Assessment of Sexual Interest in Sexual Offenders* (D.R. Laws, Chair), Symposium presented at the 2006 American Psychology-Law Society Conference, March 2006, St. Petersburg, FL.

Iacono, W.G., Carlson, S.R., Taylor, J., Elikins, I.J. and McGue, M. (1999) Behavioral disinhibition and the development of substance use disorders: findings from the Minnesota Twin Family Study. *Development and Psychopathology*, **11**, 869–900.

Jansen, D.M. and Frijda, N. (1994) Modulation of acoustic startle response by film-induced fear and sexual arousal. *Psychophysiology*, **31**, 565–71.

Janssen, E., Vorst, H., Finn, P. and Bancroft, J. (2002) The sexual inhibition (SIS) and sexual excitation (SES) scales: II. Predicting psychophysiological response patterns. *The Journal of Sex Research*, **39**, 127–32.

King, M.W., Patten, K., Hecker, J.E. and Parisot, M. (2005a) *Professional Practices in Sexual Interest Assessment Among ATSA Members*. Poster presented at the 24th Annual Research and Treatment Conference of the Association for the Treatment of Sexual Abusers, November 2005, Salt Lake City, UT.

King, M.W., Scoular, R.J. and Hecker, J.E. (2005b) *Eyeblink Startle Reflex as a Measure of Deviant Sexual Interests: Resistance to Faking*. Paper presented at the 24th Annual Research and Treatment Conference of the Association for the Treatment of Sexual Abusers, November 2005, Salt Lake City, UT.

Koukounas, E. and McCabe, M.P. (2001) Sexual and emotional variables influencing sexual response to erotica: a psychophysiological investigation. *Archives of Sexual Behavior*, **30**, 393–408.

Koukounas, E. and Over, R. (2001) Changes in magnitude of eyeblink startle response during habituation of sexual arousal. *Behaviour Research and Therapy*, **38**, 573–84.

Lalumiére, M.L. and Rice, M.E. (2007) The validity of phallometric assessment with rapists: comments on Looman and Marshall (2005). *Sexual Abuse: A Journal of Research and Treatment*, **19**, 61–8.

Lang, P.J. (1995) The emotion probe: studies of motivation and attention. *American Psychologist*, **50**, 372–85.

Lang, P.J., Bradley, M.M. and Cuthbert, B.N. (1998) Emotion, motivation and anxiety: brain mechanisms and psychophysiology. *Biological Psychiatry*, **44**, 1248–63.

Lang, P.J., Bradley, M.M. and Cuthbert, B.N. (2005) *International Affective Picture System (IAPS): Instruction manual and affective ratings* (Technical Report A-6). Center for Research in Psychophysiology, University of Florida, Gainesville.

Lang, P.J., Greenwald, M.K., Bradley, M.M. and Hamm, A.O. (1993) Looking at pictures: affective, facial, visceral, and behavioral reactions. *Psychophysiology*, **30**, 261–73.

Langevin, R. (2003) A study of the psychosexual characteristics of sex killers: can we identify them before it is too late? *International Journal of Offender Therapy and Comparative Criminology*, **47**, 366–82.

Larson, C.L., Ruffalo, D., Nietert, J.Y. and Davidson, R.J. (2005) Stability of emotion-modulated startle during short and long picture presentation. *Psychophysiology*, **42**, 604–10.

Letourneau, E.J. (2002) A comparison of objective measures of sexual arousal and interest: visual reaction time and penile plethysmography. *Sexual Abuse: Journal of Research and Treatment*, **14**, 207–23.

Looman, J. (2007) Response to Lalumiére and Rice: further comments on Looman and Marshall (2005). *Sexual Abuse: A Journal of Research and Treatment*, **19**, 69–72.

Looman, J. and Marshall, W.L. (2005) Sexual arousal in rapists. *Criminal Justice and Behavior*, **32**, 367–89.

Marshall, W.L. (2006) Clinical and research limitations in the use of phallometric testing with sexual offenders. *Sexual Offender Treatment*, **1**, http://www.sexual-offender-treatment.org/marshall.0.html (retrieved 24 January 2007).

Marshall, W.L. and Fernandez, Y.M. (2000) Phallometric testing with sexual offenders: limits to its value. *Clinical Psychology Review*, **20**, 807–22.

O'Donohue, W.T. and Plaud, J.J. (1991) The long term habituation of sexual arousal in the human male. *Journal of Behavior Therapy and Experimental Psychiatry*, **22**, 87–96.

Over, M.E. and Wong, S.C.P. (2006) Psychopathology, sexual deviance and recidivism among sex offenders. *Sexual Abuse: A Journal of Research and Treatment*, **18**, 65–82.

Patrick, C.J., Bradley, M.M. and Lang, P.J. (1993) Emotion in the criminal psychopath: startle reflex modulation. *Journal of Abnormal Psychology*, **102**, 82–92.

Quinsey, V.L., Harris, G.T., Rice, M.E. and Cormier, C.A. (1998) *Violent Offenders: Appraising and Managing Risk*. American Psychological Association, Washington, DC.

Scoular, R.J. (2006) *Startle Modified Eyeblinks as a Possible Measure of Male Sexual Interest*. Unpublished doctoral dissertation, University of Maine, Orono.

Seto, M.C. and Lalumiére, M.L. (2001) A brief screening scale to identify pedophilic interests among child molesters. *Sexual Abuse: A Journal of Research and Treatment*, **13**, 15–25.

Sewell, K.W. and Salekin, R.T. (1997) Understanding and detecting dissimulation in sex offenders, in *Clinical Assessment of Malingering and Deception*, 2nd edn (ed. R. Rogers), Guilford Press, New York, pp. 328–50.

Singer, B. (1984) Conceptualizing sexual arousal and attraction. *Journal of Sex Research*, **20**, 230–40.

Smith, J.C., Löw, A., Bradley, M.M. and Lang, P.J. (2006) Rapid picture presentation and affective engagement. *Emotion*, **6**, 208–14.

Smith, J.C. and O'Connor, P.J. (2003) Physical activity does not disturb the measurement of startle and corrugator responses during affective picture viewing. *Biological Psychology*, **63**, 293–310.

Stanley, J. and Knight, R.G. (2004) Emotion specificity of startle potentiation during the early stages of picture viewing. *Psychophysiology*, **42**, 935–40.

Chapter 11

POSTSCRIPT: STEPS TOWARDS EFFECTIVE ASSESSMENT OF SEXUAL INTEREST

DAVID THORNTON

Sand Ridge Secure Treatment Center, Mauston, WI, USA

D. RICHARD LAWS

Pacific Psychological Assessment Corporation, Victoria, BC, Canada

This book describes the development of a number of new methods designed to assess the sexual interests of sexual offenders. The central idea underlying the different methods is that sexual interest will affect the cognitive processing of material related to that interest. A number of tasks derived from mainstream social and cognitive psychology have been adapted for this purpose. Ultimately the intention is that this process will culminate in measurement procedures that can make a useful contribution to the assessment of sexual offenders' treatment needs, response to treatment and risk for re-offence. Achieving this involves accomplishing a number of distinguishable but demanding tasks. These include the following:

1. An idea for a new assessment tool is derived by combining knowledge of sexual offenders with theory and research from social and cognitive psychology.
2. This idea is turned into a specific measurement task that allows interesting aspects of the participant's performance to be quantified.
3. The task is refined through pilot work and initial studies with convenience populations.
4. A study is conducted showing that relevant aspects of performance on the task statistically differentiate a group of offenders from non-offenders, or differentiate among different kinds of offender.
5. Differences between groups on the measure are cross-validated in independent samples and by different research laboratories.
6. Refined studies of construct validity are carried out identifying the affect of various artefacts on performance on the task, and testing specific hypotheses

regarding what the task measures and why it differentiates offender groups.

7. Conditions that limit the task's validity are determined.

8. Robust versions of the task are created that are sufficiently user-friendly that they can be applied and interpreted by clinicians rather than research laboratories; the reliability and validity of the robust task as applied by clinicians is determined.

9. Norms are developed for this robust version of the task with relevant offender and non-offender populations.

10. Prospective studies test the instruments' ability to predict recidivism.

At some point after step 5 clinical paradigms for using the instrument begin to be evolved and the development of these paradigms accelerates after step 8.

The work described in this book represents real accomplishments, but it refers mainly to the first four or five steps. There is thus considerable work still to be done for any of the new tasks to become fully established.

At this stage, it is hard to judge what the eventual value of the different measurement tasks will be. At present, the new task that has made most progress through the above ten steps are variants of the IAT.

Multiple laboratories have replicated the difference in IAT responding between convicted child molesters and non-offenders. The measure also differentiates between different groups of sexual offenders and seems able to differentiate sexual offenders even when they are in denial. Thus the effect seems to be robust. It reflects more than a simple effect of being imprisoned. And it appears to offer more than self-report. On the other hand, we do not know whether performance represents a sexual interest in children as opposed to the idea of sex being made more salient by thinking about children. And if the latter interpretation is correct, would professionals who routinely investigate the sexual abuse of children, or who provide treatment for offenders who sexually abuse children, also show aberrant performance on the IAT? And if their IAT performance is aberrant, what does this imply about the significance of what is being measured? Is it just an epiphenomenon or something that is more causally linked to offending? This kind of consideration highlights the need for further studies of the construct validity of this measure.

Although it has been less researched with sexual offenders, we believe that applications of the Stroop task show particular promise. Potentially, this task can both pick up the direction of sexual interest and the degree to which sexual ideas preempt attention.

We are more cautious with regard to the rapid serial visual presentation task, mainly because of concerns that the effect may be fragile especially in populations where significant numbers have mental illness, are on medications or vary greatly in ability.

Tasks based on the slowing of response while making attractiveness judgments (Abel, Affinity, Choice Reaction Time) clearly have some promise. However, as the critical review of the Abel task shows, there is considerable work still to be done to fully establish this paradigm. In our view, the Abel paradigm has been extended into uses that go beyond what is presently justified by the data.

Finally, we would recommend that researchers pursue the development of batteries of these new tasks. Since they are mainly fairly brief to administer this is practical in terms of assessment time and batteries are liable to yield combined results with higher overall validity than any single method.

INDEX